The Sharp Edge
Of Love

The Sharp Edge Of Love

the erotic passions of submissive women

by Galen

The Sharp Edge
Of Love

the erotic passions of submissive women

by Galen

Published 2000
Published by Galens Realm, USA. ©2000 Galen. All rights reserved.
No part of this publication may be reproduced, stored in a retrieval
system, or transmitted in any form or by any means, electronic,
mechanical, recording or otherwise, without the prior written permission of the author.

ISBN: 0-7394-1546-8

Manufactured in the United States of America

About the Author

Galen

Galen is an advocate for sexual freedom, honesty and tolerance. He is, as well, a Dominant and Mentor active in the BDSM scene, a member of the NLAI, an entrepreneur, web marketing consultant, writer, inventor, and proud father. For more info go to http://www.GalensRealm.com/.

For those interested in suspension bondage, but don't have a space to set up their "home dungeon", the Tetruss is the first portable, light-weight, free-standing suspension system. "Dungeon in a Box!! ...the Tetruss is sheerly amazing. If you want to own one piece of BDSM equipment, this is it. Recommended! " Robert Dante, Bullwhip.net. See it on my website's free galleries.

You may also be interested in Submit your Secrets, a newsgroup defined as a safe place to express your hidden desires, without fear of discovery or judgement, perhaps for the first time. You will find more info on Submit your Secrets on my website. Go for it!

TABLE OF CONTENTS

Preface

Erotic submissives are not weak or inferior women. In my experience they are quite strong, intelligent, noble, spiritual and very clear about who they are sexually. They come from all cultures and spectrums of society

They are willing and desire most of all to give themselves totally to their Dominant counterpart - body, mind and soul. It is in their blood, their genes and their souls to do so.

How a Dominant/submissive(D/s) relationship is manifest is defined by the individuals involved.

Some submissives reserve this aspect of themselves entirely for the bedroom and their monogamous marriage partner. Some go so far as becoming part of a "stable" of slaves, and consider themselves the property of their owner, willing to be used any way their Master sees fit.

Most enjoy erotic punishment from mild to extreme, and the feeling of giving up control, or being told what to do. There is a broad range of fantasy role-play involved, the blending of myth and ritual. The realm of D/s is an exotic and rich culture, expressed in endless creative combinations. There is no one way, in my experience, that a D/s relationship is defined.

For the women I have met, their feelings of submissiveness were not triggered by some trauma in their lives. They did not choose this path in an attempt to hide from life's responsibilities. They were not forced into this lifestyle by an abusive partner who controlled them by fear and physical coercion.

It is simply a part of them, that they know is true, and for the most part have known in some way almost all their lives. They offer themselves of their own free will to one worthy of their gift.

Entering the world of Dominance and submission is a journey. It doesn't begin or end at any particular place. Many carry these urges

that they could trust to honor their secret desires.

It is my goal that this book serves as a gateway for those who have wandered in shame and silence, who have kept their sexuality hidden, to enter here and freely shout the joy of their own truth.

Galen.
Feb.14, 2000

Introduction

Be warned! You may find a part of yourself craving what follows in this book, or you might stop reading in disgust. I wonder which it will be. Any secret sexual desires lurking in your own heart? You'll likely find them here, if you have any perversity at all.

The in-depth accounts in this book are true. They reveal in decadent, poetic and graphic detail, a generally hidden aspect of female nature - a craven desire to be treated like a submissive sex slut, and more, or less, as the case may be.

Please don't get excited, as the politically correct tend to do, and confuse sexuality with sexism. This book has nothing to do with oppressing anyone. It has nothing to do with sexual abuse. Quite the opposite, in fact.

Also, try to keep an open mind about the language and role-play personas depicted in this book. Remember they are of a consensual nature. Some women find the "drama" of erotic submission quite a turn-on, and enjoy taking on the role of a "slut" and much more in many cases.

Not all women are submissive, obviously. Some are quite Dominant in the bedroom and/or the boardroom. Some women definitely aren't sluts!

With the onerous social taboos against being honest and proud of your sexual identity, it's often a surprise to discover someone's private perversity(Don't you just love to see one of those ever holy evangelists or righteous political figures get exposed in some lewd and scandalous behavior!). Most individuals keep their sexual truth hidden deep in the shadows of shame and guilt. In current society, with its current definitions of "normal", an individual's sexual tastes are generally required to be kept secret, sometimes even from oneself.

Not so, in the true stories of the women written about here.

I solemnly and secretly desired women like this all my life. I've always known I needed a woman with an edge to her sexual passion. What a shock to discover that at last, thanks to the Internet, I could have what I always wanted.

I am of a genre of sexual preference known as D/s, Dominance and submission. Those of us who are in this lifestyle perform rituals of BDSM (bondage, discipline, sadism, masochism). People's tastes and styles in this realm cover a broad spectrum.

I am a Dominant. What does that mean? Many might judge it depraved and loathsome. You might find I lift the veil masking your own dark desires.

I train, mentor, or have relationships with women who, by their free choice, desire to serve as a sexual bottom, submissive or slave, for their Top, Dom or Master (the distinctions between these three will be explained within the stories in this book, or see the resource list at the back of the book.). These women seek erotic torment, mental subjugation and spiritual fulfillment through their submissive desire to serve, sexually and otherwise.

How pleasing it's been to discover and meet women who offered themselves for erotic pleasure or punishment, like a sacred gift, or a total slut.

I've had contact through the Internet with over a hundred submissive women, and met with a variety of them for play, as we call it, who desired to serve a Master for life, or who were just out for some anonymous thrills.

There are millions of people exploring this clandestine lifestyle, or numerous other fetishes, on the net and in real life. The Internet has spawned the first safe environment for the repressed sexual shadows and fantasies of the human psyche to gush forth. It has allowed individuals the opportunity to reveal aspects of themselves that have remained hidden all their lives.

The anonymity allowed by the Internet lowers the barriers of shame, guilt and judgement, that has retarded the sexual truths hiding within many individuals. These truths, in my judgement, are a rushing torrent that won't be held back, a torrent of honest sexual liberation, expression and exploration.

Millenniums of repressed sexual energy, the urge to get kinky, are about to emerge in the new millennium, despite the strong backlash likely, by paranoid and hypocritical moralists. Sexuality has become the free-wheeling frontier of human personality. I like to call it Y2Kink!

At first, I was startled at how readily and easily many of the women I've met surrendered themselves to me, body, mind and soul. I would admonish them for their imprudent surrender. Only after they had, of course! I knew they could trust me. (There are basic safety guidelines that cover ways to make arrangements for a first meeting, posted on many D/s sites. See Appendix.)

Barely knowing me, trusting their instincts, they gambled with their desire. These women sought the feeling of surrendering control, being told what to do. They sought to be bound and gagged, spanked and whipped, adorned with nipple clamps, slave collars, eager to fulfill my most perverse pleasures, and their own dark desire.

They've included lawyers, engineers, artists, entrepreneurs, college students - all seeking mental, physical and spiritual subjugation, on some level. A majority were newbies (no or little R/T [real time] experience).

It was always a thrill to see how far these women were prepared to venture in the first meetings, though not amazing. Most, like myself, had been preparing all their lives, after all, on one level or another. Once they found a safe environment and the trust of a compassionate Dom, there was nothing holding them back.

I hope to glorify these women as a group, though not all, individually, were so glorious. Some were as noble and mythic in the

pursuit of their dark passion as Joan of Arc.

It has been significant for me to discover on this path, that the gift of submission can be the foundation of a poetic, ritualized love, deeper than any I could have ever known. This is what I seek now, my submissive soulmate, though the sluts are always a pleasure.

The stories told here describe real encounters, told through correspondence and journals, as I've searched for my ideal submissive soul mate. Of the many encounters to date, I have chosen four that are the most personal and intimate, and give you a well rounded glimpse of this secret world.

While three of these four encounters did develop through the Internet, one special relationship in my local community came about through a poignant irony. I met her through circumstances surrounding my bitter and painful divorce. Circumstances that were designed to humiliate and destroy me publicly, by viciously outing me to my family, friends and professional associates.

It was directly through my ex-wife's efforts in this regard, that this special woman approached me. How this happened and all that resulted from having my sexuality portrayed in such a twisted light are woven into the encounters I describe here.

These four episodes contain all the elements of life: forbidden sex, elaborate hoaxes, true poetic love, pathos and tragedy, being "outed", scorned and ostracized by friends and family. These stories are about heroic, exuberant freedom-seekers exploring the true nature of their sexuality.

While this book inevitably has to reveal my own secrets, and my own trials to get "clean" about my sexuality, my revelations are simply ephemeral. The forbidden passions of the women described herein are what's interesting. I get to be the leading man, or the dark, desirable, forbidden Lord, but they are the stars.

I ask you to be patient as I take you on this path to discover what I did - extreme sex, decadence, fantasy, romance, passion, tender

6

soulfulness, treachery, and betrayal.

Come with an open mind, before you judge. It's just life really, but drawn in vivid, tantalizing flavors. If you can observe the events described here without prejudice, there is much to discover, maybe even about yourself.

In part, these encounters describe the mythic, ritualized romance between a man and a woman, as male Dominant and female submissive. These dynamics can go the other way, Femdom/malesub or be between the same gender. Some people, called Switches, go both ways.

This book deals exclusively in the realm of Maledom/femsub.(Note: There is a convention that came about on the Internet chat rooms of capitalizing references to the Dom and using lower case for the sub. Not all adhere to this, some are totally opposed to it, as presumptuous and without meaning. When used by those who do, it is meant as a form of respect and designation of position. I personally enjoy the ritual nature of this formal protocol. Most of the writing here will use this convention)

The exchange of power between a Dom and sub is something, I believe, that is at the core of our spiritual identity. Something that was in the natural order a very long time ago. It still seems a very important part of our psyche, though in modern times, it's buried under layers of guilt, shame, political correctness and the hypocritical and mysterious "sexual norm". What the "norm" is has always eluded any clear definition.

In the U.S mainstream, it is surreptitiously defined in shadow. It is taboo for adults and even marriage partners to comfortably discuss or explore any of their true fantasies, and other kinky "abnormal" desires, without risking severe judgement or ostracization from one's family, friends, co-workers, or either the political right or the left.

The BDSM culture in particular, is generally viewed right down their with and even below rapists, murderers and child molesters. It

should be noted however that the climate is slowly changing to match the times. The American Psychiatric Association recently removed consensual BDSM activities between adults from its list of pathological behaviors. D/s as a lifestyle preference is about where the gay movement was forty years ago.

It is my belief that the repression of one's true authenticity, sexual and otherwise, has led to the acting out of destructive and increasingly violent behavior in our society. Our culture allows and accepts an incessant bombardment of titillating and provocative imagery, through the mainstream media, while expecting individuals to maintain an outmoded posture of prudish propriety, no matter what the truth of an individual's sexuality might be.

This is my opinion: Nonconsensual violence against another is the most perverse form of abuse. Playing a role, exploring the drama of our darkest urges, with the willing consent of an adult partner is the healthy and exhilarating foundation of Dominance and submission.

I don't pretend to know much about, nor am I attempting to describe the full range of the D/s lifestyle in this book. My style is personal, evolving, as are most others. I borrow what is pleasing to me across the spectrum.

My credo is tolerance, though intolerance and sometimes vehement disagreement are still imbedded within the BDSM community. These are primarily cyber turf wars - my kink is OK and yours is not. Egos battling on the field of minutiae. Hang out on any BDSM newsgroup for a while, and you'll get the idea.

There's no escaping the mammalian, territorial nature of humans, I guess. On the whole, though, the ideal of tolerance is still strong within this lifestyle. My view is that when I'm this perverted, who am I to judge?

D/s is a generally noble pursuit practiced by people from every political, social and economic spectrum. The code of honor and trust is preserved in three sacred words - Safe, Sane and Consensual(SSC).

It seems there are always efforts to etch doctrine into stone in any culture. For me the notion of SSC is to be defined by the individuals involved in the activity, not by any group or individual claiming their truth as the one true way.

But be cautious. Having someone include SSC in a personals ad does not automatically mean that they are safe, sane or consensual. (you'll see SSC encoded in most ads on D/s personals sites, should you ever happen to look one up. Scoundrel that I am, I've listed a lot of interesting sites that contain personals and other scene info, in a resource list at the end of the book. NOT NOW! Read the book first. You can also go to my website, http://www.GalensRealm.com).

There is a public BDSM "scene" in most major communities, worldwide. Attending munches (casual socials that welcome "newbies") and local events are a good way to plug into your local scene. Most people, for good reason, choose to "play" privately. There are hundreds of ways to meet others, from personals sites, chat rooms, bulletin boards etc., for those who wish to explore in the safety and anonymity of the Internet.

Getting involved in the world of Dominance and Submission is a lot less risky than say Skydiving, Base or Bunji Jumping. Of course, anything you undertake involves risk. In my experience, if you follow common sense and study the numerous guides to safe meeting on the Internet or in Real Time, the risks are almost nil.

Statistically, you'll find the numbers of "battered" submissives are few and far between, compared to the number of "battered" spouses living under the guise of "normal" vanilla relationships. Most people in the D/s lifestyle hold sacred to the principles of Safe, Sane and Consensual conduct.

If something about this lifestyle stirs that hidden place where your deepest fantasies lie, know that you are just like millions of other people who have been shamed into feeling it is wrong to be this way.

Now, maybe for the first time, should you step into the pages of this book, know you are among friends. Your fear, shame, guilt, doubts, questions, shock and every perverse desire of a consensual nature are all welcome here.

It takes tremendous courage to explore the realm of the D/s lifestyle. The challenges of integrating one's vanilla appearance socially, with the delicious, secret life, are many. I've had to face an unfortunately large number of these challenges personally. I've survived them all (so far).

Even though some of my experience has been personally devastating and painful in the moment, what I've learned has aided me in living my life with authenticity, dignity and passion.

The encounters described within are really about discovering and living your truth, no matter what obstacles stand in your way. If I can help another Dominant, submissive, or any freedom-seeker find their way to the truth, sooner than I did, that is a cause I pursue with a passion.

Chapter 1

The Evolution of my Perversion

I first noticed my sexuality at five years old. I knew instinctively, had already picked up the cues, that sexuality was taboo. I hid it right from the start. I would sit unobtrusively on the floor within a room of grown-ups, observing things that interested me from that vantage point. This is where I started my fetish for nylon legs. I snuck looks at them as they sat, got up, walked by. I was an unde-tected voyeur.

Occasionally, when the nylon legs rose from sitting, I could see a little farther into that dark forbidden zone between them. Some-times I would go to the sofa, from where a woman had risen, and lay my head down like I was napping. I could feel the warmth of her behind against my cheek, and an aroma that I breathed deeply. I was so enticed by the nectar of a woman's scent. I was a "seat sniffer!"

Even though I've come quite far in my journey, I still feel somewhat embarrassed to say that. More sophisticated pleasures weren't readily available at the age of five.

When I was 14, I can still remember my father's attempt to explain the facts of life to his only son. It was 1964.

I could see how excruciatingly awkward he felt at the task. After his brief technical duty was accomplished, I felt I had confirmed my belief that my mother was still a virgin. I thought this with some potential for fact. My sister and I were both adoptees.

What he told me then, had no impact on my life, whatsoever. I was way beyond any stingy details he might have dispassionately revealed that day. I was already deeply, secretly and instinctually into sexual passion and fantasy.

At that point, I knew little but raging desire and fascination. I sought the mysteries of the female at her most seductive. From the time I was nine, or so, I was in a constant state of arousal. I began masturbating on my sister's dolls, fantasizing about them as real girls I knew. The dolls were quite small and ill equipped, but I had a huge imagination!

Before my teens, I experimented with and perfected the use of my Dad's shop vac in the basement. That versatile appliance could send me reeling into intoxicating orgasms, even before I could ejaculate. I would damn near pass out from the ecstasy. (I know this was nonconsensual sex and it was wrong, I just didn't know any better at the time! My apologies to Sears and the whole Craftsman family.).

I couldn't wait to have my first ejaculation. When it finally "came", I was ecstatic and relieved. I was now armed and dangerous. I swelled with pride and joy for my deliverance into the wild jungle of male animal prowess.

At the same time, I lived in terror that my secret life might be discovered. I suffered the strong repression of these instincts and pleasures by my Catholic upbringing. The fear, shyness, and shame of revealing my desires to others, kept my true sexual nature deep in shadow. This secrecy strained my psyche and my soul.

As a Catholic, I had to deal with confession and whether I should receive communion at Sunday Mass. If I didn't go up for communion, my family and everyone else in the Church would know I was in "mortal" sin. How would I explain that? If I did go to communion, and I had not done the "bless me father for I have sinned" routine in the confessional beforehand, then I would be committing another "mortal" sin, by receiving communion in am "impure" state.

What if I got killed in a car accident on the way home from church! I'd go straight to hell, suffering eternal damnation. Unless I was lucky and a priest got to my side to offer absolution before I gasped my last breath.

You can see how complicated it was, being a Catholic and a Pervert at the same time.

Throughout my teens, I maintained this image of a good Catholic, clean-cut boy, nurturing my perversity in shadow, never imagining then that, someday, openly, before God and the world, my darkest desires would ever be known, accepted and welcomed by others.

Starting back there, somewhere in my young life, the roots of the events that led to this book took hold.

****

My father was a timid, unhappy alcoholic. He was smart and industrious in many ways, but he was extremely shy, socially. He had a distorted piety and religious zeal that were a manifestation of his own insecurity. His father had died while grandma was still pregnant.

He'd been raised by his mother and her "good friend" and companion, a widow, like herself. The two women had lived together over 25 years. By the time I was born, the friend was long dead, and only referred to as, "Mrs. Keough." I always wondered about Grandma's and Mrs. Keough's relationship.

My father had been spoiled rotten from what I could gather. And as I was growing up, he still was like a spoiled, unhappy child.

My mother was an even weaker being than my father, and I'm sure that's why he chose her. She was not very educated, sophisticated or cultured. But she was a kind woman.

It was a cruel relationship for her - no affection, no tenderness, no friendship. It was shocking how loyal she was. She would defend him, when I would tell her to leave him for being such an asshole to her. Can you hear it? "Don't talk that way about your father. He's a good man." I didn't see her point. At that time I hated my father, and his cruel, loveless, tight-reigned hold on my, my mother's, and my sister's lives.

My mother's pleasure, besides her love for her children? She consumed piles of pulp romance novels. Mostly historic, period types, with covers depicting a woman in a revealing or torn blouse, her breasts half exposed, shoulders bare. Her slender arms were gripped in the strong hands of a man behind her, his handsome, rugged face about to nuzzle into her neck like a vampire. The look on her alluring face would be a rapturous canvas of pain and pleasure. Her soul seemed to be torn apart by something she desperately tried to hold back. That look turns me on to this day.

I always felt a sorrow for whom my mother must have been inside, in her hidden fantasy world. What she must have longed for, what she longed to give.

****

After hiding in shame and secrecy most of my life, I am finally learning to become authentic in all areas of my identity now, particularly my sexuality.

My conscious acceptance and pursuit of the D/s lifestyle came at the most terrifying and painful transition of my life. I was at the crossroads, the crisis point. Two paths lay before me. My old one, filled with shadows, secrets and skeletons. Or the new possibility that I had repressed all my life: to become authentic, heal deep wounds accumulated over my lifetime, to get out of my head exclusively, and into my heart, and face every fear and limit I hid from myself and others, pretending I was OK. I chose the latter.

I've been aided on this path to authenticity by a group called the "Mankind Project"(mkp.org). They have nothing to do with the D/s lifestyle, but instead are an international organization dedicated to aiding individual men, no matter what their orientations in life, to be authentic; live in integrity; repossess the sacred, powerful masculine; heal and explore ancient wounds; and have a man conceptualize and then live his mission. They also have a women's component called, Woman Within, as well as coed programs.

The unconditional support I've received from this group and other

14

wonderful allies I've met along the way have been my life preserver in the truest sense. What I've learned from them has kept me afloat, carried me through the most turbulent rapids I've ever been down. Class 5 and above in some cases.

The most prominent has been my struggle through the intense awkwardness and isolation of being publicly and nonconsensually "outed", painted in the most vile, despicable terms.

I had left my wife after putting up with sixteen years of emotional abuse and belittlement. Now that my sons were older, I'd had enough. I had always tried to make our marriage work, even when it seemed impossible. I was a devoted father and it was difficult to consider tearing apart the fabric of my son's family foundation.

I was not a perfect husband or father. I strove for equity and balance in my relationship. But with my ex, there was no compromise, no balance, no negotiation about how to get what we both needed. She simply refused to discuss anything important in a reasonable, mutually accommodating fashion.

My desire to leave had little to do with my sexuality. I simply could no longer survive in a spiritually dead environment If we had had a loving relationship, I might never have entered this phase of my life.

My ex discovered my "secret" shortly after I left her. At that moment in time, we still owned a business together. She was snooping around my office one day when I was out. She uncovered several correspondences I'd been having on the Internet with submissives, as well as the erotic stories I was writing, within some of my personal computer files.

She felt horrified and humiliated. She proceeded to blame my sexuality as the cause for my leaving her, and every other problem she'd ever had in her life it seemed. She made copies and took computer disks that were my property. She tried to turn these into a strategic weapon and began her efforts to destroy me publicly and in our divorce trial.

During the time it took to go from separation to divorce, she waged an emotionally violent slander campaign to all her family, my family, my two teenage sons, the employees of our business, all our friends, the judge in our divorce trial, and just about anybody else she could spread her malicious gossip to...how sick I was, how disgusting, my violent hatred of women, that I was a threat and a danger to her, my kids and society.

After the divorce, she won custody of our kids. The judge "punished" me by providing an unequal distribution of property in a no-fault state(very rare, and in this case, contrary to the law), and by some severe restrictions on my visitation rights. I was limited initially to seeing my sons every other weekend from noon Saturday til 6pm Sunday.

I was not allowed to have anyone else in my presence while with my kids, assuming anyone I might be with would be a threat to my kids moral character. Later, I was able to get some of these restrictions upgraded to "no one with a romantic interest", and added one night per week to go out to dinner. It was a desolate feeling to suddenly be reduced to an occasional visitor to my children, who I had literally spent everyday with for 16 years.

But my ostracization was not yet complete. Soon thereafter, my kids wrote me an email, and told me they didn't want to see me again, until I got counseling for my "addictions". It was a devastating turn of events.

I had made a conscious effort to in no way involve or discuss the divorce or their mother with my kids. I asked them often if they had any questions or issues they wanted to understand more about, or tell me their feelings about mom and dad's divorce. I knew at least certain parts of her slander would be filtering down to my sons. They were living with her, and her family were frequent visitors and guests throughout her "ordeal".

For me this was a matter for two adults to deal with, not something that should involve their children. It was not my sons' burden. My ex took a different approach.

As painful as that has been for me, I in no way judge my kids about this. I know they are doing what they have to do, living under their mother and her family's judgment of me, to protect their own vulnerable psyches. I honor their decision, and know at some point, we will be back together. I love them and support them tenderly and unconditionally.

I am a pariah, now, in my old circles. I live in a fairly small city. After nearly twenty-five years as a professional in this town and having been an active parent in my sons' school, sports and social activities, I know a lot of people.

Literally, not one person in those circles ever came to me and asked about the things my ex was saying. They all took her side. Their superficial liberal natures could not cope with the volatility of who they thought I was. Perhaps, in the hidden shadows of their psyche, they were secretly terrified of their own dark secrets. They them-selves may get called onto the carpet by this witch-hunt hysteria my ex was breeding, should they even go so far as to get my side of the story. Though it hurt a lot at the time, I have no remorse over losing friends of so little courage or integrity.

Before I began learning about the empowerment of authenticity, this much severe judgment and loss would have killed me. I have withstood this barrage, taken every blow. There's been plenty of damage to me emotionally. Coming to terms with the truth of your sexuality can be traumatic, even in a supportive environment.

I became impotent for nearly a year, another of many ironies in my evolution on this path. At times, I thought I would never recover, or survive the relentless attack I was under, the loneliness and isolation I felt. Plus I was struggling with the grief and loss of my former life, and having given up my role in our business, was now facing financial devastation as well.

There was a lot more going on in my quest for authenticity, than my immediate tumult. Issues stretching back all the way to my birth, were also at hand. Survival now meant facing every haunting

imprint and fear within my psyche that held me back from being authentic. My face was to the wall. There was only one direction to go.

I chose to turn and walk forward into my truth. This and the support I've received from my allies have literally saved my life. For all the terror and pain my spirit has been subjected to, I would never desire to go back to hiding from others and myself. That was a much greater agony, really, to not be who I truly was. As Nietzsche said, "What doesn't kill me makes me stronger."

My mission now is to shed every shame, guilt, judgment or embarrassment about my or anyone's sexuality. It is my intent to no longer hide or hold back anything that I truly feel. I have that courage now. I did my trial by fire, and came out the other side, tattered, but clear in my identity.

In seeking to be totally honest and authentic about my sexuality, to honor it, I am not alone.

Episode 1

Sharah

The events surrounding my encounter with sharah changed my life almost overnight, for better and for worse. If you can picture novelist Elmore Leanord, writing one of his offbeat and sharp-edged suspense thrillers with a BDSM theme, you'll get the idea.

At the point of my contact with sharah, I was already into my transition "plan" to leave my wife. I made a lot of stupid mistakes at this moment in my life. I was reckless and naïve. I was at a point where I didn't really care about consequences. I was determined to change my life.

If I had seen what was coming, I'm not sure my courage would have been enough to keep going. Ignorance wasn't bliss in this case, but it did lead me forward.

Here's the background that led to my meeting sharah, and jettisoned me, without a parachute, from my past life.

I had been miserably married to a woman for 16 years, who attempted to defeat every part of me that she didn't understand. These things she feared in me had everything to do with my soul, my passions. Most were not related to my sexuality.

My ex approached her task of annihilating my spirit, with relentless criticism, emotional distance, soulless insensitivity, and in the end a raging, dysfunctional brutality(that gruesome depiction is rendered more explicitly in the Arlana and Kate encounters). You might question which one of us was really the sadist. I felt like I was living with the enemy, and she was slowly winning the war.

I stayed in the relationship as long as I did, in good part, because of my two wonderful sons. As an adoptee. I had a strong sense of how important a father and mother's relationship to their children can be. I missed having the compass points of a biological family, with the culture and ancestry to help anchor my life and identity.

I got my sons to the ages of 16 and 14, but I couldn't take it any farther, without irreparably harming my self, or jeopardizing my ability to help them more in the future.

I had planned a 6 month schedule to leave my wife. We owned a business together. It was fairly successful, despite our inability to communicate about how to manage it. My goal was to set that business up to run without me, while I developed a business of my own. With this decision, I also knew it was the chance to get honest this time around about my D/s sexual identity.

I began to respond to ads from submissive women I found on Internet personals sites. I was pleasantly surprised with the reception I received from those efforts. My plans to depart my marriage, and pursue my truth, seemed to be on track. I had planned a smooth transition. It didn't happen that way.

At 48, starting my life over, was a daunting endeavor. I was excited and terrified. Was I just chasing a lifelong fantasy, or was my sexuality an honest, valid and powerful dimension of my soul.

I found sharah's ad listed on a D/s personals site. She was from New York, and I had a business trip planned there, so I sent her my profile and a kinky short story I had written.

New York came and went. Then a few weeks later, I received an email from her. It was six pages of the most enticing vision of submissiveness I could have imagined. sharah was incredibly kinky and perverse, a supreme slut and slave, intelligent, sweet.

Despite the age and distance that separated us, I took a cavalier, "what have I got to lose approach." I jumped into this boiling lust and desire, without giving much thought to the consequences. Looking back, I see where I should have heard some alarms go off. I was too new on the Internet to know any better.

This is the story of sharah - 23 year old ballet instructor, Daddy/ daughter slave. You'll never see what's coming in the erotic,

treacherous, twists and turns of this intriguing tale.

This is the ad sharah placed on the D/s site. I responded to it. Who wouldn't have? (I don't really need to know who you are!)

A girl who knows her place.

i am a young (23), pretty (5'3", 104lbs., reddish-brown hair, blue eyes), highly-sexed, very loving, very obedient, very submissive female, longing to serve a dominant, highly-sexed, real Man (or Men) with a macho attitude toward women (or a Gorean attitude toward females, if you know what that means.)

There is not a feminist bone in my body. i do not wish to be a Man's equal. i want to be the property of a Man or Men who feel they are entitled to own and use a female however they please. i truly believe i exist for the pleasure, amusement, convenience and comfort of Men. i was taught my place by an older Man some time ago and have served eagerly, ever since, whenever given the chance.

i respond gratefully to orders and to all reminders of my status as a cunt, whore, slut, fucktoy, and slave to Male dominance. i know it is my place to keep myself fit and attractive for Men, and to learn how a Man likes to be pleased. i understand discipline and punishment are sometimes necessary if i fail to be perfectly pleasing or, simply if it suits a Man to punish me.

i cook well and am a diligent housemaid, but my strongest talents are as a sexual servant. i can travel to serve or entertain at bachelor parties, poker games, etc. and can relocate for ownership and whoredom. i especially dream of being owned and used by a very dominant, older, Daddy, but i will serve, respect, love and worship any real man who owns me.

"Please, Sirs, give this girl a chance to live in her proper place."

Subject: Handsome Erotic Dom
Date: Thu, 29 Oct

Dear sharah,

I was very attracted to your ad. I found your submissive nature very compelling. If you're attracted to my profile that follows, it would please me to hear from you. This is my standard profile. If you respond and intrigue me, I will write a very personal response. I am planning on visiting NYC in a few weeks. Are you from the city?

I am a professional/entrepreneur, youthful 48, fit/athletic, 6'2", 195lbs, blue eyes, very handsome, bigger than average equipment, highly intelligent and creative, with a good sense of humor.

I am newly experienced, playful and loving, yet strict. I can patiently respect, but push a submissive's limits. Although I am a kind and considerate gentleman in many respects, sexually I am a confident Dom, and have strong interests in BDSM from mild to extreme.

I enjoy women who are otherwise charming, highly affectionate, good listeners, romantic, literate and cultured, and who possess a generous and gracious "spirit". I am a bright and accomplished man whose company you would enjoy both in and out of the bedroom. I am safe and sane, totally kinky and devoted to the lifestyle.

I seek a submissive who enjoys the thrill of erotic desire and freely exploring every dark and mysterious realm of BDSM to safe extremes. Someone who has escaped or is seeking to escape the guilt, shame and judgment-centered aspects of vanilla culture. Someone who enjoys an everyday lifestyle enshrouded in the constant tension and desire of a D/s relationship. While you enjoy the beauty, romance and tenderness, the intellectual exchange, the

humor and passion of life, you also love and crave to be a Dom's slut, and eagerly surrender to his sadistic passion, using you for his pleasure.

I don't believe anything is perfect. I know I'm not. I have an ideal that I strive for as a Dom and a human, and seek the same effort from my ideal submissive partner.

As a compassionate Dom, my main goal is to assist sexually submissive women to have a safe and exciting outlet for their desires, if they're not finding it elsewhere. Consider me like a highly skilled coach or "personal trainer", preparing you well for your true Master, if it is not me.

Physically, I prefer shapely legs, trim body, average to large tits, medium to long hair, pretty face, alluring eyes, and an easy smile. But the true heat of attraction is a mystery, I believe. The soul and mind are equally important. Preferred age, late 20's to 40's, under 5' 9", and hwp.

My BDSM pleasures include: creating light to intense emotional/ mental Domination experiences, cascading orgasms, or denial of orgasm, nipple and tit torture, pussy torture, clamps, tight bondage, gags, suspension, erotic dance, high heels, nylons/garters, short skirts, spanking, whipping, anal, verbal, toys, role play, and more.

A Master and slave, 24/7 relationship with formal, ritual behavior, is a possibility, but to me that is a very complex, though potentially pleasing dynamic, that would require extensive exploration.

I'm including a short scenario about a fantasy scene I've enjoyed with other submissives. Can you picture yourself as the starring attraction? What would you add or subtract, if you were in this scene? If this message struck your fantasy, reply for further discussion. I also like to share thoughts and feelings and learn more about the mental aspects of BDSM, as well as hot email. (I like to write stories about submissive fantasy). Send me a picture, straight or otherwise.

"Scene 1"

Everything about you is so sexy! Seeing you stand before me, a willing and anxious-to-please submissive, excites me greatly. The point of your desire is to please me. You wish to release your slutty submissive nature. And so, I think of you as you will be, my total and personal sex slave.

You will learn to obey willingly, seek to please my most perverse play. You will desire to be tightly bound, pleasantly whipped and tormented. You want to be consumed by your own perverted lust. I will joyfully play with your body and your mind. You are my sexy pleasure toy. You will dance for me, be lewd...suggestive. You will voice your desire to please me. And then you will please me. You'll be dressed in black spiked heels with a strap around the ankle, black seamed nylons, and a lacy garter. You'll wear a low-cut push-up bra. Over these, you'll have on a revealing blouse, and a short skirt with a revealing slit up the side. There is a sensual groove coming from the stereo.

"Show me the kind of whore you are, sweetheart, dance for me." I look at you, piercing right through you, it feels.

"You know what I want, show it to me." I am sitting, facing you in a straight-back chair, smiling. You begin to feel the music and start to dance suggestively. Your smile shows you're enjoying this very much. Your anticipation is strong, and you feel your body start to flush with lust. While you dance you emphasize your tits, your ass and finally your cunt. Still clothed, you rub each of these against my crotch, telling me about your growing need to be my slave. You desire to please me in every way. You feel my desire for you hardening between my legs. I encourage your slutty desire. Your cunt is wettening as you sense the potential of my desire for you. Your surrender slowly begins.

I tell you to turn around and bend over. You wave your tight ass and expose your cunt to me, still dancing to the music. You're looking at me, your hair hanging down, swaying against the floor. I

watch your eyes saying all those special prayers, petitioning your lord for pleasure.

You address me, "Master, please fuck my hot slave cunt." Your fingers move from your exposed, inviting cunt and you roll a finger around the rim of your asshole. "Shove it up my ass, please Sir. I want you to take it, Sir! It's all yours. Please take it! Fuck it, right now." You groan, your eyes are glazing, you pant with the thoughts of your lust.

"Oh! I will fuck you up the ass, sweet bitch. In my own time."

You slap your ass hard with your hand. I smile at the pleasing sound that rings from your firm ass. Your smile is so encouraging. Your eyes are begging. Your ass and cunt, your tits, your mouth and your mind are becoming one thing. The one thing. You feel all hesitancy escaping. "Yes" is the only thought you have. You are drifting closer and closer to your true sexual identity... you're a slave and a slut, and you know you need a man who will treat you as such, so that you may be satisfied in the truest sense.

I reach down for the crop I placed next to my chair. Without a thought, I bring the crop down hard on your prayerful ass. Your flinch of pain is reflected in my knowing smile. Your eyes confirm my growing control over you. You know in your whore's heart that you will beg for the torture and abuse that will send you to the edge of your limits, and eventually beyond.

I'm beginning to enjoy your potential as a slut that I can use and abuse for my pleasure. I am quite pleased with your expression of submissiveness. I whip the crop hard on your ass again, followed without hesitation by a stinging assault right on your cunt. Your pain releases with the rush of your restrained squeal.

"Stand up! Turn around!" I command. You face me. My face is gentle, pleased. "You are so beautiful, so sexy! My cock is grow-ing harder, as I look at you." Your eyes are beckoning more, but reveal an uncertainty. You so want to please me.

"Yes my lovely slut, you're a fine whore, aren't you?" My eyes devour you from head to toe, examining your body. The pleasure and confidence in my inspection of you, excites you. "I think its time we crop your tits. Don't you? Slip them out of your bra. Let's seem 'em, my beautiful whore."

Your slight hesitation is met with a crisp blow from my crop smack on your cunt. You jump. You grimace. You quickly undo your blouse and pull your tits from your bra, and bending slightly, offer them to me. You savor what's coming.

(Interested in what happens next? Hint - think suspension, whipping, forced oral! Let me know)

And you, sweetheart, should know that it will require more than a few sentences to attract this Dom's attention. Think carefully, then tell me some things about your past, your training, or if you're new, what you feel your current limits are, what are your current beliefs about and goals for a D/s relationship, what are your favorite submissive pleasures, or anything else you like. What did you think of my story? I expect you to express herself explicitly, and in detail.

Galen

Subject: Your grateful girl
Date: Mon, 16 Nov

Dear Sir,

Thank you so much for contacting me and for the beautiful domination fantasy you wrote. I felt as though you were allowing me to serve you while I was reading it, and that was an honor for me. I am now dressed as you described in your story, in order to write this to you. I want very much to please you. My cunt has been wet since I found your letter in my mailbox. My nipples are standing at attention as I write this.

You seem like a wonderful man, strong and sexy. I wish you were using me right now.

My real name is sharah (at least until I am owned by a man who changes it.) The physical description in my profile is accurate. I'm 23 years old, 5'3", 104lbs, 34C-22-35, I have reddish-brown hair and blue eyes. I make my living teaching ballet and jazz dance to young girls (ages 7 - 16, and occasionally an adult class.)

I sometimes dance in bars and clubs too, but I haven't really pursued that, professionally. Dancing for men gets me too turned on, and I have a very hard time stopping there. Club owners don't look too kindly on a slut like me, though the audience usually loves it. I prefer private parties where I can dance and then be used by men. Nothing makes me happier than dancing for men, then getting my nipples clamped and spending the rest of the night fetching drinks, emptying ashtrays and sucking cock.

I have a very submissive nature, obviously, and I truly love serving men. It is not just a physical experience for me, my heart is literally filled to overflowing when I am following orders and making a man feel like a king. I get my needs fulfilled by serving others.

I'm pretty much that way outside of the bedroom, too, and not just with sexual partners. I love cooking dinner for my friends, and giving back rubs, listening to those in need, offering my help with anything I can. I'm a good, hard worker, and I want to contribute everything I can to the world.

I volunteer a lot of my time at a children's hospital and other causes, too. I know it may seem strange to some people, but I discovered a long time ago that I am happiest and most fulfilled when I am giving. By far, the most important service to me, though, is truly serving and obeying a man. All of the other things I do would have to come second to any man who decided to take possession of me. If he didn't want me to spend time on those other things, as far as I'm concerned, that would be his decision, and I would obey willingly. I really do believe that is my place, and I take that very seriously, in my heart.

I don't want only to serve blindly, I want to love fully. I know I am very capable of it. One man I served told me I was the most loving and submissive whore he had ever trained.

That was music to my ears. I was trained pretty young and I'm very grateful for that, because I have never felt any doubt or confusion about how I want to live my life. I never felt the need to go out in the world and compete with men and climb the ladder of success.

I'm no airhead, I'm a bright girl, literate and observant. I know how to behave in public, and how to hold an intelligent conversation. No man I've ever served has been embarrassed by me in front of his friends or family. But there has never been any doubt about who is the boss in the relationship, either.

About the only thing I think I couldn't do to please a man is to try to pretend to dominate him. I just don't think I'm capable of it. I'm too much in awe of men, and feel too feminine to ever think about trying to get my way. My place is to please a man, and to obey without hesitation. I know that a lot of BDSM is about acting out fantasies and I love to do that, but it goes pretty deep for me.

Even if I end up in a traditional marriage with a husband and kids, where the only obvious domination takes place in the bedroom, I will still be, in my heart, his property. And I will still make pleasing him and obeying him, the main focus of my life. I'm sorry to go on and on about myself like this. I just wanted to explain a little bit about what my submission means to me and how profound a part of me it really is.

I'm not one of those girls who try to control a man from the "bottom," by telling them how I want the domination to take place. As far as I'm concerned, what you say is going to happen, is what happens. Some men do like to understand their girls and what their fantasies and dreams are, though. If a man asks to know about me, I tell him the truth. If he doesn't want to hear from me, I keep my mouth shut and do as I'm told.

My first Master sometimes loved for me to talk and talk, and sometimes he wanted me kneeling quietly at his feet, waiting for his next order. He sometimes used a gag when he wanted to make sure I was silent, but usually I knew when he wanted to hear from me and when he didn't.

Since you asked me about my fantasies, I thought you might be pleased if I continued the one you started. I hope it turns you on, Sir.

sharah's Scene 2

...i arch my back slightly, allowing my tits to dangle, offering them to you for your use. i see you smile as you raise the crop, flicking it quickly down, stinging across both my tits. my nipples, which have been at attention since you called me into the room, are swollen and aching for your touch.

You bring the crop down hard, again. Then again. Again. Harder and faster with each strike. My teeth bite into my pouty, red lips; the stinging pain in my breasts is searing through my whole body. Suddenly, you insert the end of the crop into my mouth.

"Hold onto that for a minute, whore," you order me, then you grab both of my nipples, squeezing them roughly between your thumbs and forefingers. i moan and bite down on the crop, being careful not to leave my teeth marks on your property. You twist my nipples harder and the erotic charge goes straight to my wet cunt. i feel a drop of my own juices leak out of my whore hole and drip down my inner thigh. i want to beg you to fuck me again, but my mouth is full of stiff leather. You see the pleading in my eyes, and it amuses you.

"I see I'm not the first to train you in the use of these toys, am I, cunt?" you ask me, laughing.

"No, Sir," i try to mumble, but muffled vowel sounds are all i can manage with my mouth full.

"No?" you repeat, still grinning and pulling my nipples. "Other men have shown you what a whore's tits are for. I see you learned your lesson, well. Your cunt is dripping all over my floor, slave. You'll be licking that up later. Right now, I have other plans for you."

You reach into your pocket, and before i can see what you have in your hands, i feel the sharp bite of the clamps. First on my swollen left nipple, then on my right. The pain is intense at first, but soon fades to a constant erotic reminder of my status as your decorated fucktoy. i am falling into a trance, becoming only an object for your use and abuse. i am still bent over slightly, but i am unconsciously beginning to sway my hips, and undulate my body, dancing for you, performing like the trained slut i have always been.

"Strip!" you growl at me. "NOW!" You add emphasis to your strict commands by grabbing the crop from my mouth and giving me a hard smack on my clamped tits. i rush to remove my blouse and skirt.

"Leave the rest of it on." you command. "I like looking at you, decorated and dressed for me."

i do as I'm told, standing in my heels, hose, garter belt and bra; my tortured tits pushed up and out of my bra. i arch my back again to present myself properly to the incredible Man, standing before me. Before i realize what is happening, you are standing behind me, threading some kind of wire through the loops on the nipple clamps you placed on me.

You are pulling a chain and i feel myself being pulled upward. Even with four inch heels on, i am soon standing on tiptoe, with my nipples being pulled upward, stretched farther than i thought possible.

i know i am being put on display for your pleasure, and even though i am in pain, i don't make a sound. i am going to be the best little cunt you ever used. i won't let you down, Sir.

30

Next you are shoving something large and round into my mouth, and tying something behind my head. You are gagging me, I soon realize. You have heard enough from me for a while. i realize there must be more coming. i will be brave. i will be used properly and i will love it, because that is what my Master expects of me.

Then there are leather straps being wrapped around my waist, a collar around my neck, my wrists and ankles are bound, some kind of thin strap is being threaded through my collar, wrapped around my breasts, pushed into my cunt and ass like a thong, and attached to the back of the straps at my waist. You are binding me thoroughly, methodically. Occasionally you slap my ass or grab my clit roughly, sometimes even kissing my neck tenderly as you prepare your slave cunt for your use.

Without warning, my feet are swept from behind me, and i am suspended in the air, facing the floor. my hands are tied tightly behind me, and being pulled up toward my head. my back is severely arched, and my nipples are still being stretched toward heaven.

i am in pain, but it is not unbearable. i realize you are not punishing me - or else i am sure i would be in much more pain. You are only expertly putting me into a position of complete surrender, complete ownership, total slavery. i am now your property to use as you please, or simply to be kept on display.

You walk slowly around me, admiring your lovely new possession, estimating my value, deciding how you want to use me first. You still have the crop in your hands, and your run the tip of it slowly around my pretty face, giving little tiny stings, not hard enough to mark your property, only little reminders of your dominance over me. You walk out of my sight for a moment and return with a small whip. i gasp, when i see the look in your eye, afraid of what your might be planning.

"Don't worry, little one," you tell me, soothingly. "You've pleased me, so far. I only want to redden your ass a little before I stick my

cock inside it." I relax, and take a breath, waiting for the first blow, waiting for the moment you will finish and be ready to take my whore's ass. i squirm a little, without meaning to, and moan quietly at the thought of being fucked by such a demanding, strong Man.

The beating lasts longer than i expect, and by the end of it, my skin is alive with sensation. You walk in front of me again, and it is immediately obvious how much you have enjoyed watching me squirm under your capable lash. Your cock is already sticking straight out of your fly, and you swiftly remove the gag, grabbing a handful of my hair and jerking my head back.

"Kiss it, whore," you coo at me, rubbing the head against my soft, painted lips. i obey instantly, barely able to contain my excitement. i lick and kiss, worshipping your magnificent, hard cock, whimpering and pleading.

"Oh, please let me suck it, Master. Please fuck your little whore in the mouth."

"Open wide, bitch," you say with a slight sneer, and i eagerly comply. You slide your cock slowly but steadily all the way down, pausing only momentarily as you bump into my tonsils.

"I said OPEN, slut! Make your throat into a cunt for me to fuck."

That's all i need to hear and all barriers are removed. i am, from head to toe, an open, dripping, sucking, massaging, whore hole for you to use. Every nerve in my body is concentrated on giving you pleasure. You are pumping my throat mercilessly, your hard cock coated with my thick, clear saliva. my body is twitching in mid-air, straining against your home-made harness. my mouth is an open tunnel to my cunt and ass, and i feel your cock filling me everywhere, fucking me in every hole.

"Yes, you beautiful little whore. You love your Master's cock, don't you? You love it when I fuck your little whore mouth. That's exactly what that mouth was made for, isn't it. Get my cock nice and wet, little cunt. It's going up your ass in a minute. I don't

intend to use any grease. I won't need to, will I, my little fucktoy?"

i am almost out of my mind with desire. I can't see anything or think about anything. i can only feel myself being used by a Man. That is what i am here for. You pull out of my sucking mouth with a plop, and walk around behind me. i am taking deep gulps of air; i don't even realize that i have not been breathing for several minutes. i did not need air while my Master's cock was in my mouth. He was feeding me everything i needed to survive. i feel your thick fingers probing my glistening cunt, pinching my clit. i spasm involuntarily.

"Careful, bitch!" you snap at me. "You don't come without my permission. Is that clear?" The slap on my ass is definitely hard enough for me to know you mean business.

"Yes, Sir," i squeal. i control myself and remember that i am here for your pleasure. i admonish myself silently and put my concentration back where it belongs. Your have four fingers inside my cunt, now, and your thumb is deep inside my tight little asshole. You are holding me like a suitcase, spreading me open, wider and wider; preparing me to be used. i feel you rub the head of your hard cock all around my labia.

i feel you step away, but before i have time to wonder what you are doing, i hear a sound and suddenly, my legs are being separated, and pulled apart. my feet are still tied to the chains, still suspended, but now i am spread wide, on display like the slut i am. i hear you chuckle at the sight of me, so vulnerable and ready. All at once, with no warning, your thick cock is shoved all the way inside my tight, wet cunt, in one hard thrust. my entire whore body wants to begin its convulsions, but i know better than to give into my orgasm. i will do as i am told and wait for your command to cum.

You are pumping my willing pussy so hard, and i am using my cunt muscles to squeeze and caress your beautiful, Masterful cock. The squishing sounds coming from my cunt are almost deafening and i can feel my juices squirting out of me, covering your cock and belly. i know i will have a lot of licking to do when you are finished

with me.

i am in constant danger of slipping over the edge; your fucking is so powerful, but i will not disobey. i know it is pleasing you to watch me holding back and that is all the pleasure i could ever need. You are such a magnificent Man, and i feel like the luckiest girl in the world.

i want to cry out my love to you, but you have not given me permission to speak. Then, my cunt is empty. i moan, involuntarily, and wiggle my ass, praying for you to re-insert yourself. i feel bereft and in total despair, but i do not have to wait long.

"Now, I'm going to fuck that pretty little whore ass, bitch. You're going to open right up for me, aren't you, my obedient slut?"

"Yes, Sir." i begin, but before i can complete my answer, you are splitting me in two with your hard, manhood. Your cock is coated with my spit and cunt-juices and the force of your thrust is enough to open my tight rosebud. A hot, searing pain shoots through my body, and causes me to arch and tense.

"OPEN!" you bark at me, and i concentrate on relaxing and welcoming you inside me. You are all the way inside me now, and i swear i can feel your cock filling my belly and snaking its way up to my throat. The pain is subsiding and you begin your pumping in earnest.

"That's it, slut." you groan at me, slapping my ass for good measure. "I own you, now. I use that ass, whenever I please!"

Your pelvis is slamming into me, faster and faster, harder and harder. my cunt, my tits, my ass, and my mouth are all salivating, are all on fire with pure love and lust for the magnificent Man i am being permitted to serve. Once again, i am on the verge of losing control and losing my mind in a series of earth-shattering orgasms. Just when i think i can no longer hold on, you abruptly stop thrusting. my body is still swinging in the harness. i hear you breathing hard behind me.

34

"Lift your head. Arch your back." you are ordering me, and i quickly comply. "Now," i hear you explain, "you do the work. Move your self in the harness. Fuck your hungry whore ass with my cock."

It is difficult, but i soon understand how to make my body swing properly, and am able to ride your cock up and down. i can feel you smiling down upon me, watching me work to please you, and i feel that you are happy with your obedient, loving, eager slave. i begin using my ass like a milking machine, hoping to thrill you with my slut talents.

"That's it, baby girl," you moan deeply. "Yes! Suck my cock with your ass, bitch. Show me what a perfect little whore you are."

After what seems like forever, you can no longer contain your primal instincts. You growl deeply and grab both of my tits in your big hands, pinching and pulling my clamped nipples, and begin pounding my ass like a jackhammer. my whore body is vibrating at a fever pitch.

Just when i think i am about to disobey you against my own will, you shout at me, "CUM FOR ME, BITCH! DO IT! NOW!!!!"

i am blinded. my body is convulsing, twitching, arching gro-tesquely in mid-air. i couldn't stop now, even if you commanded it. i am a helpless, fuck-toy, performing for her Master, cumming non-stop, producing quarts of feminine liquids, unable to breathe, think or hear anything but the sound of your voice. Unable to feel anything but your cock, filling me, fucking me, owning me. You pull out suddenly and rush to the front of me.

"OPEN, CUNT!" you command. my mouth stretches wide, and my tongue presents itself, instinctively. Your face is red and twisted; you are staring at me as if i am only a pretty receptacle for your pleasure. You are holding your blood-engorged cock in your fist and pointing it at my open, eager, pretty little whore-mouth.

The first white glob shoots with violence out of your cock, and splats on my forehead, running down my nose toward my waiting, open mouth. You move a step closer and rest the head of your spurting cock on my extended, pink tongue. The next few squirts, hit the back of my throat, and slide past my tonsils, down my gullet and into my tummy. Your cum is pouring like hot lava into my mouth, and i almost start cumming again at the strong, salty taste of you.

"That's the way, cunt. Swallow every drop of it. That's your reward, my little whore. Don't waste any of it."

i am in heaven. i have never been given so much of such a precious gift. Tears are streaming down my face, tears of gratitude. i wish i could hang here, tied and clamped by you, swallowing your delicious cum for the rest of my life. i would do anything for you. i am your property. i love you, Master, with all my heart. Soon you are petting my head and stroking my hair tenderly. You slide your cock, once more, all the way down my throat and allow me to suck the last few drops from your softening cock.

"Good, girl." you are soothing me. "Good little baby whore."

You release me from the harness and untie my hands. i almost collapse from exhaustion but i manage to keep myself kneeling upright before you, thrusting my clamped tits forward for your visual pleasure.

"Go get me a soda, sweetheart." you order me. As i hop up and run into the kitchen, i hear you call after me, "And bring Daddy a cigar."

When i return with the soda, cigar, and clippers, you are reclining in your favorite chair. You look so handsome and satiated, i begin to weep again with love for you. i kneel at your feet and clip the end of the cigar, exactly as you have taught me. i watch you light up and sit back, puffing and relaxing with a contented sigh. i am so filled with love for you, and so grateful that you have allowed me to make you feel so good. You are a king to me. You are a God.

i can't help myself, i collapse onto my belly at your feet and begin kissing and licking them, worshipping you as you deserve to be worshipped. You look down at me and smile paternally. You did not order me to move, but you have already forgiven this transgression. You know how much your girl loves and worships you, and you know sometimes she can't help the spontaneous expressions of her complete submission to you.

"Come here, baby," you say gently and reach down for me, pulling me up into your lap. You wrap one arm around me protectively, resting it on my ass and gently press my head to your shoulder. i curl up into your protective embrace and let my tears fall quietly on your strong shoulder. i breathe deeply, inhaling the smell of your sweat, your cum, and your cigar smoke.

"You please me, little one." i hear you say, as i close my eyes, and thank God for you. "You're a good girl."

Well... there it is, Sir. i hope, with all my heart, that my little fantasy gave you pleasure. Please let me hasten to add again, that i am not trying to tell you what kind of scene i need. i am not like that. What takes place between a Man and his girl is up to him. These are just some of the things i have been trained to do, and, the truth is, this fantasy is a peek into my slave-girl/Daddy's girl heart. i truly worship strong, dominant Men, and i pray to be owned by one again, someday.

If there is anything else you want to know about me, or any other way i can serve you, please let me know. Any girl who has the opportunity to please a Man like you is going to be a very lucky girl, indeed.

Gratefully yours,

sharah

Subject: soulful submissive
Date: Mon, 16 Nov

My dear little slut,

Your lovely, seductive letter pleased me greatly. Your description of your soulful, rapturous submissiveness was exquisite. I appreciated the tone and style of your writing, the intelligence behind the surrender. Your sweetness and intelligence moved me.

It was uncanny how similarly your rendition of scene 2 paralleled my own, from start to finish. I will confess that if I had a choice, I would choose to be the Master in your enticing story ahead of my own. My compliments, slut. I am enclosing my scene 2 for comparison.

I will look forward to learning more about the lovely slave, sharah.

Warmly,

Galen

"Scene 2"

Your hands are raised above your head, each wrist within a leather brace with cords that connect to a pulley in the ceiling. You are hanging, suspended a foot above the floor. Your tits are tightly bound with velvet cords. They are very swollen and engorged, each nipple clamp a sharp reminder of the flogging your tits were given before I began to concentrate on your reddening ass.

"More! Please Master, whip my ass more, and harder, please Master. I'm so hot for you!"

Not that I needed any encouragement. I bring the flogger hard across one cheek, and watch with great pleasure as the flesh quivers and your body sways above the ground from the force of the blows. Ten hard strikes on each cheek, then several to your upper back,

several more to the back of your thighs. Your moan is steeped in pain and desire. You look back at me, watching me with both excitement and torment, a loving, impassioned gaze, wanting so to please your new Master.

The pain is different than you imagined. It has built gradually and you are pleased with how far you've been able to let it progress. Your lust, you realize far outweighs your discomfort. Your mind wants more, and your body is the vehicle that delivers this painful, intoxicating pleasure.

"You look very beautiful, my slave." I admire your lovely body suspended in air, your black high heels dangling above the floor, your legs, so desirable in their black nylons attached to that whorish garter, that accents your wonderful ass and aching cunt. I rub your ass softly with my palm, then reach from behind through your legs, gripping your wet pussy tightly. You turn your lust-filled face to me and we kiss passionately, your wild desire transmitted through your searching tongue deep within my mouth. Our eyes are open, inches apart and you feel yourself disappear within my dark lusty gaze.

I put each ankle in a brace, and draw each cord so that your legs are drawn apart and up towards the ceiling, your body now suspended face up parallel to the floor. It feels quite comfortable, like floating. Your arms begin to relax now that your weight is balanced with the support of your suspended ankles.

I place a huge dildo between your spread legs. It is mounted on a post attached to the floor. Your eyes widen with expectation.

"Not quite yet, my lovely slut. First I must warm up that hot fucking cunt of yours. Won't that be nice?"

I adjust the cords around each ankle so your cunt is spread as wide open as your straining legs will allow. I grab the crop and place a sharp blow right on your cunt lips. Your body writhes and sways as I continue to deliver my well-aimed blows on your exposed cunt.

"I can see your cunt getting wetter. But I think it will require a few more, don't you, slut?" As each blow was struck, your pain was soothed somewhat, as your cunt brushed against the rigid shaft of the dildo while your body danced from the delivered blows. You are determined to get your reward for your obedient suffering.

"Yes Master. You can do anything you wish to me. My cunt is your pleasure. I want so much to please my handsome Master."

"Good, slave," and I deliver several more blows, taking great delight in how your body involuntarily jumps and arches, suspended above the floor.

I step between your legs. You shiver as I grab your hips and thrust them towards the waiting dildo. It slides easily to the hilt deep within your dripping cunt.

"Oh god! Yes Master, shove that fucking dildo into my cunt. Have I pleased you, Master? I am your hot fucking slut. I'll do anything. Anything."

I walk behind you. You tilt your head back and see me remove my hard and hot cock from my pants. You open your mouth in a wide "o".

"Will Master fuck my mouth now. Please fuck my hot little pussy mouth. I want it so bad. It looks so beautiful. Please, Master. I'm a good cock-sucking slut."

You realize that with the dildo mounted as it is, you can thrust back and forth with your hips and fuck your cunt. Your hips develop a strong rhythm, which because you've been such a good girl I allow. Your mouth still begs for my cock. I step towards you, and grab your hair in my fist, and let my cock lay across your face. The tip is right above your mouth, and you are desperate to lick it, and get it into your mouth.

"Tilt your head back, slut." My voice is rough, as is the yank I give your hair to put your mouth into the proper position. "Open that hot

little cunt mouth, sweet bitch." You obey readily, your mouth already sucking the air, panting sounds come from deep within your throat. I yank your hair towards me and shove my huge cock all the way in. Your eyes are wide with desire. Your hips trying to shove your cunt deeper onto the dildo. I watch your tits bounce and jiggle without shame. They are still bound and clamped. I have the crop in my other hand.

"I'm going to whip those fucking tits, my whore. They look so beautiful, so perfect." I begin to deliver blows to each tit. Your body jerks involuntarily with each cropping. Our hips are in rhythm. I'm shoving my rock-hard cock down your cunt mouth, your cunt rocking violently on the dildo.

You are lost in your heat, and your mind is swirling in pain and pleasure. We are both disappearing in our passion. "I'm going to whip those fucking tits till I come all over your face, bitch. You little fucking whore, suck it you bitch slave. Take it you fuck…". and you feel the hot squirt of cum in your mouth, and it continues to shoot loads on your beautiful face.

"Yes Master. Give me your cum. Thank you Master. Yes Master. I love you Master!" And in your gratitude you sweetly lick the last drops of cum from my cock.

Subject: Daddy of my dreams!
Date: Fri, 11 Nov

Dear Daddy,

You have no idea how thrilled i am to have been found pleasing by You. Your little girl is dreaming of you, Master, and thinking of ways to make herself a perfect little cunt for her Daddy. i am working on a proper response to your last letter, but i have very limited access to a computer right now. i have to use the one at my dance studio when no one else is around.

i am also working on having some proper pictures made for you. my sister knows a photographer who might be willing to take some slutty pictures for your enjoyment. Then, i am working on getting another e-mail account on a friend's computer, so i can send you pictures and e-mail to your regular e-mail account, without everyone at the studio being able to read them.

i could lose my job if i'm caught, since i work with children. i'm so sorry for the delay, Daddy. Your little whore has not forgotten her place and will send you another letter as soon as she possibly can.

Your dripping, trained, obedient slut-daughter,

sharah

Subject: patience without virtue
Date: Fri, 11 Nov

Dear little slut,

You're making Daddy very intrigued by how open and desirable you are in your submission and fantasies.

I know your hot little cunt would be so right for your Daddy. You've shown what a perfect daughter/whore you could be for my pleasure. I already feel a warm tenderness for my special little girl, as well as a huge hard on that I can't wait to show my daughter.

A pic will be so enjoyable so I can better picture you doing all those perverted pleasures we've already agreed would make us so happy. Ours is a noble pursuit to unlock the mystery of our sexual psyche, to revel in the pleasure of the flesh, and forbidden fruits of lust. The bottom line is mutual pleasure, joy and freedom.

I was just in NY, so we missed a chance to meet then. I'm going to spank you on your bare little bottom for not contacting me sooner. You were a bad girl. No excuses. Just accept your punishment and

don't let it happen again. Understand my little slut?

I'll be in Florida the first week in January. If it seems right, perhaps Daddy and his beautiful slave daughter might have a joyous "re-union" there. So don't wait too long to get back to Daddy or I'll have to punish you for that as well. But I know how you long to obey. Just do it, my little cunt!

Just a few parting thoughts of pleasure.

Well my lovely slut girl, I could quite easily picture you, with luscious red lips stretched around a huge ball gag. Your mouth is stretched wide and I picture the way it would be to look at your sexy eyes and that huge ball sticking out from the middle of your face, expressing your submissiveness for my pleasure.

Your arms would be tied tightly behind you at the wrists and the elbows with velvet cords. There is a stretcher bar between you spread legs at the ankles, that is bound tightly around each ankle above your black stiletto heels. You have on a very short skirt and black nylons and garter.

You hoped you looked slutty enough, to make your Daddy want to bind and gag you. You were obviously successful. There is a cord around your waist, very tight, cutting into your flesh, and it has been brought down the center of your fucking hot ass, between the cheeks and back up through your cunt, between your lips, pressing down hard on your clit, as it is tied back tightly to the cords around your waist. Your pussy is so hot for Daddy. You've grown to the point of agony in your excitement.

Your Daddy's hands have been all over your body, as he roughly put you in this bondage. And now you beg to touch him, and yourself, but your hands and feet are bound and your mouth is tightly gagged, and your pleasure is rushing forward and being held back at the same time. You feel a drop of your juice slither down one leg and soak into the top of your nylon.

Daddy finishes tying the cords that criss-cross under your flushed

tits and you groan through your gag, as he cinches the last knot as tight as it will go.

"You're my beautiful little girl," he says, smiling, pleased, and raising your head to meet his loving gaze with the leather crop under your quivering chin.

I wait with a Master's patience for my little daughter's further response to my last letter.

Hurry, little girl,

Daddy

Subject: Your daughter's pix
Date: Sun, 22 Nov

Dear Daddy,

i know i will have to be punished for taking so long, but i finally have my own e-mail account. Now, my Daddy can find his little cunt at sharah@******.com.. i am writing to you from my girl-friend holly's computer. she lives pretty close to me and says i can pick up my mail here. i still won't always know when i can get on for sure, but at least i have two options, now. i especially wanted to get my own e-mail, so i could send you some pictures of me, and could see yours, if you have one. i would love, love, love, seeing the Man i hope to be serving in person, soon.

By the way, Daddy, your little girl has already asked for the first week in January off, so she can visit you in Florida and begin serving her Daddy the way a little whore should be serving, clamped, tied, gagged, beaten and dripping, in person.

Second, i must tell you the truth about how many Men have written to me, and what i have done about that. i have seen a few D/s sites on the Internet, and was shown how to get on-line by one Man i

served temporarily, last year. But i have never placed an ad before now. i had no idea i would get the kind of response i've gotten. The last time i was able to check my mail at the studio, i had received over forty responses, so far. You were the second Man to send me a message.

i was taught by my first Master NEVER to show disrespect to a Man when he speaks to me, so i have been trying to answer every letter i received. i'm afraid that is turning out to be impossible, since i don't have my own computer. i wrote long responses to You and to several other Men who wrote to me first, but i have written a short, respectful note, explaining my situation to all the other Men who were kind enough to notice me.

i was so upset and overwhelmed by not being able to write proper responses. i am not used to not obeying Men. my Master died two years ago, and since then i have only met Dominant Men by being recommended to them by other Men i served. i usually just get a phone call from a Man who is planning a bachelor party or a poker night or something, and has gotten my number from someone who has used me for such things before. Sometimes, more Dominant Men who are at those parties see how submissive i am, and call me for private service. i wanted so badly to meet another Master, but so far, no one has put a collar on my neck permanently.

i called my sister (who is also a slave, and owned by a Man in Ohio) when i got so many answers and didn't know what to do. She's just like me, so she understood how terrible i felt, but she told me that sometimes us submissive girls have to make our own decisions when we are not owned by a Man. my first Master chose me. i guess it never occurred to me that i would have to make a choice.

her Master got on the phone with me, when he heard what was happening, and gave me a lecture about being careful. i know He is right. There are a lot of crazy people out there, and i don't want to get really hurt or marked up and ruined for my eventual owner. He was kind enough to say that he would be my temporary mentor and that I was to check with him before i served anyone or allowed myself to be permanently collared.

He also told me that i wasn't to serve at any more parties, until i am owned by a Man who could protect me. He explained to me that some Men may not want me if i had been used by too many Men. my first Master had me serve other Men pretty often, but he was always there to watch out for me.

To tell you the truth, i was very relieved to get his orders and know that i am (somewhat) under his care for a while. i do love sex and serving Men, but i was getting frightened sometimes at the parties. So i was told to tell you that my sister's Master is named Joe, and he will be advising me from now on about who seems safe to serve.

He said he won't read your letters, unless you give your permission, but that i will be reporting to him and you can send him messages, through me, if you want him to know anything. He said the ultimate decision will have to be mine, but that he won't allow me to serve anyone he thinks is dangerous or wants to truly harm me.

By the way, Master Joe told me that i should mention to you that i have been tested for HIV many times, and that it has always come back negative. i have not served any Men since my last test which was six weeks ago. Actually, i have not served a Man in over five months, and your little slave-daughter is getting so desperate to meet you, Daddy.

These two photos I'm sending are about a year old. They are from a modeling composite i had made when i worked for a print modeling agency. i've done a few ads for a perfume company and one for Banana Republic. i can't really be a fashion model because i am too short.

My hair is longer now than it was in these pictures, although it wasn't as short as it looks in the photos, even then. They had me wear it slicked back, because that was the "in" look for models. My hair is just past my shoulders, now. i do hope you will get the pictures correctly. i got my boss at the studio to scan them for me and show me how to send them, but i've never done this before.

i would send you properly open and slutty ones, but i don't have any other nude photos yet. And i couldn't get my boss to scan them, even if i had them. You should have seen his eyes pop out when he saw the nude one. The studio i teach in is mostly for children so i have to be careful. But this one was in "good taste", so he didn't mind. He just told me to be very careful who i sent it to.

He doesn't know anything about me being submissive. Anyway, after receiving your last letter, i wanted to show myself to you so badly. i hope i did the right thing by sending them to you and i hope you approve of my looks.

If i were your little girl, you could have me dress or groom myself any way you preferred. My hair grows pretty fast, if you prefer me to have long hair. And i am good with make-up and can make it very subtle, like in the photos or more whorish, if you prefer. my first Daddy liked for his little bitch to wear lingerie at home, so i have quite a bit of it, already. i was never allowed to wear pants, in public or private so i don't own any slacks, only skirts and dresses.

So, i hope this is acceptable to you, Daddy. If it is okay with you, and you like my pictures, i would like to still see if i might someday be the right slave for you.

Oh, Daddy, some things you write make me feel so filled with longing. i can't stop dreaming of being your property and being your obedient little whore-daughter. i miss that part of my life, so much. i miss cleaning my Master's house and getting his dinner ready, then getting dressed for him and meeting him at the door, on my knees and ready to serve.

He would often use me right away, right there at the door, and feed me his cock before he had even taken his coat off. Then i would serve him his dinner and wait on him, hand and foot for the rest of the night. Do you think that would ever be possible for us, Daddy? Even just a few nights a week, someday, if i moved to be nearer to you?

i dream of being tied up tightly and bound between your legs all

night long, serving you over and over again, having you shove your cock all the way down my throat, and waking up in the night to grab my hair and say, "Suck it again, bitch!" It thrills me beyond belief. The thought of being that fully your slave and your property to use at your will is such sweet nourishment to my feminine soul.

In the morning, you could untie me to make your breakfast and get you ready for work. Would we have any mornings, Daddy? Would there be any opportunities for you to use me all night long? i wish we had already met and that i was already your property, your little trained cunt to use.

i have been a submissive little slut for as long as i can remember, Daddy. i guess i believe that i have always understood the difference between Men and women, and was always the way i am now. my Father was a very Dominant Man, and i'm sure my mother was probably his slave, although they never did anything graphically sexual in front of my sister and me.

We were taught that a Man is the boss of the house, though, and my mother obviously adored and worshipped my Father. He also obviously cherished and loved her and considered her his property. my sister and i have talked about it many times (she's five years older than me) and we both believe that our parents had a D/s relationship.

So i met my first Master when i was only 15, although he didn't begin to use me sexually until i was 16. He was a friend of my Father's and i'm pretty sure my parents knew what was happening, though my Master never told me for sure. i was allowed to move in with him when i was 17 and my parents both approved of him.

i know this would be considered sick by a lot of people, but my Master loved me, and took such tender care of me. He was 100% dominant over me, but he protected me fiercely, and always made sure i knew how much he loved me.

And i believe i was truly ready to be a sexual creature and knew exactly what kind of relationship i wanted. i don't think he would

have trained me if i wasn't emotionally and physically ready, and i don't believe my Father would have allowed it.

Since i teach some teenage girls, i've thought about it a lot, and i can say that i think most girls wouldn't be ready at that age, but some are different. The ones who come from secure, loving homes, seem to be the most prepared to enter into an adult relationship with a Man.

i think most girls are pretty confused about the relationship between Men and women. They feel the natural pull of their submission, but have been taught to be too worried about equality. i just think feminism is a big mistake and is causing a lot of unhappy and under-developed girls. And frustrated Men, too, of course. i just think we might all be a little more at peace if we recognized the biological reality of our natural impulses.

i have lots of girlfriends who aren't in touch with their submission and their sexuality, but i can see it in almost every one of them, and i feel so bad for them that they feel they can't be fulfilled.

Anyway, if what i just told you worries you, just know that i have been to a therapist and talked about it a lot after my Master died, and he did not think i was damaged or sick. i am just an unusually nonconflicted girl who is deeply submissive and loving, and was very sexual at an early age. Obviously, i have a pretty big Daddy fixation, and i'll confess to you that i often wish i had had the chance to serve my real Father.

i did start to find ways for him to see me naked when i was 15 and i believe now that he noticed. That was when he introduced me to my former Master, but i sometimes wonder if he was still alive, if i might have been allowed to serve him after my Master died.

i hope this isn't too shocking to you, but it's the truth. i think most girls are looking for their Daddy, and my therapist said it's perfectly normal. In my case, because of my Father's loving, Dominating, presence, it led me to a very loving, healthy relationship.

my Master always had me call him Master until after my real Daddy died, and then he sensed the void in my life and had me start calling him Daddy. i think that's when i truly became his property.

my sister also has a wonderful relationship with Joe and he is a wonderful, protective, but demanding and strong Man. They have been together for eight years and are ecstatically happy. So i think the house we grew up in was very, very healthy for both of us.

So, Sir, i hope this helps to explain me, and what is happening right now. i hope you still find me pleasing and that you like my looks. Something tells me that you would be a wonderful Master, and that i would be proud to be your girl, and your slave.

i am secretly praying that you will want me to visit you as soon as possible and that you will want to collar me and move me into your house shortly after that. i think Master Joe would approve of you, because you don't seem like you want to harm me. i hope i can see my new Daddy/Master very, very soon.

your loving little cunt,

sharah

Subject: A "Father's" concern
Date: Sun, 22 Nov

Dearest darling daughter,

My patience has been greatly rewarded (though my patience has a price, which will be considered at the proper time-grin.).

You have rocked my wickedly and delightfully perverse, sexually dominant nature and my loving heart, darling. I can barely type, so consumed is your Daddy by thoughts of you, both nasty and passionate. You move me like no other woman ever has...I want to be with you...right now!

I have several projects I'm in the middle of right now (though none as important as you,), but commitments nonetheless, so I may not be able to say all the things I would like to right now.

First: I can't wait until January to have my way with my beautiful daughter. You're so gorgeous, such beautiful eyes and sensuous mouth, that full lower lip. I pictured you kneeling before Me, begging Daddy to put His cock into that sweet hole.

I share Joe's concerns for your safety, and the need for caution...building trust. You are so precious. I felt a Father's concern over his little girl taking such risks, but at this point am in no position to advise you how to run your life. I know this would get worked out, should we develop a relationship. I am glad Joe is there for guidance...until I can take care of you.

You are free to pass along anything I write to you for his review...free to ask any questions...address any issue. I am a man of integrity, though far from perfect. I aspire to have a loving compassionate relationship with the world. I have a strong spiritual nature, though not in the western Judeo-Christian sense.

I meditate, practice positive affirmations, and have a strong sense that there is a spiritual reality beyond our physical senses. How else can I explain the fortunate events that led to us meeting! Perhaps if I had been the 100th man to respond to such an inviting ad as yours, you might not have even noticed.

There are many serious issues for us to deal with before we might consider a relationship. Some that may prevent us from fulfilling our destiny together, though nothing that true passion cannot overcome. Is this true passion sweetgirl? I already feel such a great tenderness for you.

It's inexplicable how a few e-mails could impel me to say such a thing. I have never been so responsive emotionally to someone I have never met...and sexually...well there's no question how strongly you attract me there.

I have had about 20 submissives contact me, many of whom offered themselves as my servant and whore, but none who I felt I might fall in love with in the classic sense. It hasn't even been a prominent thought for me, that I might also fall in love.

I had been searching for my soulmate since my early youth. By my thirties, I was resigned to settle for modest sexual gratification as the best life would offer me, and my sexual appetite is huge and ongoing. But I knew that I needed a totally submissive woman with desires as perverse as my own to find true fulfillment. Until the Internet, I never met a woman who offered such. It is quite thrilling at this stage of my life.

Since I was a child, I've been kinky, very sexual. More than just the typical guy obsession, but never met a woman who in any way hinted or expressed her perverted pleasure. Believe me, I searched high and low, prowled relentlessly, to no avail. Let's say I'm meeting women now, whose perversion quotient matches or exceeds my own. But none dearest daughter who has compelled me to express the thought of love...except for you.

But being a mature man, though a reckless youth at heart, all of these things I am feeling, things rushing so fast, give me pause. I want to accept you as you have offered yourself to me (how could I refuse?) but at the same time, my practical, logical, skeptical mind says, "Look out, dude! Be careful," though nothing you have said has seemed inconsistent, or aroused any particular suspicion.

Some of you behaviors and inclinations have shocked, though not disturbed me. I find your perversion fascinating, actually. I believe I offer a significant latitude in what is acceptable sexually. The fact that I am literally old enough to be your father, raises numerous issues. But that is obviously part of the attraction as well.

It's just the whole thing altogether. Could the universe be offering this incredibly precious gift to me, my beautiful submissive daughter, whore, slut, maid, companion, friend, spiritual ally, all in one package? No strings attached? All issues happily resolved? I want

to find out.

One of the spiritual principles I believe in is acceptance. You might want something, but until you believe and accept it with your heart and soul, it cannot come into your life. This is why I am so openly expressing my need, desire and love for you. I choose, right now to accept you in my life, knowing that all will be resolved to allow this to occur, no matter what obstacles might appear in our way.

There is nothing you have told me, except for your own lack of concern for your safety, that has displeased me. In fact the more you reveal, the more excited I become. It is clear, you are so attractive on every level that you will be left with many choices in your quest for your perfect Daddy/Master. I am pleased to be among them. Let your heart guide you. If it is to me, let the universe rejoice with me.

I have to go now, my little darling. I have included a recent photo, a new story and my love...

Your loving Daddy,

Galen

"Cocoon"

It feels, you imagine, like a cocoon...total quiet, darkness...you can feel the canvas bag Master stuffed you in, pressed all around your fetally curled body...knees pressing into your tits, wrists shackled to your ankles...the chain from your collar, connected to the chain between your anklets, your hooded head drawn down sideways upon your knees. The hood, with an opening only for your mouth and nose, was placed after Master had flogged you mercilessly, and then you were flogged again after the hood was positioned.

Master had made you stand, without restraints, and commanded you to not move while he worked on your tits and ass, and just about every other sensitive area. Intermittently, Master would reach between your legs, and massage your clit tenderly, kissing you

passionately through the opening in the hood.

"You are such a pleasure, my beautiful and obedient slave."

His words caused a glow in your submissive heart. Despite the numerous flinches, you felt you had stood pretty still, "especially trying to balance on these spiked heels Master gave me to wear." Then he got the bag, cuffed and collared you, stuffed you roughly inside, and hoisted the bag off the floor with a pulley. You couldn't think of anything you did wrong. Master was simply taking his pleasure you thought.

It's been some time since Master left the room...but you really can't sense time in this eternal darkness...you can't move...every part of you is restrained...the bag squeezes you tight...it is difficult to breathe the little air that the thick canvas allows inside. You can tell from your sense of gravity (the only sense that isn't being deprived) that you are hung, nearly upside down on your back. You wait with a slave's anticipation...you know not what...or when...but Master has something in mind...

You suddenly feel the bag sway slightly...you didn't hear him enter...you feel a sharp whack right on your ass...sharp even through the canvas...a long number of blows follow. Then you hear the sound of canvas being ripped... you feel the cooler room air on your mouth where Master has made a small opening in the bag... you go to breathe in the fresh air. Just as you begin the intake, like a swimmer that's just broke the surface after a deep dive, you feel a hard round shaft forced to the back of your throat, choking off the air you craved. Master's cock!...savagely pumping your little cunt mouth...no this is too solid and now the taste...a dildo!...probably the huge black one.

After several timeless minutes, your jaws aching with the fatigue of your mouth being forced open so wide, the pumping dildo stops, but stays deep in your mouth. You know you dare not let it go, no matter how bad you need that fresh breath or how bad your jaws ache.

You hear and feel the canvas being torn again. This time you feel the cool air of the room, grazing across your exposed ass. Master's fingers grab your cunt lips and spreads them roughly, pulling them away from your entrance. You feel the sharp bite of the utility clothes pins placed on your cunt lips...several on each side...then Master tapes the ends to your thighs and ass...your pinkness exposed...glistening now in the light of the room.

Suddenly there is an explosion of sensation right on your cunt, flashing like a bright red bolt in the darkness of your mind. Another and another as Master crops your pussy right on that tender pink flesh. If you could, you would jump up, try to get away from the searing sting of the crop. But you can't even move. Then another object, another dildo, you realize, suddenly penetrates deep into your cunt, sliding effortlessly into the soft tissues soaked in your growing heat. You almost explode, desperate to hump that shaft. But you can't even move. Then the whip is raining down hard on your exposed ass, stinging left and right. It stings so bad. But the whipping is far down your list of concerns. All your thinking of is that dildo in your desperate cunt, wishing only that Master would fuck you with it!

The whipping stops. Silence...then you feel Master's strong hands gripping the sides of the bag by your hips...the probe of his cock...definitely his...pressing at the entrance to your asshole...then his cock driving into you, deep and you feel his hips banging hard against your ass cheeks, driving his cock mercilessly over and over again into the depths of your ass...then you feel the dildo start in your cunt... fucking you harder and harder. You feel both probes pressing through the membrane that separates your ass and your cunt as the huge objects fight for space within your tight but liquid openings...and then your mind turns to liquid and color and your whole consciousness becomes like one cascading orgasm of pleasure...release...freedom...within your enslaved body.

You feel Master heave his own bliss, deep into your ass, and you feel him, panting with the end of his passion as he embraces the canvas bag, squeezing tightly. After a few moments of embrace, you feel Master withdraw. Gently, Master removes the dildo still

clenched tightly in your mouth, kisses your mouth deeply through the opening in the canvas, and quietly leaves you in your other world.

Subject: tears of gratitude
Date: Wed, 25 Nov

Dear Daddy,

You've left your little girl dripping wet at every end with your last letter. my little whore's cunt feels like it's on fire, and tears of gratitude are streaming down my face. i want to be on my knees in front of you now, so, so badly. i want to be dangling in that canvas bag, sucking on that big, black dildo and getting my ass reamed by my Daddy.

i need you to use me that way, Daddy. i need it more than anything i've ever needed. i didn't think i would ever find a Master as strong as you again. i didn't think anyone could ever understand me the way you already do. i want to be every kind of trained cunt you've ever dreamed of owning.

i will do whatever it takes to prove to you that i am real and mean every word i've written to you. Every cell of my body, mind, heart and soul is a slave, Daddy. i will only be fulfilled when i am the property of a Man just like you.

Now that you've driven your little cock-starved girl mad, she has to rush to the airport to go visit my sister kathy and Master Joe for the weekend. i'm going to beg Master Joe for permission to send you my phone number, if that's all right with you, Daddy. i want to start being available to you whenever and however you say.

Oh, Daddy, i wasn't able to view your picture on holly's computer for some reason. It downloaded as a "98" file, and i don't know what that is or how to view it. holly says you can send a regular jpg. or gif. file and that she has pkzip if you need to compress it as a

zip file. i don't really know what all that means, but, please, please, please send it again, Daddy. i want to see my Daddy's face so i can dream of you when i'm pumping my wet cunt, eager ass and whore throat with a big dildo.

Also, Master Joe says i can pick up my mail while i'm at His house, so if you want to send it, go ahead. i guess you should know, i will be serving Master Joe while i'm there. He always has kathy and me dance for him and put on a show for him, and he says he will continue using me until i am collared by another Man. i hope that won't upset you, Daddy.

i have to go now. You've got your little slave-daughter exactly where you want her, Daddy. i am tortured with my need for you, now. And yes, my heart is about to burst in two with feelings of love for you, too, Daddy. Isn't it amazing? i never dreamed i'd meet a Man like you.

Thank You, Daddy. Thank You, Master.

Your new toy,

sharah

Subject: twist of fate
Date: Wed, 25 Nov

My Darling Daughter,

I had already written most of what follows before I got your lovely and joyful (to me) letter. Something happened today…and I'm somewhat devastated. It's too complicated to explain, right now, but I will as soon as I can sort it out and understand fully how to explain it.

But don't worry daughter. It will not affect how I feel for you, how I need you. In fact it will ultimately strengthen and quicken my

desire to be with you. I wish I could leave here right now, to be embraced in your loving daughter's heart…heal Daddy's pain…nurse me back to full strength…be wrapped in the joy and rapture of my prized possession. I will write more soon, hopefully yet tonight, if I am able.

But trust me, dear, everything will be all right. I desire and need you more and more, with every passing moment. Write as soon as you can. It keeps me strong and determined to overcome this wearying dilemma.

Here's what I wrote earlier

Daddy's Home

How's my precious little daughter doin'? Daddy's been thinking of you sweetheart. Especially after today. It was a spectacularly bad day, and I need to vent. This story is how I soothed my rage. Understand my, perfect whore?

Prepare yourself slut. Know it is time to serve Master. Be ready for Master's wrath, asserting his complete and vicious control over his personal property. You see it in my eyes and hear it in my voice. You feel yourself beginning to tremble. Your heart is racing, a strangeness in your gut. You feel your nipples start to perk, and something else between your legs. You keep your eyes cast down…waiting…Daddy's coming!

Daddy stood across the room, handsome in his business suit. He removed his black leather belt. "Get over here and kneel, you fucking bitch!"

You immediately begin to walk from across the room, as you've been taught, head high, tits projecting forward in an obvious display, hips on automatic within your skintight short black skirt.

"Stop, cunt!" Daddy shouts, before you can begin your second step. "Did I tell you to walk? You stupid fucking little girl. How do you know yet, how I want you to come to me? Tell me that, will you,

bitch?"

You hesitate, eyes cast down, shaking with fear and now doubt. In a second, Daddy is before you, yanking your head up by the hair. You feel a hard slap across your cheek.

"What kind of fucking daughter are you? You think you're so fucking smart. You don't know shit, slut."

Daddy's face is covered in dark red anger. His nostrils puff with his venting breath. He is right in your face, screaming at the top of his lungs.

"You keep fucking up tonight, cunt, you'll be really sorry. Daddy promises you that. And you know Daddy keeps his promises, doesn't he, daughter!"

Tears are weeping from the corners of your eyes, falling down your cheeks. You can taste the salty fluid as the trails cross the corners of your quivering mouth.

"Yes Daddy, I'm so sorry. I'm just a stupid cunt, Daddy. It won't happen again, I promise, Daddy. I want to be your good little girl."

You so wanted to embrace him, soothe him, throw yourself before him and beg him to take it all out on your cunt mouth till he explodes his angry cum all over his little girl's face. But you dare not move. No more mistakes, you affirm to yourself. But you are still totally unsure what to do. You've never seen Daddy so upset, so cruel.

"Now where was I?"…his voice less harsh…"Oh yeah. Right now cunt, down on all fours like the slutty fuck-pig you are," his tone back to full strength. At the same time he grabs the back of your neck, fingers digging in, forcing you down to your pig position.

Instinctively, you raise your ass up as high as it will go, and hear the whoosh of Daddy's belt as it cracks through the fabric of your skirt. It stung, even through the fabric. You reach back quickly and draw

your skirt up over you ass and another crack stings as sharp as a burning iron. You'd done your best not to flinch, without permission, as you've been trained. But you were imperfect.

"Move again, bitch and I won't stop beating that fucking ass until my arm breaks"…he strikes again…even harder…"understand bitch!" You don't move a muscle.

"Now, I want you to crawl forward, first with your left hand and leg, then the same with your right. I want you to sway your hips so it first swings your ass to the right, and then to the left with each stride. Don't you dare take the next stride until your feel my belt strike you. You think you can keep that straight, stupid daughter? Or is that a little too much for your meager little cunt brain."

You've let your head drift down to the tops of your hands. The belt cracks once again.

"You must like Daddy's belt, bitch. Is that why you keep fucking up!"
You had already brought your head up even with your shoulders, face forward in the direction you are pointing…why am I being so bad…better straighten up…he's right though…I do love Daddy's belt…maybe I'm doing it on purpose….

"Please, Daddy, I'm so sorry. Please don't hurt me, Daddy." You realized your mistake at the same instant that you felt the blows begin, and continue through Daddy's shouting.

"You stupid fucking cunt. You're really pissing me off, daughter. What the fuck are you doing? Did I say you could speak? You telling your Father what to do? You disrespectful little whore. I'm going to really beat that ass now, bitch!"

But your secret mind knew exactly what it was doing, what it wanted. And it tricked the scared little girl, down on all fours, with Father towering over her, beating his bad little girl's ass.

Then the belt suddenly stopped. Daddy paused, staring down at

your reddened ass, pondering. You sensed him kneel down behind you…silence…then his fingers grasp you cunt. He feels the dripping lips. The silence breaks like a sheet of shattered glass, falling all around you.

"You whore!" his voice even angrier than before. "What is your fucking slutty mind thinking? You think I'm doing this for your fucking goddamn pleasure! You think your Father's stupid, slut! Stand up!" And he yanks you off your feet so fast by the hair that you are stumbling and falling and you're being dragged across the room, Daddy pulling you forward by the hair, tears of pain dripping across the floor, your cunt dream lost in the terror.

"We're going to the dungeon right now, you fucking goddamned bitch of a worthless daughter."

Daddy had left the dungeon nearly an hour ago. You were like in a dream, floating in and out, steeped in an intoxicating consciousness of submissive pain, cushioned by a euphoric cast of an owned and dominated contentment.

Daddy appeared at the door of the dungeon. You had heard him draw a bath, a forgotten while ago, heard other things in the outer rooms, heard his confident smooth voice, talking on the phone. He had changed from his business suit. He had on black jeans and t-shirt, and his black leather jacket. His hair was still slick from the bath. Oh, Daddy, Daddy is so handsome, you think. He stood and looked at you. No, inspected you. No not you, you didn't exist. He viewed you, hanging there, contemplating a piece of sculpture that he had created.

Daddy had bound you from head to toe, quite roughly. Ropes everywhere - pinching, squeezing, immobilizing - a huge red ball gag, leather straps criss-crossed over your face, scrunching down your hair. You were hung upside down...clips weighted on your nipples...thin cords, attached to the clips drawing your nipples fiercely away from your tits, and attached to eye loops in the floor. There was a zipper of clothespins encircling each tit. The flesh dented and very sore after so much time.

Out your ass was a 2-inch wide candle, only a few of its ten inches sticking out. Wax drips, now hardened, swam away in every direction across your ass and a thick solid puddle nested between your burned cheeks. More zippers of clothespins ran down your thighs. There were clamps on each cunt lip, again heavily weighted, and again cords stretched the lips out severely, and up towards the ceiling. Your cunt was filled with a battery-powered dildo, still humming away inside your mind, which was now centered in your cunt. Master had saved the biggest and tightest clamp and weight for your clit…and it pulled and hung down from that intriguing little treasure like an anvil.

Master spoke. You heard him from inside your cunt mind.

"I had this real hot slut e-mail me today. Wants to play." His voice was drifting towards diabolical, the effect heightened by his black attire.

"Left her phone number. Besides being a total pain slut for your Daddy, she said she also Dommes an even bigger whore than she is. Wanted to know should she bring her along."

Your cunt mind came alert. "Coming here, Daddy!"

"I told the slut, sure, why not. I told her I had my daughter visiting. That you were just hanging around, looking for something to do." Daddy laughed, like it was really funny.

"Now this cunt sounds like a real hot slave bitch of a woman, not some stupid cunt brained little girl, like someone else I know. You gettin' the picture, now daughter? I noticed that got your attention. Daddy's goin' to have some fun tonight, bitch. The party's only just starting, my beautiful daughter." Daddy rubbed his hands together, in lewd anticipation.

"I feel so much better."

Subject: I am sorry!
Date: Thu, 26 Nov

Dearest Daughter,

I am so sorry. I fear my previous letter may have tainted your reunion with your sister and Joe, if you in fact had time to read it, before this letter of explanation had arrived. I have inadvertently entangled our tender relationship in my own mess. My intentions were much different. Please read this entire letter before you pass any judgments.

I am in a marriage that I had been planning to leave in a few months (planned well before you and I met.) It has been a devastating 16 years, the purest form of personal lonely hell and depression I could ever have been involved in. Today something happened that has tossed everything I had planned out the proverbial window...how I would leave...how I would tell you...how I found myself stuck here for so long...how did it ever begin, and how does it involve you? That explanation will follow.

My wife called me at my office today. In the mail had come a bill from a medical lab. Among other things, it listed an HIV test (negative) I'd had done a month ago. I had taken steps to keep it discreet, going directly to the lab office, paying for that test in cash. It was supposed to be removed from the invoice that went to my house, but it didn't. Busted!

I had a rare! (besides 10 years ago in Hong Kong) and very brief encounter (blow job with protection) with a prostitute in Atlanta earlier in the year. I had checked with 3 separate HIV clinics and was told there was virtually no chance to contract HIV under the circumstances I described. I still worried about it in the back of my mind, when I went to my doctor for my annual physical, I had a test done, then boom!

You appeared, though thankfully, somewhat prematurely. It has only been in the past year, that I have come "back" to terms with

who I am, sexually and otherwise. I had been on a path of dedicated discovery since an early age, though my altar-boy, Catholic upbringing (till 8th grade, I considered being a priest, can you imagine!) kept it in deep space until my late teens, except for within my deepest secret masturbation fantasies.

I have been a "student" you might say, of BDSM for over 25 years. My awareness of my powerful sexuality began before the age of 5. A while back, I got on the net and found several D/s personals sites. I was fascinated by the ads from submissive women. I began placing ads, responding to ads, writing stories and sending them.

The responses I received, both in quantity and content, thrilled me. It's been amazing how easy it's been to meet the type of slutty submissives I've craved, compared to all the years cruising nightclubs in my wild days.

I was never into prostitutes. Paying canceled out the desire quotient on both sides of the equation. (There is a great irony in that statement now) I will tell you what resulted from these contacts at another time, if you wish. But I want to stay focused on you dear (in every possible way!)

In order to leave my wife and family (I have two teenage boys; I wouldn't actually be "leaving" my boys, whom I love dearly,) I have some very complicated financial issues to deal with. My wife and I own a business together. (God! there's so much to explain, but I 'm trying to get back to you, so I will and explain more later in this ongoing tale.)

I made it my goal, to establish two other businesses I'm developing, patent an invention, set up my jointly owned company so my wife could run it without me (primarily to preserve my sons' life in our beautiful home), give notice to my wife, move out and begin my life as a lifestyle Dominant.

After getting on the net, I was very confident of finding the pleasure and lifestyle I sought, even at the age of 48 (which I had been concerned about.) Then you appeared, like a beautiful dream within

the nightmare, and everything moved very fast.

I wasn't sure if I should tell you about my wife, before we met or after we had some time together in Florida. I rationalized that I wasn't being dishonest yet, since the subject hadn't come up. Strategist that I am, I was waiting to see how things played out a little longer.

If you let me be who I am, sweetheart, I will never lie to you. But that's changed now (going to Florida.) My original purpose for going to Florida, on business for my mutually owned company, has likely changed.

I had wanted to make a clean break. That didn't happen.

Bottom line, I don't know what's happening next. Fortunately my wife had already planned to take the kids to her father's, about 100 miles north. I'm supposed to go up tomorrow (holiday weekend with her family.) She had called right before she left to pick up the kids in school, first crying and screaming, then yelling and screaming.

I haven't talked to her since. I don't want to go through any more shit, I don't want to go to her father's, the dam has broken. I wish she would just say she wants a divorce, I'd say great, we'll work it out. But she's not like that.

Why don't I just leave? Right now? Why haven't I left before? My kids and the financial situation, and other things. But I might be out by the weekend.

I worry about how my boys will react, if it all blows up, right at their holiday/family time. Instead of a clean break, now it's brought down to, "Your father fucked around with a prostitute, he lied, he betrayed me, he ruined my life, and yours too (to my kids,)," or something like that she will smear. That's what my wife is like.

I need to talk to you on the phone, this is too cumbersome trying to write it all.

I have been so moved by your letters and responsiveness. I feel it so valid, so powerful, finding you, all we shared in so brief a time, the unremitting power of my desire for you, that I know we can work this out. But then, because our relationship is so fragile at this early stage, you might feel you have better options than to be involved in such a complicated mess.

I don't know what for sure will happen, now darling daughter. The when's, the how's, all unknown. It's suddenly and unexpectedly become the most complicated knot I've ever had to deal with. Please know that with all my heart I am fighting to get free of this, and make you, along with my boys, the most important part of my life.

Other than to let you know how strongly I feel about you, I cannot place any expectations on your response to this. If your desire for me is stronger than this mess, I would be the happiest Daddy in the world.

Please contact me soon. I'm giving you my home phone number. Call me between 8 & 9am sharp, if you can, (no later than ten) West coast time. You can never use this number again, without my explicit permission. I know I can trust you. I want to hear your voice, no matter what you have to say.

Your loving Master/Daddy,

Galen

Subject: missing you
Date: Thu, 27 Nov

daughter,

Maybe it would have been better not to have told you anything about what's happening now. Like you said, "isn't it amazing."

Life twists and turns, and sometimes, I guess the binder becomes bound. I realize that what we have shared so eloquently in fantasy may not be what would happen in reality.

If we met, in 10 minutes, we could find out nothing is as it seemed. But I refuse to taint my thoughts of you, with such bad thinking. We have shared more intimacy and honesty in a few messages than many would in a lifetime. I choose to believe that what we have felt and shared is really how it would be between us.

I just talked with my wife. It was very difficult. I agreed to come to her father's, but we talked about those things...how could I do that...do I still love her...do I want a divorce...am I using my indiscretion as an excuse to leave her...is there something I'm not telling her?

I told her we can't talk about it now on the phone and then have me go up there and pretend everything is as it was. I couldn't tell her I love her, or I don't want a divorce, but pauses and silences spoke loudly.

I wanted to say yes I want a divorce, no, I don't love you, but how can I say that and then go to her father's. I told her we need to talk and that we have to bury the subject if I come there. Which I know won't happen, she'll need to know, and I understand that. I shouldn't go, but… "everyone's here waiting for you, your boys want you here. Please don't leave me here alone, under these circumstances, don't turn this all around on me, I didn't do anything wrong."

I've been here before, now she's scared I'm serious. She'll straighten up her act, even though she's hurt and feels inadequate, because I "had to go to a prostitute," and she has a right to feel hurt. She'll be nice for a while, stop her constant complaining about everything under the sun, never satisfied with what she has, never appreciating how much we've accomplished. She's very materialistic. We have a $450,000, 4000 sq. ft home, new cars, travel often, and she still complains like we were Bangladesh refugees.

I won't be able to check my e-mail again until probably sometime Saturday. I don't know what will happen over the next few days. It is very painful for me to tell her I want out. It will, at least temporarily, shatter her, and she'll plead and cry and promise, and guilt trip, and accuse and plead some more.

Why she wants to hold onto something that has provided so little soulful harmony, intimacy and respect is beyond me. I've been through this with her dozens of times. I know if I am pressed, and don't see how I won't be, I will tell her that its over, I want out. It is not going to be as smooth and as painless as I had planned. I can barely think of how to tell my kids, without terribly hurting and confusing them.

But I have to tell you that this is not some married guy, out screwing around on his wife, breaking up his home and then rushing into the arms of the first person that comes along. I don't need you here, in order to make the changes I must make in my life. These things began a very long time before I met you, dear one. And I know most armchair psychologists will warn you you're looking for trouble to get involved with a married man, no matter how short a time I may remain so.

You simply came like a gift out of the blue. Unless I'm missing something, I can't think of a woman/daughter for whom I am better suited. Not just sexually, you have shown me much more. Your skill at writing and your ballet skills shows a highly evolved creativity. You have a keen intellect and a compassionate, loving, beautiful, freedom-seeking spirit. You are courageously honest. And more. You would find me equally fascinating outside the bedroom. Our life could be a continually evolving and incredible adventure.

I am sick that this mess is happening before we have the chance to probe deeper into our budding and beautiful relationship, daughter. I pray we get past this and give ourselves the chance we deserve.

Love,

Galen

Dear daughter,

Though it's breaking my heart not to hear from you, no matter what the reason, my will is as strong as ever, and I have a very strong will. The will to own you body and soul, the will to correct the mistakes I have made in the past, the will to unravel my "mess" here now, and be completely free to own you, use you, enjoy you, and be the most loving and exciting Daddy you will ever have the pleasure to know.

Don't you or anyone else dare to judge me so quickly. There is more complexity here than you know, or can judge about who I am as a person and a Master, or about my current relationship. Have I judged you? Getting a call from a stranger, got your number from some guy you served, and be willing to serve him; whoring at parties for strange men; going off to whore for Joe; wanting to serve your true father. If you can be so judgmental and disrespectful of your Daddy, perhaps I have misjudged you, daughter.

Do you think I am is not a strong and powerful Dominant man? You cannot fathom the strength it took, to retain my quest for being true to myself, and at the same time sacrificing my pursuit for reasons I consciously chose - to attempt to preserve for my boys, a strong sense of family, love for them, security for them. This was something I felt very important, and that was missing from my own sonship.

I've never met my real parents, I did not have a positive relationship with my adoptive father, and so I was determined to provide my sons important things that were not provided to me in a father/son relationship. That, as well as it could be done, has been done. I feel I can take the next steps I need to take for my life, and though

painful for them in the short term, I know that the strength and their awareness of my love for them will continue to flourish in the long run. For this I am thankful.

I am a Dominant. You are an admitted slave. As a slave whose mission is to serve and respect all worthy Masters, you must obey. And as a totally subservient creature who answers to the call of strangers to serve them eagerly, it would be the greatest disrespect and a dishonor to your kind to not contact me immediately.

Galen

Subject: so close
Date: Sat, 28 Nov

sharah dear,

I'm still thinking of you! Think about how close you were to your secret passion. Wasn't it exciting…special…rare… how close and intimate we could be?

…and ironic…think of the power in the fate that brought us together…was it just random luck…or did we attract each other through some subtler channel that guided me to you…and the strange twists of fate that have ripped this splendid, otherworldly love and pleasure from our grasp.

I want you to know how proud I was of you. I respected your courage in revealing to me what a sweet and exciting submissive you long to be, and your greatest desire to serve your Daddy so completely.

When one longs for the truth, to be true to their nature, no matter how society may judge them, this is the noblest of pursuits. I know how you desire to be set free, to serve a supreme Daddy/Master, to become entwined in the dark mystery of his soul, to become his prized possession. I know how you crave to learn more about being

a total slave to your Master's desires. And I know that over time, step by step, as you are ready, you will find fulfillment.

I was impressed by how open you were able to be in expressing your submissive daughter desires to me (as well as really turned on by the thought of the way you wished to dance for me, dress for me, be tied and gagged, suspended and helpless, taking my hard cock in your slave mouth to suck the pleasure from, to be tortured in all those ways that made you so hot and wet with desire!).

But what stopped you so suddenly from continuing this beautiful exploration? I deserve to hear your story. I really want you, have a special tenderness for you. you moved me with your passion and desire and openness, devotion, and love, dear daughter.

I'd like to reach my hand between your lovely legs and feel just how wet you would be. But I bet I could make you even wetter. You'd like that, wouldn't you? You do want to be the submissive little whore I've described in my writings, don't you?

I can feel how it would be, doing those things to you, feeling how you feel, watching the desire grow brightly in your eyes. I know how you need to surrender, to be my slut, my little girl, unashamed and proud of your submissiveness. I know how you long for it to become more and more real.

Don't you want to step a little beyond your caution and feel, feel again the pleasure that I offer? I know you do. I know you desire to really please me, to be lovingly dominated and made to surrender to your most hidden and darkest desire. I can tell how that excites you. Don't be so reluctant, daughter. Let me take you there.

Daddy's Daydream

I want you to dress up for me as I described in high heels, sheer black hose and garter under a tight short skirt, revealing blouse and bra. I want to see your lips, bright red, and bright red polish on your fingers and toes. I want you to meet me in Florida. We'll meet first, in a public place, a restaurant, a bar or hotel lobby. I'd

have you sit across from me with a perfect view of your legs and follow the line with my eyes, from your crossed legs, where it disappears into the wettening mystery between your thighs. We look at each other and talk, with both our words, but more with our eyes.

You know you're my slut daughter. I know you're my slut daughter, but right now we just chat, getting to know each other, while underneath your skirt, you are remembering things I've described that you hope I still want to do to you. You imagine being with me in private.

You feel me place the gag in your mouth, draw it tight, caress your cheeks lovingly with my lips. I command you to bend over. I draw your very short skirt up above your waist, revealing a black thong brief that disappears between the cheeks of your lovely ass. I kneel down, and playfully nibble on one of your ass cheeks.

"What a nice ass you have. I can tell you enjoy having Daddy inspect his daughter's ass so approvingly. I never imagined my own daughter could be my perfect little nasty slut. Do you know you're making Daddy's cock hard, little girl. You're such a bad girl for making Daddy's cock so big. I know you can't wait to see it. Are you going to suck Daddy, my little cunt face?"

You're gagged, so instead of saying it, you think this…"I want my Daddy's cock in my mouth. I'll suck it like the hottest slut, Daddy. Whenever you want, just force it into my mouth, please, Daddy, as hard as you want to fuck your daughter's pussy mouth, you just do it to me, Daddy."

Daddy, being a highly intuitive Master, knows you well, senses your thoughts. "I'll keep that in mind, slut. I am pleased that you came to me, dressed as I requested. You look like a real fucking whore, and of course you are, and you will be treated as such. That's what you want my hot little bitch, isn't it?"

You can't speak because of the gag tight in your pussy mouth. I slap your exposed ass once with my bare hand. "Answer, when I

speak to you, slut!"

I slap your other cheek. Now you nod your head vigorously, and look back towards me with apology in your eyes. You so want to please me. To do whatever I tell you to do. I slide my hand between your sexy nyloned legs, feel your wetness soaking into your thong.

"Grab your ankles with your hands, you sweet little cunt." I reach down. I tie each wrist tightly to each ankle. I stand up to admire you.

"I think you look like a perfect whore, my slave. This is a good way to expose your ass to me. You look so inviting. But I can't see your dripping, fucking cunt. You should show it off to me, like the prize for the Master that it is. Don't you agree, slut?"

You fail to nod. And I immediately slap your perfect ass, holding you by the thong so you don't lose your balance. You get the message and nod vigorously. I rip the thong down, and expose your hungry cunt. I rub it tenderly with my hand.

"Your cunt looks very sexy, sticking up in the air like that, daughter. I like your pussy shown off this way. It's perfectly submissive. What a good slave girl your are becoming for your Master."

"You please me greatly, whore." Daddy reaches down between your legs and pinches your clit forcefully. He bends down, you feel his wet tongue gliding down the crack of your ass, and suddenly he buries his tongue into your deliciously hot cunt. You gasp, tears of pleasure and ecstasy swell in your eyes. You have never felt more cherished than right now with your Daddy.

I can offer no guarantees…relationships become…whatever they are destined to be. I feel a potential with you…that is so strong…I want you…to respond.

Galen

(Note: I sent this letter below to Joe c/o sharah's email address)

Subject: ATTN – Joe, are you there?
Date: Mon, 30 Nov

Joe,

If you are involved in screening sharah's mail please respond to this message.

If you have an opinion on sharah's and my relationship that is preventing her from contacting me, I request that as one Dom to another you address your concerns directly to me. I ask that you judge neither so quickly nor harshly these recent events in my life. I have been preparing for my life as a Dom for many years, and now I have taken the final steps to allow that to occur, giving it my full and dedicated attention.

What has occurred in my brief encounter with sharah has been totally sincere and of the highest passion. While you are now mentoring her, you cannot be her Master. But I can be possibly the best Daddy/Master she would ever find. I doubt that you could know for certain, if this were true or not, based on the little you know of me.

I ask for you to withhold judgment. If you have concerns, address them to me directly. I ask that you give sharah approval to continue discussion with me, and let things evolve in their natural course. If we are not meant to be together, let us discover this ourselves.

It is highly unethical and cowardly not to allow any response to my sincerest efforts at open and honest communication. I deserve an explanation. I am open to your concerns, and feel you should be open and interested in my response to them.

I look forward to your reply.

Sincerely,

Galen

(Note: First letter from Joe)

Subject: an explanation
Date: Tue, 1 Dec

Galen,

Just got your message to me from sharah's mailbox. I wrote the message below earlier today. I do not have a problem with you so don't worry about that right now. The following will explain why you have not heard from her.

Joe J. here. I am sharah's brother-in-law and guardian. It is my understanding that sharah informed you she was staying with her sister and myself and that she did not explain the circumstances.

sharah was severely beaten and attacked with a knife by someone she met last week without her sister's or my knowledge. This guy got a hold of her number in New York and called her the night before she came here to stay with us, a real maniac who beat the crap out of her and cut her up. Thank God he let her go before he did too much damage but she was injured and will have some scars.

Apparently she walked some distance and was found outside a hospital emergency room sitting on the street, in shock and bleeding. She has a broken rib, broken cheekbone, stitches on both breasts and some internal cuts. When the police called us from the hospital I made arrangements for her to come here the next day. She tells me that she wrote to you just before she left New York but didn't tell you what happened. She seemed all right under the circumstances, on the phone, just shaken up, naturally.

When she arrived here she obviously was not herself and had to be

taken to the hospital again shortly thereafter. She is still hospitalized and pretty sedated most of the time. They think she will be
released in a week or two but probably to my custody for a while.
I'm sure she will recover but I have no intention of allowing her to
go back on her own until I am sure she is fully recovered and able to
make safer judgments.

sharah was able to give the guy's address and the police arrested the
sicko that cut her up but I am told he is already out on bail. My
wife and I will be personally going back to New York with her if
she has to make any court appearances.

I retrieved her mail for her yesterday and told her who had written
but have not allowed her to read anything. I'm sure you can understand my caution under the circumstances.

sharah is really not in a state to make rational decisions right now
and I don't want her to have any more pain right now. She did
specifically ask me to contact you and explain what happened.
When I think she is able to handle it, I will pass your letters on to
her and when I am sure she is fully recovered, I will not attempt to
keep her from contacting you, if that is what she wants to do.

I apologize for the interference but her sister and I feel she must be
protected right now at all costs. You have to understand this is a girl
who literally doesn't know how to say no to a man when she is
given an order. She has been on her own for a couple of years and
gotten in trouble a few times before though nothing this bad. She is
a beautiful, sweet, true submissive soul and she is like a daughter to
me. I couldn't have prevented this but I am going to make sure
nothing like it ever happens again even if I have to retrain her
myself.

I will keep her here with us for as long as I think is necessary. I will
be keeping her e-mail account open for a short time in case that sick
bastard tries to contact her again, but I will probably cancel it
eventually until she is ready to make her own decisions.

You probably won't hear from me again unless there is a change in

her condition that I think you should know about.

On a personal note I want to tell you that I am sorry for your personal troubles right now. I ended an unhappy marriage eight years ago myself and had two teenage boys also. I understand how hard a time you must be having. I'm sorry to add to it with this news about little sharah, but it couldn't be helped. She specifically begged that I write to GALEN and explain what happened.

I will tell you that since I collared my kathy and became the full time Master of my house I have never been unhappy again. My boys forgave me and can tell the difference between being around a happy contented marriage and the one they grew up around. I'm sure in time everything will work out for you. I will keep your letters for sharah.

Take care of yourself.

Joe

PS. As I said I wrote that earlier today. I have spent most of the last two days going through her mail trying to piece the story together for the cops and for myself. I don't know how he got her number. She did not give it to him or anyone else in her letters. You mentioned that I might have concerns about you in your message to me.

Under the circumstances I will say that it is obvious you and sharah have feelings for each other, but I must protect her right now. I will tell you that I have known sharah for many years. Knew her father and her former Master and I know what kind of slavery she has been exposed to and trained for. She has only had mild exposure to pain and serious torture until this sick bastard got a hold of her. If she gets better and decides to accept a collar, what goes on between her and her Master is their business.

But if it is someday you, I will offer you the chance to feel free to ask me anything about techniques or about sharah's history you want to know. I don't know how much actual experience you have with torture and it is not my intention to insult you.

I'm just a little touchy right now about anyone torturing this little girl. I'm sure you can understand my position. I can tell you this: sharah is not likely to say no to anything or to let you know when something is hurting more than she can stand unless you specifically order her to give you signals. My kathy is the same way but she is a little older and more sensible.

Not that she could have helped what that bastard did. I'm sure he doesn't know the meaning of being someone's Master. No one is EVER going to damage sharah again if I have any way of preventing it. So don't be too proud to ask about what you don't know.

I'm taking that as a lesson from this myself. I'm 55 years old and have been practicing this lifestyle for 30 years but there are things I still do very cautiously. Don't mean to insult you. Just can't get over this shit yet. Feel like I'll kill that son of a bitch if I ever get a hold of him. I'll try to keep you posted if anything changes.

Take care, son.

Joe

Subject: shock and relief
Date: Tue, 1 Dec

Dear Joe,

First, tell sharah (if you can) that I care about her greatly, and I'm here when she is ready. And a very, very close second: THANK YOU for looking out for sharah. THANK YOU for sending me all the background in such a compassionate way. Third, if you find the perp, would you be so kind as to wait until I can get there to serve justice on the fuck, with you? It should be extreme, don't you think?

The news of sharah was a real shock. She sounds in better shape than your description of the attack might have indicated, and for

that I am thankful (feeling a lot of thankfulness right now.) She didn't give me a clue in her last letter, but some things she told me about earlier, raised many concerns for her safety. She's a wild child, but what I know so far a very loving, generous, devoted, intelligent, creative woman. I don't need to tell you about her sexuality.

Joe, you were so kind to write me. You can sense what I may be going through, and while it's not all bad, I can say I haven't slept much this last week. From my volume of e-mails this last week, you can tell how much of my sentiments are directed at sharah. I was never more relieved than to get your letter. I know sharah well enough to know it would not be like her to not contact me at my request (repeated), no matter what the news. I was prepared to let it go, but it just didn't make any sense, unless she were physically unable to reply.

I really appreciated your offer to help me should sharah and I continue to develop a relationship. In no way could I ever harm a creature as beautiful and precious as sharah. Guidance on techniques and cues and equipment et al, would be warmly welcomed. I have a strongly developed sensibility about being a Master, cultivated over many years of observation. But I know I have a lot to learn in the realm of experience. I would welcome you as a mentor in that regard, and would feel quite fortunate if that occurred.

I accept your terms for future communication with sharah. She and I are very lucky to have you there to protect her. There is more I'd like to talk with you about, but I'll leave that for another time. When you can, tell sharah I'm thinking about her, praying for her quick recovery, and that I love and miss her.

You are a remarkable man, Joe.

Galen

(Note: At this point, I started sending letters again, directly to

*sharah. I tried to aim them as healing missives to her wounded
psyche. I did not yet comprehend the full extent of the harm done to
her. I knew she would not read them soon, but I thought they might
help her later, to realize that I was still connected to her through all
this.)*

Subject: you are a blessing
Date: Thu, Dec 3

Darling Daughter,

When you are ready I know you will read this. I hope it is soon.

I'm thinking of you, sweetgirl. I'm visualizing you vibrant and
smiling and beyond all past events. You are surrounded by the
power of love and the strength and devotion of those who love you.
Nothing can harm you now, or ever will again. This is the truth.

Your devotion to men and ultimately to your true Master has not
been betrayed, daughter. This vile evil that attacked you was not a
man. He was a piece of shit that squirmed out the wrong hole of his
mother. He should be flushed like any other piece of shit...from
your life, from your mind, from your heart, and from this existence,
if the opportunity presents itself. A true man will never harm, and a
true Master will never cause that type of terror in your tender heart.

Joe wrote me about what happened, and other things. I think Joe
and I would get along great. He's been a blessing to me, in your
absence. And I am so thankful you are now under his protection.
You are blessed, daughter, though I know you might feel otherwise
for a while.

The first time reading Joe's letter, I got some of it and some things
didn't really sink in, because part of me was so joyful, just to
understand that it was impossible for you to contact me, and that
you were going to be all right. Then he told me you were having a
hard time, and that you might be in the hospital for several more
weeks, and I started to picture what you must have had to endure.

80

I suddenly went to a depth of anger and horror...it enraged me to think of it. You are so precious sharah. Don't ever do anything like that ever again. This is the first and most important order your future Master gives you. And I already know that Joe has laid down the law as well.

I'm still hoping that you can meet me in Florida, though I have no idea if that will be possible. If not, when you are able, I'll make another arrangement.

I'm staying with a good friend of mine for a few days. Then, this weekend, I'm moving into another friend's house. It was up for sale, after he moved to a new place. He's taking it off the market, and I made a deal to rent there for the near future. Then I'll see what happens down the line. It's a 3-bedroom, with room for my kids, if at some point they want to visit.

My oldest son hasn't talked with me since the weekend I moved out. I've called several times to say hi, tell him I love him, but he's really mad at me and won't talk or even let me take him out to dinner. My younger one's a little warmer, and we set a dinner date for next Tuesday. He's snowboarding all weekend so he's <u>busy</u> till then!

I have so much shit here to deal with. I have to heal my life with my kids, ultimately heal with my former wife, so we rationally take care of our kids needs till they're on their own, major financial entanglements. I don't have a bed, or sheets or pots and pans. I might have to shut down the business we own, sell our house, liquidate stocks, and pay off my share of the debts. There are likely to be some sticky, ugly issues to contend with before it's all over, and that's a painful thing to think about and do.

But I'm okay, hanging out with guy friends, who've made me laugh about a lot of this shit (they only know about the HIV test and my leaving, not the D/s part.) My new business deals are still perking. I'm getting stuff done, though I don't know how. I get only a few hours of sleep, before my restless mind overtakes my weary body,

and I know I'm exhausted and drained, and I'm determined tonight to sleep all the way through, and start to recover my strength and concentration.

I'm ready to unleash. Already I feel the surge and excitement of my true self re-emerging. I just need some sleep and to have sweet dreams of you, daughter. I know you'll contact me when you can.

Love,

Daddy

Subject: keep faith
Date: Fri, 4 Dec

Galen,

Glad I could ease your mind a little, son. Sorry I didn't get to you sooner. Try not to worry yourself. I'll keep in touch and let you know as soon as she is well enough to get letters, calls, etc. kathy has been with her all day today and I'm going to see them in a few minutes.

kathy says she woke up for a little while today but started crying again so they had to put her back under, poor little thing. Breaks my heart to see her like this. You normally have a hard time getting a frown out of her. Sweetest little girl you'll ever meet. She's okay for a few minutes when she first wakes up. Smiles up at us and starts talking, but then you can watch her crumble up right in front of you and then she starts crying and can't get her to stop. Now my little kathy is all messed up too. I got an upside-down house here with two hurt women and several businesses to run.

My oldest boy is having some troubles of his own and now it looks like I might have to go up to New York in a day or two to deal with the cops. They were right on it at first, but now are starting to imply that they may have trouble prosecuting because sharah went over

there and consented to sex with the bastard. If they won't prosecute him I swear to God I'll find the sick fuck and take care of it myself.

Yeah, I'll call you and we can pay him a little visit. I say we cut his dick off with his own goddamn knife and shove it down his throat while he bleeds to death. I swear I see fucking stars swimming around my head when I think about what he did to that sweet little girl. I can't fucking breathe, right now.

Anyway, don't worry if you don't hear from me for a while. I'll take your letters to her when she can read and stay calm. I'll take her your picture first and see how she does with that.

Easy does it son.

Joe

Subject: caretaking
Date: Fri, 4 Dec

Dear Joe,

It's hard not to worry about sharah, not hearing from her directly, more than a week later. Your description of her state of mind tells me her scars are much more than physical. It didn't really sink in at first. Then I started thinking about "internal cuts" and the knife, and there's only one way I can (barely) think of for that to have happened.

Sometime, somewhere justice will catch that sick fuck, and squeeze the life out of him, as painfully as possible. I'd enjoy seeing the terror in his eyes before they closed for the last time.

Hopefully, she is recovering and gaining strength everyday. I know it will take time, and I know she's in the best possible situation with you and kathy for that to occur. I wish I were there to help; I know and appreciate how much effort you're putting out on all fronts.

sharah and I had planned to meet in Florida in about 4 weeks. I don't know what her prognosis is, or if there is anyway that will be possible. My goal now, if it were at all possible, would be to totally support her recovery. I'll be in Ft. Lauderdale at the Marriott. She could kick back at the pool, all day, bake in the sun, read a book, and just totally relax, while I take care of business.

I'll be at a trade show during the day, and if she wanted, she could come and hang out there with me as well. Then we'd fly to Orlando, where I have just a few appointments. We could mostly relax, and I could devote my attention to her care, until I return home on the10th day. sharah's and my sexual interests would be put on hold until she was both physically and mentally healed.

I bring this up now because of the busy travel at that time, and I would want to secure her a plane reservation. I realize you may not know yourself if sharah should make such a trip, or you may know already that she shouldn't. If you can trust that my intentions are honorable and I could provide kathy and yourself a needed break from caretaking sharah, I would be happy to provide sharah all she needs to make the trip. That is if she herself wishes to go.

Let me know what you think.

Galen

Subject: tender embrace
Date: Fri, 4 Dec

Dearest Daughter,

Can't stop thinking of you! I'm so sad and angry about what happened to you. I want to take you in my arms in the most tender embrace, feel you nuzzle into me, look into those lovely blue eyes and with just that look, heal your wounded angel heart.

Daddy's so worried about his little baby. It's hard to be here, day after day, knowing how much you are suffering, and not be able to do anything. Hoping that when I check my mail, I'll see your name, and know that you are going to be OK.

What a strange, strange week it's been. And I'm so tired. Didn't sleep again last night. Seems like every day, it just gets stranger and stranger.

But the good thought is that if you're reading this, I know that you are healing, and feeling all the love and warmth and passion that your Daddy can offer. I want to feel your heart pressed against mine, sharah, in an embrace that will last a lifetime. Sweet dreams, sweetgirl.

Love,

Daddy

Subject: rescue mission
Date: Sat, 5 Dec

Dear daughter,

See, daughter, what this has become, is a rescue mission. All this strangeness has happened to us both, at the same time, the synchronicity of meeting when and how we did, the explosion of passion and understanding, the hot sexual tension of Master and slave, Daddy and daughter, then suddenly the horrendous tragedy all around...and now, the rescue.

That's what I'm going to do, sweet daughter. Rescue you. Heal you. Protect you (and honey, you do need protection in the worst way). Love you, and restore your tender soul that yearns for her true Daddy's ownership.

You are remarkable, sharah. How on earth did you write that letter

to me Wednesday, after what you were going through? You were so passionate, so loving, beautifully slutty, (makin' Daddy's cock hard), and so wounded on so many levels. It made Daddy cry when I realized what you did for me, my sweetest daughter.

I know you can feel me in your heart, dear daughter, as I can feel you in mine. There are many passions yet before us. But right now daughter, Daddy is focused on helping you recover. I am here for you daughter, like the good Daddy I am. For some reason, we were meant to start from this point. We know where we're going. I'm ready to start, and I know you will soon be, too.

Love from your Daddy

Subject: I'm freakin'
Date: Sun, 6 Dec

Joe,

You gotta help me out here, Joe. I'm starting to freak. It's been almost two fuckin' weeks. It can't be physical at this stage. That's got to be healing. What did this sick fuck do to little sharah?

I need to know how she is. I know that if she can't write, or send a message, then she's got to be really out of it. Why isn't she re-sponding, Joe? Is she still totally out of it? Isn't she getting any better? If she's not coming around at all in a few more days, I want you to consider the possibility of me coming to see her. I feel so out of touch with the situation there that I don't know if that would be a good idea or not.

But I'm feeling a little more than concerned for her, now. I'm fuckin' worried! But if nothing else is working, I want to try, Joe. sharah and I became incredibly close in spirit in a very short time. I haven't a clue what that really means right now, or what our desti-nies might be. But I want to help this precious girl heal, in any way I can.

86

I was thinking the same thing about the shitbag. He's tasted blood, if not for the first time, it's certain not to be the last. If the cops don't shut this fucker down, he'll go farther next time. This guy wants to kill. I've never seriously desired to kill someone before (in a furiously slow manner), but I've changed. I don't know how smart it would be to do it. But I sure do desire the pure pleasure and vengefulness of it.

Galen

Subject: healing
Date: Sat, 6 Dec

Dear daughter,

I'm fighting for you, little darling, with everything I've got. This was one event in your life, an incredibly tragic and horrendous one. My focus now is to heal you, little daughter. Don't you worry, little sweetgirl, your lovin' Daddy is the remedy you need.

Do you know you're the most incredible little daughter that your Daddy can think of? Every day I haven't heard from you, my hate and desire to fuck up the shit that hurt my little girl eats at me. I am strong for you daughter. My heat for you is intense. I want to be by your bedside. Walk into your room, and see you look at me, and feel us melt away all that's gone on in the past, in that one look.

I couldn't look at your pictures again till after I got Joe's first letter. I was in that state of mind where all I knew was that you had stopped writing me, after your last letter, filled with passion and desire and love. Now I look at them every day, and see you exactly as you are...happy, devoted, joyful. All I see is my lovingly submissive daughter. Sweet dreams, daughter.

Love,

Daddy.

Subject: New York
Date: Mon, 7 Dec

Galen,

Running out the door to go pick kathy up and see sharah at the
hospital. I'm going to New York tonight to talk to the cops and get
some things from sharah's apartment. I should be back on Tuesday.
Not much change in the little one's condition. She did let me hold
her hand for a couple minutes today. Now she's losing it when the
male doctors and orderlies come into the room. She's not too bad
with me though.

Her face is looking better. Some of the swelling is going down.
There's still a little hemorrhaging from the internal cuts but they
assure me those will eventually heal. Yeah, you got the picture
about the vaginal cuts. I don't know exactly what she did to keep
him from killing her but somehow she must have handled him
pretty well.

Anyone who could do something like that to a woman, what's to
stop him from going all the way and killing her? I can only figure
out that she kept him happy and he figured he wanted to keep her
alive so he could use her again. I can't imagine what it was like for
her but she got herself out of it alive. Sweet baby girl. Breaks my
fucking heart and makes me want to fucking go berserk. I've had to
be real careful with kathy the last few days, not to get too close to
the rage when I'm using her. She's all spooked too but she's doing
okay.

Can you imagine what kind of mind could do that to a woman?
Filthy fuck has fucked up more lives than just little sharah's. Mine,
yours, kathy's. I've got the scumbag's address. It's all I can do not
to go over there and rip his fucking head off. Can't do that yet
though. Have to stay calm and let the system do what it will do. I

88

would just end up in jail and leave kathy and sharah when they need me. They are my first responsibility right now.

I swear to Christ though, buddy, if the legal system won't serve justice on that piece of shit, I will someday, somehow, finish the job myself. He WILL do this to some other woman if he gets away with it and the next girl may not be as submissive as sharah and will end up dead. Not on my watch!

We will be patient for the time being, but I'm not going to wait forever. That's why I'm going up there myself. Try to get this thing moving and get the DA off his lazy ass and get that fuckhead locked up again. Have to calm down before I get to the hospital. kathy knows me too well and I don't want her scared <u>and</u> alone for the next few days. Driving me crazy to leave her right now. Can't stand to let her out of my sight.

Anyway, buddy, I don't know what to tell you about Florida. The way she is now I have a hard time imagining it, but who knows. They're moving her out of intensive care tomorrow and I'm going there now to try to keep them from putting her on the psychiatric floor. I don't want her around a bunch of loonies. That can't be what's best for her right now.

If I have to fucking pay cash for a private room I'll goddamn well do it. kathy's got a good idea about getting her close to the kids' ward so she can take her over there to watch the kids or near the babies and so on. I'm going to see what I can do about that too. That's the right idea as far as I'm concerned. sharah volunteers in a terminal kid's ward up in New York. If anything's going to snap her out of it that's what will do it.

So hang on for a few days and I'll write when I get back from New York and see how she's doing. kathy put your picture in a little frame and took it over to her by the way. I saw her looking at it on her table a few times. I told her it was you, and kathy said "Daddy", but I don't think she's figured it out just yet. She's looking at it though and not getting crazy, so she must like your looks. You look a little like her old man to tell you the truth. kathy

89

saw it right away. Owen was a buddy of mine. Sit tight for a few days. I'll get back to you as soon as I can.

Joe

Subject: general alarm
Date: Mon, 7 Dec

Dear Joe,

Hope you had a safe and productive trip. I fear no news is bad news. Every day not hearing from sharah, my nightmare of how much damage this sick predator has done to her escalates. How can she not be incredibly damaged? I picture her tied up, watching, knowing, fearing she will be slaughtered mercilessly. The horror of it shakes my soul and in my heart I feel the greatest sadness. But then there's something else to feel as well.

Short of putting out a contract on this inhuman shit, I'd like to post everything we can learn about him on every relevant site, bulletin board and newsgroup I can find. Pictures, physical description, addresses, occupation, place of employment, both to fuck him up in every area of his life, but more to protect other potential victims.

Let's put this guy out of circulation with a general alarm. Maybe some creative soul will figure out how to get this asshole, without risk to himself. Make him suffer everything thing he's ever dished out, before his lights go permanently out. What do you think?

I sure hope to get a message that sharah's coming around. I'll do anything I can to help.

Warm regards,

Galen

Subject: you are protected
Date: Mon, 7 Dec

Dearest Daughter,

sharah, I want you to take my picture, and look at it, then read this
letter. Know this is your Daddy talking to you, darlin'. Or maybe
kathy can read it to you.

I know that you must be filled with truly painful thoughts, right
now. I sure wish I was there, and could cuddle my little daughter in
my strong arms, and gently hug all that pain from you. I'm not, but
I will help you get through this. Trust Daddy, sharah, you (we) will
get through this.

The first thought must be the terror, with that scary movie playing
over and over in your head. But now, sharah, listen to your Daddy,
the keyword is "movie." It's just a very mad, bad movie now. And
the movie's over, darlin'. You will never have another experience
like that again.

You are now under the very capable protection of Joe. Soon, you
will be under the protection of your loving Daddy Master. There
will be nothing that can break through the barrier of strength and
love that surrounds you. You are now safe forever. Your devotion
to your life as a submissive daughter will move forward, joyfully.
Trust Daddy! Very soon, all this will be true.

There might be other things as well roaming through that thoughtful
mind of yours. Are you worried about your physical body, sweetheart, about scars and pain, about your worthiness to serve. Not to
worry dear. I'm certain you will be quite fine, and will soon be as
beautiful as ever.

Physical attraction is only on the surface. Though it is a strong
aphrodisiac to lure a Master's eye, it has nothing to do with the
exquisite depths of pleasure between a Master/slave in their hearts
and minds.

It's interesting, we've never had our relationship on a physical level. You zipped right past that, straight to the heart, and my mind readily followed. So don't worry, daughter. We go deep, sharah. I know you can feel that. Grab hold of that feeling, sweetheart. Hold on and it will lift you from where you're hiding, where you're just wanting to be safe, right into Daddy's arms.

I can't wait to read your letter, or hear your sweet voice. Talk to me, sharah. Daddy will help you.

Good night, daughter.

Love,

Daddy

Subject: trying to be patient
Date: Tue, 8 Dec

Hi Joe,

I know you'll send word when you can. I just feel like I've been holding my breath since your last letter. I've got plenty else to occupy my mind, but I can't stop thinking (and worrying) about sharah.

So, I'm writing more to assuage my own need to "do something", than to try to hurry your response. I don't like where my thinking's going on this. I fear the worst. Hopefully, when you write, you'll have some positive news.

Had my first bright spot in a few weeks. Took my kids to dinner last night. They're totally cool! We were loose, and joking and laughing, absolutely no problem. Their mom's the drama queen. We're just guys that want to have fun. I'm taking them and a couple of their buddies snowboarding this weekend, to a beautiful

ski area about 3 hours from here.

So, now I've got my boys back, hopefully my "daughter" will be back soon, too!

Talk to you soon.

Galen

Subject: owning you
Date: Tue, 8 Dec

Dearest daughter,

You are the truest slave/daughter I could ever know, sharah. You have the most courageous slave soul in the world. You are the most beautiful slave daughter I've ever laid my lustful eyes on.

There is nothing in this world that will stop me from owning you, daughter. I know your slave heart is mine to take, and how lovingly and submissively it is offered. I take it and cherish it, and make it my own. I will protect you from every darkness in our future and heal you from every darkness in the past.

Listen now, carefully, daughter. This is a direct order. Take my picture and gaze at it, then read further, and know that as you read you are hearing my voice, and in your mind you can see me as I give this command that you must obey.

I know how hard it is to concentrate, but Daddy is here now to take away all your fear and doubt. Picture Daddy opening his strong arms to you, commanding you to come into his embrace, and in that embrace you feel the warmth and power of me, you absorb my scent, and feel the surge of energy flowing from me into you.

Feel all my love and power over you flowing into you, and now, sharah, I command you to understand that you will be all right.

Nothing has changed the strength of my desire for you. Nothing physical nor emotional, no fear you may have that can penetrate or diminish my total love for you. I command you to come to this understanding now, slave. Do not dwell on anything other than where you and I as Master/slave, as Daddy/Daughter, as Soul/soul are heading into the future.

I know how much you love your true Master, how you long to please me. I know when I give you a command you will readily obey. That is why I choose you as my slave daughter. Your collar is waiting. But you must obey your loving Master, right now. This is your next step towards the future you have always longed for, dearest daughter.

Your next duty: send me a personal message of any length or content you desire. I am waiting for you daughter.

Daddy

Subject: The Full Story
Date: Wed, 9 Dec

Galen,

I'm gonna try to be organized about this so you don't feel so left in the dark. Sorry you've been so frustrated. I've been doing my best to keep a lot of balls in the air here and take care of the girls. I know my letters to you have been all over the place and sounding crazy. Not half as crazy as I felt I can tell you.

I got back from New York last night and have been getting caught up in my business and trying to take care of some new developments at the hospital. This is the first time I've had a chance to sit down for an hour in the last week and a half. Unfortunately it looks like I might have to go right back to New York as soon as I get sharah squared away here, either in a different hospital, or at home with us.

First I'll give you a report on sharah's condition. Then I'll try to piece together as much of the full story as I know. Then I'll tell you what just went on up in New York.

sharah's physical condition is improving though not as fast as we hoped. There are complications with that due to some of her reactions to the trauma. She will eventually be all right physically. She has a fracture in her left cheekbone (which I will explain when I tell you all that happened to her.) Her face was badly bruised and swollen for a while but that has mostly returned to normal. The fracture will take some time to heal though since the cheekbone is a difficult place for a break. Not much they can do about it.

Most of the cuts and bruises on her face and body are healing and won't leave permanent marks. There are a few deeper cuts that needed stitches and those scars will have to wait for a while before a plastic surgeon can take a look at them. Those are the ones on her breasts and around her nipples. The subhuman scum apparently tried to carve his initial on one of her breasts. I didn't want to tell you about that one because I knew it would upset any man and I am hoping we can get it taken care of with plastic surgery.

I will pay for any surgery our baby girl needs to help her forget what that fuck did to her, but that is the least of our worries right now. Her ribs are healing slowly and are obviously causing her quite a bit of pain when she is alert enough to feel it, which isn't too often. The vaginal cuts are also not completely healed yet though they stopped the hemorrhaging while I was away by going in and re-stitching up the worst spots.

One of the reasons the injuries are not healing as fast as hoped, is that sharah is still pretty hysterical when awake. She has panicked a few times and reinjured herself by trying to get away from whatever demons are chasing her. When any man other than me walks in the room, if she is awake enough to realize it, she starts crying and struggling to get out of bed, etc. When I go in I have to start slow and talk to her for a while before she will stay still and let me hold her hand.

95

Her emotional state is very inconsistent and unpredictable. There are times when she seems like the sharah we know so well and other times when she is unrecognizable. I've had long conversations with her and had her laughing a couple of times, then you can see it come over her like a shadow. She sometimes starts talking about that night, but most of it is incoherent and half the time she doesn't know who's in the room.

Once she begged me to use the bat again and hit her, instead of more of the knife (Jesus H Christ, I still get sick to my stomach thinking about it. She's stronger than any man I know for living through what she went through.). Then she might be almost catatonic for a while and can't look at you or talk and just lies there shaking. Then the crying starts and nothing can stop it until they give her a shot to knock her out. She sleeps for a few hours then wakes up and seems okay again and then it all starts over again.

She seemed to be doing better over the weekend and kathy got them to let her wheel sharah down to see the kids play room. She just sat there for a while but she watched the kids. Then one little boy came over to see her and kathy says she lit up like a Christmas tree. Started talking to the boy and sounded completely clear and made perfect sense.

Then she asked to see the babies and kathy took her down there, but when they got there sharah started crying again and had to be taken back to bed. Next day kathy tried to take her back to the kids but she got scared and thought "Master" was waiting there to trick her.

I can't stand that that filthy piece of shit got her calling him Master. I only heard her say it once, but it felt like the knife was going in me. I gave her an order never to call him that again and it seemed to calm her down actually. Obviously, I've been very gentle with her the whole time but I lost it when I realized he had her thinking of him as a Master.

The only other time I tried to give her an order was an experiment. I ordered her to look at me when she was slipping into one of her

trances. She didn't do it and that's when I knew she wasn't anywhere we could reach her at those times. sharah has NEVER
disobeyed an order to come to attention before.

One interesting thing, though, next day she looked at me and said I
didn't mean to disobey you, Master Joe. I thought she was talking
about going to meet that guy and I had already told her she wasn't
allowed to blame herself for what happened and she said no, she
was sorry for not looking at me when I ordered her to. So she heard
me in there somewhere.

kathy says she asked for me several times while I was gone but she
kept forgetting kathy told her I was in New York. One time kathy
told her where I was and she got to crying again because she figured
I'd gone to kill the son of a bitch and she thought he had killed me.
That's when she fell out of the bed and started the internal bleeding
again, and they finally went in and stitched up the major cuts.
When she woke up after the surgery, kathy called me in New York
so sharah could hear I was all right, but she was so gone at that
point, I think she had forgotten all about it again.

I only saw her awake for a little while today and she smiled at me
and talked for a while and said she missed me, but the trembling
and crying started again and they had to put her down. She looked
so pale and thin, it got to me.

It's what's in her eyes when the trance starts that kills me more
though. It's wearing kathy down too and my kathy can handle more
than any girl I've ever known. I'm going to spend as much of the
day with sharah tomorrow as I can and make kathy stay home for a
while. I want her to get a break and I don't want sharah forgetting
who I am and getting spooked when I walk in the room.

All right, so that's where she is right now.

Now I'll try to put together the story for you in case I left out
details, that will fill it in for you. This fuckhead wrote to her early
on at the bondage site. Came on pretty strong ordering her to write
back and send pictures. She wrote him back as ordered and told

him about her training and sent him the pictures. Then she didn't hear from him for a while and got about a hundred more responses. I think he may have written to her under other identities to see if he could get her to reveal more and give her address.

That's part of what I've been trying to untangle going through all the letters she got and sent. She was trying to be respectful and answer everybody who wrote her until I told her to stop and just make a form letter to reply with telling them she couldn't answer anymore.

Pretty soon she was getting involved with you and (don't get pissed) only answering a couple of guys. I say don't get pissed because you were the one she wanted the most and you were the one she asked for permission to give her number to.

I was bringing her out here for Thanksgiving anyway, so I told her to bring all the letters and we would look at them together and talk about it. I had read some of your stuff already and was planning to give her permission to call you from here where I could talk to you first.

I just wanted to talk to her and make sure she knew what she wanted and recommend that if she called you it be only you and she concentrate on getting to know you before you both made any permanent decisions. I told you before she is like my daughter and I just want her to be happy.

Anyway, that's the last conversation I had with her before what happened. So she had gotten another letter from the scum ordering her to give him her phone number and telling her he lived in NYC and he was collaring her and she was going to serve him before the end of the week. She wrote back and told him the god's honest truth. Told him she was hoping to accept someone else's collar and that I wouldn't allow her to give her phone number out without my permission anyway. She thanked him respectfully and apologized if she misled him.

He writes back again, all nice and understanding and says what a

shame he never got the chance to just see her dance and gets all weepy and tells her how lonely he is. Asks her would she just come over and dance for him and maybe suck him off one time before she accepts your collar. Naturally you know our sharah feels terrible and writes him back a sweet loving letter, saying she's so sorry but she has to obey me and coming over is out of the question. But she writes him a long letter telling him she's sure he'll find a good girl and she's trying to build his ego up and make him feel better.

He sucked her right in, knew exactly how to play on her sweet heart. That was Tuesday before she came here. That night, he somehow figures out how to get her number. I have no idea how, and the police don't know either. She never gave him her number, her street, or her last name. But he figured it out and called her. He gets her on the phone and orders her not to hang up until he gives his permission. He's got her right there. She's all upset and says she's disobeying me by obeying him. He tells her she's not disobeying me because I only ordered her not to give her number out and she didn't.

Now you know as well as I do that our sharah is not a stupid girl by any means. She knows that she is to follow the essence of an order, not just its letter. But since she's not technically collared by me, and has been on her own for a couple of years, she's getting confused about what to do with this guy. Then he starts playing the sweet and lonely routine again. Tells her his wife left him and he doesn't feel like a man anymore (you can say that again.)

Once again, tell our little sharah a man has been mistreated by his woman, and she wants to make him feel in charge again. He promises her all he wants is a lap dance and a blow job, and tells her... get this... he's gonna kill himself if he doesn't get to meet her once. She tries to say let me call Master Joe and ask his permission and he tells her if she does that, he knows I'm going to tell her no. Of course he was right about that. She knows it too and he tells her again he's gonna off himself. Tells her she's not collared yet and orders her over to serve him. She goes.

Most of that we know because of what she told kathy and me the

night she arrived. She hasn't been able to talk about all that happened when she got to his place, in order of what happened, but her injuries tell most of the story.

This is the best I can piece it together. So she gets there and does some dancing for him. He orders her to suck his cock. She's doing her job for him and then he puts her in cuffs. She's used to that, so it's no problem. Then all of a sudden he pulls her off his cock and she sees something big in his hands and he's swinging it at her face.

The fuck, the filth, wormy sorry ass excuse for a piece of shit, swings a baseball bat right into her face. Knocks her out cold and breaks her cheekbone. That could have killed her easily right there. I don't know what the fuck saved her. I guess he didn't swing full force. She lost one of her teeth in back. Bit her tongue pretty bad and fractured the cheekbone. Jesus, I'm shaking with rage again. A fucking baseball bat! Right at her head.

All right. So she comes to and she's cuffed to a hook in the wall, ankles cuffed spread eagle. She wakes up and he's slapping her repeatedly in the face and using her body as a punching bag. Somewhere in there he brings the knife out and tells her she has to service his "friend" too. He starts cutting her, little cuts all over. Then he starts the deeper cuts around her nipples. She's begging him to stop, tells him no man will want her anymore. He tells her that's the whole idea and then sticks the knife in her pussy. Jesus. Have to take a break here. Can't stand to write this.

Okay. Had to go hug kathy for a while. I'm going to finish this though. If anything is going to happen between you and sharah you need to know all this. Put it down and walk away from it, if you can't read it. Take it in small doses. That's what we're all having to do right now. So she's screaming and begging him to stop. He tells her he'll stop if she'll agree to wear his collar and never see me or kathy again. She says okay and he pulls the knife out and starts carving his initial in her breast.

She's crying and he tells her to shut up. She can't stop crying, so he gets his bat again and takes a big swing and breaks two of her ribs.

She manages to stop crying and he gets his "friend" again. He gets it inside her and little sharah figures out what the guy needs to get him to stop.

She tells him how much she loves him and what he's doing to her. She begs him to fuck her now, so he can feel her blood on his cock. He likes that idea but can't get to her the way he's got her positioned, so he uncuffs her. She keeps talking to him while he's fucking her, telling him about the 24" dildo she's got at home. That she wants him to use it on her while she services him and his "friend." He cums and falls asleep on top of her for a minute. She's trying to figure out if she can get out and he wakes up.

She starts working him again, begging to go home and get the toys and another knife she has at home. He gets into the idea again and lets her put her dress on, but no shoes. He lets her wash the blood off and put bandages over the worst cuts. Then he gives her a tampon. Proof that he's done this before and was prepared. He sends her home to get the toys and tells her if she's not back in twenty minutes he's coming to kill her.

Just had to take another break and go lay down with kathy again. I haven't sat down and put it all together in one place like this before. Even with the cops and the DA.

I saw my best friends get their heads blown off in Viet Nam and I didn't feel like this. I can't believe that sweet little girl had to go through that. No wonder she's in the shape she's in. Amazing she has any sanity left at all.

She wandered around for at least an hour as far as we can tell. She found the hospital but she didn't go inside. Just sat on the curb in front of the emergency room and waited to be called in. I asked her why she didn't go inside and she said she saw two kids in the waiting room and she wanted to make sure they got helped first. And her dress was covered in blood on the front and she didn't want to scare the kids. And... this is the part that breaks my heart into a million pieces... she said her predicament was her own fault because she disobeyed me and she didn't want me to find out what she did

and she knew no man would ever want her again anyway, so she might as well just die.

I have been spending most of my time with her trying to convince her that it was not her fault. She has got to believe that. It is the only way she is ever going to get better. You have got to promise me whatever happens between you two, that you will never NEVER punish her for this. NEVER make her feel like she caused this to happen to her. I have to have your word on that or you will never meet sharah.

Sorry. Didn't mean to threaten you. I just can't stand the thought of that poor little girl suffering any more because of what that fuck did to her. Yes, she disobeyed me but that doesn't mean she deserved what she got. I will never believe that as long as I live. You and I have to make her see that too. We get that through to her and she just might make it.

Anyway, they found her and got her inside and called the cops when they saw her injuries. The cops came and interviewed her and she was completely coherent and gave the guy's address and everything. They went over and arrested him that night. The hospital called us and told us what happened. I was ready to get on a plane and come get her myself, but she sounded fine on the phone and said she was coming out the next day anyway. I talked to a doctor in the emergency room and he said she was beat up, but okay to fly, and that she seemed perfectly calm and rational.

Neither sharah nor the hospital told me the full extent of her injuries. I didn't know anything about the baseball bat or the knife until she got here and told me. All I knew was she got beat up and had to have some stitches.

She knew the guy was in jail already so she wasn't even afraid to go back to her apartment and get packed and ready to come to us. kathy was on the phone with her every half hour the next day until she left for the airport. kathy seemed more upset than sharah did. She stopped by her neighbor girl's apartment to write you before she went to the airport.

When she got here I couldn't believe my eyes. Her face was badly swollen and she was black and blue all over. She could barely walk and I couldn't believe they didn't tell me how bad it was, so I could come get her. I can't believe now they didn't fucking keep her in the hospital even overnight. But she was still rational when she got here and I made her tell me some of the story. When she got to the part about the knife though, that's when she started to crack. She managed to hold it together until she got to us, but once she was here and knew she was safe, she started to go fast.

We stayed up half the night with her trying to help her calm down and she finally cried herself to sleep, we thought. She woke up a couple hours later though, screaming at the top of her lungs and fighting and kicking. She was hemorrhaging and had the sheets covered with blood and I thought she was dying. I just grabbed her and put her in the car and took her to the emergency room. I didn't even take time to put a shirt on. Barely got my pants on.

We got her there and they had to give her two shots before she fell asleep again. They admitted her and put her in intensive care so kathy could stay with her round the clock and they could keep an eye on the bleeding. We never left the room, except to go to the john for the first 36 hours or so. She knew when one of us was stepping out and would start crying hysterically till whichever one of us it was, came back.

Finally she got some real sleep and when she woke up seemed herself again. That's when she asked me to write to you and I started getting more of the story in bits and pieces. I don't remember what day that was anymore, but I wrote to you within a day or two of that and have been trying to pull this family back together ever since.

Got to take another break now and get some sleep. I'll try to finish this in the morning, or I might end up waking up later tonight. Been having a few sleepless nights myself. Hang on. More coming.

9 Dec., con't (Joe)

Here is the second part. Guess I needed sleep bad enough. Managed to get through the night and only woke up once or twice.

Took kathy to the hospital and saw sharah for a few minutes this morning. Looks like she had another bad night but we got her to go down to see the kids with us again. She looked like she still thought he was going to be there, but since I was along she stayed okay. Kept looking over her shoulder though. I don't know how he got tied up in her mind with the kids but we got to put a stop to that. Can't have that ruined for her too. She calmed down after she was with the kids for a while. By the time I left she was giggling and acting like sharah again.

I'm going back in a little while to relieve kathy and I might spend the night with sharah if kathy can stand to stay by herself. I want my girl to get one good night's sleep for a change.

sharah got out of intensive care on Sunday and we managed to get her to a private room on a regular floor. I want to get her home with a private psychiatric nurse as soon as we can, hopefully by the end of the week. They are fighting me on that at the hospital, but I have a lawyer on it and he says as long as we get a certified nurse full time, they should let her go. I want her home in familiar surroundings.

So I spent most of Saturday with the detectives and met briefly with the DA. The cops were better than I expected, but the DA was an insinuating fat bastard. He says they can't get a conviction on attempted murder because he let her go. And they can't get rape or sexual battery because she consented to the sex part. The most they are going for right now is assault. They may get some other charges because of the baseball bat.

The knife doesn't mean that much to them because they are saying that was part of the sex. Unbelievable! That slimy fat bastard looked me right in the eye and said, "Well, that's what you people are into, isn't it?" I just about lunged over the desk at him and one of the detectives grabbed my arm and told the fat fuck to back off.

So it's like I thought and just because sharah is a submissive, they haven't got the balls to really go after this piece of shit. The cops are pissed too, because they know this guy is going to do it again and worse.

Sunday I spent going through her apartment and met up with a buddy of mine from the service who is in the FBI up in New York. We went over to the scumbag's apartment and he wasn't there. Steve got the building guy to let us in and we took a look around. I kept hoping the scumbag would show up while we were there but no such luck. The cops did a good job of getting all the physical evidence. They got blood samples and proved they were sharah's and got the knife and the bat and cuffs, etc.

But get this. We're looking around and find this box on the counter with six or seven knives of different sizes and blades. They just left all these fucking knives for this guy to use on some other girl. If sharah hadn't gotten out of town right after, you know that fuck would have come to get her and finished her off. We cleaned the place out of knives and anything else he could use as a deadly weapon.

Not that he can't get what he wants, but I didn't know what else to do with the shit. Steve kept it all in case the cops get word of what we did. He can't do much unless the guy takes off out of state, but he got an unofficial surveillance on the guy and they supposedly are following him. The thing that really got me though was at sharah's apartment.

This psycho left her fifteen messages on her answering machine. Some were from that night and the rest were from after the fuck got out on bail. Can you believe the balls? I took the tape to the cops and they said they could bring him in again, but he'll probably be out on bail again in a few days.

How the fuck are we supposed to protect girls from this scum if the legal system won't do it and we can't put the fuck out of business without getting locked up ourselves. This guy knew just where to

go to prey on submissive girls and he spotted sharah right away. He knew she was the real thing: a true slave who puts all her focus on pleasing a man. I've always loved this girl and kathy for how completely submissive they are, but I've always feared for sharah because I knew she couldn't protect herself.

I should have collared her myself when Owen died, but I thought she deserved to have a Master who could give her his full attention. kathy's been wanting me to bring her here and collar her so they could be close to each other and because she's always been worried about sharah too. I should have done it.

I'll tell you one thing. She is not leaving us again until I know she is in your collar permanently or someone I can trust to protect her.

All right. So here's what I think we should do. I'm going back to New York in the next day or two to talk to the DA again about that fucking tape, and see if I can put pressure on them to get that fuck locked up again. For one thing if he found sharah's number what's to stop him from finding out where she is and getting my number and calling kathy and starting his shit. He knows about us and has probably figured out where she's gone. I'm protecting my own house now as much as looking for justice for what he did to sharah.

I'm also way ahead of you about putting out an alert about this guy. That's another reason I'm going back up there. My FBI buddy is gathering all the info on this guy that the cops won't give me. He says we have to be careful about what we publish about him, because if they do prosecute the fuck, his lawyers could use it to tangle things up even longer.

He says we can post some stuff and he's working on finding out all the different identities the guy is using online, and whether he hangs out at the D/s clubs in New York. When I have all the stuff Steve says is okay to post, you and I can talk about where to put it and maybe split the workload up between us. So hang in there for a while longer.

When I get back, maybe we'll have sharah home and we can talk

about bringing you out for a visit. It all depends on how she does. I figure if she meets you now she'll most likely go crazy like she does with every other guy. Maybe she wouldn't if she realized who you were, but then she's so afraid you won't want her anymore and she was convinced the night she got here that she didn't deserve you anymore.

Let me get her settled enough and feeling safe so I can give her your letters to read. Then she'll know you still want to meet her. But you think about it real carefully, all right? I mean it. You think about everything I told you here and whether you can handle every thing that happened to this girl and what it could mean.

I believe that sharah can eventually get past this and be the perfect submissive little girl she was before, but I have no doubt she will carry the emotional scars for the rest of her life. Who knows how those will manifest down the line.

I don't have to explain to you that owning a girl is not the same thing as a vanilla marriage , especially a girl like sharah. The responsibility is huge, even bigger than raising kids sometimes. Girls like sharah and kathy are less independent than most kids. They are smart girls and both very creative and dependable but they need a man to make most of the decisions and to be able to enforce those decisions. They give themselves to us completely and give up most of their ability to protect themselves.

I've worked for years to train kathy how to take care of herself if anything ever happened to me or when I'm out of the house, etc. But Owen didn't worry about that much with sharah. I guess he figured he was going to be around a lot longer to take care of her and liked having her as submissive as she is. He passed her around too much for my taste too, but I guess that was his business. Problem is, it left her thinking she had to serve any man who snapped his fingers at her and didn't teach her how to recognize filth like that scum that almost killed her.

So you think real hard about whether you want a girl who is that submissive and whether you can spend the time to take full respon-

sibility for her, not just her physical safety, but the whole package. I can tell you if you someday own sharah, it won't just be her body you own. That girl gives it all without limits. A man could break her in half and destroy her soul, without ever lifting a finger to harm her body.

Can you handle that kind of responsibility? Can you handle any physical scars that might be left? Can you teach her how to take care of herself if anything ever happens to you? I'm not asking you to answer these questions before I arrange a visit between you and sharah. I'm just asking you to think about these things. I know you're a decent guy and have thought about this for years. I'm sure you have what it takes to be a lifestyle Master.

Just remember this girl is not and never has been a part time play slut. That's why I didn't want her dancing at those parties any more. She thinks all men are born Masters and can be trusted to be responsible for her. She actually believed that she hadn't been collared again because she wasn't pleasing enough to the guys she served. Trust me, she couldn't be a more delicious little slut. She wasn't collared because there aren't very many men who want more than an occasional play partner.

All right. Enough of the lectures from me. Don't take offense, buddy. I just have to be fully responsible for this poor injured girl and make sure you understand the full situation. You think about it and write me again. When I get back from New York, maybe you and I can sit down and talk on the phone for a while. I'll get you caught up again on the situation and we'll talk some more about a possible visit. If you come out here to see sharah, I hope it will be as my guest. We've got plenty of room and live in a rural area with private land and great places to take walks in the woods, rivers, etc. kathy's a great cook and she'll wait on you hand and foot, except for her duties to sharah of course.

I've even given her orders that she is to disobey me if she thinks she needs to do something for sharah right now. No explanations, just do it, and explain it to me later.

But maybe sharah will be home by then and we'll all be here to keep an eye on her. Maybe you and sharah can even get out of the house sometimes and spend some time alone if she's able. I don't know. There's no way of telling what state she'll be in.

I know you believe you can help this girl heal and kathy and I both think you're probably right about that. But the timing is too important to fuck up. If we put you two together too soon, it could ruin both your chances to get past this. I'm thinking about you too here.

I know I'm not your father and you're about the same age as me. To tell you the truth, I'm feeling protective of the world right now (minus one that is - make that two - the fucking DA too.) I guess I've been worried about you too. I know you can take care of yourself, but I've been where you are now and I want to help if I can. Nothing would make me happier than someday turning sharah over to you and knowing you were the one who was going to own her and take care of her for the rest of your life. Knowing that the girls would still be able to visit each other and you and I were good friends and could trust each other with our property.

We've all got the same goal here I think. You and I both know things can change and happen in this world and in families. We both know it in our guts for sure now. But nothing can take away my responsibility to both my girls now. I wouldn't call myself a Master or even a man if I couldn't shoulder this responsibility.

You take care of yourself. I'll get back to you when I can.

Joe

PS. kathy wants me to tell you that sharah still has your picture on her table and she's looking at it more every day. We're pretty sure she knows it's you now. So I'll take a couple of your letters to her tonight and see if I can read them to her. I'll do the best I can for you. Also that's great news about your boys. I figured they'd come around.

Joe

Subject: rage and tears
Date: Wed, 9 Dec

Dear Joe,

It was nearly impossible to keep reading, tears begging to come from every pore, but the rage came out on top, until it swung back to sharah's personal struggle. The full force of both leaves me feeling very strange right now. I understand and appreciate a lot more about what you've been going through, though for you, I know, it's magnified even more.

Well, your letter(s) leave me with quite a pile to sort through. I read the first, had a meeting with my production managers (the mind is an amazing tool), then read part two.

I'm trying to give you my short responses right now. I've got to finish a presentation to a new client in the morning, and a half dozen other things in the next two hours, but I want/need to respond.

Tell sharah I love her, forgive her, want her, need her, and will do everything in my power to help her heal.

Thanks so much, once again, for the awesome amount of aid and love you and kathy are providing (sharah and I both).

If it can work out for me to visit, between both our situations, I'll be there. Thanks for the offer!

I'll help put this guy out of business anyway we can, with pleasure!

All these events of the last few weeks, have clearly taken the edge off my D/s relationship with sharah, and everybody else for that matter. And I obviously can't think of sharah in that way right, now, so that's probably good.

I've tried to think hard about what's happening in sharah's mind and what to say to her, in my letters of late. I've come on strong as "Daddy" the protector and unconditionally loving father, because I sense she needs that. I figured if I can supply that to her and help her that way, then no matter what eventually becomes of us, if it helps pull her out of it, that's the best I can hope for.

For a while, if not forever, sharah has been altered. An event like this can totally reprogram the brain, and imprint a new personality.

Am I strong enough to reach into her and reprogram her to the way she was? I honestly don't know. My energy for sharah and her for me before this happened to her, was at such a high level, I thought it was going to progress quite naturally. We had the fantasy and soul energy, the same sexual bents, and I figured we'd meet in Florida in high gear and know pretty soon if fantasy and reality would be the same. But this is virgin territory for me, on top of considerable other challenges I face right now.

It's been tough to be here, without ever communicating with her directly, and know exactly what I feel anymore on those other levels. I guess I've just shut off those other feelings right now. I might be more in big brother mode than Daddy, just wanting to protect and heal that sweet girl, and seek revenge in any way possible. I guess I just have to hang in there and see what happens. It has nothing to do with the damage that might have been inflicted on sharah's body or mindset.

It's more what do she and I together add up to now. What is my own situation going to be here, in those practical day-to-day ways, from this point forward, that will affect when it might be possible for sharah and me to be together on day to day basis. I guess what I'm feeling in sum is that whatever sharah needs most in the near future is the most important issue, but I'm not backing away from what could be the most important relationship I could ever ask for.

Another thought about the scumbag... After I hadn't heard from sharah, those first few days, though I had decided I wouldn't resort

to it (but I might have changed my mind), I thought to just start dialing up dance and ballet studios around New York, and just ask if sharah was there. I would have tried to bullshit a phone number out of somebody, if I found the place, and she wasn't there. That's one possible scenario of how he got her number.

Got to get back to business, Joe. sharah wouldn't stand a chance right now, if you and kathy weren't there for her. I can't thank you enough.

Galen

Subject: tenderness not punishment
Date: Wed, 9 Dec

Dear Joe,

Harder to write now than it was before. I had to fight not to puke all day, and I've got a wrenching gut-ache like a piranha's chomping away at my intestines from my asshole to my stomach.

Then I had to read your letters again tonight, because I knew I had spaced out most everything but the absolute horror suffered by my little girl (I skipped those parts tonight.) I understand now how easy it is to block everything important to you out of your mind, with the relentless rage to kill someone like the shithole predator.

So here's further comment on some issues you raised, but I gotta try to be short, because I'm nearly doubled over, my gut's going on so bad.

I give you my solemn word. I agree sharah deserves no punishment.

That had to be totally weird being in his apartment, and then the phone messages. But I'm very impressed by your modus operandi. That ought to freak the perv out nicely, knives missing, knowing

somebody's onto him. Let him know something's coming, but not knowing, when, how or what. I'll be happy to share in the workload to destroy that bastard.

I'll save all that deeper stuff about sharah and I in the future, when we can talk by phone. I really can't think or write anymore tonight.

I hope you're drawing energy from somewhere, my friend, because you sure are pouring it out! And who knows where the tide will run next. I'm here to help in every way I can. You and sharah can count on it.

Galen

Subject: Bingo
Date: Thu, 10 Dec

Galen,

Had to let you know. Bingo!

You hit the nail right on the fucking head with the phone number. I just got off the phone with sharah's work and somebody called looking for her one day that week, saying it was for some modeling job and they had to reach her right away. The little girl answering the phone thought she was doing sharah a big favor. They won't be giving out any more numbers after the noise I just made.

I can't believe I didn't think of that and I can't believe the cops didn't. I can't thank you enough. You may have just ensured this guy's prosecution, because now it's more proof that she didn't give him her number herself. Makes it look less like she wanted it. Let's hope for the best anyway. Good work! Jesus, I'm impressed and very fucking grateful to you.

I read a couple of your recent letters to sharah last night and she did pretty good with them. She cried a little bit at the end, but I know it

113

did her some good.

You're batting 1000 today, my friend. Thank you for everything. Sorry you got the gut crud. Take a damn day off if you can. You've earned it. Heading back to New York tonight and thanks to you I feel like I've got some ammunition to go with. I'll let you know when I get back.

Joe

Subject: I need to talk
Date: Thu, 10 Dec

Dear Joe,

Heading into the 3rd week, without sharah. It's getting more and more difficult to feel connected to her. To feel the realness of it, to know it's truth, while we are so far removed from each other on every level. I understand quite well why she can't communicate with me, and if I were in different circumstances I would handle it better than I am. But like sharah, I am a wounded animal, trying to find a safe place to heal up and get back in the hunt.

My wife is already causing me some major headaches. I got sloppy recently, used my home computer, which I rarely do, and I believe I left a trail that led her to my personal ad on a D/s site (I had used my real initials - pretty stupid). That really set her off. She now thinks I'm a slimebag pervert, who's been cheating on her forever, in the most perverse way, and she doesn't want my kids to be around me. She's told everybody in her family, and told me they think I'm the most disgusting thing on earth.

Plus, I got a reference of it from a guy friend, whose wife told him, she knows something about me, but she can't tell him, because it's too horrible. I can handle the public outing in one way or another. I don't care what people think. If my kids find out, well, I'll deal with that too. I'm past feeling any shame or embarrassment, and

that's why I decided to move out anyway.

Now I've got to think about what all this might mean legally in a divorce proceeding. I've never told any of my friends about my sexuality, because you can predict someone's reaction to this lifestyle if you know them well enough.

My financial picture's not looking so good right now, either, in the short term, but that's another story.

I need to talk with you, Joe. I need most to know how sharah's doing.

I called this group called the Ministry of Prayer and asked them to pray for sharah. They do what they call a spiritual mind treatment. They believe that there is only one mind, that each individual mind is part of the one mind, that thought is creative and healing takes place by meditating on the truth that all is perfect in spirit, and everything physical is the out-picturing of spirit, etc.

I'll go with anything right now, as long as it might help sharah. But I've had some direct experience in this and I'm praying right now that I've got what it takes to pull through all this shit I'm in. I pray that sharah starts to heal up, and somehow the two of us can pull a life together like we imagined before all hell broke loose.

I've been in kind of a daze and a funk since your last letters, I can't sleep again, and I know I've got to get on top of this because I've got too much to do, too many responsibilities to take care of to be so spaced out, right now. But there's a part of me that doesn't want to do or think about anything else, until I can hear from sharah.

I know it doesn't help sharah to let my shit start sliding all over the place. I just need to hear something from sharah soon, Joe. I need to know that somewhere within all that tangled up terror, wrapped around her mind, that she can still feel me in there, that she knows when she's ready she can reach out for that and pull herself out of her hiding place.

I'm sorry, Joe. I'm not meaning to dump this load on you too. It's not directed at you, personally, so please just let it slide off. You're putting out a heroic effort.

I'm going to give you a business number and the number where I'm staying now. Wk: ***-****; hm:***-****. If I can't talk, I'll tell you I'm in a meeting, and will call you back. If my secretary answers the office phone, just say you're a friend. If you get the answering machine at either place, leave your number if you're comfortable with that, and I'll call you back.

I'm staying at my friend C's. I finally told him yesterday, some things about sharah, that I met her on a dating service, that she liked older men, that we hit it off and planned to meet in Florida, and that she was brutally attacked and raped, and has been out of it, ever since.

If I weren't so painfully connected to it all, this would make for one helluva movie script. You know the kind of ending I'd write.

Talk to me when you can. I'll be OK, eventually.

Galen

Subject: a message from kathy
Date Fri, 11, Dec

Dear Sir,

This is Master Joe's girl, and sharah's sister, kathy, writing to You. Master is in New York City again and He told me to respond to your last letters to Him and sharah.

Please Sir, may i first say thank you for what You did for sharah and Master by figuring out how that person got sharah's phone number. He left for New York feeling so much better about everything and not so helpless. i'm so grateful to you for that because i was so

afraid of what Master would do if they don't put that person in jail. So thank You so much from the bottom of my heart. Master promises he will call You as soon as He gets back and has some more news.

Thank You also for everything that you mean to sharah. sharah told me all about You before this horrible thing happened to her, and i know she already felt that You were her owner. i believe that You are going to be the only thing that can bring sharah back and Master agrees with me.

We are doing everything we can think of to help sharah reach the point where she can communicate with You again. Master has given me orders to read Your commands to sharah tonight when i go back, and see how she takes it. i have to stop if she gets too scared or confused though. i think she is ready to hear it. i know how much it would help me if i were in her position to hear my Master's commands.

Master said You might visit us. i hope so, Sir. It would be an honor to meet You and i think it would do so much good for sharah. i would truly love to meet You. I don't know if sharah told You but You look sooo much like our real Father. It's uncanny. We are hoping that sharah will be home with us next week when Master is back. If You came to see us, i would try to make Your stay as comfortable and enjoyable as possible.

By the way, sharah is a wonderful cook, Sir. she puts me to shame in the kitchen and she loves cooking for Master and other Men so much. i have this idea that if she really gets into making one of her special multi-course dinners for you and Master, and if she sees You really enjoy it, it will work wonders for her self worth and the rest of her service would naturally follow.

i just know that if she was in the presence of her real Master (You), she would get better so much faster. sharah is even more profoundly submissive than me Sir, and that is hard to do. i can see the flashes in her eyes when she looks at your picture and that is my real sister, not the scared girl in that bed.

117

i shouldn't speak out of turn here Sir, but i know sharah is in love with You already and is trying so hard to fight her way back to You. i just know it. i know how hard things are for You right now, Sir, but please come when You can. It would mean so much to all of us. i am leaving for the hospital again and will read Your orders to sharah. i will take down her message back to You and send it tomorrow. i am so excited to do this for You both. And thank You again for what You did for my Master. He is so much happier now.

kathy

Subject: I need a response, NOW!!
Date: Sat, 12 Dec

Dear kathy,

Thanks so much for you kindness and encouragement. But you said you would contact me this morning and you must understand, in the state of mind I'm in, that not hearing anything leads me to think the worst: my precious sharah's no better and possibly worse.

My understanding of the full horror of what she endured has left me in the greatest rage and despair of what that shit fuck has done to her. I need you to tell me as much detail as possible about sharah right now. Is she sedated full time? Is she healing physically? Is she ever coherent? If she is, what does she say? Has she hurt herself further? Does she show any signs that she wants to get through this? Does she know how much I'm thinking of her? What happened when you read my commands?

kathy, my worst fear is that she becomes suicidal. I can almost feel that happening, and I couldn't bear that further tragedy. I'm feeling pretty helpless right now, kathy. With Joe's permission, please let me know all you can, no matter what it is, as soon as possible. The more I know, the more I might be able to help.

Tell Joe that his letter about the phone number clue cheered me up a bit. I'll do anything to bring that bitch down, but I can't feel anything but torment, until I can feel that sharah is making a turn for the better. Except different ways to fuck up that subhuman piece of shit that's putting all of us through this unbearable hell.

I'm out of town till Sunday night. If Joe's back and e-mails me a phone number, and the best times to call, I'll try to call.

Galen

Subject: e-mail's still active
Date: Sat, 12 Dec
kathy,

I just wanted to let you know that I can still check my e-mail, before tomorrow night. Actually I'm going kind of nuts. I've probably checked my mail a dozen times today. Hoping that sharah can send a message that she's getting better. I don't have any choice but to tough it out. Usually there are choices. I know how to deal with that. But I'm not having an easy time of it, I am heartbroken that after nearly four weeks sharah is still suffering so, and I can't do a goddamned thing about it.

If for some reason (and I say this only because clearly anything can happen, no hidden messages, just being practical) you stop hearing from me, you can call my friend C's. He can probably fill you in on anything about me. He knows about sharah, except for the D/s side of the relationship, but you can ask him anything, or tell him anything you want. He's "straight", but cool.

Galen

Subject: panic alert
Date: Sun, 13 Dec

kathy,

Now I have to worry that something's happened to you and Joe. It's Sunday about 10am. I've fought off the panic and frustration, and I will be fighting it until I hear from you. It's much worse now, than when I didn't hear from sharah that first week. I pray you're both all right, and sharah is too. But so much bad shit's been happening I don't discount anything.

If I don't hear from you by tomorrow night, I'm going to start calling every hospital in Ohio. Then all the dance studios in NY, but that will be tough after Joe read them the riot act. Then the NY cops, until I can track sharah down and find out what's happened.

Though I'm sure there is some explanation, if I finally hear from you, not hearing from you now makes about as much sense as when I didn't hear from sharah initially. There's only one explanation that I can think of, and I pray to god it's not so.

I've hung in the background until now, but it's time for me to draw closer. I ask that you give me sharah's last name, her address in NY, her work number, the cops involved, names and numbers, any lawyers involved, the name and number of the hospital sharah's in, your phone number, and address and any other info or people I should know about, plus the name and address of shit fuck, and the number of your FBI friend. If something happens to you guys, I'll pick up the ball, and see this thing through, wherever it's going.

I've barely slept since your last contact, I can't think straight, I feel like shit, I look like shit. I've struggled through a lot of disappointments in my life, fought through it, kept going, determined to get where I'm going. Now I feel like everything's collapsing, and the struggles behind me are nothing compared to what lies ahead. Please contact me immediately. If I don't hear anything by tomorrow night, I'm shifting to plan B.

Galen

(Note: The following is a letter I sent to various BDSM sites, when I thought I'd lost touch with Joe and kathy. My first goal in plan B was to alert the D/s community about the predator. Then I began compiling a list of hospitals in Ohio, and Dance Studios in New York City. I felt like a character in a kinky twilight zone episode written by Joe Esterhaus. I sent this letter out Sunday afternoon, not willing to wait till Monday night.)

Subject: Predator Warning !!
Date: Sun, 13 Dec

I'm going through a tragic experience right now. A slave/daughter, with whom I am very close, was viciously raped with a knife, has a broken jaw and rib, and right now a broken mind. She's been under heavy sedation in a hospital for almost two weeks now, because every time she wakes up and sees a male orderly or a doctor she freaks out.

This vile evil that attacked her, and she was the sweetest, most giving submissive I've ever encountered, doesn't deserve to live. He was neither a man nor a master. He was a piece of shit that squirmed out the wrong hole of his mother. He should be flushed like any other piece of shit, from her mind, from her heart, and from this existence if the opportunity presents itself. A true man will never harm, and a Master will never cause that type of terror in the heart of his slave.

This shit fuck's tasted blood, if not for the first time, it's certain not to be his last. If the cops don't shut this fucker down (he's already been released on bail!) he'll go further next time. This guy wants to kill. I've never seriously desired to kill someone before (in a furiously slow manner,) but I've changed. I don't know how smart it would be to do it myself. But I sure do desire the pure pleasure and vengefulness of it.

When I track down this sick fuck's name and e-mail address, I'm

going to publish it on every D/s site I can find. Justice will find this piece of shit, somehow, somewhere. I hope to be there, watching the terror in his eyes, as they close for the last time. Please be careful out there, at all levels. I'm grateful to be on this path, and I appreciate all the beautifully submissive women I've met, some briefly, some wonderfully ongoing. You have all added to my life and pleasure. So continue on your courageous journey, and be very, very careful in choosing whom you serve. It's all about trust!

Galen

(*Note: These are some responses I received from my post. I was touched by the passionate concern and offers of help from total strangers.*)

Greetings,

Thanks for the effort to deal with this. I found your message so painful and disgusting I have a hard time even re-reading it. I am writing to offer my assistance, as appropriate. I am a lawyer with access to private investigator resources not easily accessible to the public.

I also have some Internet contacts that are unusually good; I went to Stanford and have lots of Silicon Valley buddies who make an extraordinarily good living off their websites. I do not want to put out a lot of money for a stranger but I am willing to offer you and your friend some assistance in dealing with this guy. This is the sort of person I would like to put out of business, in more ways than one. (I am a sexual Dom but mostly a mental one; I actually hate violence and the infliction of pain on anyone for any reason, and I especially despise cowardly men who get off on hurting women to prove their . . . you know, all the clichés.) If your friend and this sick f— are on the West Coast and you all want some help in dealing with this guy, let me know. I may or may not be able to help. I can look into it a bit. As I tell my clients, don't get mad, get

even.

SD

Greetings,

If you do track this piece of maggot shit down, please inform me for I will also aid you in getting the word out on him. Plus there are other options available to deal with the likes of this dung pile. This post has caused my heart and soul much grief, my prayers go out to the dear victim. When a submissive's gift is abused it puts a dark shadow on us all.....

with my deepest respect,

Master S

Hello,

What a terrible story.

"When I track down this sick fuck's name and e-mail address, I'm going to publish it on every D/s site I can find."

You are welcomed on my site http://come.to/xxxxxx-personals.

Also, you may publish your warning at the soc.sexuality.spanking and soc.subculture.bdsm-bondage newsgroups (there are probably thousands of readers for each one.)

Hope this asshole will be raped in prison many many times.

D

Sir,

I can feel your pain and anguish in your message. The miserable little puck that has inflicted such a horrible act does not deserve to exist in the same world that you and I share. I received your message through a friend (my sub) and would offer my empathy to you in your situation. I would also offer any assistance in helping you locate the piece of rat shit, you seek, as that is what I do best. I'm a "Hunter," I can and DO find anything or anyone I pursue. If finding "it" is truly your objective, send me as much info as you are willing. This is my personal e-mail address and is "for my eyes only." If you are merely venting your anger, and understandably so, and I do not hear from you that is how I will take it.

I pray that your friend can make a reasonable recovery from her ordeal, for there is no "total" recovery from which she has endured.

My best wishes to you and yours...

R2

Sir,

You will understand if I am reluctant to get sucked into a scam. There are so many on the Internet, and many of them originate with addresses such as yours at hotmail.com since that is a free email account on the Internet that anyone can access. Before I am willing to forward your information to anyone, and I have substantial contacts within the OHIO BDSM community, I need to know if you're legit.

How did you get my email? Who else did you write to in Ohio and can any of them vouch for what you wrote in this mail? What is your "real" screen name?

What is the name of your ISP? (You do realize that you need an ISP

and an email account to get a hotmail false front account, don't you?

If I don't hear back from you by 6 p.m. EST Tuesday, I will consider you a hoaxster and so inform anyone else who asks me about this email.

NN

Subject: there's been some trouble
Date: Mon, 14 Dec

Dear Sir,

i am so sorry i didn't get back to You before. Something bad happened in New York but my Master will not tell me what. i was ordered to stay off the Internet until today. Master is coming back late tonight and He said He will contact You tomorrow. He told me to tell You to please be careful what You write about that person because this account is probably being monitored. That is all i am allowed to say about that.

i did read your orders to sharah and i think they did her a world of good. she picked up Your picture when You ordered her to and she made it most of the way through without crying. This was the message she asked me to send You:

"i love You, Daddy. i miss You so much. i'm sorry i let that Man ruin Your property. i'm trying to get better. i still want to be Your little slut and i promise i will obey You. If You don't want to use me after You see me, i can stay with kathy and Master Joe, so don't worry about that. Maybe i could cook for You a few times and clean Your house before You send me back."

She got pretty upset then and couldn't go on. i know it doesn't sound so good, but that is more than she usually says once she starts crying. And the next day she was holding Your picture all day and

talking a little more. she even let the male doctor examine her without trying to get away. And He used the speculum and everything. Usually they have to give her a shot before they can put anything inside her. she cried a little but was very brave. she even looked at the doctor's face and said thank you to Him.

Since then, i've been reading her a little bit from Your beautiful letters every day. she is definitely listening and You are getting through to her. i think Master wants to check her out of the hospital this week and bring her home.

Master will call you tomorrow.

kathy

Subject: I'm so proud of my daughter
Date: Mon, 14 Dec

Dearest daughter,

Daddy is so proud of his good little girl. I am overjoyed just to hear your loving words to me. I understand what you're feeling, daughter. I know how hard you are struggling. But I know what a fighter you are, and I order you to keep fighting every day until you and your loving Daddy are finally together. With the wonderful progress you're making dear, I know that will be very soon! Won't that be wonderful, daughter! Just do what your loving Daddy tells you to do, sharah, like the good little slave you are for me, and all will be well.

Listen to me sharah. Know this is the truth. Daddy's heart is surrounding you, protecting you, loving you, needing you, desiring you, planning so many delightful adventures with my sweet slave toy.

So, you are already planning to cook and clean for your Master. That's very good progress, daughter. And, you will serve me my

126

dinner, slave, and serve me in all those other ways I already told you about, as well. Remember the cocoon story, daughter! Daddy's going to have a lot of fun using his sweet little daughter for those delightful pleasures you offer.

So listen up, slave, this is an order: You are not allowed to do or think anything that slows your healing. You got that, daughter. I order you to focus only on the things that will speed you on your way to your Daddy. I demand that you meditate each day. Get comfortable, sit up if you can. Take Daddy's picture and press it to your slave's heart. Start taking long, slow, deep breaths. Let your mind start to slow down.

After a few moments, close your eyes. You will instantly see me, just as I am in my picture. I order you to come to me. I gather you into my strong arms and gently hold you. It gives you a warm feeling all over your body, and your mind relaxes. Keep breathing long slow breaths. Repeat these words slowly, in rhythm with your breath, slowly, over and over for about ten minutes. Remember, it is important to go slowly. These are the words I want you to say: "I am calm. I am loved. I am healed. I obey my Master's commands. Nothing will stop me from being owned by Master Galen."

Second Command: At least every other day I want you to send me a message, daughter. You are serving me very well when you send me a message. It helps me to feel you, sweetgirl, and Daddy loves that feeling of passion you stir in me. For the time being, I want you to express whatever you wish. Maybe comment on some of the writings I sent you so far.

Soon, I may send you some specific instructions, my slave. I am setting a goal for you too, and I will prepare you for it step by step. The goal - within one week or less after you go home with Master Joe, we will speak by phone.

Now these are my commands, slave. You need to work hard to please your Master. But you must also pay attention to your health, daughter. Pay attention that you do not push yourself too hard. It will not please me if you do that. You must make progress every-

day, a little more each day, at the pace that brings us together as soon as possible. I'm counting on you to obey these orders, slave. Let nothing interfere with your dedicated service to your Master. I expect you to please me in every way. And I know you will.

All my love,

Master/Daddy

Subject: What happened in NY
Date: Tue, 15 Dec

Joe,

Sorry I jumped the gun there and sent out that post. I didn't reveal anything significant about the perp. I hope you understand. I pulled up 600 hospitals in Ohio, and if it came to it, I'd have called every damn one of them. But I figured I'd try to work a little smarter. So, I contacted about 6 Ohio BDSM organizations, about 20 individuals in all. I only described sharah's situation, no details on the perp. I received 5 or so replies which might have been helpful.

They all worried that I might be a hoaxster, guess that happens a lot. Then I had to consider it too. Could sharah, you and kathy, be just some sick asshole somewhere, playing all the parts, playing me for all its worth? You'd have been pretty damn good.

But too good, I'd decided. Then I heard from kathy. To paraphrase Hemingway: The yo-yo also rises.

Tell kathy she's done a great job with sharah in your absence, and thank her from the bottom of my heart for delivering sharah's message to me. That's been the hardest part for me. Not being able to feel a direct connection to her. I couldn't write her over the weekend. I just didn't know what to say, anymore, what could get through.

kathy's letter and description of sharah's responsiveness has put me back on track. Hearing sharah's words to me made me so happy, but also sad, because it was clear how tentative she is. She's blaming herself, feels like she's ruined and worthless. But she's fought her way back, has some level of faith that I could still want her, and I'm going to build on that.

I hear something went down in NY. Hope you're all right. What happened?

You can try to call me tomorrow. E-mail me to set up a time if you can, so I make sure I'm available.

Galen

Subject: precautions
Date: Wed, 16 Dec

Galen,

The events of the last few days make it necessary for me to stop our communication for the time being. I am truly sorry but it is for your security as well as my family. I assure you this has not been a hoax and you have not been toyed with. No one involved has had any deceitful motivations.

I would like you to know that there is no longer any physical threat to sharah. That is guaranteed. I'm sure she will continue to improve and I will contact you as soon as I am sure your safety and the safety of my family will not be compromised. I give you my word on that. I have been careful to make sure the authorities do not know about your connection to sharah or to me. Stopping our communication for now should insure that.

Should the police contact you, do whatever you need to do to protect yourself and your family. But that is unlikely. In any case

we both know you have nothing to do with any events surrounding sharah's attack. The telephone is definitely not a viable means of communication between us right now. You must try to be patient and trust me and know this is for the best of ALL involved. If for any reason I am unable to contact you at the appropriate time I will instruct kathy to do so. Take care of yourself, buddy. Try to be patient. Everything is going to work out fine now.

Joe

(Note: I responded within a half-hour of the time/date on Joe's farewell.)

Subject: I want sharah's info!!
Date: Tue, 15 Dec

Joe,

I can't accept this. I hope you are all right, and I won't dwell on what happened, but I can imagine. Please, if you have to lay low, I understand. But I must have sharah's last name, the city, and hospital, the hospital phone number, and the name and phone of sharah's work.

These can be sent through an outside computer to either of my email addresses, or you could have kathy go to a secure phone, and call any number I gave you. I will use these only in the event I don't hear from you. If something happens to you and kathy, there's no one left to take care of sharah. You've got to find a way to do this, or I will do it myself. There should be no additional risk in doing this, after all the contact we've had so far. Don't let me down, Joe.

Galen

(Note: Sensing my connection with sharah was again slipping away, I immediately sent out a second call for help over the net.)

Subject: A desperate call for help to the Ohio BDSM community.
Date: Tue, 15 Dec

I'm going through a tragic experience right now, and I desperately need the help of the BDSM community in Ohio. A slave/daughter, with whom I am very close, was viciously raped with a knife, has a broken jaw and ribs, and right now, a broken mind. She's been under heavy sedation in a hospital in Ohio for almost four weeks. Every time she wakes up and sees a male orderly or a doctor she freaks out.

The perp was arrested but released on bail, because she went to see him voluntarily (much longer story here). The attack occurred in NYC.

There are some new and I fear dark developments. I need help, locating the hospital she's in now in Ohio.

The sub I'm seeking ,and I, had grown quite close. It's a long story, but I'll try to be brief. We hadn't exchanged last names, or phone numbers, yet. Everything developed through e-mail and photos.

She has a sister who's also a sub. Her sister and her sister's Master live in Ohio. I know them as Joe, and kathy. He is about 55, she is about 28, and have been together 8 years. He claims to have been in the scene for 30 years. They live somewhere outside an urban area in a rural or wooded location. Probably not too far from a major airport, as he has flown to NYC 3 times in the last 4 weeks, to deal with the cops handling her case.

My sub friend, whom I'll refer to as "s", is now apparently under Joe and kathy's care, but as far I know, is still hospitalized, possibly in the psych ward and still heavily sedated and over the edge of sanity.

I've developed a very close relationship with her sister and Master, via extensive email communication. s had told them a bit about me previously, and I knew of them, but we'd had no contact, prior to them contacting me about the attack on s.

The Master in Ohio has been understandingly protective, she's like his daughter, and has both taken care of s's treatment, and has gone to NYC several times to deal with the cops. He needed to feel absolutely certain he could trust me, so we only communicated through e-mail up to this point.

Today I received an ominous email from Joe, stating that he had some problems with the police in NYC that related to the perp, and they needed to lay low. Consequently they wouldn't be able to contact me for a while. Immediately after, their email was disconnected.

I fear this story may be taking another bizarre turn. If something has happened to them, then I fear for s, even more, because she will be left all alone in a psyche ward. I need to find her as soon as possible. Her sister and Master told me they felt the only hope for s coming out of this was through me, but she was still too freaked out and we felt it best to try to get her calmed down a bit, before I went to see her.

Can you help me find s? Can you put this message out throughout the BDSM community in Ohio? I'll give anyone who can help all the info I have, but it's skinny right now. I pray I hear from the couple very soon, and all this gets resolved that way.

But everything about this has been so strange, and I can see no good reason for them to have dropped out of sight. I've never needed help more than I do now. If something has happened to them, then it will be up to me to take charge of dealing with s's welfare from this point.

I've got to locate s! I realize I'll have to prove this isn't a hoax, or that my intentions aren't other than I've stated. I will give my personal phone number to discuss this in further detail to anyone

who feels they can help me locate s. This is a life and death situation.

Galen

(Note: this begins a long correspondence with my personal guardian angel, sleuth and good friend, who went by the handle - Unknown.)

Subject: RE: call for help
Date: Wed, 16 Dec

Hi Galen,

Your letter was forwarded to me by a friend in Ohio. I am familiar with psychiatric facilities in Columbus. The one associated with Ohio State is Doane Hall; the one that is private is Harding Hospital where worst cases are. Both Riverside Hospital and Mt. Carmel have semi-services.

I do not know if you are real. I do not know if this person you seek really wants you to find her. I do not know if you could have abused her emotionally. I do not know if your email was a way to find out about people in the D/s community in Ohio, but they are concerned enough to turn it over to me for assistance, as they do not wish a sister to go unaided or a brother to go uninformed if it is real.

If you have an address or a phone number for her, I can do a criss-cross. I can get you a full name.

I can get you phone numbers of hospitals and outpatient clinics. (You can also, if you wish, on the net.)

We have some connections at facilities......we just need more info. Are you certain she is in a facility? Who would be paying for it?

I hope to help you, if you are sincere. One time, I made a similar call, miles from home, as my own daughter had been kidnapped. A private-eye spent three weeks and did not charge me a penny. The least I can do is return such favors.

Yours,

Unknown

Subject: thank you!
Date: Thu, 17 Dec

Dear Unknown,

Thank you for your compassion. Many responses I got from my call for help were concerned if this was a hoax. Now I am too. But it's so elaborate, so fantastic, so bizarre, and gruesome, and took someone so much time, it would be totally amazing if it was.

It would make quite a movie. It's a fantastic, erotic and horrible story. Whether it's true or not has not yet been concluded, but because it keeps getting more complex, now my own suspicions are aroused. You seemed genuinely concerned. I've appreciated your kind words, and offer to help.

If it's not a hoax, then my search for sharah, must continue. After I finally heard from kathy on Monday, I was relieved. Then I heard the last from Joe, and if what he said is true, then I'm freaked out again. Now his e-mail account has been canceled.

If you'd like to confer by phone, let me know and we'll arrange a time and I'll give you a number.

I'm sending along the transcript of all the correspondence I had with them. I'll bet you won't be able to stop reading. It's quite a tale…so far! A couple of questions: Are police reports public record? If they are, I would try to confirm the attack on sharah,

somehow. Is there any way to dig more info about someone from their email address? I would still like to confirm the existence of Joe and kathy through the OHIO BDSM community. I hope you will offer your insight. Thank You.

Galen

Subject: tears and rage
Date: Fri, 18 Dec

Dear Galen,

My daughter's kidnapper just got 6 consecutive life sentences...seven years and $200,000 or more cost. Nothing in return. Yes, I do know tears and rage. And to think Paula Jones got $850,000 for copping a peek and a second one of the Pres.

I have forwarded your message to the group.

You should have included all the e-mail addresses of all of the people you mentioned in your original message. Also inclusion of your telephone number would have allowed a more rapid and accurate response to your search request.

Who is your source of information concerning her response to the male orderlies or doctors? They should also have been capable of immediately providing the name of the hospital to you!

Do you know what city?

If they have a Children's Division, it would be Children's Hospital, as the other hospitals are called young adult I believe.

I do not know how to help if no phone numbers. I am a bit con-fused as to whether she was from Ohio or NYC. Do you have any of her mail which may give a clue?

What is her email address?

Do you think this could be an elaborate hoax?

Do send the Joe and kathy mail.

How are you doing?

Unknown

Subject: what a movie!!
Date: Fri, 18 Dec

Dear Unknown,

Thanks for your support and good ideas and thoughts. How am I doing? Besides feeling stupid and now paranoid, a little heartbroken as well, I'm determined to bust this sick fuck. I don't know why he's wasting his time fucking people around, why not go to Hollywood and pitch the next Basic Instinct sequel. I've got to admit he/she is good. He definitely sucked me in and kept me there at his mercy.

So now I've got some worries. In prep for phone contact I gave him my business number and personal number. I also told him the hotel I'm staying at in Florida. The flags went up over his last letter, so I'd better watch my back. Besides feeling stupid, I'm not wanting to become a victim as well. After all, I'm a dom (note the small d…until I get over this!)

Here are the e-mails: Joe@***.com; sharah@***.com; both disconnected. I answered her ad from zyx.com. This was her ad, it's still active. (*sharah's ad*)

I'm including my letters I received from sharah, and all the ones from Joe and kathy (brother-in-law and sister). My responses are interspersed between.

If you have time, (it's quite a pile), and can read through them, and come to the conclusion that its all been a hoax (not by me, but on me), I sure would appreciate your feedback.

I don't know if sharah is real or not. Maybe she is and this guy did kidnap her, and he's still got her. Maybe he made her up, along with everything else. Or maybe somehow it is legit, and sharah is still in a psyche-ward somewhere.

I feel he'll contact me again, after awhile. He's obviously very smart, and now on the alert, since I brought up the hoax aspect in my last letter. That's probably why he canceled his e-mail. If he does contact me, I'd like to set him up somehow, and then bring him down. What would you do?

I can't thank you enough for the aid you're providing. I haven't confided in this to anyone, except one friend, whose knows a little bit generally, but none on the D/s level. He's vanilla.

I know this is taking up your valuable time, but if you can stay on board any way you can, I sure would appreciate it.

Galen

Subject: hang in there
Date: Sat, 19 Dec

Galen,

Will cull my records for the name at AOL. How difficult would it be to trade hotels? The one you are staying in may have and agreement with another hotel and will gladly change you. Just a thought.

What were the screen names she used? If you have no problem, I will see if anyone in any of my own connections (nationwide) have

heard of any such person or similar scam. Have they asked you for money? Do they know your last name? How difficult would it be to change your phone number? Or have it forwarded to a cell phone or something?

Keep me informed and hang in there.

Unknown

Subject: is this my worst nightmare??
Date: Sat, 19 Dec

Hi Unknown,

Thanks again for you help. I already changed hotels. Phones - I'm going to sit tight for a bit. I imagine it wouldn't be too difficult for someone with the know-how, to backtrack to an address, and if this is my worst nightmare movie, then I guess anything could happen. It's a scary thought. He doesn't know my last name.

Assuming you've had a chance to read the transcripts, it's quite a story, isn't it? Not one readily accessible r/t clue to nail it down. I had requested direct contact info on sharah in a letter on Saturday, in case something happened to them and sharah was left on her own.

No response or mention of that in last 2 letters, which is suspicious, after we became so "close" and with the concern for sharah para-mount. I e-mailed within an hour of Jame's last letter, demanding this info again, saying if I didn't hear by Thursday, I was beginning my search again, but the account had already been terminated. What do you think?

The question is, why am I worth all this effort? Then I considered there might be more than one of me. A lot of the story could be boilerplate, and he patches in little personal particulars from what I write about. Still a lot of effort for an audience of one, or a dozen.

Maybe I should offer to be his agent and co-writer, and set Hollywood afire! Money hasn't been involved in any way (yet), and that's why it's hard to figure it as a scam. What's the return on investment?

sharah's handle at the personals site was subsharah. I don't know if she had ads anywhere else.

Although any man would, I grew particularly fond and protective of this "little girl." I still worry that she might be real, and in danger. Until I am sure, I can't let go of the desire to help her, regardless of whether she and I would ever be together. There's something sinister looming here. This guy is a sick fuck, no matter what the truth of it is. Maybe he even is a predator and possibly a murderer.

So, to start to figure this out, I need to determine if sharah, Joe, kathy, or the perp exist. If you have the contacts and can put out an APB on Joe and kathy in Ohio, that would be a big help. If they exist, and they're in the scene, even quietly, somebody somewhere has to know of them. I sent an initial message to 5 or so Ohio based D/s groups, and a couple of places I'd have to look up, and that's how you got a hold of it. Everybody that replied was very suspicious. No one has responded to my further requests for help, and I can understand that. It's a crazy story, and possibly even dangerous.

sharah apparently worked as a dance instructor at a ballet and dance studio or school in New York. There was a letter that referenced how I came up with the way the perp got sharah's phone number. After sharah dropped out of sight at Thanksgiving, I had thought of calling ballet schools in NYC and just ask for sharah. I was surprised at the time that "he nor the cops" had thought of that. It wasn't that big an idea, it was a fairly obvious thing to do. But if this is a scam, then I thought maybe he's covering his tracks, in case I tried it now. He'd hope I would think he already set up the studio to be paranoid about giving out any info on sharah.

It would be amazing if the one guy could play all three characters in the story. They're so well developed. I'm a thinly published though serious writer and have studied writers and writing for a long time.

Except for a few possible slips, I've noted, this is a very tight and while unbelievable, plausible story, except for technical details you pointed out.

Can an e-mail be traced to the phone line where it originated? Will AOL give out that type of info, or be able to track that past or future? My account is at hotmail. Can I request they monitor my account and trace the originating phone number of the message? I guess I'll have to inquire. Maybe the "fun's" over and I'll never hear from any of the players again. But if I do, the more I know about them, the safer I'll feel.

Look, if we keep communicating, and I hope we do, and I suddenly disappear, and I hope I don't, will you do whatever you can to follow through on this? All the records of my to and fro correspondence with everyone involved are on my office computer and on my notebook. They (files) shouldn't be too hard to find. If they need a password, try ****. I'll tell you that I live in ****. The first two letters of my last name are **, my first name begins with **, my ex wife's name begins with *, and I have two sons, x years and y years, whose names begin with * and *. The local paper is the ** and you should be able to find the obits online. Morbid thought, I know. Just covering bases.

Keep in Touch,

Galen

Subject: book on hoaxes?
Date: Sun, 20 Dec

Galen,

Have you read the Slave series by Anne Rice? Any similar literature? Have you read The Story of O?

Some things ring similar to stories there.

I do not think the guy is all three. Could be he is doing a "story" but my own intuition is that he is some sick perv and is getting kicks out of what he is doing. You aren't writing a book about this, are you? What type books do you write? I have 3 children's (pre-school) books ready for a publisher. Haven't gotten the nerve up to send them anywhere yet. They are good, however. LOL. The right publisher would like them I am certain.... just needs the cutting edge house.

Let's not worry about your safety at the moment. I think the sicko is playing mind games. I too continue to worry about the girl (if indeed she exists). Am also wondering if it could be an Ohio Penitentiary person (one is at Marysville).... thus the reason for on and off screen names (Perhaps a call to them would ascertain what server they use.)

Sorry this is disjointed.... am watching bombs fall in Iraq as I write this. Keep your chin up. I think at least half of this is a hoax, but we need not drop it. Also, if you choose to write a book (each chapter being hoaxes on Internet) I would love to co-author. Have experience with 5 women being engaged to the same man who came off as a millionaire (showered gifts and trips) - all on borrowed money from the previous woman. In three cases, he asked the women to give their children up. Two did.

One has lost her children, her job and her home, as she was to move to be with him, and marry him. It is so very very sad. I am a moderator of a support group for them. Problem is, there is nothing really that can be done. The emotional damage on these women is so severe.

Unknown

PS. Did you send all the email correspondence to AOL? They need to see what is going on.

Subject: please call me
Date: Mon, 21 Dec

Unknown,

Thanks again for sticking with me. I just got off the phone with
AOL. Without the cops, no help. They can answer most of the
questions regarding where and who accounts are billed to, phone
numbers where messages originated etc. I really need to verify if
any of these people exist, what "facts " do check out. For sharah's
sake, I've got to do this. You mentioned a cop friend. Can he help?

I'd like to talk with you about this in more detail. I'll give you my
cell phone number, if you feel comfortable, please call me. You
should be able to reach me most of this afternoon, or email me a
time convenient, and I'll email back if that works for me. I have a
tentative appointment with my kids for dinner this evening, but I
should be available until 4:30 West coast time. Please give me a
call.

Galen

Subject: my ex knows about sharah!!!!
Date: Mon, 21 Dec

Dear Unknown,

Forgive me for using you for therapy (about to,) but I need to get
this out somewhere, so if you don't wish to read what I'm about to
tell you, just putting it into words was what was needed (by me).

My ex called C(my friend's "halfway house", where I'm temporarily residing) in a tirade. On a disk she pilfered from my office,
she found out about sharah, Joe and kathy. I'm not sure how much,
or what parts, maybe about a third of all of our correspondence, plus
numerous other contacts I've had with other submissives with very
nasty content.

Plus, somehow one of the 8 women that work in our shop found something about something, I don't know what, but referring to BDSM and me, and called my ex about it. None of them knows (or knew) that I had split from my wife. We hadn't told them yet. My ex has her office at home, and doesn't really go to the shop, so no one knew the difference. Tomorrow evening's our company Christmas party. Ought to be fun, Ho! Ho! Ho!

Finally, my doctor wouldn't release the HIV test results to her (I need to go sign for the documentation personally), so she's concluded I have aids, and so does she!!

She also wishes I were dead. That's what she told (screamed at) C on the phone, and a lot of other shit. C told me about her tirade, when I got back from my office. C was cool, but he hadn't known about my sexuality. I'm sure it was quite a shock to him. And I still have to tell him the whole story. He let it slide tonight, and I thankfully went to bed shortly after I got there.

That was a lot to get hit with all at once, on top of everything else (understatement!) All along I hoped to make this transition from my ex, in a smooth, painless manner. Fucked that up pretty good, didn't I? I've always been a relentless competitor in my life, when it would come down to it, toughed my way through a lot of shit. But somehow my relationship with my ex has been this continually escalating erosion of my very life force. And now the struggle with her gets even more intense.

I don't want to go to the office party. How the hell is that supposed to work? Nine women with their husbands or boyfriends, my ex, me, her mother and stepfather, and one thing on everybody's mind! Great situation for small talk. I guess I could ask them for a couple hours of their time, and lay it all out for them, just be honest. That'd be easy, compared to the devastating drama of those unspoken looks, snickers and low whispers.

I might just have to get out of Dodge, now. Next thing I know, I'll get the morning paper and there I'll be in the headlines,

"SLIMEBAG PERVERT TORTURES LITTLE GIRLS, DE-STROYS FAMILY - WIFE SAYS HE GAVE HER AIDS!" Let me know if you see anything on CNN(at least I can still attempt some levity, even if it's a fleeting whimsy!).

The absolute worst of it is my kids. I don't know what they might know. They know something. That was obvious, when they told me that they couldn't see me for dinner, as we had planned. They were incredibly nervous and evasive on the phone, with their mother probably nearby. My ex's the type that, if she doesn't say it outright will get it across how fucked up their dad is by not saying it outright. But, I understand her rage. All of it's true. I just have a different spin on it.

I should have never married her. I knew it was wrong. This one thing will devastate her in major ways, while her methods of destroying me have been much subtler, doing it a small slice at a time over all these years. I am sorry about this in both cases.

I've aged a couple of years in the last month. More high drama than I care to experience in a lifetime, let alone a month. I look in the mirror and know what the terminally ill reflect on each day.

I've got a lunch presentation tomorrow with a company that designs merchandising and trade show displays for adidas, nike, benetton, etc. Pitching them on adding an interactive capacity to their displays. Almost have them in my pocket. This is for one of the new companies I'm trying to launch. Do you think I might be distracted?

Until tonight, through all this to now, and everything that's gone before, I always took everything that life dished out. I was always too stubborn, to proud to let it show, to yield; go ahead and break me if you must, I'm not giving in.

At 48, I don't have the reserves of youth, so I'd better find something else. I know I'm supposed to rely on wisdom now, serene cunning, versus kick-ass testosterone. I feel I'm coming up empty on both counts.

This really complicates the financial picture, but that, as is everything right now, is another long and complicated story. This plot
has thickened around me like quicksand. Like in those old jungle
movies on TV, Saturday afternoons when I was a kid. You sink.
There's no escape. Maybe during the commercial break, I'll be able
to write in a miraculous rescue by the loyal chimpanzee, if I haven't
pissed him off too!

I referred to you as my angel in the darkness, now I guess I made
you my shrink as well. I hope you don't mind too much. For a
Dom, I'm sure generating a lot of masochistic karma. I guess so I'll
know what it's like for my suffering beauties in the future.

May it be soon.

Galen

PS. Thanks for listening - I really mean that!

Subject: You are not a villain!!
Date: Tue, 22 Dec

Galen,

I have tried numerous times to reach you today. Are you OK?

Your presentations will be great - sometimes adversity brings out
the best.

I am mildly amused at the thought of you at the office party etc. Do
you actually think there are not a couple of these individuals who
know and possibly enjoy your style of life? You MUST realize that
what you do and feel is not ABNORMAL. Yes, to the vanilla
community it is, but not to everyone.

Keep these things in mind -

You are NOT weird or perverted. You are NORMAL. You are the same person you were before they "found you out." You have nothing to feel guilty about. You need not change your behavior.

What is it in you that you need to feel guilt? Why would you need to flee due to your sexual inclination? Have gay male acquaintances in your lifetime fled? Why are you beating yourself up?

You see, what you do and feel is so normal to much of the world. The sooner you realize that and come to accept that YOU ARE OK, it all will be fine.

Let the people talk. They will believe what they want to believe. Keep a smile. They probably won't even believe half of it. LOL. DO NOT CHANGE YOUR ATTITUDE.

Regarding your children: they would have felt some hostility if you had left for ANY reason, so it has nothing to do with your sexuality. Quite honestly, there will be a time when you can explain D/s to them and do the scene justice so they will not feel "perverted" if they have such feelings.

I hope I hear from you soon, and I do hope you contacted J at AOL

Unknown

PS. You have never LIED to the children, have you? You have not destroyed their life.

(*Note: letter to J at AOL, a friend of Unknown's, after a brief phone conversation*)

Subject: Hoax on AOL?
Date: Tue, 22 Dec

Dear J,

Thanks for whatever help you can provide. I received my last e-mail from sharah on 11/25 (but you probably know that.) This should have been her last message to me or anyone else, originating from that account, certainly none after the 25th, as she was in a hospital the next 4 weeks. Just a thought. Let me know what you can.

Happy Holidays,

Galen

Subject: no police reports
Date: Wed, 23 Dec

Galen,

Regarding the policeman...he checked for 2 weeks, to see if there was any police report of a similar scene.... none. NY is large. Was it Manhattan? Queens? Brooklyn? LI? He checked Manhattan. If you ever change your user name on AOL, could you inform me of them? If you feel comfortable that is.

Unknown

Subject: not guilty
Date: Wed, 23 Dec

Dear Unknown,

Just a quick thanks for your support (once again). Traffic must be heavy on the net - just got the email you mentioned in your call. It pepped me up. I know I'm not guilty, evil, or abnormal. No, I haven't lied to my kids. I know I can't deal with these things only on my own terms. Stuff's going to happen. Ultimately, I don't give a shit what others think.

But I lapsed into that concern in my letter last night. Partly because I'm sick as a dog the last three days, my energy's low, and partly because I wasn't ready to deal with all that outing all at once. That's the price of admission, though. Pretty cheap really. I'll let you know if anything turns up at AOL.

Galen

Subject: Happy Holidays Galen
Date: Mon, 28 Dec

Don't worry so much. :) Unfortunately, without a police search warrant, AOL cannot provide you personally with any info on AOL members. We have the background info you provided, but because there are no illegal activities involved, there's not much more we can do at this point. Trust that everything will be OK. Say Hi to Unknown for me!

J at AOL

Subject; Are you OK
Date: Tue, 29 Dec

Galen,

Are you OK?

I am beginning to think that <u>you</u> were not real.

Interesting.

Unknown

(Note: Unknown IM'd me online one afternoon, and we had a brief chat, which resulted in this email from her)

Subject: You sound wonderful!
Date: Tue, 29 Dec

Galen,

You sound wonderful. And you seem to be putting all the pieces of the puzzle in slowly, but in the right places, and apparently you have a conceptual image of what the total picture looks like. It is great to see.

Don't worry if you get stymied at spots. It will all come together.

Regarding subs, I still do not know what your r/t experience is. Be careful and know that many are looking for "something" and they DO NOT really know what it is.

Always play safe. Always let someone know where you are. Always have a time to check in with that person, so if you DO NOT, they can come or send the police.

There are many men on-line posing as women. There are even more half sex-change individuals who believe they are women, but still have a penis. There are those who have had a sex change and call themselves women, only to tell you they were men some time down the road. This is tough on the psyche.

There are groups and ways, in all cities of the USA, to reach out and see if the individual you are playing with is "in the scene." The fact that a partner may not be known does not mean they are bad, but suggests they are newbies. Perhaps such as yourself? Or are you really more experienced?

Usually people who have been in chat rooms with certain names have also corresponded with people online or in D/s groups. For instance.... NO ONE.... absolutely NO ONE.... knows of sharah

..... or her sister and brother-in-law. We have had feelers out in Ohio and NY ever since you wrote. Nada, more nada. Some interesting and similar scams, but not the same names.

Be safe, be sane, be consensual.

Have a very happy New Year. Will you be near a computer?

Unknown

Subject: Happy New Year
Date: Sat, 2 Jan

Galen,

Let me know how you are, and how the year is going so far. Did you have the opportunity to see your children over any of the holidays? Is anything settling down on the home front? Are you still involved with a business with the wife?

Remember, you had these desires when you were married, living with her and carrying on as "she" expected you to. NOTHING has changed except her knowledge and perception. OK?

Hope you were safe in Fla.

Unknown

Subject: It's a New Year
Date: Sat, 9 Jan

Hi Unknown,

I'm still in FL. Not so tropical here, the last few days.

I saw my boys for the first time on New Year's day, since I took them snowboarding several weeks back. They didn't want to discuss their mom and dad's differences. They seemed OK, and we had a good time. My ex keeps saying how hurt and depressed they are, but she always paints the picture dark, and then exaggerates from there. She's as crazed and neurotic as ever. And she thinks I'm the one who has problems. I've never felt better!

You were curious about me, r/t. My education and Dominant mentality is better developed than my r/t experience, which is sparse. But I've had several subs that enjoyed long, intoxicating sessions with me, including mental subjugation NT, TT (clothes pins and clamps, breast bondage), spanking, paddling, flogging (ass, tits and cunt), gags, dildos, vibrators, various bondage, slut wear and high heels (mandatory) and of course cocksucking on demand. These are things that I enjoy, and happily, the subs were eager to oblige.

I've gotten several new inquiries to my ad, that sound interesting, two of whom are talking with me seriously and want to meet soon, (one in Dallas, one in LA).

I just entertained a sub here, near Ft. Lauderdale. A 30-year-old lawyer, who only wanted a spanking, and discovered she wanted a lot more. Now she realizes she's got a submissive slut hiding inside. I was the first to bring her out. I guess I just naturally have that effect on women(weg!).

She's driving down to see me again tomorrow night before I head up to Orlando. Still coming up short for a sub on my home turf. But I'm keeping pleasantly busy. I enjoy my work!

But you, mystery woman. You've been quite cautious in telling me about yourself. You know my biggest secrets, wildest fantasies and my true nature. It's time to tell me about yourself. How are you so involved and connected to the scene. What is your orientation and experience? I'd like to start planning to attend some of the most interesting scene events this year. Got any recommendations?

Know that I feel you are a special woman, no matter what flavor you are, and I am truly grateful to have had your wonderful support in my darkest hour. That's behind me now, except for the gory details of unwinding the financial and legal entanglements of my marriage and business relationship with my ex. My other business deals are chugging right along. Life is good. I hope yours is as well.

Thanks for the roses.

Galen

(*Note: Unknown and I had several conversations by phone and IM's, during our correspondence, so you may have noticed a few lurches in the email exchanges. She sent me an email bouquet, and that's the reference above about the roses. She got me online on AOL Instant Messenger, a few days after my last email. We shared a few laughs, and planned to keep in touch. She had just changed her email address, but I lost track of it. I am forever thankful for her support and encouragement. It greatly restored my faith in humanity.*

I was firmly convinced at that point, it had all been a hoax. I have not heard from any of the characters in this plot since.

This was not a typical encounter. Please don't be intimidated. Be prepared. Do your homework. Study and learn the rules for safe meetings with online contacts. Though you are likely to encounter some obnoxious and flaky people online, on the whole you'll meet people as sincere, friendly, intelligent and most importantly, as perverse as you.

In the remaining three encounters you'll meet three of the loveliest women I could ever desire to subdue!)

Episode 2

Arlana

One of the brightest blessings I've ever received lives in Canada. She was an angel brought to me at my darkest hour, my deepest despair.

She is a talented artist, deft intellectual, soulful ally, international beauty and fetish model, and a submissive of the highest rank, though she can be a cruel Domme bitch to lesser subs.

We tussled together like two excited panther cubs, clashed and harmonized intellectually, crafted prose as romantic, lyrical and poignant as a John Fowles' novel. We developed a sacred trust that allowed us to reveal our deepest wounds, and found them soothed in the ointment of tenderness.

Arlana and I survived several lurching episodes of impatient bickering, during our cyber dance. We both struggled to hold our individual ground in the delicate negotiations of D/s passion. I felt her as deeply as I've ever felt anyone, heart, mind and soul. Could this translate to the body as well, when we finally met?

How could all this passion and romance be so true in a cyber relationship, in a random encounter over the internet. . . the greatest love, highest respect, deepest desire, edgiest D/s?

After a torrid 10 months of email and a few phone calls, the two "Superpowers", as we indulgently referred to ourselves, negotiated a first meeting. The delicate web that enshrouded us had been shred and repaired several times. It would be reinforced with a pact of "no expectations," of what chemistry might occur in the flesh.

We had both carried each other over the roughest terrain of our personal tragedies. We'd snuck behind enemy lines (our own doubts, fears and disillusionment's) to rescue a weary but gallant warrior from doom. We met soul to soul in a modern dance of the

spirit, sparks flying everywhere. No matter what happened on earth between us, nothing could defile what had been wrought in heaven. After our first meeting, that heavenly bond held true.

Subject: Little girl's replies
Date: Sat, 16 Jan

Hello Sir,

I found your ad to be most interesting and stimulating in many ways. I am educated, cultured, attractive and crave mental and physical relinquishment. I would enjoy further discussion, if you honor me with a reply. I am eager to learn and deepen my submissive self.

respectfully,

Arlana

PS: I check my e mail once a week or so.

Subject: Relinquishment
Date: Sun, 17 Jan

Dear Arlana,

Well, just by replying, you intrigue me a little, dear. I will appreciate if you are intelligent and attractive, but you need to tell me more to capture my attention. Are you beginning on your path of relinquishment? I do like the word "relinquishment". Is there anything I wrote before or what follows, that is beyond your limit, presently? Are you inclined to cyber, r/t or ltr?

The little girl replies fits well with the Daddy/daughter stratum, of

my D/S persona. But I don't want to raise a daughter, I already did my major parenting. I am pleased you enjoyed my ad. But did the other two Doms who received your reply, write the same ad as well, or was theirs different? (grin! – the email address box noted two others your first response had been sent too.)

I'm including a short scene for your pleasure.

Master Galen

(*included Scene 2*)

Subject: Visceral submission
Date: Tue, 26 Jan

Dear Sir,

Thank You for your message and the juicy and exciting story. There is nothing in it beyond my limits, except that I do not tend to swear as the slave in the story did. I am not looking for a Daddy per se, I was only employing the language You used in Your ad.

I only answered three out of what seemed like a sea of notices. One of those ads struck me because of its use of words. The definition one used was admiringly accurate, the other simply made me curious. In any event, I have nothing to hide- it was all out there in the open, right?

I am not beginning on the path of my relinquishment. I have been living the lifestyle 24/7 for the past two years, although SM fantasies have always been a part of my sensual landscape. I have been fortunate to play with some very experienced tops during these two years whom have taken me far in my path. I believe that I have grown and learnt a great deal and want to continue to do so.

Cyber domination is not something that I have experienced, but it must provide some intellectual stimulation, I imagine. I love and

need the physical, throbbing, visceral part of submission. I crave pain though I have learnt that it is not for my pleasure or desire, but rather to indulge my Top- the Beloved Guide in the labyrinth of this most thrilling way of life and love.

I hope that this reply has answered some of Your questions and that it has pleased You. I apologize for taking so long to answer.

respectfully,

Arlana

Subject: A certain zest!
Date: Wed, 27 Jan

Dear Arlana,

I did like the thought of you as my daughter. And other thoughts as well. I like the tone of your "voice". I appreciate that you are very respectful, deferential, but with a certain zest. Most important, I appreciate that you are past your interest in your personal desire for pain/pleasure, and recognize that it is really from being pleasing to your Master, that you draw your pleasure and strength.

By the way, you mentioned why you were drawn to the other two Dom's ads, but not what drew you to mine.

As I stated, in my first letter. I seek most the slave I will collar. But, I am always open to new experiences and do provide a high quality r/t experience for those seeking to explore or sharpen their experiences. I'm backing away from heavy cyber, too time and energy consuming, but a great way to get started, towards real time in the not too distant future. Like you, I do love to, and do provide the "physical, throbbing, visceral part of submission"-nice description!

So tell me more about what you are about. What type(s) of relation-

ship do you wish for; how would you describe your current limits; what types of BDSM have you experienced; do you desire to experience; why do you feel you would be a good slave possibility for this particular Master; where do you now live? Can you travel, have guests, relocate?

I am committed to safe, sane and consensual conduct, and will gladly cover all those issues if we should find ourselves with the need for serious discussion.

Are you currently in any other relationships? You probably looked at my picture at ****. com (go to personals, Doms, late December). Can you send me a recent picture? Is there anything that I've told you so far that raises an issue for you? You may ask me anything you wish, sweetheart. My stories tell a lot about me, but not much of the total possibility I offer.

Galen

Subject: Your answers, Sir
Date: Wed, 3 Feb

Master Galen,

Thank You for your pleasing e-mail. What attracted me to Your ad was the tone, content and confidence it emanated. I did not see a picture of You and have not yet seen one.

Yes, I do indeed recognize that it is really from being pleasing to my Master that I draw my pleasure. You see, I want to please Him because He is my guide. I figured this out after a session that was so good, so difficult that I was illuminated, as a pilgrim is, who sets eyes on Holy Relics or something soul shattering of the sort.

The Master is the Sensei, the Guide, the Teacher, Guru: the King. I have grown through these kinds of experiences. Great physical and psychological torments have changed me. The Master involved in

providing this intense training has left me a much improved slave. I have learned a great deal and am eager for a worthy successive episode . I feel alive when I live the intensity of my submissive nature.

I am owned by a Master here who is very kind, tolerant and liberal minded when it comes to sharing all of me. He is often very busy and cannot be here, Himself. There is no lying or disrespect between us. In fact He and the Other were great friends, and I think that They will remain so for life.

I adore relinquishment, as I have told You before. The love and gratitude I feel for what my Master is giving me makes me obedient and compliant, though I am an independent and willful woman in life. Mental games are as important as the physical. A purely sensational scene will leave me emotionally cold and often mentally distant. The greatest tool to "break" me I have found, besides fear and great pain, is tenderness. This, mixed in with fine cruelty as a seasoning has given me some of the most memorable moments of my life.

Practically speaking, I have enjoyed all types of bondage, saran wrap, cords, shackles and cuffs. I also have experienced: needle play, nipple training, vaginal lip training, urine retention, corset training, as well as urethra play.

I have had to wear plugs and love balls out of the house, been told how to dress and been ordered to meet in strange places where I have been dominated, tied and left for a time. I have been in a body bag, donned a latex mask with only a tiny hole, been wrapped in a body harness under latex sheets (little air), ridden in the trunk of the car- blindfolded. . . (yum), and have been whipped paddled and flogged with a cornucopia of instruments.

I have indulged in some edge-play, but have done this only twice in my life and only with very experienced partners. I have been zapped and taped, teased and taunted. I have an abduction fantasy that has yet to be lived and a few others.

I have been trained to be a proud slave, not a groveling one, and have also learnt to be proud of my sexuality in all its respects. I cried more freely with this latest Master, because he tapped into my heart and psyche at the same time.

I am not the housecleaning type of submissive. Sub-slaves and foot-boys do that for me, but I love to sit at my Master's feet as He reads the paper or sleep at the foot of His bed or even on the floor if He chooses. I would adore a cage…sigh.

I have few physical limits except: scat play and lasting scars on my body. I love pain and fear, and have good days an bad days, but am considered to be on the heavy side of tolerance. I do enjoy soft humiliation but no face in the toilet scenes, or extreme names. My threshold is beautiful bitch, little slut or the like. My being does not illicit much more than that anyway.

I do consider myself to be classy, but I can be dirty too. I enjoy getting roughed up, as the physical strength of a man in contrast to my own is exciting. I don't mind being slapped in the face by my Master and I guess I deserve it sometimes, but would leave a vanilla boyfriend for doing so.

Have I described myself to You yet??? I live in **** and can travel and can have guests. I live alone in a lovely condo in the center of town, with fireplace and private roof patio and a little Jacuzzi and have a cat called Felicity. I speak French, and several other languages. I would like to grow, learn and be taken to the sensual, dangerous Country of Passion and Peril. Few women have been there. There, I will travel side by side with my Guide, glorious at His side, to make Him proud, to cry, come and bleed for Him.

Respectfully,

Arlana

PS: if You send me a P. O. box address, I can send You a photo, otherwise I will go to a friend's one day soon and scan You one. Where can I find Your photo? I hope that I answered some of Your

questions, Sir. I will fill in the blanks where You request.

Subject: Are You upset?
Date: Sun, 7Feb

Sir,

Are You upset at me??? I didn't want to offend with my last message. I only wanted to be frank. If you are not angry, please- only a couple of lines. I do need your aid to wade through the mire and find your photo. Also I raised a few pertinent issues I am eager to hear your spin on. Thank you.

warmly,

Arlana

Subject: Universe of Passion
Date: Mon, 8 Feb

Dear Arlana,

Why stop at country, sweetheart, when you can have the whole universe? The heart is an erogenous zone. Tenderness? I understand tenderness, dear slut. I offer and require it.

I am assuming that you didn't receive this e-mail last week. So, I 'm resending it with some additions, including a photo. My computer with my picture file has been in the shop until this weekend, so am now able to send. If you did receive my last email, and your last message was a response, I would require further clarification. I don't understand it?

Either way, what was it in your previous response to this, that you felt might have offended me?

You sound exquisite on my computer screen sweetheart, but then so do I on yours, no doubt. I try to weave all these elements of you into a picture, and though I can't see you, I get a sense (not visually) of Ingrid Bergman, who I hold as a classy, intelligent, passionate babe, if she was a hard-core submissive slut. Wouldn't that have been something, to have seen her in a BDSM film!

Until I verify that you are a real, sincere submissive of integrity, dear, as much as I would crave to gush forth my dominance upon you, I do not offer the full power of my passion as a Master. The right match for my Dominant persona, will thank God (and me) to have met her Master. (I indulge my arrogance on a regular basis!). But I'm sure you're very aware of how much fraud and hoaxing and general coo-coo's there are, running rampant on the web. Therefore passion must suffer for prudence.

I'll wait for your scan. I don't have a PO, and I won't, now reveal my street address. I'm still perplexed where you saw my ad. I didn't remember posting one that included Scene 1, but your first letter seemed to indicate you read Scene 1, I know Scene 2 was included in my first reply to you.

For your pleasure, daughter, I've included a scene called Cocoon at the end of this letter. If you liked the body bag so much, you're going to enjoy this one.

Language. Well dear, I am verbally abusive at times, but only within a scene and only with consent. But like a tender caress of your cunt, interspersed with a hard flogging, sweetens the pain, I'd sweeten the harshness, with tender, loving words as well. After a certain stage, I don't think you'd have a problem with it. You would understand and trust Master, at the point it would occur. I would respect this limit, if it was one, initially.

I appreciate how you described your Master as a Guide. I relate to that thought, well. But I require feedback and insight, to understand the mental landscape and it's inhabitants. I can't dominate a statue. I enjoy a slave who voices her passions and her lust, from sleazy to

eloquent. It turns me on and also inspires me. Intuition requires these things to weave together seemingly disconnected aspects of submission in a creative way.

Now for some Q&A(and a few comments).

You enjoy fear. Broad category. Fear of embarrassment, rape, harm, pancakes? (That's a joke, I swear. I've never used pancakes to instill fear!)

In what ways have you changed from "physical and psychological torment? How were you before and then after?

"Mental games are as important as the physical. " Give me some glimpses into your most enticing mental games.

Tell me a little about your abduction fantasy. If you aren't preserving it for your own writing, I might create a scene from it.

I like that aspect - your pride.

Sub-slaves and foot-boys, really?

At night, you would sleep close to me, it's easier to use you should I care to during the night. I like the closeness of you as well. Now a cage, that's a nice idea. A good place for you when you've been a bad girl, or on my whim.

Tell me more about how you enjoy being "roughed up". I can rough you up, good sweetheart.

I want to understand more clearly your relationship to the current Master you mentioned. Are you under his ownership? I would understand this to then be defining your interest as casual. I would be fine with this, if we came to that stage, but I am seeking my slave/soul mate.

I'm curious and attracted to electric and fire play scenes I've seen depicted in SM porn videos. I am not an experienced edge-player,

and I wouldn't attempt edge-play without proper training. I've been subscribing to several email lists on them. Doing my research, you might say.

Until I get your scan, describe yourself physically. Are you bi-sexual, curious or straight?

You may answer these questions all at once, or a few at a time. But I expect clear, straightforward responses. You may expect the same from this Master.

This next scene will perhaps give another small glimpse of this Master. There is much more to understand.

Galen

(*Note: I included the Cocoon scene here*)

Subject: The whole universe
Date: Tue, 9 Feb

Dear Sir Galen,

Thank you for the photo. I did receive it. Its arrogant indolence is suggestive of a cruel self-indulgent Pascha, kind of hatefully sexy and remote. I like.

My last reply was to this same letter. I did get it last week and answered You.

My turn. Get thee to a scanner Arlana, and then after, if You trust me a bit more, and if You like what You see, I shall begin to get deeper on the questions. Like I said in my last e-mail, I did raise some issues, last week, that I would be grateful for You to address in the meantime, if You would be so kind. *Merci*.

I am surprised You did not understand. I felt that I was speaking out

rather boldly in my communication to You, almost angrily, certainly beyond what I thought were the proper parameters. Perhaps to see what You would do to a bold slut!

Guess that the sedate screen cools the fire. I thought that the first paragraph, where I unburdened myself, was the one that was iffy. I assume that it didn't upset You, and I am glad that I was able to get it off my chest without causing damage. Do You understand now, dear Sir?

ardently,

Arlana

Subject: Pascha rising!
Date: Tue, 9 Feb

Dear Arlana,

First, you're proving to me that you are reliable in your communication, and my trust that you have a serious interest is growing. I am pleased with you.

OK. Got the sequence of events straight. You'll have to specify the issues you want me to respond to. I reviewed your letter and my response, and didn't understand what issues I didn't respond to. Put them in the form of a question and I'll respond.

Pascha! Had to look that up. I was doing my best to project sweetness in the photo, but I guess the truth shines through, doesn't it! That was one of the nicest things ever said about me!

I detected no anger, nor did I read anything that might have required it. I appreciated your honesty, and how you defined yourself as a woman and a submissive. I love boldness. I react to it aggressively. The most fascinating slaves are those who have few physical limits. It means they have a highly developed submissive consciousness,

that I find very erotic. It's a strong attraction.

The only thing I want on your chest is what I put there. And it's not removed with out my permission. So anything else still on your chest should be removed immediately. i. e. I expect honesty at all times. Who doesn't?

I still don't get your "unburdening" and "causing damage" perspective relating to the first paragraph or any other. I thought you were just telling me about yourself. Why would I judge you for being a profound submissive when that's what I seek? What exactly were you worried would cause damage. Be honest and direct.

When you respond to the questions I raised in the previous letter, use the latest version I sent because, I added, deleted and changed the questions. If I am pleased with your next response, our worlds will draw closer.

Master Galen

Subject: Exquisite
Date: Thu, 11 Feb

Dear Sir,

You do indeed sound exquisite on my screen and I must tell You that this is the first time that I have engaged on any such cyber connection with anyone I didn't previously know, let alone a Dom. I am surprised that You do not sense the sincerity and veracity of who I am. How does one do that?

Since I am new to this type of "getting to know" someone. Can You not tell from my "voice"? What about Your gut feeling? (hell- all the capitalizations should set You at ease right there, Sir !) Or is it that women are more in touch with that type of intuition?

I imagine that exquisite Doms vibrate with near extra-sensory

perception when it comes to feeling the other out. It must be that you have met many quacks and wanna-be's on your Internet adventures. I assure you that I am a jewel. Want references or what!!! I am somewhat ruffled.

Would I invest so much time writing to You if I was a nut, Dear Sir? or give You my real name? You err on the side of caution. Wise. The wild will have to wait. Yet, what could I possibly do to harm You???

Why am I not cautiously skeptical? This is an interesting interaction, thus far. Theoretically, You have a far greater potential to harm me. That unleashed passion You spoke of is not intended for the little screen anyhow. I liked the arrogance You displayed- enticing, strong and sexy. You must have the goods to back it up. I am sassy tonight, *n'est cepas*?

I would have You know that for every message I send you I must make a physical trip to this computer. My home computer is primitive and I only use it to word process. I will be getting a new one next year, but am waiting to avoid a potential Y-2K disaster. I am very busy and neglect real life friends at times- yet I compose thoughtful and well-intentioned messages to you. I hope this counts for something.

Also, please, You should know that all I read about You, were a few lines of a Personal Ad, no more than two sentences, no story, Papa. I will try and surf around and find the site and I will let you know. I can't even recall where it was. You see, it is true that this in an unprecedented event.

You are the only one I am corresponding with. I cherish Your stories but really trip on Your own communications to me. They're more exciting than anything else. I feel better having written this paragraph. I hope it retained a sense of respect in spite of its candor.

The ****. com site is too vast for me to find You. I do not know where You are in there- there are hundreds of ads and I do not know

if pictures are attached. A guide of sorts would be helpful. Help please, thanks

OK. I am 5'8" of Arabic origin- exotic looking with almond shaped eyes, that look amber in sunlight. I have long black hair with a pink streak in it that is just rebellious enough for my fancy. I sport no tattoos or permanent piercings, yet. I dream of getting a triangle one day.

I style my hair straight or leave it naturally crazily curly when I feel like it. It is a big lush mane that You would no doubt enjoy pulling. I weigh 127 pounds and have a curvy behind and long muscular legs. I am a 34B- the girls are very sensitive- nipples discreet and diminutive. I am closely shaved about the pussy- just a tiny little triangle of hair.

My tummy is flat and a light down covers my limbs and has driven some lovers crazy. I have a pale olive complexion and have been told that my skin is gorgeous. I am self-conscious of my butt and fear the ripples that age may bring or shadows cast, but I care well for myself and no one is perfect.

I am well groomed at all times and have a wardrobe full of clothing from slutty to couture. It is almost funny that Your skepticism has made me afraid that if You saw my picture You would be convinced that I am a real lying coaxer. Could you think that a picture is too good? Oh, now I really am at a loss!!! Do I try and send a semi-botched photo or a fabulous wet-dream one and risk Your prudent retreat??

If You chat with anyone who is anyone in the Fetish community here, they will tell you that Arlana is a real person and that my description is accurate. I do not have a scene name. I am proud of what and who I am, and prefer not to hide behind a pseudonym. Besides, there is not much need to do so here.

My nose is aquiline and classic. Cheekbones are evident and a pointed chin frames my small but shapely mouth. I have little dimples that sometimes show when I laugh. My teeth are perfect,

167

top row for sure, and I have a long, elegant neck, which looks lovely in collars of all types. I hope you like the description.

I am not a statue and love to express myself to my Dom. I need to share even the thoughts behind my thoughts. On passionate nights after the air has vibrated with my cries of pain, pleasure and passion I love to cuddle and talk.

I like the description of how You sweeten the harshness. Excellent. I guess after a certain stage, I would not have a problem with anything, really. Eloquence, You know I posses, and when things get really hot I can certainly talk dirty. Bergman spouting sleaze, perhaps. I just don't gush like a Penthouse letter. Certainly, I might beg to be fucked harder or urge my lover to climax, but cartoon trash-mouth lingo is beyond me.

I say pussy, for example, but get a shiver when mine is called a cunt. I enjoy objectification. I have been called a lovely creature, and like the animal implications of that, as well as those of feeling that I am a toy or a prize. I am like a highly bred horse that needs to be ridden hard. I come from a long unmixed bloodline. Pure Arab.

No more for now. I am eager to have overcome some of your concerns. I will answer the questions once we have surmounted the trust barrier and have examined one another's pictures to see if there is chemistry. Though so far, the mental chemistry is compelling.

Arlana

Subject: March salutation
Date: Tue, 16 Feb

Hello Sir,

Just a hello to check if You received my last e-mail- it is the long, long one. Do let me know please, I did put a lot of energy into it. Thanks. Hoping to hear from You soon.

Arlana

Subject: Long long letter
Date: Tue: 2 March

Dear Arlana

I've replied 3 times to your query about the long, long letter, which
I never received. Are you "tied" up, or are these messages not
coming through?

Master Galen

Subject: Missing letter
Date: Sat, 20 Feb

Dearest Master Galen,

Sweet Sir, I indeed did not receive them! Please note: only You have
this address and that I access my Hotmail account once a week or
so. There are frightening viruses out there and I am more cautious
than usual. Did You send it to my Hotmail account or here?? This is
a better address in every respect and I have my privacy here as well.
I miss Your letters. . . Hope to hear from You soon. Anything is
possible as long as we keep our minds and the channels open, right?

I did get a pic scanned. Hope you approve, Sir.

Bonsoir, Monsieur. . . x o o x

Arlana

PS: I just attended a cocktail party given by the British Consul-
lovely party, a jazz trio, wine and tasty bites. . . It is so cold out and

I feel randy and willful. .

Subject: Udjat eye
Date: Sun, 21 Feb

Dear Arlana,

What an enticing pose, dear. I found you poised with humility, respect, erotic beauty, ready to be led to Master's Holy Realm, your dark submissive soul begging from your serene Udjat eye. Proceed, sweet slut.

Master Galen

Subject: Dear slut proceeds
Date: Sun, 21 Feb

Good morning Sir,

Thank You for your responses.

I am glad that You liked the photo. Did You send the revised questions to my Hotmail account? Corresponding with me at this address is much better as You are the only person who sends me e-mail here. My Hotmail account is deluged and often I don't have the patience to access it, and going back and forth to answer questions is easier this way.

Ok. Some of my issues of the past letters…

Didn't Your gut give You a feeling about who I am??

Do You have that second sight as a Dom??

Have You had many quack episodes on the web? How could I harm

You?

Did my photo match my description??

Does compassion live in Your heart? Is the continent of Your heart on the equator or the North Pole? I imagine that You are as sensitive to the vibrations of the sub's spirit, heart and mind as to the body, no?

I guess that I was a bit ruffled when I wrote that paragraph, I spoke of, but now somehow, I am out of touch with that feeling. My indignity was roused, after all. I am honest to a fault, especially when it comes to this cyber talk, and the real thing! I feel much better and am glad that nothing upset You.

Replies:

FEAR.
Hmmm. . . I enjoy apprehension, truly fearing what my Master will do to me. Fear is the righteous tribute His superiority merits. This also means respect and fear of displeasing Him because it will be bad news for me. I enjoy fearing His imagination. What will He do next???

Suspense I enjoy less, as I have a very active imagination and sometimes I make it much worse for myself, until fear takes a hold on me and sweeps me along like a raging river. Still, I know that I must endure this too.

When I fear, it means that I am overcome in a way- this means that a broader force is controlling me and thus I can let go. I never let go to lesser beings or feelings. My individual fears I shall leave for You to pleasantly discover.

*note- the Marquis de Sade used to serve piping hot omelets on the buttocks of his victims. I don't think I would like that at all-food and sex- not my thing. Although, on one occasion, Master Lothaire (the sadistic edge player who lives dangerously himself. He is a former deep sea diver who lived in Malaysia and now is somewhere

in South America) sent me out at six am into the cold Canadian fall morning and made me pick blackberries in the nude. I walked over sharp gravel in my bare feet in the rain, getting torn on the brambles and thorns. I presented them to Him and He made me lie on the wet wooden deck of our hotel suite.

My entire body was in goose flesh. He then bade me to distribute the berries on my myself for His breakfast. This repast He leisurely consumed off of me. I nervously kept looking up to the windows and doors of the chalet, fearing that my vanilla friend would wake to this unlikely spectacle.

Lothaire kissed my mouth lovingly afterwards and covered me with a towel. Each mark on my body was precious to me, even though He told me to take no trophies. Still, in my heart, they were treasures. Interesting, no?

The grand Dominants can make you love something you thought that you disliked and push you past such barriers as modesty, self-consciousness and fear: another limit to be conquered, but one of the *big ones*, as You know, that we subs struggle with constantly. Let me know if You want to hear more about fear.

PHYSICAL/PSYCHOLOGICAL TORMENT
These have changed me in that I feel like a deeper submissive. I have looked my mortality in the face and have plumbed the recesses of my soul. I have crossed thresholds that I didn't imagine existed and feel less animal hunger for domination. Now I am patient enough to wait for the right partner(s) and exquisite and rare domination.

This I have discovered through the physical torture that I have experienced. I think that the desire to please the worthy Master is what makes me strong and helps me endure. I can let no lesser Tops touch me now.

I have been sanctified in a way: a loss of submissive innocence if you will. The down side, if it is a down, is that I think my body has retained the memory and the fear of these great ordeals. You have a

lot to work off of, dear Sir.

I was prepared for hours before these great cataclysms and was ripe for them when they arrived, though at moments, I wept with dismay and howled with pain. I feel changed, in that I feel grander, more experienced and selective now.

I want to continue on this path that I have begun on. I want to rush towards my fear and clash with it in a brightly glinting sword fight of the psyche. I crave to slay it, though it always resurrects like some immortal monster. This is the psychological and physical dimension together.

In life, I calculatingly and pragmatically have severed love from sex and am always the emotional and often, the sexual top in relation-ships. The Master Lothaire experience threw me for a loop because "making love" did not happen, though some sexual domination did, but love itself did bloom in spite of my resistance to it. Don't get me wrong. I can and do love, but the feeling of "in love" is what I have avoided as it has always caused havoc and disorder.

Psychologically, it was a tormenting revelation to feel this love and loss of control and it made me hate Him. (Lothaire). My Master Martin slapped me in the face when I shouted: "I hate Him! I hate Him!" I meant it. Love and hate are so close.

I have changed because now I know that I can let myself fall into that kind of love again. It is as painful as any torture I know, but has made me feel so alive. I was able to live fully in the moment, which is rare as I have a vagrant and perpetually mobile mind, always thinking.

I had let myself go to the point where I toyed with the idea of leaving behind home, hearth and reason and just following my passion and flinging myself into the arms of danger and folly. He ran. He did nothing. He was cryptic instead of practical. Was He afraid, I wonder??? He was and is an unfathomable mystery to me.

RELINQUISHMENT

This is a topic dear to my heart. This is the abandonment that my whole being craves, which happens when I totally trust and give myself to someone. It is when the Top is truly the one in charge- it is amazing how much control I have had from the bottom!

The potently effective Top has the intellectual arsenal, steely control and tenacity to make me into a willing puppet. He does not hesitate nor flinch, which I can sense in a New York minute and get blazingly rebellious at, and yet, He is sensually strong and loving. He is always one step ahead and is constantly surprising me. (rare, rare, rare!) It has been hard to find emotional and intellectual equals, let alone superiors. Relinquishment is what happens when I do.

I am up so early it is still dark. . . I do not know why it is that I cannot sleep. . .

ABDUCTION

Yes, this is preserved for my own writings, Sir. Still, I imagine being taken, blindfolded to an unknown place. I imagine it to be of stone, a room with no windows, shackles everywhere- a kind of *Roissy*. There, day would be indistinguishable from night and I would suffer sensory deprivation, hunger, sexual torment and abuse. Totally dependent. My Master would show up from time to time. I would know Him from the smell of His skin or the touch of His hand on my body or His hand around my neck. I would thirst for His kiss more than for water though I'd be parched at times. Kind of a cliché fantasy, *n'est ce pas*?

PRIDE

Yes, I am proud. I have been called prideful and willful. Surely, I am proud to be who I am and proud to endure and please. It does take will to suffer, grow and fence with fear. I would have no one divest me of these noble traits. How can a glorious and powerful Top crave a cowardly, soft slave. ? I am as spiny as a cactus and venomous as a snake(my Chinese astrology sign).

It is always below the surface. I hope You will feel it one day as You tame me. When I sublimate my savage side, I am proud of my

174

self-control. It is and always will be a gift because it is so hard. It is part of my nature-yes, but I always like it to be difficult and somehow, a challenge.

What is your Chinese sign by the way, Sir???

ROUGHING UP
I like to feel the strength of the male against me. (not just a top-even an ordinary toy or casual lover) I enjoy a kind of struggling for a time- i.e.: having my hair pulled a bit, being choked, squeezed, slapped about (not crazily hard), jerked around roughly to be positioned for sex, kissed until my lips bruise etc. This makes me feel small and female. I like that feeling. I am a strong and statu-esque woman and this is a rare feeling. I have scared many a man, too.

I was once dragged and thrown in the snow for being too bold. I fought like a hellcat, but was docile as a kitten afterwards when the Master laid His body on mine and kissed me as the snow melted off my teeming body.

I like bucking and fighting and feeling my wrists pinned down by the superior male brutality. Sometimes I get a pleasure from seeing my partner sweat and toil with me. In public a mighty bruise inducing squeeze of my arm, just to remind me of who I am can mightily excite me and wet my panties(when I am allowed to wear them!).

I enjoy You saying: "I can rough you up, good sweetheart". . . . sigh. . . Perhaps I can make You sweat a bit, Sir. Its nice and cathartic, good for the heart and all that.

Is this sufficient for now, darling Pascha? This odalisque shall take a walk in the frigid morning air to find a *cafe au lait* while I wait for the world to wake. Where was the picture taken, in your house? Do you trust me enough to tell me whereabouts You live, just the state or something? I will not stalk You, I promise. I am simply curious.

Sometimes I am so hungry for pain, love and sex that it swells

inside my body and hurts me from within. At other times, I feel like I am suffocating. My Master is so busy and seems to have settled down to a comfortable state of complacency with me, though He cares and still finds me a "magnificent beauty" as He says. Does it bother You that He exists?

Perhaps one day, He himself will pass the leash over to You and hug you (they do that here- very Latin and warm of them). You have kept some of my sanity afloat as my mind is titillated and my body pines. Thank You for that.

FOOTBOYS

Yes, I am such a glorious slave! They don't mind one bit that I am a submissive, only they are too squeamish to watch a session. The little foot boys (6 foot tall babies), do like to come over, clean my house, shine my shoes, do the dishes, serve tea to my girlfriends and me, answer the door, massage my feet, serve as footstools, carpets or ponies, paint my toenails and brush my hair.

They persist in calling me Mistress, or my Queen. Who am I to argue? I do like a clean house for my Master and myself and a nice pedicure and manicure are important. Its just a question of hierarchy. I certainly am and do feel above them in the pecking order.

I worry that I have become soft and need to build up my strength. I do have days where I am a powerhouse of endurance and others where I do not: emotionally and physically. I think that this is cyclical or something. I am not the same person from day to day. I hope that this is acceptable to You.

Limits, I do not set. Why should adventure be censored in advance?(apart from scat, disfiguration, extreme humiliation and major scarification) One guy in the scene here actually cut off part of his little finger as an "experiment". This is a little too far for my personal taste. Mental amputations of a kind can be much more difficult and effective without spoiling my body for You.

I have been writing since 6:20 am or so. I think that I will try and hit the slopes today.

Affectionately,

Arlana

PS: whoever told me that e-mail should be brief and full of mistakes is wrong! Bye for now.

Subject: the molten core
Date: Tue, 22 Feb

Dear girl,

The "continent of my heart" resides not at the north pole nor the equator, nor anywhere on the surface of the earth, but at it's molten core.

It was worth the wait to hear from you, sweetheart. Deep space rising. I'm on alert, after so many mundane contacts with other subs. I'd become lulled until connecting with the cosmos you are. But there are other reasons why I hold back presently.

My second sight, as you call it is normally very keen in 3D. Recently I was blind-sided by a primary passion and desire that came down in cyberworld. I took a big hit right to the heart and soul of me. Someone I met on-line. I've concluded my radar doesn't in fact penetrate the (computer)screen.

It's a bizarre story of an ultimate betrayal of trust - not the kind you might think. I haven't tried to describe this before, it is so huge and complex, I'm not sure how to describe it simply. It will reveal more of me and there's more as well that this episode created in my life, and I will try to bring that out for you also. Here's the short version.

I began exchanging mail with sharah, age 23. She was the most exquisitely submissive slut I'd ever encountered. I would send her

a 3 page scene, she'd respond with 6 or more pages, taking the scenes further, more elaborate, and spinning them into these Daddy/ daughter scenes that drove my passion through the wall.

In her last letter we had confirmed an arrangement to meet in Florida. I had told her the hotel I would be at on a business trip the following month, and we planned to meet there. She was leaving the next evening for her sister and brother-in-law's (also into D/s) in Ohio; she was from a NYC, where she taught at a ballet school, and would contact me the next day. She had expressed the hope that I might be the Master she had so longed for.

No word for a week. Then I get a letter from James, her brother-in-law, telling me not to worry. He tells me that sharah is in intensive care and under psychiatric care as well. She apparently went out with the wrong guy, posing as a Dom.

He raped her with a knife, sliced up her cunt, torso, tits and nipples and tried to carve his initials into her. He broke her ribs with a baseball bat to top it all off. James said that she was in his care now at the hospital. He wouldn't reveal where. sharah had told him a bit about me by phone, before this happened, and in her brief moments of lucidity at the hospital begged him to contact me, though she feared I wouldn't want her anymore because she'd been disfigured.

He wouldn't give much detail, but reported that sharah was under continuous sedation, her mind and body presently shattered, and consequently he wasn't trusting anybody he didn't know, for her protection. He told me to be patient, and that he would give me more information, as he felt it was safe to do so.

My rage and feelings of helplessness were boiling. I wanted to kill the sick fuck that did this, and Joe(who was feeling the same) and I, began to discuss ways to deal with the sick bastard. The guy had been arrested, but his lawyer got him released, and James was flying to NYC periodically to deal with the uncooperative cops(reflecting the: "she agreed to meet the guy for kinky sex, attitude.")

He also was able to check out where the guy lived. Joe went there with an FBI buddy, who he'd been in Vietnam with and with his buddy's credentials convinced the super of the guys apartment to let them in, but the guy wasn't there.

When Joe was away, kathy, (sharah's sister) would write, and tell me more about sharah. How she cries and screams every time a man comes into the hospital room, how she looks at my picture, which kathy placed by the bed, for hours everyday, but maybe doesn't realize it's me. kathy thought her sister recognized me and how this seemed to calm her, but she wasn't sure.

She related that sharah had confided in her, before this happened, that she hoped I would be the one to collar her, after her former Dom had died 2 years earlier. He'd been her Master since she was 17.

She wrote me that it was uncanny how much I resembled their father, and finally, that they wanted me to come to Ohio, because they eventually became convinced that I was the only one who could bring sharah out of it. We had gotten to the point where we needed to contact one another by phone, and I gave them my number.

Joe didn't call at the arranged time. kathy wrote and said Joe had gone to New York and something bad had happened, and it was necessary for them to disconnect their e-mail and Joe would contact me soon. Several days passed, and I got mail from Joe. The "sick fuck" predator wouldn't bother sharah again, and Joe "believed the cops didn't know anything about me." He couldn't be sure. He thought they might have been monitoring his email. He would contact me as soon as he felt it was safe.

It was all an intricate HOAX! Why? I'll never know. There was no money involved. At that time I was quite worried, because I had given them my phone number and where I was going to be in Florida. I've only scratched to surface of the full story. My thought was why did they waste all this effort for an audience of one? They could have gone straight to Hollywood with this script. Sometime,

if you're interested, I'll share more.

I had to do a lot of investigation, on the chance that there actually was a sharah and she had been abandoned in a psyche ward in Ohio. I had to be sure a real human wasn't left in such a tragic situation. After I verified it was a hoax, it was clear how much I had exposed myself by revealing my phone number (which a decent hacker could possibly derive an address from), and Florida hotel location.

Because real violence had been such a prominent part of the drama, and that these were unscrupulous perverts, a part of me had to consider that there might be danger coming. Consequently, I am cautious in the cyber world. I've had a number of other strange episodes as well, but none as vividly rendered as this one.

Intermission: It's late and I have plans this evening. I will stop here. You've provided a revealing and abundant glimpse into your submissive soul, that I wish to ponder more, before I respond further. I will write more tomorrow. I have another story I'll send as well.

You've developed quite the lifestyle there dear slut. Perhaps I will soon see it close up!

Master Galen

Subject: Bravo, Sir
Date: Wed, 23 Feb

Dear Sir

I received Your reply, *merci beaucoup*.

The molten core. . . luscious and dangerous- excellent and exciting answer. Bravo Sir!

I am so sorry to hear of the rotten tale- how twisted and depraved

they were! What kind of satisfaction could they get? On my honor as a slave, a human being of value and who cherishes honesty and *noblesse d'esprit*- I am real. As I told You, please feel free to contact anyone within the scene here. I want You to feel at ease about me.

I don't know what will happen with us, but I have always been and will always be real with You. This is one of my credos in life and especially within the scene.

A Master should have reign over the very imagination of His sub. No hallway of her mind should be invulnerable to his patrol. This sharah creature, was an exquisitely accomplished fake! These generous adjectives were too good even for the idea of her!!!

Perhaps these degenerate fools have nothing better to do than playing pathological pranks and are deeply disturbed and jealous of You. They are spineless! One day, they will get their just dessert! Thank God they didn't get to You in person!!

I am so new to all of this online stuff. Your story is sobering and has made me cautious of others. My instinct tells me that You are as real as me. Your last sentence about "seeing my lifestyle close up" titillated me and made me shiver and smile at the same time. Thank You.

Au revoir for now,

sincerely, (cross my heart)

Arlana

Subject: Out of my head…
Date: Sat, 27 Feb

Lovely Whore,

You're a sweet girl and a delicious slut. I appreciate how you respond to my thoughts about you and other things.

My interest in play partners has been rapidly diminishing over the last several months. This shocks me, because I was driven by casual play, vanilla and finally D/s throughout my sexual life. I still remember getting turned on the first time as a clever, though deviant, voyeur/toddler. Sitting on the floor as a five year old you can get away with a lot, and you have a great view up women's skirts as they walk by or stand, or when they sit without closing their legs tightly.

Lately, I've acknowledged the pain my soul suffers from lacking that element of passion and desire that's stronger than any physical sensation, or visual stimulation. Stronger even than that rush of power, knowing you have taken complete control of a slave. I know my soul and its full passion needs it counterpart to awaken the volcano in my heart.

My desire goes beyond a D/s relationship. I seek "higher intelligence". Soul to soul contact. Everything, nothing less. I may have created this lack of it in my life, but as well, the opportunity hasn't thrown itself before me, either. Especially, with the D/s aspect.

Until I got on the Internet, and met women cultivating their submissiveness, this aspect was never expressed in my earlier partners. I was always and easily into the pleasure of sex. Nothing else was required. I could be passionate about sex, and sex alone. But I find myself going through this change now, and I'm clearer about what I desire.

I settled for less, only once and it was a mistake, though I did receive two lovely sons out of the deal. Might not have happened any other way.

I had been in this phase, before I got "caught" by marriage, where I was trying to define for myself, my life as single. I felt I could love a variety of women(and people). What was this limit that I should only allow only one person the depth of my heart, or only receive

one heart in return?

I was committed first to developing the life of the artist/outlaw. I rationalized that to support the time my art(music and writing) required, initially, I either had to have inherited wealth, or I became an outlaw. I didn't inherit wealth. It was a romantic though flawed notion. Facing 40 years in prison helped clarify my mistake.

Now, I want to get out of my head, go beyond pure physical prowess, and more into my heart. I realize now that my head, no matter how smart, cannot reach to the soul. I can only connect to my soul through my heart. And I cannot connect to another soul without the passion, mixing heart and soul creates.

I am slowly opening my heart to you, sweet slut. I desire your intellect, your body, your devotion as a slave, but I need the passion of your heart and soul. I sense it there. I feel no impatience with our pace. I'm enjoying the process, the expectation of your replies, a growing trust and attraction. I will follow it wherever it leads.

There's more I want to say. I've only gotten out this serious tone, while there are several octaves of more delicious thoughts of you, singing in my mind. But my brain is mush. Busy week on the business front, only a few hours sleep the last few nights, and woke up this morning with some kind of bug. I'm exhausted. I wanted the pleasure before I went to sleep of knowing you might be reading this, this weekend.

Have faith luv,

Master Galen

PS: I'm including a new story here about a very irate and mean Daddy!

(Note: I included "Daddy's Home" story here.)

Subject: Tired Tiger
Date: Sat. 27 Feb

Good morning Sir. .

I'll try to be more me in this, more relaxed and open as You were.
Thank You for opening Your Heart to me; maybe being tired,
relaxed You more. There is one volatile composer friend of mine I
prefer to meet in this state, for we argue less. It is pleasurable and
good for all of me to write to You also. Our pace is fine, our
interplay, delightful and inspired!

I can just picture the burgeoning pervert sitting on the floor and
looking up women's skirts. Nice early start Sir (smile). Is there one
event in particular, which made You begin to lose interest in casual
play a "few months ago"? I am curious about this, or did the
realization begin to creep up on You like a slow sunrise until You
were blinded by the light?

I realize that we are very similar in many ways. We have both,
through will or circumstance, avoided or been avoided by passionate love and fulfillment of the soul. We are both artists, and if I may
say, dreamers, in the Jungian definition. I am delighted to find you
in the family of the creative where roam my favorite people. Oops,
I'm beginning to sound stiff and formal again!

I am thrilled that we share the same creative passions for writing
and music. But I never use the past tense about artists- the inner
persona of the creator is always there, no matter where our material
travails may lead us. I stubbornly have pursued my artistic dreams
for years.

About a year and a half ago, everything collapsed before a big
round of auditions to Europe. I split with the man I was living with
for several years. I've never been wed and have no babies except
feline ones.

I routinely "settled" all the time, to protect my heart and to keep on
the artistic path. Since passionate love caused me such pain as a

young girl, I decided to break the pattern. When I felt that passion well up- I ran. I thought this was smart since I didn't want to be led by my hormones like so many *hound dogs* I sneered at.

So, I looked at all the sensible things, family background, education, gainful employment/ goals, and how nice he was to Mom. I supplemented my dreamscape with a lover here and there and tried to teach my partners S & M. I had to Switch to do this. Vile necessity!!

This was fine for awhile until the big collapse. Suddenly, no more security, I had to do it all on my own(I just couldn't continue with him and had become involved with heavier and sometimes public play and came home bruised etc.). It was more complicated, but I won't get into all that. I had always had help along the way. I didn't inherit wealth either, but come from a comfortable family that always was there to help cover the tracks of their eccentric and rebellious daughter.

The last year and a half has been a crazy struggle, so much so that I have had little time or inspiration for my art. Since this has about killed me, in many ways, I have to continue this struggle to keep my art alive. It is a crazy life and everyone is worried, but I have to be me. In this respect, I am an outlaw, though not an out and out criminal.

You found D/s on the web how long ago, cruel Sir?

I was attracted to D/s early on, in the convent. Yes, You heard it right - nuns and all - to images of the missionaries and the Indians transfixed with arrows, or tied to posts. Now I know that this turned me on. When I played doctor with other children I always was the patient.

With my parents, I was the doctor, though. In my life, the nuns did strike me, rebellious impertinent sprite that I was. At home, my strapping father (no pun intended- ha ha) did strike me on the ass, pull my hair and generally scare me into trying to obey. I needed a reason, and this brute force only made me wild. He wasn't being

fair. He was just being a domineering Arab male and I sensed the unfairness of it.

Boys were my rebellion and escape though I managed to preserve my maidenhood until adulthood. My first boyfriend used to tie me up a lot and well, the rest is history.

Your eloquent picture of the pain in Your soul, is a description of longing for love. It is noble, touchingly honest. It is great that You uncovered the circuitry of bliss -the heart to the soul. You cannot give the heart without the passionate inspiration. This is rare. I thought that I had found it. He flew away, from the danger of it, from the possible pain and from Himself (this is the worst!) I don't think He admits to himself that His wound is deep and bleeding.

Still I am glad to have felt this for a time. At least I am still capable of it. The mixture you speak of takes the playing, love and giving to new heights. It feels like a religious experience. . . ready to give all, suffer all.

Now I am a lady in waiting (not for Lothaire!). I have no taste for lesser experience now. Mind and body are the minimum now, still without the passion (heart and mind)- the magic just doesn't happen. My mind still cautions me though, telling me that it cannot be.

Did I mention that Lothaire signed his last letter with "luv"! He often also said, "have faith"! Seeing both of these together at the close of your e-mail really sent me. One, or the other would be ok, but both, at this time!! No one in my life until him has written "luv" to me!!! And then You do, a short time after his cautious letter! This is not a coincidence to me, very strange. . . I wonder if it is a cosmic message. Oh oh, she's sounding new age! Even my British best friend never calls me luv. Sometimes he calls me "mate", jokingly. Let the theme of the year be faith.

Would you tell me your Chinese sign if you know it, Sir, pleeeeazze. ??!!??. . .

Superstition does not rule my life, only it is fun trivia and I would

like this tidbit. Thanks. I presume that You did not answer some of the other questions because You did not want to. This is Your prerogative, Dear Lord.

Last night, I dreamt I sang an opera in England and it was a great success. Cut to:(all my dreams being cinematic, you see) the Royal Palace. I am dressed in a great and huge period gown as is every-one else. We are in the past, but this looks like a two floored elegant shopping mall! The music from the opera I just sang in is being piped in from somewhere, and I begin to sing from the second floor of the mall where I am standing.

A couple of people realize that a live voice has playfully joined in with the recorded ones and begin to look up and applaud. There is a great noise then mass confusion suddenly. The Queen has arrived. It is Queen Elizabeth. (our very own) and she is beautifully gowned as we are. I run down the stairs to intercept her passage, curtsey, and lift the back of her gown. She walks so slowly, my liege, I know that I am a handmaiden to her and proudly place myself next to her favorite. I am a lady in waiting.

From the upper floor someone is trying to get my attention. It is a man smiling and pointing at a calendar agenda. I look up and read Matinee Performance. I have another show to sing. I am happy and nod my head. I awake.

I don't know why I shared this with You. Are You good at interpret-ing?

Sorry to hear that You are feeling a bit ill. Crazy schedules and little sleep tend to lower the resistance to bugs. I am also thrilled to be able to distract You enough to stimulate these layers of different thought in You. Thank You for managing to write even though You were out of it. It is a great way to start my weekend. Sweet dreams, Sir. I nurse you with my thoughts.

faithfully,

Arlana

PS: I loved the story, but would personally be too angry/upset/ distracted to function after being called a "fucking goddamn bitch-slutty fuck pig or a stupid cunt"- this is beyond my limits. I don't mind being deprecated when it is softened by things like little, or beautiful or perfect. Slut and whore, I can swallow in small doses.

One day You will write profanities on little pieces of paper and make me eat them right??? Maybe you'll make me write all kinds of vile profanity on a big blackboard until I can't stand up anymore. I don't think I will inspire these expletives in You, even if You are acting in a persona. I would pass out on the spot if anything was hooked onto my clitoris. It is way too sensitive (even all around) I would buck like a wild stallion! I have the world's most delicate nub!

Subject: Hungry Tiger
Date: Sun, 28 Feb

Sweet snake,

So, I'm a Tiger (Chinese sign) and you're a snake. It wasn't a highly recommended relationship, from what I read about the combination on an astrology site. But I've never used esoteric criteria to make decisions, just what my heart and mind tell me, fuzzy and as conflicting as that logic might be when it comes to full spectrum relationships. I believe that's what we are discussing, isn't it?

Love and hate and sex - a jagged triangle. Jealously, possessive-ness, rejection, insecurity – all dangerous bio-chemicals, injected into our thinking and feeling when love goes awry. Good reasons to avoid it.

But if you catch the right wave and your cycle is ready, you can ride it a long time. Maybe not until death, or maybe longer. But that instinct to merge with your soul mate is irrepressible. It won't go

away. It's primordial. A profound spiritual event. The culmination of the soul.

I've avoided it as well a good part of my life. Independence is hard to give up. I take no pleasure in all that drama and pathos, the loss of dignity on either side. I stayed single until my early thirties, when a twist of fate snagged me.

I sense you're in a phase of change, the end of a cycle. I know that is an un-fulfilling and restless place. I accept that part of you sweetheart.

I enjoy the complexity and challenge of your nature. I appreciate that you have a strong intellect and spirited opinion. You are a deep channel submissive, with a craving for extreme excitement and devastation, which is alluring. Your courage and desire to attack what you fear, or surrender to it, were splendidly stated. You're an exotic beauty.

Would we be good for each other, dear? I understand things about you that give this Master's heart longing. I dwell often on the thrill of using you, overpowering you, relentlessly driving you past the pain I would inflict, with tenderness and cruelty, passion and compassion. I revel at the thought of engaging your keen intellect, and sharing culture and other delights. All these aspects keep me on the pursuit.

Now I'm going to give you another side, both from what you've revealed about yourself, and other things about myself, and why this Tiger and snake might have problems. This is meant, not to discourage you, but to bring us to the threshold of our feelings about each other. After this you'll either come crawling, at least a few steps closer, or you'll change your email address and go into hiding. That wouldn't be necessary, though.

These are my judgments: You have high expectations. You group yourself in the elite. I recognize a star quality about you, and I appreciate the woman you've described, but there can be a dark side. This may narrow your objectivity, cause you to make quick

189

comparisons. I will not react kindly to comparisons, subtly or overtly stated.

The Tiger's paw, claws extended, would strike you harshly, his powerful jaws would clamp their authority and threat around your slender neck, his great mass would press down on you, and you would either submit or slither away. But you wouldn't escape unscathed.

I am a unique Master. I am a deep and complex man. I've covered a lot of ground in many areas of my life: I was a musician/composer for over twenty years, have always written, done a lot of photography, studied more than most about art, science technology, philosophy, politics and business.

These things I am may not be what you expect. I am not always "on", expressing my A personality. I can be withdrawn, cautious, cool. A lot will have to do with our chemistry. Being judgmental will not serve you well with me.

I can be quite poor at banter, and clumsy at repartee, usually because I don't feel enough passion to care, even when under attack. When my passions are roused, either love or hate or both, the Tiger's unleashed, or Bull/Taurus, if you prefer. Unconditional love and an eager passion to surrender, releases the Tiger's heart.

I don't dominate to entertain someone. What I do is for my pleasure. Where I take you will be different than others. How I take you will be different. When I'm not in the mood for play, you will need to sense that. Though I expect you to always offer yourself wantonly and with discretion, without getting caught up in rejection. This ability would please me.

Sometimes I can be distracted, or moody, and an eager reception can swing my mood, and click me instantly into Domspace. Although I always am "on" at some level, it takes tremendous energy and concentration to be a good Master. I need time to recharge. I also have many other responsibilities that require my devotion.

But I do believe in the right relationship, energy is generated on both sides, rather than consumed.

You've caught me in a low cycle, sweetheart. This isn't an easy nutshell to describe either. Let's see how you handle it.

My D/s life has been led discreetly. I live in a small city in ****. I had been in a vanilla marriage for 16 years. The marriage was an "accident" arranged by the universe. She was pregnant, I told her no way did I want a relationship. Shortly after, I was busted (I'm a reformed outlaw) for narcotics distribution, facing 40 years.

Between legal fees and confiscation of assets, I was wiped out. I was a wounded animal, and reached out for the only branch offered. I thought well OK, there's something here I need to pay attention to. Maybe I'm supposed to work this out. I married her two months before our first son was born.

The next month at my trial it was discovered that the narcotics agent that busted me, had ripped off the evidence and substituted an inert substance and charges were dropped. Whew! Thank you, Lord.

Within a year I was ready to leave the marriage, but then she became pregnant again. I was given up at birth, didn't have a close relationship with my adoptive father. I was determined, as I realized how important a father is in a boy's life, to stick it out, "until they were older. " I chose what I thought was the lesser of two evils for the sake of my sons.

I am so happy I made that decision. To stay for them, be a father, watch them grow up, participate in so much of their lives. That part was the best and happiest experience of my life.

In my late teens, I had become compelled towards BDSM and knew that my sexuality lay there. Throughout my 20's, I had a lot of sexual adventures, but none fulfilling my D/s desires. I never met a woman so inclined. I continued to study it discreetly, throughout my marriage.

Sexually my wife was mildly submissive. I took her whenever I wanted, not always how I wanted: mild spankings occasionally, forced oral, a few attempts at anal. D/s wasn't her thing. She thought it disgusting. She wasn't a sub.

She was non-negotiable in all areas of our life. She was relentlessly dissatisfied, endlessly critical, took no joy from our prosperous life. I couldn't "beat" her into submission without getting arrested, although I came as close as putting my fist through the wall right next to her head. My ability to maintain, in this emotionally abusive relationship deteriorated continuously, as did my spirit. And I stayed.

When I decided to leave my wife. I also decided it was time to get honest with myself about my sexuality. I got on the net, began answering D/s ads and started corresponding with submissives online.

My extensive background study of the lifestyle over many years, natural passion for BDSM and my inborn Dominant tendencies, proved quite satisfying to both myself and those who submitted to me. While my realtime technique and mechanics have only begun to develop over the last year, my spiritual nature as a Dominant has been refined over many years of thoughtful study.

Not long after I left her, my ex discovered a disk in my office, when I wasn't there, that had the whole story of sharah and Joe and numerous other encounters and stories. She told everyone we knew, gave it the worst spin, suggested I might want to leave town, is using it against me in a long dragged out legal battle of our personal and business assets.

Using falsified testimony, she filed restraining orders, that barred me from of our mutually owned business, and tried to have me arrested for trespassing when I was on the premises, and then again for domestic violence(a FAPA order), though I never laid a hand on her. She also told quite a bit of her "horror story" to my kids. I've been ostracized by many of our friends. It's popped up in several social situations. I had planned on a clean and tidy break. That's

not what happened.

As an entrepreneur, things go up and down. I basically abandoned everything when I left, and until the legal deals are finally resolved my share of assets are tied up. So I've started over.

I've developed a business plan for a web-based business. I just received a provisional patent on a product I invented, I should have a prototype done by the end of the month, then I'm going to shop it for a licensing deal to the top manufacturers in that category. I'm working on another patent as well.

Meanwhile I pick up business as a marketing consultant and multi-media development, as an executive producer. I'm living comfortably now, but still along way from where I was, or where I plan to be within a year.

But this is the nature of being an entrepreneur, no matter what the circumstances. Usually, everything's on the line. It can be a game of nerves, but it's who I am, and I'm good at it.

All these things have been a load on my spirit. Doing it alone, being cut off from all but a few of my closest friends, none of whom share my D/s nature; financial pressures, legal pressures, trying to rebuild my relationship with my boys (now 16 & 14), all have taken a heavy toll.

You've experienced my strong side to some extent in my previous writings. Those are my passions and desires, the writings squeezed right out of my heart and onto the page. Now you know some of my dark side.

Can you handle that sweetheart? It's a package deal, the good with the bad. In truth that's always the way it is, always and forever. I don't need to fly to where you are to find a sub to Dom. I can find that much closer to home. I am seeking the passion, love and power of two souls whose sparks of desire set their world on fire.

If you feel this potential, sweet slut, I'll welcome your response or

further questions, like a hungry Tiger.

Yours,

Galen

Subject: Stretching the borders
Date: Wed, 3 Mar

Sweet slut,

I wasn't able to cover all my thoughts in my last letter. This captures a lot of them.

You've stretched the borders, of what I thought I was seeking in a D/s relationship, sweetheart. I'd abandoned as inconceivable that at this stage, I would find a soulmate that matched my interior spirit. I was planning to find a sweet, reasonably intelligent, attractive, lusty explorer, devoted and sexually servile, a submissive slut girl Friday. I stopped believing these other levels we've broached, would be reachable.

Previously, I had cultivated the idea that unbound intimacy in a relationship started on the foundation of a liberated sexual passion, which in turn would trigger connections and liberation on other levels. I feel we've jumped right over this process.

In my Domspace, I am, by definition ultimately selfish and in control. In subspace, my slave will be ultimately selfless and yielding. This will come through trust. I am cruel in my way, but it doesn't extend to crushing the journey of your noble spirit, because it may detract from having your total attention on serving me. And this is a conflict, because I also do expect to take control, and for my slave to serve me at every level, according to the terms I dictate.

What you've stirred in me is too new at this point for me to understand how this might balance out to where we both were happy.

This doesn't mean that I would be a wimpy Master, or that I would allow you to manipulate me. I would hold sacred your limits, and consider your desires. This could ultimately become a conflict, where either of us cannot compromise or yield to the desire of the other, because of personal ambition or style.

I haven't totally unraveled the mystery of why I degraded my spirit so severely by staying in a poisonous marriage for 16 years. During that period I felt like I had abandoned everything connected to my soul, little by little. I let my spirit erode moment by moment over the years, until I could no longer recognize, barely remember my truth.

Self-sabotage is the greatest tragedy. It's damaged me. I've a lot to repair. That's what I'm doing now. I want you to know how important you have been in this brief time in that process. The noble Tiger had skulked too long in his cage at the zoo. Your encouragement and challenge excite my passion and confidence. I'm loving it, sweet slut. I want and need the stimulation of your spirit.

You asked for instruction on how to be more pleasing. Come from the heart. Show tenderness, compassion, be complimentary regarding my intelligence, creativity, D/s perspectives, stroke my vanity, provide eager expressions of your desire to be used and abused. These all work readily.

But they must be honest. If who I am in your feelings, doesn't elicit this from you naturally, I don't expect or desire hollow accolades. I could pay a prostitute for that service. But you are more and more pleasing, these ways dear, very pleasing, and I can feel how you yearn to give your full expression and I recognize that for both of us, it will take time to trust that who we might be together is worthy of our golden treasures.

I had never abandoned my awareness of my sexuality. Possibly if I had a half way meaningful relationship with my wife, I might have sacrificed it altogether. But there was a point where I finally gave up on the relationship, and developed my plan to leave.

Thus freed in spirit, I instantly rekindled my D/s exploration. I began exploring D/s personals sites, responded to ads, wrote stories, devoured information, started collecting toys, and found a fairly responsive number of subs desiring real time contact.

These I would meet when I traveled on business, anywhere from three days and nights to a one-nighter. None that I cared to get deeper with, though several stay in contact.

Even as a newbie, I was a powerhouse of Dominance and Mastery. It was totally natural. Besides being already well developed mentally, and well studied in many of the arts, I was fearless, adept, and centered. I was in my realm, taking control was my right. I instinctively knew how to strike the sub's deepest chords, applying the flogger, paddle, bondage, ball gags, dildos, vibrators, clamps, clothespins, proper attire, or hot wax with a natural skill.

I found it easy to read their natures and guide them, step by step, threshold by threshold to submissive ecstasy. I soon understood the principle of sweetening the pain as we progressed, lubricating any resistance that still remained.

My pleasure came from turning them on, and the knowledge that I could and did do anything I wanted to them mentally or physically, within their stated limits.

I still consider myself a novice in many areas of technique and equipment, but feel well advanced in the mental and spiritual aspects relative to what I've read of other Dominants and the responsiveness and appreciation of the subs I've played with. But I am still learning and growing in this regard as well.

As for my art quest:

I have great love of literature and the creative arts. As a young man, I aspired to write both fiction and journalism, and did accomplish a handful of short stories, and published a small variety of interviews and features in both national and local publications and public radio.

I had outlined and drafted 2 novels, but the tides of life pulled me to other things.

One of my short stories: "First View of the Blue Water", was about a
teenage boy's close encounter with his 30 year old cousin, an attractive, provocative divorcee from the South. It was my "coming of age" story.

I loved most, though besides telling a story, getting lost in the entrancing rhythm of words.

Some of my favorite books and authors - A Moveable Feast, Hemingway - full of anecdotes about famous authors artists and young lovers in Paris during the 20's, almost all of his short stories; The Magus- John Fowles: a young woman's exploration of her submissive sexual nature. You would love this exquisitely rendered story by one of the best male writers on women (also French Lieutenants Woman); Sons & Lovers - D. H. Lawrence; Steinbeck - Grapes of Wrath; More recently, Get Shorty, Maximum Bob - Elmore Leonard: greatest writer of dialogue I've ever read, street smart characters, will make you laugh out loud as you read.

In general I classify all these as writer's writers, people you might want to study to learn the architecture of good writing.

I was also a musician and composer for 20 years - all original, lyrical, rhythmic jazz, with a quartet, with guitars (me), electric and acoustic bass, drums and congas, and a horn player (alto & tenor sax, clarinet, flute and recorder). I preserved the best of it in an album titled "Diamond Lake". We played a lot of festivals and concerts in this region, and nightclubs.

I also got to perform several special solo performances on a cultural exchange for musicians, on a trip to China in the mid 80's.

Later adding photography from my travels, and works from other photographers, I created multi-projector slide shows, that wove together with twenty-minute sets as part of our group performances.

These were quite moving to the audience, based on their response to the darkened stage and the images and light and music blending and connecting into their consciousness, drawing meaning for themselves like a multimedia Rorschach test.

I've been to China 3 times, hustling up business deals, exploring, and have spent
time in Fujian province, Shanghai, Guanzhou, and of course Hong Kong.

I also lived in Mexico for 6 months in the late 70's and have visited there numerous times. I love both Asian and Latin culture, and found the women, beautiful, alluring (*eyes*), passionate, exotic in both similar and dissimilar ways.

So I know as well the hunger and pain of abandoning my art. It's like sacrificing a child. There is no greater sorrow. Tell me more about your art, dear. I still seem to have left so much unsaid. Other tasks require my attention, now, though none as important as you.

have faith luv

Galen

Subject: The Struggle for Joy
Date: Tue, 9 Mar

Hello my dear. . .

The tone of your last messages was sublimely touching and profound. I guess I had to be brave to have engaged in some of the things I have done and others I would love to do with You. I also have been feeling a sense of admiration for You, and respect. I feel that it is Your due to hear of my vulnerabilities. My psyche should be the romping ground of Your mind and my body; the playing field of Your desires.

The struggle for joy has always been there. I need for life to be large and its colors bold. This has turned me into a rule breaker, rebel and a dreamer, as I mentioned before. When things become dull and normal, I die a little inside and then burn with dissatisfied restlessness. The interest and beauty of my life are upheld by marvelous beings who, like you, are extraordinary, creative and intelligent. Simply, being thus surrounded, I feel special and can at least laugh and cry at it all.

Step into vulnerability darling, I am there too, holding Your hand. Whatever happens, this is good for us. Somewhere it keeps us alive and nourishes our sanity while feeding the furnaces of our respective fires. We burn. I will always be honest with You in this journey. I promise! All that I possess is at Your disposal as a balm, for You are a superior man; the kind that deserves much, as he inspires it.

Please don't let my few limits obscure Your desire or curb Your will. The few things I outlined are just guidelines, but, as You say, in the right circumstances, You could probably get me to agree with anything.

As for the pointed verbal abuse, I don't think I would inspire that in You, as I said before. In a real role playing scene it could be all right, i.e.: tonight you are a prostitute that I have hired and I am bringing you home. Could such theater be the ticket, my roaring Tiger? Just whhhhoa on my little volume knob or I'll huff and puff and bloooww your house down!

Question marks. . . I wonder what You smell like, what the texture of Your skin is? How deep Your eyes and profound your patience? How twisted Your perversion and fiery Your love?

We are different in that I never allow my thoughts to be tainted by the rosy fantasies, no more than You can let those negative scoundrels color Yours. I believe that I will jinx myself if I let myself dream like that. Perhaps Your way is more evolved . This means that You are better and braver than I. Hope can still burn through the murky clouds of all that You have endured. I feel that every-

thing will turn out to be as You wish, because You can still believe in it. You still yearn, and best of all, You have the faith You call up in me.

I keep trying to have this also, but am sometimes so tired. I am weary of dancing the dance and playing the game. It is like a world war that never ends. I perpetually am surrounded, but for what reasons? I become tired of being a sex object or the projection of an ideal to some men, just because of my exterior.

Unlike You, they never bother to explore the inner continent of me, thus missing the entire point. This is why I have become cold and cynical and compartmentalized love and sex. I have found that men work like tenacious little devils to get me, and once they have, fall into comfortable complacency. This passive neglect is more insidious and damaging than the table smashing, wall punching sort of mishandling.

Sometimes I worry about what will happen when I am older. Will I be alone? What of the crowds, will they dissipate? Men can still attract with their power and status in our world. Unfortunately, a woman's status is often directly proportional to her looks. Money does go a long way in that sense also, but women don't buy mates as readily as men do.

Who will be brave and smart enough to get beyond my face and body? The ones who think they love me for what I look like are too vapid to realize that what is charming them comes from inside. That is what makes me sexy. I will never allow myself to fade within. Who will be noble enough to cleave to me when time has altered the shell? My parents have this deep love and friendship, so I know it exists. It is rarer and rarer these days. We cannot dwell on these questions everyday. It could drive you mad.

Just beat me my dear, until Andromedea meets Cassiopia and Your face becomes my Universe as every other care fades away.

love,

Arlana

PS: I'll be back on the computer on Thursday or so. It's kind of a crazy week and I caught a cold. Maybe in sympathy to Yours.

About the "soul-mate matching my inner spirit"- I am glad that I redeemed Your belief in one. I never give up on this point because I require the entire connection to achieve the delectable heaven that I so crave. There are no half measures anymore. Sex only, or empty domination cannot trigger liberation or qualities which were not there to begin with. I can smell this from afar and am politely unavailable most of the time.

I wouldn't have proceeded and spent so much time on us, if I thought that You were not capable of such a voyage. Be selfish, my Sweet, take full reign, let not one breath of mine, one thought remain mine! I like my spirit to break but the noblesse will not be marred because it can't be! I am a sub, but never sub-human.

I know You have understood this, thank you! You don't want to distract me by totally getting me angry and out of my own self. I am only sharing this with You for our mutual benefit, though, I know in principle that this is a mental subtlety that I am speaking of, while most people only delineate physical limits. I am giving You the tools to be aware.

You, whimpy- never!! Your entire tone is one of confidence and ease. Tell me though, how could this ultimately "become a conflict in my own desires"? Is it the verbal thing? Or do You wish to scar me, zap me, humiliate me? I sometimes think that men who over-desecrate a female submissive, unless she is base, are punishing womankind through one martyr. I could be a Joan of Arc, but for a grander cause, *seulement*. (I am smiling now.)

I can help You to find things out about Yourself too, if You'll allow me. You have a lot to get out of You and the load You carry on Your heart and soul is tremendous. I want to be the silky unguent for the warrior's wounds. I am glad that I have put you more in touch with the torrid and powerful creator You are.

Only, I am afraid that this holding out has made me weak in body. As I told you, I think that my body has retained the memory of this year's cataclysms. I have talked to others about this and we have agreed on it. The "innocence is bliss" saying is true, when applied in this way. The innocent sub, who has never felt the pierce of a needle or pinch of clamps, will not be afraid or feel his/her body recoil on instinct. Mine (traitorous body!) does. Sweeten liberally, Sir!

I'll tell you more about my art at another time- but can tell you a bit now. I have two degrees- one in Journalism, and one in Music. I have lived in New York City (4 years- singing pop) lived in Milan for one year (studying opera) and the rest here. I have done movies (I sang on one soundtrack also. This movie was nominated for an Academy Award.) I studied dance while in New York and was also in a few music videos.

I have toured the world twice, once with an opera company and the other, a theater company. I've been to Australia, Tokyo and most of Europe and would love to go to China! I also have sung in my own jazz ensemble, a trio- *moi*, piano and upright bass (who had a tenor sax to blow on the slow sexy tunes). I have a Musical company with other artists and we sing for children.

Now I am in an artistic vacuum due to the $ difficulties of life. I am so grand and impractical for these petty and vulgar fiscal details. I should smarten up because I want to be independent and happy and still remain an artist.

When I feel backed up against a wall I sometimes think the blackest thought. Where are the admiring crowds then? I feel the ticking of the clock and am like a rabbit caught in the headlights. Can I do it? Do I still have it in me? How to manage it all? You see, even preparing for auditions is an investment- coaches, teachers and pianists. Oh. . . I feel a headache coming on.

One day I will sing for You. I have a gorgeous voice still. Now I take a few singing engagements but have not returned to voice

lessons since the big breakup. I teach a few students, pose for sculptors and painters, and do the odd TV show, as I did this afternoon. I dream of returning to my training and doing big auditions and of completing my master's degree in voice performance. I am also working on a project of original music. (a whole other story.)

I am starving now, oh mortal body, and so, will say *adieu* for now. I wanted to end the letter with stars colliding. This, after all is just the beefiest postscript that You ever saw.

I am thrilled You are a musical and literary man. I have read several of the books you mentioned. I love reading. I am a fan of medieval literature (I read old English like people read the paper) and stories, some poetry and lots of fiction. Some authors (I'm not in my Library to find some of the titles I am forgetting) I like: Marvin Peake (very strange) some Kafka, both Brontes, Tolstoy and other Russians like Dostoyevsky and Nabokov (genius), Jean Genest - Querelle de Brest, Our Lady of the Flowers, Rushdie, J. P. Donleavy (very funny),Gabriel Garcia-Marquez, Dumas (love all his stuff), Anne Rice (the most pop- ish stuff that I read- those vampires are sexy! and her sexy "Beauty" Series under A. N. Roquelaure)- the most recent book I have loved is called- The Alchemist- Cohleo- a beautiful fable that made me cry. It is written in the tone of Khalil Gibran's The Prophet and Exupery's The Little Prince,(which is the hit of hits here and in French speaking countries).

I have read many of the *classics* and read historical novels for light entertainment (content- not the weight of the books- most weigh a ton.) I am so pleased that we can share all of this! Like You, I love language and the word. I have several friends who are writers and love to share this love with them.

I speak four languages fluently, *Anglais*, of course, French, Arabic and Spanish, and can understand Italian very well and speak it with reasonable ease. I also read German fluently even if I don't know what I am saying. I can speak it a bit, though I must learn more vocabulary to feel more at ease conversationally. I can identify most languages I hear spoken. I love doing this. It is like music to

me!

What did You think of the snake? hisssss hisssss.

I live with two pussy cats, one whom is leaving soon, I fear, to return to his other keeper.

I'd love to own a Saluki, a kind of Arabic desert sight hound, that is the epitome of elegance and grace for a canine. I fell in love with this breed by pure chance and didn't know until I researched it that it was the dog of the Bedouin Nobility. One day I'd like a snake too.

Oh, oh I must liberate the phone line. #O'=!!*&#"^+!!!

A kiss for You

Arlana

Subject: Cultured wench
Date: Fri, 12 Mar

Dearest,

I am so proud of you my little slut, such an accomplished and cultured wench. I will very much enjoy hearing you sing, whether you be under my whip, or on the stage, or in the car on the way to the coast. You can sing me all the opera you please, but opera is something I know little about. I would enjoy the jazz.

There was something I was not clear about in your last letter. "You don't want to distract me by totally getting me angry and out of myself. "

I do not believe it possible or wise to try total take control of you without having an intimate awareness of your limits (which I feel fairly well versed in sexually), and aspirations. A long term rela-

tionship involves much more than in scene play. The conflicts could be many, not the physical pleasures, so much, but more in the domestic sense for one, or competition between competing interests

If we were living together or spending considerable time together (where/when will that ever occur?), I expect to be served and treated royally. Someone has to manage and take care of domestic duties. It won't be the Master.

You mentioned that you do not think of yourself as a house slave. This might be a non-sexual limit for you. If it was, and I loved you as deeply as I hope to, and I felt you should be elevated beyond this level, I may arrange for a slave/maid to be part of the household (see how practical I am!). But it would be up to you to manage that end. Would an idea like this work for either of us, I don't know.

You have personal artistic aspirations that are very important to you. They define you. I do not begrudge this and would in fact encourage you. But I have my own ambitions as well. Would these compete? Until some of these situations came about, and we found otherwise, I trust they can be managed.

You do help me so much already - healing my spirit, firing my creative soul. Knowing you care enough to offer such devotion and compassion moves tenderly across my wounds and soothes and sweetens me.

Again, I love you for that sweetheart. I stand at the edge of possibility now, as free as I've been in a long time to choose my path. My struggles through this lonely, dark jungle of the last year, nearly did me in. They are not over, but my faith is strong. I haven't done it alone. I have been blessed lately with the coincidence of some very powerful allies and guides, none as lovely as you. You're the only one having to do with my D/s life.

What did you mean by, "What did you think of the snake?"

One part of the fate I am still interested in, is where did you see my ad. How did you come across it. What brought you to that place in

your mind, to peruse ads for Doms that day?

How I long for that kiss, sweet snake.

Keep faith luv

Your Master

Subject: Speedy Sunday
Date: Sun, 14 Mar

Hello Sir!

I'm rushing around, but missed You and had to check. I am awaited at this very moment. Everyone wants to see me before I leave. They sound charmingly provincial! I am only going for 10 days.

I would love to sing jazz for you. I can swing, but I really am hot in ballads and love to sing the *Evil Gal Blues*.

What I meant is that I do not want to get upsct to the point of leaving my submissive space and thus totally out of the scene and out of the right mind-space.

You are so considerate! I am a royal cook, and quite neat, but the big jobs, I am not partial to- managing staff and making sure everything is just so- no problem. I am civilized and tasteful in that respect. I love beauty and order(not obsessively.).

Aspirations make us interesting- we should always encourage one another.

I meant- what did you think of the sign of the snake? The descriptions of the snake's personality and character??

I was just randomly surfing and browsing around. I can't really remember where I was. I think it was ***** BDSM page, but then

again, maybe not. I had not read any ads before (except a few random ones in news groups) and have not read any since. I was not searching for Doms or anything. . . but , when I saw where I was, I decided to scroll through them to see if any seemed intelligent and enticing to me. Yours was so short and almost quiet- in its own way. . . I didn't think, I just acted (perhaps this was Divine intervention) and wrote to You.

Hope you will like that kiss, darling Sir.

x o Arlana x o

Subject: Travel advisory
Date: Mon, 15 Mar

Dearest Sir,

I got Pasha rising and Hungry Tiger, which I just sent You a reply to…just checking that everything's getting through OK.

I look forward to Your next communication. I just wanted to let You know that I will be in Mexico from the 26th of March until the 4th of April for some scuba diving and relaxation. The winter really is too long here. I will answer any more questions if You like.

As I am going to a primitive little island and staying where there is not even a phone, I will not have access to a computer. I apologize for this hiatus and hope that it will not dampen things. I could later e-mail you a snapshot of me in diving regalia or while sipping a *Pina Colada* or petting an iguana, or any pose You would like to have me take while in Mexico. I am glad for the time to dream and the time to long for you

bye for now.

Arlana

Subject: backtracking
Date: Mon, 15 Mar

Dear Sir,

Sorry for this third note in one night, only I was re-reading Universe of Passion and wanted to ask you about what you meant by:

"I am not an experienced player, but I'm curious and attracted to electro-play and fire-play scenes I've seen in S/m porn. I wouldn't attempt them without proper training etc. . . "

Do you mean that You are not an experienced edge player??? Please clarify. Thank You.

Also, I owe You a couple of more answers myself. Ok, this is the last one for tonight.

truly,

Arlana

Subject: Tiger Shark circling an isle in Mexico
Date: Mon, 15 Mar

Dear daughter,

I'd prefer you here, petting my iguana, while I sip a *Pina Colada*.

Mask and snorkel - have to ad that to my toy collection. I could picture your face squeezed by the mask, your succulent lips clamped around the mouthpiece, naked except for your slave hue radiating from subspace.

No, you'd have fins on, and I'd make you run in that clumsy way,

and I'd chase and catch you and throw you down to the sand at the edge of the surf, and prey upon you like a Tiger shark on a sleek furred seal.

See how you affect me, sweet slut. The wild man in me begins to stir from hibernation.

You understand why I am cautious, but perhaps you are also beginning to glimpse into the depths of my soul and it stirs something in you. Love is a strange and rare chemistry. Without it, my power and passion are diminished. I want and need to feel that sense of pure joy. I've sought and fought that connection all my life. Can passion meet passion and align, create harmony, bliss, and journey courageously to the darkest reaches of Eros?

Perhaps there are a lot of reasons, perhaps most to do with my own slow responsiveness, but you hold back from me as well, dear. This is a very cautious dance. But you keep responding, and this heartens me greatly.

A part of us are like two worldly diplomats in the "cold war" carrying on delicate and complicated negotiations before the two Superpowers can meet. We negotiate your surrender! Your struggle was brave, but Master fights dirty and won handily.

That was my meaning: not an experienced edge player, but seeking to learn. I've been fascinated by slaves in electro-torture scenes from SM porn videos, the exquisite expressions on the slaves face as the juice is applied(weg). I'm just such a twisted sadist, don't you think!

As a Master I enjoy entering that state of objectivity, a pensive immersion into deep Domspace, while playing with the slave.

Perhaps you will awaken tomorrow and this will be there for you. It is my pleasure to greet you as your day begins, sweetheart. We should start talking about what is left to discuss before we consider meeting. And yes, I want you to be very cautious in all your online communications.

Master Galen

Subject: You Tiger Shark!
Date: Tue, 16 Mar

Good morning Sir,

I just happened to sleep here last night and was on the computer to
see Your message come in. What a nice way to wake up. Thank
you.

It is interesting what you say about love. It is also a connection that
I have fought all my life. What bliss to give in once in awhile
tough. Can passion that has created harmonious bliss be sustained
though? That the answer might be no, haunts me. No one has gone
there with me yet. They run or fall into complacency. I rage and
burn silently. It is better to wait than to settle.

Perhaps You interpret my polite literacy as holding back. I do not
mean to do this. Please instruct me on how to let go a bit more to
please You. I love your analogy about the cold war…Superpowers.
. . I like thinking of myself in that light. I e-mailed a dive shop in
Isla Mujeres to inquire about diving to see the sleeping sharks. I
think You are more dangerous than they! Fight dirty darling, that's
the best way. purrrr. . .

I just read a warning about electric currents this morning. A little
jolt can be fatal in certain circumstances. I read that one man put
probes from a tens machine in his lover's anus and in his while he
fucked her. Their tongues even tingled when they kissed! Sounded
interesting, but my experiences with electricity have not been that
great so far. I'll tell You about them one day.

I'll be back at this terminal soon, Saturday or so. I do not live here,
as I think I mentioned before. I am taking your story with me in my
purse and want to read it while in public, in a cafe, so that my face

210

will show the pleasure of the torrid story and people will wonder. I will wear no underwear and hope to feel the moisture coursing down my thighs as the excitement travels from my mind to all of my unbruised hungry body.

torridly,

Arlana

Subject: So much to say
Date: Wed, 17 Mar

My lovely slut,

I have so much to say to you sweetheart. You're exquisitely complex (like me). You have suffered and are suffering (like me). You are courageous and noble, like Joan of Ark if she was a submissive little slut. You have a sublime sense of humor: "little pieces of paper", though it does give me some ideas for the future! I respond so strongly, to your nature.

I've had enough experience with fate, to believe in fate as much as I can believe anything else. Why couldn't we both find something powerful here. We've hit some deep chords. I feel a building compassion for you, a respect, an appreciation that you're brave enough to reveal your vulnerabilities, and remain intelligent.

You express yourself wonderfully, you have the soul and emotion of the artist within you. You're a divinely submissive slave girl, with exotic tastes in BDSM, the passion of an explorer. How could I be just mildly interested in someone who possesses all that. I understand how hard you are struggling for your joy, your truth. When we're inspired, nothing can prevent creation.

I want to do this differently than I have in the past. I want to get everything clean and clear before we meet. I have to take this step into vulnerability, with you or without you, to get where I want to

be in a relationship. I want an intimate ally, a submissive with whom I can trust to offer respect and love unconditionally, with the freedom to provide insight, and creative and supportive feedback.

I require the intelligence and integrity which you possess, and I would be stupid to turn down wisdom. I need all I can get. It's all about trust. And healing. And freedom. Relinquishment. When it's right, it all combines and merges and balances at the deepest levels of the D/s relationship we seek.

What would you and I be like together in a D/s relationship? I wouldn't try to define it, now. I can catch glimpses of it. See shadowy forms emerging in the primordial ether. I would think of it as an evolving work of art. I know what I need. Where we might differ, there are creative and practical ways to get what you want, without compromising one's limits or integrity.

But when I gain your complete trust, you will eagerly do whatever I tell you to do, without fear (you'll still get the pleasurable kind), doubt or resistance (from your soul, your body can resist all it wants, it amuses and excites me to watch you struggle in vain!).

The question marks are the practical side, and that's a topic for later. I have a number of other items I will respond to later from your recent replies, which I enjoy greatly, reading into the very soul of this captivating love snake. By the way, Tiger is my Chinese sign.

have faith luv,

Galen

(*Note: After not hearing from Arlana for almost 2 weeks, I finally received this letter after Arlana sent it initially to the wrong email address – because of a typo. A lot of "cyber karma" followed this "typo" that led to a major misunderstanding later*).

Subject: Bye for a little while my dear

Date: Fri, 26 Mar

Dearest Sir,

I just wanted to let You know that I am thinking of You and have missed and will miss our contact, while I am in Mexico. I am leaving at dawn tomorrow morning. I will be back in town on the 5th and online a couple of days later as I already am pretty booked for my first couple of days back.

I was dismayed to see that I mistakenly sent this letter to the wrong address and received a stinging "Earth to Arlana" message from the inadvertent and irate recipient who urged me to "get it right" as I seemed to put so much "time and energy" in my messages.

I feel that You are part of me. I feel You inside of me, and all around me at times. It is wondrous and voluptuous. I will print Your picture and carry it with me. I will compose a segue to the naughty nun story. I bet she is hiding a lot under that habit!.

Sometimes, bits of phrases You wrote, cross my mind like deer traversing a highway, startling and thrilling me. Writing this, I feel a strange tightness in my belly. Desire can hurt. I wonder how Your voice will sound, how Your hands will feel.

devotedly,

Arlana

Subject: Mythic Virgin
Date: Mon, 29 Mar

Well dear slut,

Thank you for the sweet thoughts before your departure and the explanation of your long absence. If I hadn't heard from you by the 26th, I would have believed the snake left the clearing, slithering

back into the safety of the jungle.

The thought hurt (deeply) to have had you just disappear, without explanation or discussion, or ever hearing the "Evil Gal Blues".

You are such a lovely, lively, tender, sexy, soulful, sinful snake! I was touched by the romance of taking my picture with you. I love romance. You are in my heart as well, sweetheart. I am missing you, craving you.

We've barely touched our sexual D/s side. That feels very special to me, as that part's always been the lead and priority for me, denying any attachment, but lust and power. This odyssey with you is mythically virginal, delaying that physical gratification, forestalling your training as my pleasure slave, and mine as your Master.

As an aside, I'm not hung up on a "topping from the bottom" thing. For me, feedback, suggestions, debriefings are all helpful information, and if I don't like what I'm hearing, I'll just give you my stern, patriarchal, "Silence, slave!" look, and you'll instantly obey~ weg (wicked evil grin).

I feel this deeper love and attraction, this tension between us growing little pearls of joy in my heart. I've never met a woman who offers all that you do. I offer my heart as your refuge from that tyranny of ignorance that veils others seeing the beauty beneath your lovely skin. Shed your skin for me sweet snake, and I will embrace the raw beauty of your soul.

I looked up some info on a Chinese astrology site: Snakes - sexual, exotic, intelligent, star quality, but can be dangerous when cornered.

Chinese horoscope '99 forecast: Tiger. . . auspicious year for love; snake. . . romance in the air, could meet love of your life. Sounds promising.

Until I met you, I felt like the moon sometimes, never showing my dark side. I've felt the greatest liberation, baring all to you, risking judgment, rejection, and though my main emphasis was to "come

214

clean", to have received your compassion and trust and desire, has been the greatest gift.

We are soulful allies, and that is a great gift, an ally as alluring as you. I know we've both been in a down cycle. I think we both recognize in each other the truth of our individual power, passion, dedication, intellect, eroticism, and creativity. I think of the magic the alchemy of "us" could create.

Will meeting each other break this spell? What would this mixture of equality, respect, encouragement, support and D/s produce. How will we define your relinquishment? I'm ready to risk and accept the consequences of finding out.

My practical mind wants to dwell on the 100 or so reasons why this won't work between us, long term. No doubt your mind plays similar tricks on you. Where would we live? Could we stand being together on a day to day basis? Could we stand being apart for long stretches, etc?

Then there are other levels : Are you a poisonous snake? Should the Tiger be cautious? Will you wind up being annoying? Will I wind up being boring or dull? Can we trust enough, love enough to commit to dealing with any adversity? Not running away when things aren't going smoothly? Total commitment. Without that risk, we won't sustain and grow our passion. I'm not going any other way this time.

I say this knowing that I have felt your desire and love for me, compassion, tender emotion, and it stirs a warmth in a cold part of my heart. This is my work now. Thaw out my heart, lower the shields, raise the temperature.

I've been going deep into this process. I've aligned with some very close allies, who are creating an environment where I can safely explore all this hurt and fear of abandonment, and other issues that lock me up at times. It's been very powerful and emotional to explore these dark caverns. Starting with being abandoned at birth.

I first connected with this in my mid thirties, when I discovered my birth mother's name - Mary ****, and that she had named me Galen Robert ****. I then retrieved the non identifying information about her allowed by the adoption agency. She was 30 years old 5'2", etc.

But with just this tiny bit of data, a picture of her started to form in my mind. I began to think about her circumstances and feelings in the context of 1950 America, and all the judgement, shame and isolation she must have suffered. I realized how intimate I had been with this woman, had grown in her belly for nine months, inherited her DNA, touched the skin of her thighs after this tremendous struggle we shared to be born, heard her voice screaming her motherhood as I arrived in the world.

For the first time in my life I thought: "I have a mother. " A real person, who looks like me, and a father, and aunts, uncles, nieces, nephews, maybe even brothers and sisters. A complete ancestry of me, an entire heritage, an identity that I knew nothing about. It was a profound moment.

It's interesting that I have no legal right to my biological identity, the culture feeling it's more important to conceal the shame of unwed mothers and their families. This was a convenient solution to the worry and embarrassment those pesky, unwanted children might cause, in case they ever got curious about who the hell they were.

I'm doing some deep emotional work with issues I've carried around and buried, and which have haunted my life and led me generally to flee from commitment. My shadow took over. I became one of harsh judgments, I could hurt deeply with my brutal honesty, the first to flee, rather than do the work, and it nearly shattered my quest for the tender, rapture of love.

I am grateful and blessed for the opportunity to do this work, now. I'm on the path of the warrior, lover, magician, king. The greatest battle, facing my shadows - shame and guilt and every fear hiding within me, shadows sabotaging my nobility. My goal is to become a better man. My mission: the complete liberation of my spirit to

freely offer my gifts to the world

I have little concern about our compatibility sexually. I am a lovingly sadistic Dominant, and I will extract your total submission to me, exceeded only by previously agreed upon limits. Sounds like fun, doesn't it!

I resonate to your exotic charms, sweet snake. It will be an exquisite exploration. Intellectually I think we will do well, though we've definitely mined some different channels. You have a breathtaking scope of culture and history. I swerved over the last 20 years towards, entrepreneurism, technology, science, futurism, and of course, BDSM.

But you'll have to be a good listener, no a great listener. I tend to be a big picture thinker, and I like to think about things. You need to be able to keep up and devotedly and respectfully pay attention while I'm gathering all the pieces together. Not that I wouldn't accept input. But you need to be able to sense when I'm on a roll, and don't care to be distracted, and when I need feedback.

But my point to all of this - I am committed to developing a soulful D/s relationship, to put everything in my heart at risk to live a fully passionate life with my partner. I sense a yearning in you sweetheart, equal to my own.

At this point dear slut, the only way to know if we can bring to life what we've brought through this cyber world is to meet. Whatever issues you face before you are ready to meet, I want you to address them directly. I'm ready to get this show on the road, wherever it may lead. Are you ready for that, sweetheart.

Con't: Friday - 4/2

Dear one,

I am struggling to feel you, now. So much time and distance between us. Can it be reasonable to expect a lifetime relationship

bridging that empty span that stretches beyond the horizon, beyond my belief at times?

Can I believe this beautiful captivating cyber snake can mate in the flesh, become the undying love of this data Tiger? I am so hungry for that connection, sweetheart, to risk the danger of it. It's escaped my grasp all my life. Until now, perhaps.

More shit flying from my ex. Her lawyer sent mine a copy of an ad and photo of mine she tracked down on a BDSM site. She's trying to portray this as evidence in a legal effort to prevent me from having the right to have my sons spend the night, based on the danger they would face being exposed to my sick, disgusting, brutal treatment of women.

I remember a good friend of mine commenting before I had to decided to leave my marriage - "the only thing worse than being married to R, would be getting divorced from her." Got that right!

If our love would be true, all this gloominess, battered trust, and loneliness would dissipate like fog, when the sun catches it. You know what I really need right now, dear. I need two weeks of 24/7 love. The tender passionate touch of a woman, every need of mine being served royally, a daily regimen of debauchery, deep moist kisses, listening to your eyes speaking to me in all those exotic languages, your hands caressing, your sweet voice soothing, body pressed close to mine, passion spent.

Just me in the middle, surrounded by your gentle loving heart. That would feel like more love, more passion than I've felt in my life-time. Actually, a long weekend would do wonders! This would be the greatest gift, the most noble service you could provide as my slave, right now, dear snake.

The Tiger requires your assistance to rediscover the joy and fire of emotional love. Straight from the heart. This rejuvenated Tiger would then feast on you every moment.

Speaking of feasting on you. I want to understand more about your

body's retention of the memories of intense pain and torment, and now, against your will so to speak, flees from it. I don't understand precisely what this might mean in our play. You would have my devotion and sensitivity to guiding you through it. Perhaps, to "sweeten liberally" is the key.

I'm not worried about it, I will also be poring my love and my heart into yours. You will feel safe, protected. I know I will find you so pleasing, it will melt me into a tender Tiger. But once soothed and assured, I will continue to take you through higher thresholds of erotic torture, submission and obedience. My desires will prevail, but I am patient.

I'm trying hard to ignore the ache of missing you, my dear. Sometimes I am very good at it.

keep faith luv

Galen

Subject: Sunday night
Date: Sun, 4 Apr

Welcome home my sweet *senorita* snake. I hope you're well rested, baked and content to carry on. I've missed you and my heart is at a standstill, until I hear from you sweetheart. Send me a picture of you on the beach (naked?!!). But more than anything else, tell me how you are.

keep faith luv

Galen

Subject: I've returned from Mexico

Date: Mon, 7 Apr

Hello Sir,

I'm sending You this before speaking to my Mom, or calling my
best friend, (who has my cat, which I adore) to say hello and tell
you that I came home safely late last night. I thought of you and
have missed our contact. I look forward to hearing from you soon.
I hope that all is well with You and that we can resume as before.

all my love,

Arlana

*(Note: the following is the text from an e-card I sent Arlana shortly
after she returned from Mexico.)*

Dear slut,

There are times now that my desire burns for you, to take you,
enslave you, torture your flesh and watch the pain grow brightly in
your eyes before they fade into surrender to your Master. I want to
grab that black hair and force your face down, and use your mouth
like the cunt I intend it to be. I'll bet you're one hot little cock
sucking slut, aren't you sweet girl! I know your body thinks of me,
begs for it, wanting it so bad. I want you here now, kneeling in
expectation as my slave, longing to impale your mouth on the steely
shaft of your Lord Pasha's scimitar. Keep faith luv.
Thinking the nastiest thoughts. . . Master Galen

Subject: Good Friday
Date: Fri, 9 Apr

Hello Sir,

Thank You for the card, it made me hot. I just returned from
Church where I sang by candlelight. I have a gig out East this
weekend. I'll be back on Sunday night. I am eager and hungry to
hear from You.

Passionately,

Arlana

Subject: Ooops!
Date: Fri, 9 Apr

Oh, oh! I sent this letter below to the wrong address and just got an
irate e-mail from the surprised recipient. I am sorry. It must have
seemed like I was incommunicado for so long! Here it is darling
and sorry.

*(Note: The letter Arlana sent me was actually not what she thought
it was.*
She meant to just send an attached photo with a note from her.
Instead what I
 *received was a letter to her from a professional fetish photographer
who had "shot" her recently. I was just a little jealous!)*

Hi Arlana,

I apologize for my incommunicado-ness. I've become kind of e-
mail shy and cut way down on any sort of serious correspondence.
Please excuse me.

Well, I heard you were in LA and made a delightful impression.
And it sounded like you were carrying a picture of me. But maybe
you just e-mailed one later. I wonder what picture that is. I'm
better off staying behind the camera and keeping the beauties like
you in front. I am just not photogenic.

I'm sure you have no shortage of latex pictures of yourself to submit. But if that is not an opportunity you have pursued by now, perhaps we should seriously pursue it. I need a new latex project.

Many of the pictures I do have of you are quite lovely. Although, I don't know what to do with most of them. I'm sending one to Secret Magazine. As far as I can tell, and I could be wrong, there's not much of a market in fetish, lesbian or men's magazines, for that particular soft session we had. Some nice portraits but that's about it.

One particular problem was the cosmetic cover-up of various bruises and such. It ended up looking like you were covered with blotches of calamine lotion, you know, that pink stuff you can use for mosquito bites. It took on an off-color reflection of it's own.

In hindsight I realize that it would have been more interesting to have had you leaning over your dresser and in front of the mirror applying lipstick with those massive butt bruises in the foreground. I think that would have been a fun picture. Oh well, live and learn.

What's intriguing about you is that you can play the domineering, haughty diva just as convincingly as the kneeling slave. That might be an interesting study for future reference.

I don't know what images you've seen. Here are a few that I've already done that I can easily enough send along now.

Yes, I hope we can get together again. Please don't take my lacking staying-in-touch skills as an indication of how I really feel about you.

Warm regards,

M

Subject: S O R R Y

Date: Sat, 10 Apr

Good morning Sir,

Oh! Do I ever feel like a computer dummy right now. I was trying to send you a lovely photo that was included at the end of this letter and I seemingly did not succeed. Instead You only received the dammed letter and not the photo, when it should have been the other way around.

The note is just what the photographer wrote along with them. S O R R Y. I guess I need a little technical support. And I thought that I was sending you a nice little surprise. I guess I deserve punishment for this one.

Please don't be too mad. I'll figure it out. Please write me some more. Did you get the e-mail prior to this last fiasco of a note? I'll be thinking of you while I am gone. Please do not allow my time away and this oversight to cloud our beauty and what is to come.

yours,

Arlana

PS: The guy is a freelance photographer. The community here was all excited to have him here in town, about 8 months ago, because he has published in famous magazines. Everyone and their dog has been photographed by him, especially at our local Fetish Club. He asked me to do a shoot and I said yes.

My bum was bruised from the playing a few nights before. That and the "softness" of the shots make them unusable for publication, but I thought you might like one or two, (nothing more than breasts showing). I'll work on this for a while, but have to pack as my flight leaves at 2:15 pm. Bye for only a short little while, dear.

x o

Subject: Let's continue
Date: Mon, 12 Apr

Good morning,

I trust you got my last note, and understand the mix-up. I have figured it out and am sending you the photo I was attempting to send in the first place. I hope you like it. Let us please get back on track. I'm waiting. Let me know if You like it and if it worked!!!

with love and faith,

Arlana

Subject: Our connection
Date: Wed, 14 Apr

Dear Arlana

Something's not right here, sweetheart. I have felt so much for you, starting to glow within me, and felt something similar from you. This slow but steady willingness to trust, and ultimately love.

So it doesn't make any sense to me that I would not have heard more from you than your brief hello, and other note, as sweet as it was and several misguided missives. My letters while you were gone, were quite sincere and open. I feel they deserve your fullest response, dear.

I need to hear from you. I need that connection from you. I need to feel you. I want to loose my passion on you, but this long absence of your passion, causes me to question whether I can sustain my desire in this awkward dimension of time and space.

That's why I suggested us talking about meeting. I don't want this to just be a cyber fantasy. It's too much energy to expend. I need to

know what you're feeling, right now. Just the truth, from your gut. What do you feel for me? Do you believe that we might be destined to manifest this bond, and devote ourselves to our own special version of a loving exuberant D/s relationship?

You know this is what I seek. If that's not happening for you, then there's no reason to continue, on that level. Maybe that's not what is meant for us. Perhaps there is some other connection between the Tiger and the snake, more allies than lovers. I don't know.

I do know that I feel a lot of something for you, dear. So, I need you to check back in, and tell me what's in your heart.

keep faith luv

Galen

Subject: missing you too
Date: Thu, 15 Apr

I miss you also, sweet Sir!!

Your letter moved me so much, I cried a bit after reading it. I long to have quiet time in front of any computer, so that I can answer You in peace and quiet, slowly, fully and at my leisure.

I am thrilled and apprehensive about our meeting. I have not lived internet horror stories, only heard about them, and Yours. I trust You. You have become a part of me. I am ready to discuss the particulars of this with You.

What do I feel right now??? Hummm. . . In my own explorations, I have found out that I flee. I have run away from love, intellectualized emotions and waged war with men I've been personally involved. Like you, I am working on all of this. I determined that what I truly want deep down is: love. It is what we all want darling, is it not? I'm even figuring out where the submissive part of me

came from.

At the moment, I cannot tell what will happen with us. Sure, I have hopes and feelings, (I am smitten with You! so far and D/s and love is the headiest mixture- how could I not want that?) but I don't let them run amuck.

I thought I told you that I am superstitious about wishing for something too much in matters like this and sort of jinxing it. So, I live day by day and reign in my hopes. We can't predict the physical, can we? We certainly have laid a good foundation though.

How will the chemistry be? How will you taste? How will I feel to you? Will we thrill one another, and mesh all the other variables? I'm nervous with Your "give me your gut feeling" question, "or else there is no reason to continue"- this is premature. How can we stop what has not begun?

You are bravely seeking love, even after what You have been through.

I feel You all around me sometimes and will take whatever happens as the adventure of us. I cannot say where that will lead. I also am a thinker and like to look at the big picture, but for affairs of the heart - I leave a lot to nature, faith and fate. Things grow in their own time also, we just water the earth around us- and we are doing a great job.

Sometimes our mail gets crossed and sometimes I mistakenly have sent it elsewhere with a slip of the finger. I am often under pressure and having to use someone else's computer quickly and hence the errors. I am looking into getting a new hard drive/modem at home so that I can get onto the web in peace and in my own space. I have all the rest- right now my system is too primitive to sustain the web.

Please bear with me! I hope to resolve this soon. I am also frantically preparing for an audition the 17th of this month and will be away for a gig this weekend. Back to the airport!

I think of You all the time and am eager to meet with You also. We do have a lot to talk about, don't we?

love,

Arlana

Subject:
Date: Sat, 17 Apr

Arlana,

I feel if I hide the truth of what I feel, worried that I might jinx it, I hold back the very spark that ignites passion. Being uncertain or unclear is a different matter. I also believe though, that being uncertain can be not accepting what my heart is telling me. It might be different for you.

Thank you for the picture. You are so beautiful, my snake.

I'm going to let you set the pace for a while and see what happens.

Galen

Subject: Pace
Date: Sun, 18 Apr

Galen,

I am puzzled by Your message and new resolve. Am I to be in the driver's seat then? It's funny that we both have opposite views on "jinxing". I believe that if I let myself dream something or fantasize about a person and what might be- then I will jinx it. You feel that You will jinx it if you do not reveal it. I guess we have both ends covered.

So, you are holding back the spark that would ignite the passion? Is it the uncertainty You speak of which stalls you, or a fear of letting go, or being hurt?

What of the effusive letter while I was gone? Has Your desire to take this to another stage also passed into a state of patient observation? Do I take it from there, or from before that, sweet Pascha?

Is the passing of the reigns a way to access my desire for You? for us? Perhaps You are testing me, or lying back and letting me do the work - like lavishing You with my mouth and body as You languidly lay there, not touching me.

Sigh. . . without Your words the conduit to You seems dim, still the light is there. I have to relinquish the computer now!! It makes me so mad that I could scream. I am rehearsing for an audition on Saturday and working long hours in preparation. I wish You could hear me sing.

I miss you.

Arlana

Subject: My serve
Date: Mon, 19 Apr

Arlana,

If I serve you the ball in tennis, that does not put you in the driver's seat other than the ability to choose to return the serve or not, and what type of shot you might attempt, assuming you have the reaction time and coordination to get it over the net.

I haven't held back sparks or anything else, until my last note. What of my effusive letter? What has been the response to it? I felt that since before you went to Mexico, your passion was retarding. And this I see as a reflection of your leisurely pace and tone, of that

non-jinxing sort, or second thoughts, and a very busy lifestyle.

For myself, I feel we've gotten off track. A month ago, we were involved in this escalating passion and soul. I've felt overall, your letters since then have been oops's and sorry's and busy got to go.

I am not in a state of mind to put out so much and get so little in return. So I am upset and angry, and protective as well. I am negotiable but I will not compromise on what I ultimately will expect from a submissive for a long-term relationship.

I feel your busy lifestyle and attitudes might be an issue between us. If I am mistaken, feel free to correct me. I already have enough battles taking my attention and energy. If I am to keep this channel open, it needs to be energizing and fierce.

I brought up a number of feelings and issues in my letters while you were gone. You've dodged them, while asking me to rekindle the spark. Until you return the serve, honestly and with passion, I have nothing to offer.

That means if you have questions, doubts, issues, fears feelings or anything else that stands in the way of or encourages our meeting, this is the task at hand. I stated this clearly in a past letter, and I am disappointed that you have not addressed them to this point.

I'm trying hard not to say something I'll regret, here. Still trying to get it to come through clean, and from the heart, sans guilt trips and all that other shit. I don't want to coerce you or hurt you(well, that's not entirely true!).

I am of course, protecting myself. I've taken a beating this last year, and it's still raging. I received a call the other night from my very vanilla sister in Chicago. She's totally flipped out. She just got a copy of my ad and photo on ****. com, with a letter from my ex. My ex, out of her concern for me!!, wants my sister to come to my aid, and have me seek help for my sexual psychosis.

My sister demanded to know what the hell's going on. Fortunately,

after I explained it to her, she supports me, as weird as what I am into sounds to her. I stuck by her when our family and hers shunned her when she left her husband. We have always been loyal to each other that way.

Plus I just found out my ex stopped paying all our joint business debt that was in my personal name. Now I'm getting harassed by collectors, and have several of my personal lines of credit effected. Off to the lawyer again. I put a restraining order on my ex, that prohibits her from discussing my sexuality with anyone except a counselor. Next I'm going back to court to get some of our jointly held assets released to cover these debts, until the final resolution still 4 months away.

I greatly miss your passion. I've needed and wanted it. I don't want to abandon this effort. Are you not intuitive enough, paying enough attention to understand my needs? Have they not been clearly stated? What of your second sense and the continent of your heart? And yes, as I've already stated, I do need lavishing right now.

Galen

Subject: Feeling Sad
Date: Mon. 26 Apr

Dear Galen,

I have taken a long time to think before answering because I didn't want to write anything that I would regret later. I was upset and saddened by Your last reply. I thought we were somewhere else. Still, I am glad that You expressed Yourself.

Please listen to me when I clarify a few things with you. I am answering from memory as there have been some computer problems. I regret to hear of things that have been going wrong for You and realize that this is probably a factor in Your mood and reactions. I hope all this soon passes- and it will. Don't allow it to poison the

rest of what is good in Your life.

I feel that You have not been hearing me, or perhaps are not willing to do so at this juncture. I explained several things to You after I returned, joyfully, to contact You even before speaking to MY OWN MOTHER. No mention of this from You.

Did this not mean anything? Did this skid off Your reality like a child's rock skips over the surface of a summer lake? Look back at the replies of April 6, April 8 and the others and REALLY h e a r what I said to You.

Remember me telling You about the problems I was having with finding uninterrupted time at the computer to sit and write to You at leisure. Remember how I spoke of LONGING to do that?? Does that sound like I was willfully neglectful?

I am sorry that I did not address the feelings and issues you raised while I was away. I thought, in all truth, that they were musings and not direct questions. I always wait for Your direct lead, as a matter of respect. Even the "are you ready for that sweetheart" did not have a question mark after it. Only the paragraph beginning with questions on intense pain and torment appeared to me to be direct queries.

I attempted to touch on some of what you raised, but felt that I received no reply, no prompting me to continue. You could have just asked, my dear. I find that we are invariably disappointed when we set up "tests" in the mind, that the other person must pass. I do not let this type of dynamic invade my happiness and I will not participate in these one way trials of the mind. I am intuitive, yes, a mind-reader, no.

It hurt me that You feel that You put so much in and get so little in return. I so fumed over that one that I almost thought of not reply-ing at all. Still, I am civilized and know You deserve some explana-tions, even if it all stops here. My time is precious and important too, as important as Yours. I have put in a hell of a lot of time for You.

231

As for Your complaints about my "busy" lifestyle…how can You say such a thing? Do You want a dark stagnant pool or a clear rushing stream? If You have enjoyed me until now, it is because I am vigorous, alive and challenging. You won't get "energizing and fierce" from an agoraphobic wallflower, or are You upset to see me striving for things outside of the universe of You?

When I give myself it is a gift and should be that much more satisfying for the Dominant to know He has conquered a vital and dynamic being. I am not less important because I am the sub. My life and concerns are real and should matter in the scheme of things. I was surprised at Your lack of understanding on that point.

You say You are generous. This is an area in which it was needed. For all men's talk of love, some forget that it is about giving and suffering long. This is an analogy for generosity and patience.

I understand that this is a trying time for You and that You may lash out at females around You, because one is trying to do a number on You. (see, I consider Your current reality and even the psychological framework of Your personality, without making You feel that I am using your confidence as a weapon). Is it possible that Your fears of neglect and abandonment were running high? If so, I would guess that many of your reactions are due to that.

For the matter of needs, we all have them. What about mine? You have made me feel that only Yours matter. Offensive attacks like that just scream for a defensive reply. I have abandoned this type of outdated, destructive dynamic a long time ago. You left me in the dark to wonder, waste time fretting while You tested me. No suggestions about my computer woes and longing to write to you, no "good luck" or "break a leg", for my audition.

This is hurtful, yet I did not become upset until I received Your last letter and read Your complaints. As You bemoaned Your needs and wants, I was in the shadow of Your eclipse. In fact, the upsetting communication from You did haunt and distract me from the task of my audition. Did You have any idea? The timing could not have

been worse. I told you that it was on the 17th and the upsetting letter came on the 14th, and I got it on the 16ᵗʰ. It couldn't have been more ill timed.

If You had been forthright and clear as soon as You began to get upset or angry (offshoots of fear, I think- not weakness, just the utter unwillingness to be injured). You would have asked and gotten a satisfying reply directly. Everything was all You, even if You thought of asking about my doubts, fears and feelings. But what about what went before? Did You even hear anything or care about what was going on in my world?

The word "negotiable" offended me greatly, in reference to Yourself. Are You a commodity? What is this, a business deal?? Have You misplaced your Artist's soul? I think that the darkness took over here and shadowed Your nobility. The "complete liberation of the spirit" that You crave, involves greater delicacy and tact than this.

A great man is one who cares about the smallest others (let alone one that You say You care for) and all that they might feel or suffer. These are the great beings on earth. They uphold the dignity of others. In personal life, I find it criminal to trudge on the other person's honor or to belittle their importance through self-indulgent tunnel vision. I cannot allow myself to be treated in this manner.

I feel that when Your demons carry You away, You lose touch with what is noble, giving and beautiful within You. It takes a long time and work to transcend these patterns in ourselves. You thought that You were taking chances with me. You had barely even begun! When something did not go Your way, the unfortunate reaction happened, that hurt me and us.

Talk of love does not woo nearly as well as acts of love, and most males need to learn to OPEN up, simply and totally when things are not as they want or require. This should be allowed to happen in a natural rhythm, not meanly, accusingly and protectively, after too much time has passed and resentment has built. How can someone feel safe, protected and loved, when the lover skips understanding

and legitimization of the other and heads straight to recriminations of acts unknowingly committed?

This doesn't sound like a man who wants a soulful relationship and wants to put "everything" in his heart at risk. If it is, he has really gone astray. I know it is not through malicious intent. Love grows and develops. We cannot will it to do so by force. Perhaps, next time, You will be able to water it, shelter it, and revel in its growth. That's all You can do, and try not to stomp on it as You do a rain-dance around it.

Arlana

Subject: star of Arlana
Date: Tue, 4 May

Dear Arlana,

Quite a journey, we've taken. I am so sorry I became a distraction for your audition. It was not my intention. I am sorry to have hurt you, dear. I did wish you well in my thoughts, if not my writing.

Though I tried damn hard to be clear, I was unable to convey what was in my heart and what I desired and needed most, in that moment I was in over the last month or so. I'm learning the importance of asking for what I need emotionally and otherwise. Clarity, I'm working on.

I don't want to trade hurt for hurt with you, re-analyze the whole intricate fiasco of delicate emotions that tossed our compassion. It did get tangled up in my never lower state of mind. I'll take the responsibility and give what occurred between us, that magic, a positive, brightly colored reference point on my learning curve.

I thank you for allowing me to open before you, in a way I had never done before. You were an inspiration and a challenge and I needed both. You breathed not just life into me, but a fire, that

blazed across my parched landscape. The dried wood, thirsty for the flames of your passion. That part won't ever leave me. You were the most thrilling engagement of femaleness to occur in my life.

I hope you will not remember me only for my selfishness.

I'll be watching for the star of Arlana rising from the east.

Vaya con Dios! Break a leg!

Galen

Subject: Grateful for Your letter
Date: Thu, 6 May

Dear Galen,

Thank You for Your gracious letter. I admired the way You responded with dignity and restraint. I found it rather generous. I was not trying to berate You, only to let You know of my point of view. Thank You for understanding, though Your letter sounds rather final.

I would hope that the door will not be forever closed, at least not locked, between us. We have only scratched at the surface in many aspects and You are so compelling, rare and brilliantly attractive on many levels that it would be a heartache to lose touch with You forever. In any event, I cannot and will not forget You.

yours still,

Arlana

Subject: Fate and circumstance

Date: Sat, 8 May

Dear Arlana,

I need you to know, that under different circumstances, nothing would have stopped me from coming to you, giving all of myself, and consuming every last drop of you, had it taken a day or a lifetime.

Fate and circumstance have taunted me rather cruelly that way, dangling a prize like a carrot on a stick, while I've chased it wildly in every direction, only to have it yanked away at the last moment. I know that somehow I am both chaser and yanker.

Thank you for your note, I appreciate your generosity as well. I was resolved to not hear from you again, nor to re-contact you. The tone of finality you read was accurate, but not for all the reasons you might have assumed. There was more going on than you ever knew about, and had nothing to do with you, personally.

I, of course, couldn't sever what I felt for you, sweetheart, only the channel that conveyed those feelings.

My state of being had been pushed right to the edge by all the calamities around me, all the grief that I hadn't let gush forth. I'd become too weak, too frustrated, too vulnerable, too worthless and futile to continue. I was close to becoming an absolute zero.

Fortunately, my allies, here, were dedicated enough to connect me with just enough love, anger and fierceness to focus on a small seam in my black depression. Like a laser, it cut through that sludge that had swallowed me and I was able to escape. It's been almost two weeks (11 days, actually) and I feel like I'm on a 12 step program now, staying focused on what I have to do to survive and then prosper, avoiding the things that might suck me into that black hole again.

I've had an incredible time of deep ritual, magic and medicine, rediscovering my sacred connection to life, reshaping my state of

mind, opening my heart through myth and ceremony, touching the spirit world, grieving tears, and contacting my animal spirit in a "warrior" initiation ordeal and rebirth (Sage Panther).

I was in no shape, at that point where we went astray to continue, or to resurrect the flow. I was deteriorating, and knew that I was no good for you in that condition. I didn't feel any good to myself for that matter. I still face the same challenges I did two weeks ago, and they are formidable, from financial to health to my ex and my sons and most of all, spiritually. I will go, and need to go into some of these things with you, should there be the opportunity in the future.

There's still this tremendously impractical circumstance of time and space between us. But I do want you to know that I do care about you greatly, and so enjoy the beauty, depth and art of our romance.

I hope you are well sweet snake.

Keep faith luv,

Galen

Subject: I care too.
Date: Mon,10 May

Dear Galen,

Please keep up the fight and keep well. I understood that something big was happening in Your life and hope that I did not add to the problem in any way. I trust that we were not being spied on, but probably were.

It is grand of You to admit to being the "chaser and yanker". I saw it and wondered why. Thank you for explaining. You are brave and stronger than you know. Just dig deep and reach out to those around You who sound like they care so much. I'll tell You about

my battles one day.

You sound more like Yourself in this last letter and I am glad for it. I am here for You whenever you need to speak to me. Instead of worry, I send you love, support, belief and strength. You will get through all this. I just know it!

a tight hug from,

Arlana

Subject: Rare and glorious
Date: Fri, 14 May

Dear sweet,

Please, I wish you to confide in me of your "battles". I am past the need to express my own now, and can focus on you. If you need someone to lean on, vent, cry, rage, or express utter joy or delight, you would serve me well, to offer that to me. And I offer my compassion and attentiveness to you. I do still feel a great tenderness for you and will do all I can to soothe your soul.

I know you have been struggling, and I have been too self absorbed to be of any help, and I know I have contributed to your sorrow. I also know how noble and strong you are, and the beauty and passion of your soul. That is the truth I know about you, and it will always be the truth. You are a very rare and glorious gem, sweetheart, and I thank whatever fate has brought you so close to me.

I am much more like my old self now, only better. I've expanded, there's more room in my heart now, to let others in, with a special chamber reserved just for you.

I'm going to give you my address. If you had a tape or a CD(preferable) of you, I would love to hear you sing, or shout, coo or giggle. Also some pics would be nice. I recently had my album

from 1988 called Diamond Lake, converted to CD and I would send you a copy if you wished.

I am here for you dear, as I know you are there for me.

Keep faith luv,

Galen

(*Note: My address was included.*)

Subject: Your fan, friend, and passionate partisan
Date: Sat, 15 May

My Darling Galen,

Welcome back! It is so good to hear you back to Yourself- and in such a generous spirit of loving and giving. You are truly a man capable of much and of greatness. I admire You so much.

Please do not let the lesser spirits interfere with the beauty and power of who You are. Clouds can only obscure the sun for so long and eventually it burns gloriously through, right to the heart of the land. Your attention now is like those warm rays of the sun caressing my senses, my soul and body, warming me deeply. Thank you.

My challenges are manifold and I would love to pour them out to you: they are professional, personal (the heart), family (issues galore) and financial. It is rather a quagmire, but then, who is immune to suffering? My mother says that I am so complicated. This, I take as a compliment rather than an insult. She calls me Jezebel- to tease her I told her that if I ever have a daughter I will name her Jezebel.

I haven't been coming to this computer much, because things have cooled off with Martin. (I gave him back his house keys and he mine) He does not want to (cannot??) Dominate me any longer. He

longs for a "partner", and is tired of the hierarchy of a D/s relation-ship. He claims to still want to play, but only as equals.

He sat on this decision for so long that everything was eroded. We couldn't even speak anymore. I am glad the truth came out, be-cause at least I know that I am not nuts and my intuition is correct. So, things are up in the air.

The weekdays I spend alone, and see my friends and some family on the weekends. I am looking into getting a computer. I feel so alone at times and crushed with the weight of my own cares, ambitions, expenses, life and plans that I just become caught in the headlights and get nothing done. This lack of productivity and passive lassitude make me feel worse and is a vicious circle that I cannot seem to break through.

I suppose I must learn to take better care of myself. I enjoy having a partner around to draw strength and give strength to. To laugh, plot, bemoan and adore life and one another together. This is all too rare. I believe that humankind are social animals. Do You agree, my dear?

Now that I came so close to losing You, I am more attached to You than ever. I will not let it get that close again, and hope You cooper-ate!

Still, I enjoy everyday and drain life to the dregs like tomorrow may not come. I will be in Europe on the 22nd of May for ten days or so to visit my brother and some friends there. I will try to find a computer to drop You an e-mail. Better yet, since I have Your address, I'll send a postcard, if time permits. Thank You for trusting me enough to give me Your address. I will send You a good old fashioned letter and some photos, and my address as well.

How are Your troubles, my Tiger? I hope that things are better. You sound strong and capable now and I know You will decimate Your foes and scatter Your troubles to the wind. I hold You close to my heart and gently kiss your forehead. . .

love and faith,

Arlana

Subject: Soulful submissive
Date: Sun, 16 May

Darling panther,

I've always been chagrined at how much time I've spent alone,
when I knew I was filled with such magic for the right partner. I
wish I was in a position to come to you now, fly to London and just
play for a week together. Wouldn't that be nourishing?

We would begin working on your relinquishment. I can tell, you
need some control and discipline, immersion in "subspace", far past
the borders of mundane confusion and frustration. A little leather
and rope therapy would be good for you, and the fear/excitement
the smell of both convey.

I don't have time to write more now, sweetheart. I feel for you and
the strife you are experiencing, wishing I could rescue you, but I
know you will endure and persevere. What are these tribulations,
really, compared to what you have so bravely endured as a soulful
submissive.

I did have a little inspiration for writing, the first in many months.
It's just a short piece, but I will include it, with the hope it might
cause you to dwell on more pleasant options in your future.

warmly,

Galen

"As Master Wishes"

Master had explained to you some time ago, before you accepted

his collar (what a glorious ceremony that was), that you would be involved in finding other D/s partners for Master's pleasure. You accepted this, and obediently agreed that Master should have whatever He desires. "As Master wishes," you had replied.

You had placed an ad that Master had approved, on several D/s personal sites, and had responded to several ads placed by interesting females who sought to play with a D/s couple.

"This is what I want you to find." Master described His wishes, pacing the room, forming the picture of the types sought. You were getting aroused because as Master revealed what He was looking for, it was clear that your own moist desire was interfering with your habitual competency at taking dictation.

"I would accept a strict sadistic Domme. . . for you, my bitch", and His cruel grin sent a penetrating chill into the warmth between your legs.

"You see, it's natural for a Master to force His slave to do whatever He tells her to do. I'm sure you'd agree, wouldn't you slut?" And you knew you agreed and would agree to anything and everything, readily. You were Masters proud fuck slave, ready to surrender your ass, mouth or cunt. You were a whore and a slave, quite good at both and happy to be so.

"But to see a woman," He continued, "forcing another woman to be her slave, with all the contempt and arrogance that a cruel Domme can exert, now that's quite unnatural and perverse, a royal betrayal by her own kind, a grand form of humiliation."

Master was pacing back and forth as He talked, the leash in one hand. You were standing now, in spike heels, black nylons and garter, and your training collar. When Master came close, you would sway your cunt and tits towards Him with a sweet but wanton subtlety, a slight purring groan of desire from your throat, sometimes brushing Him lightly. Your eyes, full of desire, tracked His every move, hoping for a return glance. What His gaze conveyed did not matter really. Of course, you would have preferred

that Master used you, and allowed you to orgasm. But you thought, "As Master wishes."

Occasionally Master roamed beyond the length of the leash and you would stumble towards Him as the leash tightened and you were yanked forward by the neck. Once you stumbled right into Him, and were thrilled just to come in contact with His body. Master glared at you for breaking His concentration.

"Are you so clumsy slave, that you have to stumble around so awkwardly?"

He pulled the chain roughly towards the ground, and you were quickly on your knees before Him. You looked up at Him with what appeared to be respect and an apologetic look on your pretty face. Master's eyes narrowed sharply, and He slapped you across the right cheek. You long remembered the sting and shock of it with a certain fondness.

"Did I give you permission to look at me, my little bitch?" He asked. You had quickly lowered your eyes, but your head was roughly yanked up and back, by a fistful of hair in Master's grasp.

"Now I want you to look at me cunt! You've disrupted my concentration and I'm going to relieve my frustration in your mouth. Let me see you open in the cock sucking position." He ordered. "Come on bitch, make it nice and round, that's a good girl. What a pretty little cunt mouth you have. Keep it open dear. Ok, now take my cock out of my pants and show me what a good cum sucking slut you are." Master commanded.

As soon as you had Masters' hard shaft out, He grabbed you roughly by the hair and forced his cock all the way down your throat and held it there, as you gagged. You tried not to give in to the reflex, but it was difficult. You have since improved, but then were very nervous and rather upset with yourself for breaking Master's concentration again. It works better when you just relax, you reminded yourself.

Master drew back and you sputtered, but caught a quick breath and devoured His shaft again seeking His precious cum. Master's voice was tender now.

"Look at the pretty mouth. Come on, suck it my precious slut, show your Master what that sweet fucking mouth is for." He hissed, in a tense voice.

Master was now thrusting His hips in rhythm with the sucking, and in your mind, He was in your cunt and you could feel it. All you wanted was His cum, to receive His full pleasure. You were soon well rewarded.

"Swallow it slave!" He roared.

"As Master wishes," you thought.

Subject: Tumultuous
Date: Mon, 17 May

Dear Galen,

My dearest, thank You for Your support. Oh yes, some soulful and physical relinquishment would be just what is needed...sigh. The gorgeous transcendence of the trip of the senses we would take.

We could ride the TGV over to Paris, and gaze into one another's eyes over *café au lait* and *croissants* as You watch how uncomfortable my nipple clamps grow under my flowery blouse. Perhaps I would be wearing vibrating panties to which You hold the remote control. It would be thrilling to climax, right there on the public *terrasse* as You proudly gaze on, a bulge in Your pants.

Things are not as bad as all that at the moment, in my life, and I suspect, not as bad as what You are going through. You are sounding solid and vital again, and I feel that You are winning Your battles. Keep in up darling. My whole life has been tumultuous

anyway, so this is no different and I have bursts of creative optimism to light the darkness.

Just Your wish to rescue me, melted me and filled me with a grateful desire to please my Hero and all His whims. It would have been magical to meet in the old world and blend our aloneness into glorious togetherness. I also spend and have spent much time alone, and know how You feel.

Thank you for the story. It is very hot, balanced, and in just the right tone to get all my juices -womanly and mental, flowing. Interesting that you wrote from her point of view, I might add. I love talent, perversions and compelling power. They are truly sexy.

on my knees,

Arlana

Subject :*Bon Voyage*
Date: Tue, 18 May

Sweet snake,

"…on my knees". . . I like a slut that understands her position in life! And it would (will) be a fond pleasure to see my sweet girl so positioned. I have to tell you, dear, that I do think of the tortures I want to apply to your body, the torment to your soul, and the beauty of your submission welling in your eyes. Your pain for me would be sweet.

"…desire to please my Hero and all His whims. ". . . see above. I am going to start training you specifically in how to serve me. You have more than proven worthy, my magnificent, exotic slut. I have given you many clues into my particular pleasures in my stories. I feel it is important that you understand these things clearly, or you will not please me.

I know you understand, and will hold back nothing in your desire to serve me. I will hold back nothing in my total subjugation and enslavement of you. You will desire Master's torments and react to them with burning desire in your eyes, words, body and soul. I will draw this forth from you, encourage its growth, until my desire to be your Master is constant and unyielding.

I will provide more detail at another time, since you are leaving tomorrow and cannot respond readily. I will say that it will be a requirement of you in the future to include further scenarios and thoughts such as. . . "You watch how uncomfortable my nipple clamps grow under my flowery blouse. " and: "Perhaps I would be wearing vibrating panties to which You hold the remote control. " Arlana, do you understand how much it turns me on and why I require your ability to express such sublimely sluttish thoughts?

I know how well you wish to serve my desires, sweet bitch. You know how impassioned and loving and romantic my affections to you will be, in this blend of pain, service and romance you offer. It is late, so I'll say goodnight. Travel safe and well, dear. I sent my music CD "Diamond Lake", and if customs doesn't seize it with dark suspicion, it should arrive today.

Bon voyage,

Galen

(*Note: Arlana sent me a fragrant snail mail letter with her lovely pictures, just before she left for London. This was my response.)*

Subject: Haunting
Date: Mon 24, May

Dear sweet snake,

I just got your mail this afternoon.

That fragrance! It haunts me. Nearly brings me to tears. It is the scent of love. It takes me into an idyllic state of rapture. It has my nose nuzzled into the neck of your beauty, tingling against your skin. I thank you for that.

I am lonely for you, my slut. It is more difficult to keep my focus without the synergy of two, now. When I was younger, in my serious devotion to be an artist, I killed anything in my path that threatened my focus. That was lonely too, but I knew that agony fed my inspiration, and I stole from it(that dark and poignant solitude), as much as it stole from me.

Your lithe and lovely figure jumps out at me from the cityscape in your picture, your look, so open, vulnerable, while appealing permission to take that next step closer. Step towards me, my beauty.

Thanks for your sweet expression about my music. The production value isn't great, and I always envisioned the added energy of keyboards, lead guitar, and synths to give it punch and texture here and there.

I hope you soon return safely to me. Send me that special pleasure of you as soon as you return.

keep faith luv,

your Hungry Tiger

Subject: Back from abroad , Sir. . .
Date: Thu, 3 Jun

Dear Galen,

Thank You for your beautiful letter. I felt the Mastery and power of it. I have returned and have terrible jet lag, which I suffer more severely on the way back. I had a marvelous time in Europe and

spent a day at the cool seaside.

I was introduced, via close circles, to some people in the scene there. It was very special in many ways. They marked me profoundly. I will tell You more if You like. I believe that I had enriching moments there, culturally and as a sub, and feel inspired. I held my own and elicited favorable comments and exhortations to remember my self-worth, which had been damaged recently.

In conversation, certain subjects really got me thinking. I have not really been exhausted physically in a scene, tired, yes, but not broken by labor as they do in the army, or had my senses played with in such a way that I could not rely on them much.

The couple I played with are so beautiful and have done much that I would like to experience. Their togetherness moved me and embodied the kind of relationship I would like to have. It exists, they exist! Many of the forms of SM are developed to the point of an art form there.

Here is a story that my experiences gave birth to.

"Lord of the Manor"

You, as my Lord, and Lord of the Manor, cool as a stream, deep as the sea. My nipples harden at Your presence as You walk around me to inspect your property. I lower my eyes to conceal my agitation. You are wearing riding pants and a crisp white shirt. Guests sit nearby. I do not heed them, though I feel their eyes on my body. I am skimpily clad.

"I have an offense to punish you for, my slut." You announce.

I nod, overcome, yet thrilled. I know that I have not been perfect and cry inwardly for it. I am eager to expunge my crimes and prove my love and devotion to You through my endurance and gifts.

With a wave of Your hand, You beckon a lackey who is carrying

your instruments on a tray and standing very immobile. I look at her and wonder what pleasures You have taken on and in her lovely body. . .

You begin Your *ostinato* on my breasts which redden at the hungry nips of Your whip. I pant like an animal. "This is just to warm You up," You comment, casually. The instruments grow worse in severity and I sway with the effects of the pain. "Hold on girl, stand still for me!" You urge.

This is awful. How can I stand still under this pelting? I look up at You and see the love, purpose and desire in Your eyes and feel a fresh energy and second wind. Hurt me my love, I think, in adoring subjugation. You trace a finger over my welts.

"Very pretty." You comment and turn to Your assistant: "Get over here to rub her breasts!" You command the girl. She puts down her tray and slinks over to me. I see her stealing glances at You as she massages my torrid breasts. "Rougher!. . " You order her.

This creature then becomes a real viper of pinching, slapping and biting. This is worse than the barrage before as it is through another. It hurts my feelings. A second hand beating! The mind twist of it makes me reel. "Oh, my King, why won't you keep touching me, even if it is to hurt me some more?" I think, distraught. "Have I upset You so much? Oh, it is hard to serve and love You, as it should be."

You disappear from my view and leave me with the vixen who keeps up her abuse. I growl and snarl a bit as I am wont to do when feeling animal, and see her eyes widen in surprise. I imagine myself hurting her one day. I see You out of the corner of my vision, sipping tea and laughing with Your guests.

You absent mindedly pet the dog at Your feet. This makes me jealous! You haven't deigned to give me any physical affection today. Oh, to feel Your hand on my face, caressing me, stroking my hair and telling me that You have to make me suffer for being too beautiful and exciting You.

249

I imagine You inside my body as you push me up against a wall, standing, looking deep into my eyes. I imagine you pulling my hair, slapping, then caressing me as You thrust roughly and deeply into me. I shake my head to dispel the fantasy. You won't even look at me.

After what seems like an eternity, You return, lift Your hand to stop your cruel little assistant. You pat her bottom to send her off without looking at her. Taking Your time, You hook the leash into my collar. You slowly lead me to the manse, deep into the basement.

Unbidden, I fall to the cold stone floor and wrapping my arms around Your legs, kiss your boots. You admire the line of my spine and how my hair cascades around Your ankles. "Good little girl. Get up- fetch me that chair."

"Yes Sir." I reply, as I rush to comply, standing straight because I know You like me to have good posture. You sit down and with a sudden gesture, sweep me down across Your lap. The spanking is prodigious. The sound of the slaps resonate in the hollow darkness. Even my sighs seem loud. You allow me to wiggle as You enjoy the pressure on Your crotch and the sight of my ass undulating under Your hand.

Still slapping, You reach under to feel my sex, It is wet and dripping onto You. You insert several fingers and I moan with the joy of feeling them in me, though, You are matter-of-fact about it. "Look at what You've done, you naughty thing! You've wet my riding pants!"

"Oh, I'm so sorry sir. . . please sir. I'm sorry." "Sssssh." You order me up and make me walk over to an object that is free standing and covered with a sheet in the center of the room. You pull it off the covering and it reveals a huge phallus on a hydraulic pole. I gasp at the size of it. You press a button nearby and it lowers.

"Since you're so excited, stand over it and open for this." You

250

order.

I comply, the blood rushing from my face, back down to my crotch. I feel a drop of fluid running down my thigh and know that You can see how much I want to be impaled by this object. My desire for You is such that even the humiliating need for the huge tool is overwhelming, and I writhe in anticipation of it. You press the button again and the phallus rises.

"Bear down on it. Good." I moan as it moves within me- I feel so dirty. It is huge and I can take it all in and like the sensation. You come around back and tie my hands together behind me. I am grateful and lunge my breasts out to try and brush against You. You smile, tweak a nipple, kiss my forehead and stride out of the room.

I am left hanging there on the ingeniously sexy skewer as it increases in speed, moving up and down. I moan and look around for You. I feel an orgasm coming on and You are not there for me to ask permission. Feeling safe in my solitude I ride the phallus with abandon and unselfconscious frenzy. A flash of You as You appeared to me outside in sunlight, selecting instruments from the tray, just sends me.

It breaks over me like a thunderstorm and shakes my entire body. It feels that I just keep coming and coming- the pleasure is so intense it hurts. I scream my release out loud. The pain and tension from the long day simply evaporate in the white hot fire at the center of my release. I am limp from this ferocious climax.

The infernal machine continues. I am drenched now. Perhaps I have ejaculated, like I sometimes do. I hear voices in the hallway. You enter with your guests. "Magnificent!" a lady comments. There are hands are all over me, talking about me as though I were not there.

You lean over to whisper in my ear: "We saw it all on the camera, very nice but you didn't ask for permission, sweetheart." I throb inwardly at the sound of Your voice. I feel a tear streak down my face as I happily realize that this is just the beginning.

kissing the hand that would strike me,

yours,

Arlana

note- Hope You like my English fantasy dearest Sir and thank You for expressing Your desire to begin my training to serve You. I appreciate the clues You have given me and will strive to be up to Your standard.

Subject: Idyllic humiliation:
Date: Fri, 4 Jun

My sweet little whore,

How you thrilled me with your beautifully rendered story. I longed to be the one hurting you so royally, like my queen bitch. Exposing you to that idyllic humiliation for the entertainment of my guests.

Yes, I used that other whore. She was just a one-dimensional pleasure, compared to the bright complexity of my sweet, luscious slave girl.

I fell in love with the picture of you walking down the street. So much life in you, the supple, graceful body, your face showing me something, now that I know so much of the mystery of you, that shoots into my heart like a thousand arrows, each tip dipped in a different exquisite passion. See how you stir the poet in me. I am so thankful for that spark of life you strike in me.

Business matters require my attention right now. My communica-
tion, sadly, must be short. I will try to write more soon. I desire you so greatly dear. The spirit of you is so profound. It affects me truly. You allow my passions to rise. Your manner, so respectful, insightful, so rich, so devoted. Your soul entangles mine like an interlocking Chinese puzzle, the pieces so difficult to be undone, yet

so readily joined together.

Please tell me more about your trip, sweetheart. I am jealous of all the pleasure I did not partake in, but get excited nonetheless hearing of your exploits. I will take my pleasure on you, someday, make you suffer for my patience. I think often of the treasured look in our eyes as I sweetly torture you. The pain fierce and calmly dispensed. Our pleasure colliding in a final passionate embrace.

Goodnight sweet slut. Feel my kiss.

Galen

Subject: I embrace you too
Date: Sat, 5 Jun

My dearest,

You are melting me with Your insight and sentiment, threats and love. It is beautiful indeed. I am glad that pride and anger did not prevent us from continuing as we should. I know I try Your patience, my beloved tormentor, but I too languish. I am glad of the power of Your third eye in seeing beyond the surface. You are truly worthy.

Now, I would like to lay my head on Your chest and talk to You and tell You about myself and my life and to share my challenges and disappointments. My life is strangely beautiful, but like a stormy sea and often in a flux. Many would find this life too stressful, too dangerous. I am weary of it at times, but persevere. I must be true to myself.

My trip was lovely: I saw the sights in a more leisurely manner than I previously did. Last time, I was too busy, and had an interesting time socializing with friends I haven't seen in awhile, and generally spreading and receiving joy. I admit I like to touch people, seduce and be admired. I think we all do, to some extent. I enjoy making

people feel glad to know me. It is validating.

However, it is a poor substitute for what I should be doing on a grander scale: my performing. That is what I am truly born to do. Art uplifts all humanity and takes us beyond mundanity and mortality. The stories are so long and the jet lag so strong.

Hold me, my darling. You would stroke me and then slide Your hand around my neck and tighten, so that my face would redden and my eyes would plead.

I did go out one night and was lightly disciplined, as it was our first scene together. The Master whipped me publicly while the beautiful blonde sat on the floor under the punishment cross. Classical music came on at one point. It was so poignant. I felt a surge of pride for what I am. It was good for me to be thus displayed in public again. The play of the past year has been the kind that cannot be done in public.

We shared another afternoon and evening of gratifying distraction together, us three. It began when I arrived late and was castigated. I do not have my journal with me today and would like to copy the entry for Your pleasure if You would like to hear it. I believe that this experience was valuable for me in many ways, as it helped to overcome some barriers that had been in place for some time: electricity and the dreaded soles of the feet- my former Achilles' heel, as it were.

I was introduced to several new sensations as well, and benefited most from meeting those two truly special people. They are as keen as they are superbly beautiful, and their warmth and passion was enveloping, even in the midst of my tribulations.

I was told that I was well trained and the Dominant in question told me that he had never met a submissive quite like me. This was a fine compliment and I took it as gracefully as I could, and gratefully, I might add. It was telling and consequential for me.

I am ever thrilled by Your desire and even more so by the sparks of

inspiration that I touch within You. I feel how alive You are and how strong and potent Your prowess is. You are unmatched in exquisiteness of poetry.

This goes a long way to woo me from afar. You affect me inside and out. It feels wonderful. Thank You. I understand that You are busy. Never worry about that. A word from You is a nourishing delicacy.

at Your beck and call,

I remain,

Arlana

Subject: Mythically sublime
Date: Tue, 8 Jun

dearest slut,

I would love your lovely head on my chest, pouring your heart into mine. The thought of squeezing your lovely neck, the look in your eyes, as I slowly bent forward to kiss your supple tender lips, makes me gasp for breath. You are a mythically sublime slave goddess.

It is no doubt you are cherished and applauded wherever you go. I put your pic up by my desk, not directly in my line of site, but 3 or 4 times a day, I turn, and there you are, walking towards me. A most pleasant sensation. I attended a kink seminar recently and attended a comprehensive electro-torture and e-stim workshop. It totally confirmed my interest, so your mention intrigued me- tell me more.

Also, tell me now without any equivocation how we can bring about my sweetest desire to partake of your flesh, dear. Where and when can we arrange to meet?

Your depraved and loathsome,

Galen

(*Note: I had made my first attempt to phone Arlana,*)

Subject: Answer to query
Date: Wed, 9 Jun

Hello my dearest Galen,

It was so wonderful to hear Your voice on my answering machine! I have saved it and listen to it over and over. Thank You for that. I run around a lot and am aggrieved at times at having someone hovering over me because I am hogging the computer. Sometimes this keeps me away from my home, work and cat.

I am working on a solution for this. I am in fact, pressed for time at this moment. I know You are upset when I sound rushed. I love writing to You at dawn when there is no one around and it is quiet and I have all the time in the world. I cherish the image of You squeezing my neck as my head is on Your chest. I am glad that You like my photo and are inspired by it.

Please tell me more about the electro-play workshop and the e-stimulator. The Master in Europe had a wand. It is described as a static electricity conductor. I believe that it touched his body and made him into a charge. Then, He came over to me in the dark, touched the tip of my breasts, and zap!-sparks and electricity. I found this sexy as it traveled from body to body.

He directed His stunning beauty to hold the wand and she did so and gave me electric kisses. I lunged for her, not caring about the zap, only wanting her pretty mouth on mine. The sparks lit up the dungeon. It was very beautiful.

I need no pretext to want to meet You. I have a strong urge to look

into Your eyes and to speak to You. I must tell You that I am a bit afraid, though. You know that I love who You are and what I know of You.

I never have had this kind of thing happen to me. I feel at a loss because I have no frame of reference in this type of situation. You understand, sweetheart? We have to arrange something safe and comfortable for both of us, all right? With patience and communication, it should all work out fine.

You are not depraved and loathsome, but rather, devious and delightful. Let the weak flee and the judgmental preach. They have not the ability to live as deeply as we dare. I am tired. Life is such a whirl! Kidnap me. Just kidding, but, perhaps one day, just not the first meeting!

bye for now dear,

xo Arlana

PS: I am glad you like my voice on the answering machine.

Subject: Gleaming Jewel of the Soul
Date: Thu, 10 Jun

My sweet beautiful slave,

I am driven by the image of you, arms extended over your head, wrist cuffs secured to a rafter, forcing you to stand on the toes of your high heels. I watch your countenance slide deeper and deeper into submission, as I lay the cat on you stroke by stoke, across your ass, and tits. I kneel to place the clamps on your cunt lips and kiss your wetness tenderly. I trace the welts from my whip with my fingernails, continuing my pleasure as I torture my property, peeling your resistance layer by layer until your flesh is stripped down to the gleaming jewel of your soul.

..."I must tell You that I am a bit afraid, though, You know that I love who You are and what I know of You. I never have had this kind of thing happen to me, so I feel at a loss because I have no frame of reference in this type of situation. You understand, sweetheart? We have to arrange something safe and comfortable for both of us, all right?"

Tell me my sweet, what do you fear from me, or yourself? What do you mean that you've never had this happen before? How would you describe a situation that was safe and comfortable? I want you to feel safe and comfortable, that should be understood. Are you afraid you might become an episode on "Unsolved Mysteries" or "America's Most Wanted"?(grin). I want you to address these issues for me, so we can create an agenda for meeting, dear.

I believe Master **** was using a violet wand, as it can conduct through the body. I saw it demonstrated also, with a metal glove to caress those tender areas. One slave howled like a banshee, as her Mistress gripped her shaved cunt.

I tried it on my arm for the sensation, as well as several other painful implements. Ouch! The e-stim device is called a Tens unit. It cause sthe muscles to contract from mild to extreme. The extreme made the demo slave writhe in pain, as her buttocks contracted to a sweet pucker. Her mouth going wide in a silent, contorted scream.

I must correct you, dear. I am "deliciously" depraved and "delightfully" loathsome.

I have attached an image of my animal spirit – the Panther.

keep faith luv,

Galen a. k. a. Sage Panther.

Subject: Sage Panther
Date: Fri, 11 Jun

Dear Galen

Thank You for the gorgeous Panther. A psychic told me that it is my spirit animal, as well. Another link between us. How many more to discover?

The imagery of me suspended as You torture me is lovely and stirred me mightily.

About the comfort question, I just want to feel physically safe and relaxed. What I am trying to explain is that I have never met anyone via this type of channel and don't quite know how it's done. That's all really. I am not afraid, but just want to be somewhere aesthetic and reassuring. I will get so much from just speaking to You and looking in Your eyes. I will tell You what I feel. I will be totally open and honest.

The ravishing beauty in Europe sent me some torrid pictures and a lovely letter. I am eager to return to Europe, simply to see her. Master **** there did use the wand on me. He said I took it very well indeed. I don't think I would enjoy a huge muscle-contracting jolt, though. I understand this is difficult on the heart. It would not be a poetic way to accidentally die during play. Asphyxia is sexier to me, but just as deadly. The ideal is to stay alive for You, dear.

How do You feel, by the way, about expressions of pain. Do they turn You on? What are Your rules? Must the slave remain quiet? Can she scream out her pain and/or her pleasure?

Bye for now my deliciously depraved and delightfully loathsome tormentor.

love ,

Arlana

PS: It is torridly hot today and I can hear the race cars at the Grand Prix. I won't be around to write tomorrow, but will be thinking of You and of our Panther link.

Subject: Dance divinely
Date: Sun, 13 Jun

Sweet snake,

Slippery you are my precious, you dance divinely, even if it's over the issue of arranging to meet you.

OK, let me put it plainly. I will come to your city at an agreed upon time between now and September. I will get a hotel. We will arrange to meet in a bar with a cozy private atmosphere. You can take all the standard precautions: bring a body guard(s), arrange random phone calls to you on a cell phone, devise times you need to call in, give your protectors your exact location and temperament every 15 minutes, code 911 into your cell phone, take me to meet your parents, bring a gun, make me wear the handcuffs first, behind my back, until you feel safe. (Don't get any funny ideas, I don't have a submissive bone in my body. I'd gnaw my hands off at the wrist, and then beat you without mercy with my stumps(lol)!)

I am prepared for and would accept, if after meeting, you discovered it was all a grand illusion. I hold the same right. We would part company, and hopefully remain friends. I am sure I would find the city an interesting place to visit, even if I was on my own. If you still liked me enough to play or even fall deeper into this special love, you could take me back to your place, or wherever you felt comfortable. I would plan to "come" for four days or so, (and you should too!). Pick a date and between now and then we will resolve all the issues.

I've asked you numerous times what specific issues of a resolvable nature do you have before we meet. I ask again. What has to happen for you to feel confident with meeting. Are there any

unresolvable issues? I will not accept any further dancing on this issue, understand sweetheart? I want to develop a specific plan that covers every possible concern, and we'll address each one to your satisfaction.

You've had numerous lovers and have submitted publicly and privately from your own description to lesser acquaintances. What is it that holds you back from seeking the consummation of this glorious mystery?

Here's my phone number, ****, its both a business and personal line. If you reach the answering machine, leave a likely time to call you back, or try again.

I haven't produced "Galen's Rules of Order". They'll be created and imposed as I understand you better. As for screaming your pain and pleasure, my only concern, with a slave with your operatic range, would be for the windows or at least the wine glasses. Outside of that I would take pleasure in your screams in both regards, though I might suddenly slap your face to quiet you if that was my mood, and kiss your quivering lips tenderly.

The Panther is my spirit guide as well. It came to me as part of a ritual "warrior" initiation, in a guided meditation. I was visualizing myself in a wooded shore by a lake and asking for my animal guide to come forth.

The Panther appeared from the edge of the woods, its luminous eyes first, then the sleek athletic grace of its body as it stepped towards me. The "Sage" was added as I was purified with a sage smudge shortly after. That is my animal name: Sage Panther, the sage representing both healing and wisdom. It is how I am known to my brothers in the group I belong to(It's a warrior-guy thing!~grin). Check out www. mkp. com. It's called the Mankind Project.

So, we are both Panthers. Another serendipitous union of our souls, my panther sister. It doesn't cease to amaze me, but it is no longer a surprise.

261

Please send me to first two pictures (jpeg's) you sent before. I deleted them(it's a long story), and send anymore you think I might enjoy.

Sweet night my sleek and supple feline,

Galen

Subject: Two Panthers
Date: Sun, 13 Jun

Hello Sage Panther. . .

I am thinking of you and am not dancing when I say that I was out all day and now must run to an important rehearsal. I laughed and laughed at Your message. It was so lovely and light.

I am thrilled that You are coming here, and will discuss everything with You. I feel safe, already. I suppose that at the root of my nervousness was the desire to have the assurance that, whatever happens, we will remain as we are. I want to please You, and don't want anything to go wrong.

The fact that this is very far from a "lesser" acquaintance raises the stakes and makes the outcome more important.

Oh I am almost late dearest, but assure You that I will not shimmy around anything anymore. Just tell me and set me right. I will rush to continue this message as soon as humanly possible. Nothing will hold me back from this glorious mystery, dearest Galen. Thanks for your number. I will call.

X   oooo   xxx

Arlana

PS: Photos will come soon too, when I am calmer and less hur-

ried!! Sorry, Sir.

Subject: Our Mission
Date: Sun, 13 Jun
My beauty,

It pleases and excites me to think of meeting you, and that you are
joined in that mission. With what I feel in my soul for you, regardless if I should become tragically engulfed by some other orb of my
human emotions, nothing can go wrong between a panther brother
and sister like us.

There is no one like you on this earth, to match my soul. I don't
know how it will be in the flesh, moment to moment in our human
guise. Master and slave? That is complicated to consider with the
full range of our understanding, in any ongoing basis. I believe we
both have the ability to enjoy and create an intoxicating play scene.

Will the rest of it shine through those personal shields we might still
be compelled to sustain? It may be so, that even with a growing
desire to be together beyond a first meeting, our circumstances of
location, career and such, may prove impractical. Though our souls
may stay entwined, our bodies and emotions may drift to more
practical mates.

That would be tragic, but the beauty would still remain. I am
uncertain and nervous about these things too, sweetheart. A part of
me is afraid to risk all this passion and beauty. But to not take this
to the flesh, it's just potential gathered, but never spent. To not take
the risk would be a worse tragedy.

I crave your tender feminine hand on my cheek. I want to feel you
draw intimately close to whisper, your cheek lovingly against mine,
the breath of your words in my ear. The smell of you would engulf
me. I can feel right now, the rapture of a moment with you.

Your new picture stirs other passions, just as deep, though the flow

of tears may likely be reversed, dear slut. You are incredibly seductive and sexy. The depth of your soul peering out from your reflection, seems so far away from the earth. I can see how perfectly my hand will fit firmly around your neck, in a gently tightening grip, as my other hand takes a nipple, and pinches and pulls it steadily. I press tight against you, watching the two sensations at work in your eyes, waiting, knowing that your expression will soon change to please me in another way.

luv,

Galen

(*Note: I spoke with Arlana by phone for the first time, for an hour or so. Her voice was as lyrical, as intriguing, and as exotically foreign as her prose. She was a challenge right from the start, strong, but graciously charming as well. The thrust and parry of our relationship intensified.*)

Subject: Cowboy and stallion.
Date: Tue, 15 Jun

My decadent panther girl,

I am sorry about the difficulties you are facing with your home. Don't worry, you are creative, splendidly so. You will find a way to solve these problems.

I wish I was there to comfort you. Make you laugh. Make you cry. Make you scream in both ways we talked about. Make you sing the "Evil Gal Blues", while I play percussion on my slaves' body. I love the slow progression of the (black and) blues, don't you dear?

So I sound like a cowboy. . . who better to rope and break a wild stallion like you?

You were a pleasure to talk to. It only confirmed the spirit of you.

Showed how much there is yet to explore. There is something very special here for me.

I'm not worried at all, what happens when we meet. What happens between us physically, I feel is inconsequential. We've already transcended pure physical sensation and erotic pleasure. Though I am very confident that we will find what we seek there as well.

Our destinies are entwined now, I feel the purest love and respect and delight in who you are. Though my ultimate depravity wants to squeeze from you every pleasure you so gallantly offer.

I know you have high expectations and standards in that regard. I acknowledge your experience exceeds mine. Does that worry you? I am not intimidated by it. When I accept your submission, you will not be so bold as to turn and laugh in my face, as you boldly stated you have done to others.

You would not forget my eyes in a moment like that, nor the fierce hand across that insolent face, and being thrown to your knees by a sharp yank of that panther hued mane. "Don't move." I will tell you. You will know that I mean those two words. You will sense something uncertain in the silence that follows. Your face will reflect no more insolence.

Our phone discussion raised some concerns and thoughts, important for me to express. Some things you should know about my process: The art of Dominance for me starts with probing and clearly under-standing the slave's depth and style.

I've been at this a while now, and find, unlike you, that most subs are afraid, with a new Master, to forego safe words and hard limits. They need to feel assured that they have a clear ability to survive and not be harmed. If I stated that I don't honor safe words and hard limits, that would, in most cases end the discussion right there. What would be the point of that?

I don't have a problem not having safe words or specified limits, if you insist. I don't have a problem with them. It is an honor to be so

trusted by you, to have you offer yourself without limits. I trust my ability to stay in tune, and have the integrity to have your safety my highest concern. Ultimately that is the destination I seek. . . a trust so strong there are no limits,

I commented to you once, that D/s was like theater. I am like a method actor. I begin the drama at the point the sub is, where she is comfortable, confident. She has the opening lines. I improvise from there, knowing clearly where my character is driven to go.

This is simply my way, not what everyone's should be. But once my slave accepts my collar, she will have relinquished everything to me. That is where the live performance begins and rehearsal ends. The point where the exchange of power has been completed

But, to probe further regarding your statement that you don't use safe words or limits. What about your sensitive clitoris? You've stated a frank limit there. That it was too sensitive for all but the slightest breath upon it. Are you saying I should ignore you on that point, place it in the grip of a cantilevered clamp with heavy weights pulling it down severely, flog it without restraint?

What about your statements that verbal abuse may jar you from your "trance" and make you angry and defiant? Will you accept whatever words I tell you to describe yourself with to me. Can I abuse you relentlessly that way? Am I mistaken, are these not limits, or are there no limits? These things must be clear, very clear. I would not be pleased to have "limits" suddenly popping up at inappropriate times.

So if you do have borders to your sanity, dear, now would be the time to let me know. I know they are there. Knowing them won't spoil the total devastation I desire to engage you in. But all these things are part of the reality, love.

You have a tantalizing depth to your submissiveness, a dark erotic edginess. I literally drool at the thought of you, your "O" ness. My eyes sharpen in craven reflex to the image of you cast before me, like prey. I can taste your tender sweet flesh, even before I've

266

consumed it. It is scary and delirious, how everything about you turns me on.

Your Pascha.

Subject: Your panther girl
Date: Wed, 16 Jun

Dearest Sir,

I so loved speaking with You on the phone and also feel closer to You than before. The tone of your voice, pauses, breath and languid pace were exciting and mesmerizing. Your letter is very sexy in its own way also, as You speak of the slow progression of the black and the blues. That's some naughty double *entendre* there, Sir.

Tie me up with Your rope, cowboy, and I'll try not to buck. You will know when I am broken, by my tears and smile - often at the same time. That is a fantastic moment of release and transcendence. It is not weakness really, just relief.

I am also less worried about what will happen in the physical when we meet. This bond is solid and real and will endure if we decide to make it so. I know I have.

I love that word "gallant". It embodies some of the masculinity that I feel coursing through my womanhood. My expectations are only to learn, grow and travel somewhere wonderful with You in an adventure of the senses. I feel sure You will be able to absorb, vanquish and rule me without wavering, and with love. I am not worried.

If I feel something is wrong, I will let You know right away and we will talk. Such an event is not a limit suddenly "popping up", it is a right that I must have, especially at the beginning. It is simply the right to tell You something is wrong. It is not calling off a scene or setting a barrier. If I feel bad and need to express myself in an

urgent and serious matter, You can bet that I will. This is a rare incident, of course, but I need that avenue to remain open.

I understand Your position on safe words. It is a responsible position to take, and You still gracefully balanced it with my desire to have none. I do not have preferences and dislikes, which, expressed at the wrong moment, take us from the pleasant flow of Your rushing river. These predilections I do not consider limits, just tastes.

If things work out, in time, You will know all of these. I do trust You much already, dear. I can relinquish everything. That is the way I submit, once You know my inner landscape. These tastes of mine, do not diminish the huge playing field that Your desire can run rampant on.

I will answer all Your questions as best I can, with base language if You so desire it. As I said, I do not believe that I will inspire relentless verbal abuse in You. It would be an unpleasant surprise. Some women do just evoke it by their being. I do not. I do love diminutives added on to harshness and enjoy being called a little girl. I am expressing a preference.

I dislike strong verbal abuse. I am telling You, because if it is too much, it will jolt me right out of our torrid drama and into a resentful reality that I do not care to visit, with You. My sensitive clitoris is a biological fact. There is nothing to be gained by tormenting me there. It is like someone having a bad back. It is a simple actuality.

I admired the way Master **** warned me about his slave's tender nub and explained how she likes to be tongued below it. This is loving and thoughtful. In my long letter of introduction to Him, I had forgotten to tell him about mine, so I had to tell Him during the scene. This was not a limit popping up, just a respectful aside that served me well later. He was not displeased by my comment in any way.

Later in the scene, He applied a burning gel to my pussy and carefully avoided my clitoris. Sometime later He said: "It's a good

thing you told me. " He said, "otherwise you would have had this on your clit also. " I shivered with relief. I was already twitching like a piece of bacon on a hot griddle as it was. It was clear that I had narrowly escaped something awful and not worthwhile.

The border of the mind you refer to, to me, is the demarcation line between sanity and insanity. If You push me too close to the edge, I could go over it. I would warn You when I felt it near. This has only happened to me once in my life. It is rare, and I am quite strong. It happened when I was deprived of air, love and communication. I was utterly enclosed also.

All this came about, at a time when heavy grief constricted my heart that made it even harder to breathe. I was emotionally vulnerable even before the scene began. Everyone possesses a border to sanity. I have been told that once you go over that demarcation, you cannot go back. I would be of no use to you as a nut case. Death of the mind is not to be hazarded. The brain is at the center of too much of our fun, isn't it?

Are You ever inclined towards the macho, dear? When You called yourself a Male Dominant, I found it curious. Is there a difference? Is the male thing important? I refer to the backward Arab males around me as "Patriarchal Pigs. "

I enjoy the way You describe Your hunger in vicious animal imagery. Fierce, just as I like it.

We're rolling at a wonderful pace, aren't we dear Hunter??

Your Arlana

Subject: Honesty.
Date: Wed, 16 Jun

Dear,

I'm not in a good mood now. I have to go to a deposition this morning at my lawyer's. My wife and her lawyer will be there. I haven't seen her in over six months. It's painful to be exposed again to her energy, so hateful, scornful, so hurt herself. It's really fucked up.

You've drawn my honesty in every other regard, I have to come clean on this too.

Over the last 6 months, I've become nearly impotent. I can still come, but I can't sustain an erection. The irony is almost laughable, were it not so devastating.

It's made it difficult to get out from the shallows of my Dominant nature, and into those sublime depths. I have the mental capacity for it, but without the heightened arousal of a hard-on stimulating me, driving my passions, I cannot get completely immersed in my "Domspace. " The intensity level is diminished, like playing an electric guitar without an amp.

I fear my life could become a constant and tortuous frustration or a permanent sentence - the masochism of giving up the most pleasurable part of this lifestyle and an ultimate punishment.

I've just had a physical, blood tests- everything's normal there. Must I become addicted to Viagra! My desire has never been stronger, nor my fear and frustration.

I know when I first heard from James, regarding what happened to sharah, the horror of it sliced across every level of my psyche, but perhaps my sexuality most of all. I also know that having my ex discover all these things about me and how she has sought to literally destroy me, has taken a toll. She herself must feel so devastated, to be painting me so vilely to our former friends and family.

All these devastations, and ultimately how the situation will play out with my kids, stand guard in some way at the entrance to my true Domain, mocking me, shaming me, trying to block me from

exercising the sovereignty of my natural self.

I've suffered my fair share of loss and disappointment, over the years, but nothing's ever been able to penetrate or diminish my pervasive sexuality, until now. Unless it turns out to be physical, after all.

I'm going back to the doctor this week to see what more can be done. If the problem is mental, I feel at a loss what to do. How would I untangle the intangible, immeasurable mystery of my deep psyche?

I feel I'm generally pretty clear with myself. I can look at all that's happened and admit that it would be difficult to not be somehow affected. Unfortunately I have no plan, nor any idea of how to reverse it. How can I reconnect my mental desire to my physical body? I cannot understand why my own mind wants to betray me now too.

Galen

Subject: Domain.
Date: Sat, 19 Jun

Dearest Galen,

I hope that everything went all right yesterday for the deposition. How disruptive and consuming this must be. Do not let her anger, sully or pain You. Surround Yourself with positivity, it is such bright armor! Think of happier tomorrows.

I am touched by Your revelation and once again, in admiration at Your honesty. I do hope for You that everything is physically sound. It appears that all the tension and events have occupied Your mind and interfered with Your life force.

I will tell You a true story of a dominant man who so wanted to

perform for his lovely new girlfriend, that he was unable to do so for six months. It is more staggering when it happens to a Dominant/male - the irony of it!

When things settled down, he was able to relax and not to fear losing her, nature took over and things were ok. He said that he wanted everything to work so perfectly that nothing functioned at all. He did check everything physical out with a doctor and took medication. He even went to therapy, but when his mind was truly at ease, the rest followed. I hope, for You, dear, that this is the case. His doctor said that a greater percentage of cases are not physical.

Think of it darling, You have been through so much, there are bound to be aftershocks. Your mind is not at peace and You are in the middle of a great mess. Your boat will keep rocking until You get out of the rough weather, and then it will be overcast for a while before the sun comes out. You are strong. You are not alone.

After my relationship of eight years ended, I suffered a great deal. Not so much out of nostalgia for the love, just for the tumult of change aspect and the challenge of rebuilding of my life. I see a therapist now. It very interesting and I am growing so much. I want to know myself, heal old hurts and learn how to not repeat patterns and mistakes.

I dare say, my Panther, that You should speak to a professional yourself. The man I spoke of consulted a Sexologist and found it most beneficial, if only, to situate himself and to feel less alone while asking all of the pertinent medical and psychological questions that came to mind. There are precedents galore and much assistance. I can imagine how devastating this can be to a vital man like You. I am sure that this is not permanent, medical problem notwithstanding, and that You will not have a life "sentence".

The mind is the erogenous zone, compelling Pascha, it drives the passion from the brain downwards, not from the crotch upwards. Don't You agree? If You do, then Your Dominant self should be mostly intact. You didn't attract me with Your physical self, dear. It was with Your mind that you enticed me. That is whole and hale.

You are sexy for You are powerful there.

Do not think that this changes anything for me. I have played with Lothaire for about a year and he has never penetrated me. I am perfectly fine with playing only. In fact, if I had to choose, scenes would prevail over sex- in a New York minute!

Please feel no pressure, You have nothing to prove to me. I just want You to be well and to leave all the dark turbulence behind. One day, this will be a distant memory and even the pain of it will seem faint. I send You much love,

It's Your turn to have faith,

Arlana

Subject: Animal attraction.
Date: Sat, 19 Jun

My serene exotic panther,

You are so good to me. So good for me. I did have faith that you would serve your perspective back to me softly, sweetly, encouragingly as your noble spirit always has. I love you for that so much, sweetheart. There's not another woman in the world that I could trust so completely, or desire so totally.

I don't believe I have a life sentence. I do have faith, and then there's always Viagra- sounds so vital, doesn't it?(smile) Hugh Hefner sings its praises, as he dates those 23 year old twin bunnies.

But as you say, I still crave to "perform" on all those mythical, diabolical levels. None, more than with you as my leading lady. Script change! Make that: "kneeling" lady. The pleasure of you goes much deeper than the physical. The path to get there is through your sweet flesh and blood. The sublime rapture of that thought drives me to you as pure as any animal attraction could,

sweet slut.

I have one of your pictures up on my laptop, as I write this on my desktop. Yummmmm. I want to attack you. I see the panther in you now. I literally see the wild untamed power of you, held in check, only by the power of a superior Master, as He displays you on your leash. I like your hair long. I'm also pleased to see that serene udjat eye gazing at me again. You are glorious, dear.

Have you thought about times for our visit(no dancing).

I hope the time goes by, before we meet, like a fraction of a "New York" minute.

You are my awesome treasure sweet panther girl. Hmmm, I think I might be your panther Daddy, and you're my wild and sexy panther daughter.

Thank you so much darling, for your unflinching support and love.

Always with you,

Galen

(Note: This letter was preceded by a phone call.)

Subject: Plains of paradise
Date: Wed, 23 Jun

Dear sweet panther girl,

I loved hearing your voice again. I needed that little boost. You sounded a little forlorn.

Makes the Panther's protective instincts rise. Want to come protect the lair of my precious mate, defend her from the hyenas while she devours her kill in peace. I nuzzle close and lick your bloody

mouth clean with my long pink tongue. There is a warning growl in your throat and your claws tense and grip the kill jealously.

But I am playful today. I pounce on you. In an instant my jaws are clamped firmly around your vulnerable neck. You try to rise and this Panther tussles you onto your side, without lessening or tightening the grip on your neck. Your breathing is just slightly strained, his panting sounds hotly into your tensed, poised ear.

Just something for your pleasure, dear. Can you feel the passion dancing within me? Can you feel how I need you? Daddy's suffering a bit, missing his sweet little slut.

I am being sooooo patient dear! Papa's waiting for his girl's discussion of making my visit happen.

I try to avoid thinking about you too intensely. You hold back in your way, not wanting to jinx, but it cools my fire to do that. I'm creeping toward the point where I nonetheless would risk everything to pursue you totally, completely, whether I possessed your heart, or broke my own. Being afraid of that, is not how I choose to live anymore. I've held back always, waiting for what I want. I know that's precisely why I never captured it. My passion is now sweetheart, not later.

I want to swallow every ounce of you until I've had my fill. I want to fill your soul with my soothing love. I want your slave's soul joyously accepting my cruelty and pleasure.

Please know that I am not displeased with you, dear. I am only telling you how much I love you, to the core of my being. No one inspires me as you do. You bring out the beauty of me. It is my utmost desire to unleash all that beauty around you, and out into the world. This is why I tell you this, dear panther, I ache to let myself loose. What can I offer you in return? If it is enough, I do not know. In fairness, you don't know either. I understand…

I met with my warrior brothers tonight. It was an intensely profound encounter, as usual. Men coming clean about shame, anger,

betrayal and learning to deal with these burdens with integrity. "What does your gut tell you?" a man is instructed to ask himself. "Get out of your head man!" he is told. "What's in your gut?" he is asked.

A man might pause then, and suddenly tears might well in his eyes, his hand unconsciously gripping his shirt over his heart. "Yeah-go there brother! What is that? What is that? What is that feeling there? What happened right there?" pointing to where he clutched his shirt.

It's often just a man wanting to be loved. He's safe and surrounded by men who love him, who have compassion for him. He can admit things there. Every man in that place is committed to do his own work and to aid his brothers in theirs. We are learning how to be complete men.

I've learned a bit about Shamanic drumming from a Native American teacher. The vibrations are powerful, particularly the upper world eagle beat. This cadence is said to carry prayers to the upper world, one of the seven directions.

I sent a prayer to you, for your safety and happiness and I sent my panther spirit to watch over you also. Then, lost in the rhythm of the eagle beat, I visualized you and I as two sleek panthers racing across the plains of paradise.

goodnight luv,

Galen

Subject: Fuzzy as a peach
Date: Wed, 30 Jun

Dear,

Your neglect of the past few weeks is painful. It shatters my faith in all the love and respect you have claimed for me in the past. This

hot/cold interaction puts the fire out, ultimately. I will not repri-mand you here, but if I could be there with you now you would undergo harsh discipline. No excuses or dances required or desired.

Even your negligence inspires me, I've made further progress on a new story about a nun. It's a bit different than my past stories. A bit more literary, more character and mood, filling in the psycho-logical and metaphorical landscape. I've included the first install-ment at the end of this letter.

There are certain things in a relationship, IMO, particularly in a D/s one, that require a black and white clarity. Ours is as fuzzy as a peach, sweet as it is.

It is time to state things clearly, once and for all, where if anywhere this relationship is going in real time. I will always feel you are my panther sister, no matter whether we meet or not. I have stated where I want this to lead. That I want to discuss the specifics about arranging to come to meet you. Why do you continually avoid that discussion? And then suddenly cool off your communication, after blowing across my screen, and my emotions, like a torrid tropical storm.

Do you suddenly have some judgment about me, that negates all that has been expressed up to now? Are you trying to leave my passion to dissipate in disappointment? Do you have something festering in your own chest, that's not being expressed? Are you too caught up in all the attention you receive in your world, to be able to focus your soul on another? Is your phone out now, as well as your computer? Is the mailman on strike or tied up in your closet? I do pray that no evil has befallen you.

I miss you.

Galen

PS: Your inspiration and some of the glimpses into your passions brought me to create this new tale…Sister Christina

"Sister Christina"

The nuns sat like porcelain figurines in the front pews of the Church. From behind, their reverent countenance was shrouded in the black veils of their habits. Their faces, shaped by white linen, peered ahead like solemn theater masks.

The priest spoke Latin, facing the Altar. He had just delivered the sermon. His tall stature was bent low, his ornate vestments draping to the floor. In deep murmurs, that rang clearly in the spacious Church, he moved through the ancient rituals of the Mass.

The sermon had been in English. Something he said played over and over in sister Christina's mind. She heard it in the priest's voice, first like a cello, with ominous warnings dancing across the strings, then sweet as a *musette*.

"Let your heart be not swayed by false gods! They will drag your soul to hell. But when your Lord calls you, open your heart. Embrace Him. Surrender your whole being and He shall guide you to the greatest bliss your heart will ever know."

Sister Christina's toes curled in her shoes. She tried to stay focused on the spiritual meaning, but could not, not completely. Another spirit called to her, a seed planted from she knew not where. She was pregnant with it and she feared it was a pregnancy that could not be aborted. The seed was desire. It was need. It was flesh. It was the priest. And now he knew.

****

The nuns had taken confession, as they did weekly, the afternoon before. Sister Christina had stood outside the confessional, in the sanctity of the house of the Lord, with no conscious alert, at what was about to occur. Her mind was on her class, grading deadlines, and an unfortunate incident with sister Alma. She would include this in her confession, as a sin of pride.

Her turn came. She caught the door before it closed as sister Brigitte exited. She shut the door. The light evaporated from the small cubicle as she knelt facing the priest's cell, totally cut off from the outside world. Sister Christina pictured the priest inside his small parlor sitting on his comfortable armchair. She visualized his elbows propped up on the arm rest while the handsome features of his face rested pensively on the pedestal of his fingers and thumb.

She voiced: "Bless me Father for I have sinned."

"Are ready to confess your sins, my child?" He inquired in his rich baritone. His substance filtered across the dark screen of the confessional separating her from him. Kneeling there, she felt a yearning leap from her, into the darkness of this small private cubicle.

Suddenly, in her mind, the screen opened and he drew her within, and now she was in the same chamber as he, still kneeling, but now directly before his magnificent figure in the chair. " I have had impure thoughts, Father." She looked into his regal blue eyes, clear as a Tiger's and her look sought not, forgiveness.

"Tell me the nature of these thoughts, my child." His voice was kind, his hand gently soothed her brow.

His actual voice, speaking through the screen brought her back from the reverie, as he responded to the long pause from her side of the screen. Startled, she heard herself saying aloud: "I have had impure thoughts, Father." Still thinking dazedly of all the things she had imagined.

****

The next afternoon, Sister Christina had folded the enigmatic note she'd received, and tucked it in a pocket deep inside the plaits of her habit. Recess was over. The girls streamed back into the class-room, their faces red and their young hearts full of frolic and play. They made a jostling clatter as they shuffled and chatted. Sister Christina, from her desk, watched them pensively.

Her hand, pale as chalk, clanged the hand-bell sharply, calling them to order. Her face was devoid of the customary glare of threatening intent, that normally accompanied the bell. The children became quiet, slightly alarmed. They wondered why she wasn't giving them the "look", but after six months, the bell had become stimulus enough to assure their apprehensive response. They became quiet as mice.

Sister Christina looked out the window. Clouds covered the sky. She could no longer maintain herself. She composed a small, but adequate measure of authority in her voice.

"Take out your history text. Begin reading chapter seven. When you are done, place your heads on your desks and with eyes closed, pray for the salvation of your souls. I will return shortly. Remain totally silent! Know that God is watching you closely."

With this, she hurried towards the door, but paused at the threshold.

"Know that Satan will seek you out. Pray also for the strength to resist his temptation."

She left.

She went down the corridor from her classroom. The halls were thankfully empty. Several nuns noticed a hurried figure in black, head bowed, shooting swiftly past the open doors of their classes. She cut to her left through the door to the nun's lounge. She went to the far end of the lounge to the lavatory. Inside, she shut and locked the door. Taking a breath, for the first time since leaving her class it seemed, she removed the note. Her right hand instinctively fingered the oversize beads of the rosary that hung from the waist of her habit. Her left hand fluttered as she read the note

Sister C,
I spoke with Father Galleon, about your calling. It is important for you to make a decision now. Are you ready to surrender everything to your Lord? To suffer for His greater glory. Do you possess the

highest calling? Do you have the courage, Sister, to become the maiden, in service and devotion, kneeling to your Lord and Master?

Be at the entrance to the sanctuary at 8pm tonight, or remain as you are for perpetuity. Are you called to the sweetest suffering, sister?

Your Lord's servant,

Sister Bernadette,
Mother Superior of the Sisters of Suffering.

****

In the confessional, after her blurted admission, Father Galleon had been kind, gentle.

"And what were these impure thoughts, dear sister. Was it someone you know?" His voice was a low resonant whisper. It kindled a spark in her. Her heart froze around that tiny spark of desire for him. She was terrified to trek further, lest her next step trigger an avalanche within her lustful heart. Again, her silence brought his response.

"Do not be afraid, sister. The truth brings mercy. Denial will only ad to your list of sins. Know that your Lord loves you. Through your purification comes atonement. Proceed sister. Confess to your Lord and Master."

His voice, the supreme authority of it, compelled her beyond her logic. "It was you Father," her voice sobbed. And the avalanche swept her into a state of whiteness, its coldness burning her skin, her mind tumbling with the rush of it. It was the beginning of her descent.

****

Sister Christina tucked the note back into her habit. She hurriedly left the lounge, and managed to return to her class. Several nuns noticed the swift blur of habit again, past their classroom doors.

She arrived back in time to dismiss class at the bell, with a look that the young schoolgirls could not fathom or sense.

There was a legend that surrounded the Order of Suffering. It was about a secret group within the Sisters of Suffering, cloistered in the old convent. That stone cold antiquity sat apart from the modern structures of the parish. It was built of slate colored quarry rock. It was an ominous, yet idyllic structure with peaked windows of stained glass, depicting the stations-of-the-cross. Tall spires capped in ornate sheets of bronze jutted towards heaven from the facade. Two mammoth, weathered oak doors secured its entrance.

The only time the nuns of that secluded order were ever seen, was on Good Friday. They attended services, and mourned the crucifixion quietly, in a special section to the side of the altar. Their faces were hooded, and shrouded from view. It was strange that they each wore a chain around the waist of their gray habits, which attached to each other. They rose and knelt as one. An eerie sound came from the swaying chains.

There were hushed conversations about the rituals performed by this mysterious group. It was said that they were kept bare beneath their robes. Nervous whispers spoke of ceremonial tortures, for penance it was assumed. The rituals of purification were for atonement, driving out all remnants of secular concerns while extracting total devotion and surrender to the Lord.

****

Sister Christina knelt now by her bed in the empty dormitory, praying for the answer to her destiny. She had begged leave from the evening's community meal, claiming cramps. The dorm Superior, seeing the ashen pain on her face, and her shrunken posture, excused her.

"Dear Lord, am I worthy to receive you? It is my deepest desire to relinquish all to you. My soul begs to be taken into your glorious realm." She murmured fervently. "But I am so afraid, that I may not be worthy. Why does this desire to dwell on my flesh possess

me. Please, dear Lord, burn these devils from my soul, so I may serve only you."

With that image locked in place, recurring over and over, she chose her destiny.

****

Sister Christina had held herself back from packing until the last moment, clinging to the last breaths of the self she knew. She was driven forward by this desire she did not quite understand.

She looked at the picture of her mother on her bureau. Her mama looked out from the simple metal frame with a certain provocative, but still proper, demeanor. The picture had been taken on Christina's graduation from eighth grade. The following fall she would be in the convent.

She had asked her mother that day, "Am I doing the right thing mama? I feel so strong, yet long also to be like you mama."

Her mother cradled her chin in her hands, and spoke to her gently, "Always listen to your heart, darling. And if it changes or is drawn to a different path, follow it there as well. That is how you best serve the Lord. That's what you want most, isn't it dear, to serve your Lord."

"Yes, mama," young Christina had answered.

****

As she descended the stairs to the courtyard, Sister Christina heard the chimes of the church tower count to eight. A small terror struck her with the last stroke. She crossed the courtyard, on the path that led to the old convent. The night was cool and fresh as the light receded into the evening. Tall oaks and maples lined the path, their canopies almost black in the diminishing light.

At the great doors of the old convent, halfway up the dozen steps to

the entrance, stood a cloistered nun. Her dark gray hood drooped and covered her face, just a small irregular opening in the folds of the hood where no light entered. Sister Christina, lifted the hem of her habit and ascended the stairs. She stopped without being told to, before the taciturn nun. They stood in silence for several long moments. Sister Christina felt a trickle of warm sweat trail down the sides of her chest. The nun spoke bluntly, a challenge in her voice. "Why are you here?"

"I was given a note from Mother Superior. . . " The nun's hand shot up, palm forward, commanding silence.

"Why are you here?" she repeated, with added force.

"I was asked. . . " The nun's hand shot up again, punctuated by her sharp voice. "Why are you here?

Sister Christina felt frozen in her mind. She tried to think, to understand, but could think of nothing that would not recall that severe hand in front of her face. She closed her eyes, took a breath, and her felt her mother's voice speak from her heart.

"I am here to serve and please my Lord, sister." The hood nodded slightly.

"What time is it?" came the sharp voice from under the cloak.

"The time?", Sister Christina repeated. Nervously, she looked up at the clock in the tower of the Church, noting the position of the big hand. "It is 8:04, sister."

She watched the other nun record something on a small pad, that appeared from within her habit. She wished now that she had been more punctual. She was known for her lateness, but had never been reprimanded in the blunt way the question and the recording on the pad had made her feel.

"Go now. Stand before the doors. Knock seven times, slowly, with a pause between each knock. Wait in silence until you are told to

enter. Then go in quickly."

At Sister Christina's hesitation, the nun snapped, "The Lord is waiting!"

Propelled by her intention to serve, as well as this fevered adrenaline state, Sister Christina stood before the door and knocked as instructed.

To be continued…

(Note: I had finally reached, Arlana by phone the evening before this letter. We cleared a lot of issues between us, and established a covenant promoting her commitment to regular intervals of contact.)

Subject: First covenant
Date: Sat, 3 Jul

Dear one,

You made me so happy tonight, sweet girl. I was in a more playful mood than I have been in our past conversations. You provoke my better qualities, and sharpen them, as you deserve.

I feel that we do have many things to discuss, shave clean that fuzzy peach. I was quite pleased that we are able to dissect the subtler and more complex topics we might face.

I need to be able to make all these things crystal clear with you. To always be in that realm where we can discuss any topic or issue, no matter how complicated the nuances and have this ability together to wade through them with intelligence and patience. I trust we can do that now.

As you can tell, I'm not a phone Dom. Under the right circumstances it may be something to play with. But it's really a very

narrow channel to try to squeeze my full Dominance through. My element is the flesh.

I thought about it tonight. I would have had you get a belt and put the end through the buckle and slip it over your head and place it snugly around your lovely neck. Hold the belt where it feeds through the buckle, cinched against your neck, and begin to feed it through your hand a little at a time.

I want you to talk to me as you do this. I want to hear how your voice constrains until it starts to rasp. I want you to describe to me the rising pressure in your head, Arlana. You may touch yourself if you desire, but tell me whatever you do. A little tighter dear!

Perhaps after we meet, and I understand you better, phone sessions might serve good purpose for when we are apart. We shall see.

We have made our first covenant, sweet slut. (*Note: By phone, Arlana had accepted the first "agreement" between us.*) I expect it to be held sacred. You are never to go more than one week without contacting me. I will allow for special circumstances, arranged in advance. Know that you honor me with this gift of yourself.

You are my special panther girl.

All my love,

Galen

PS: I am including the next installment of sister c.

"Sister Christina" con't...

Several moments passed with no response. The longer she stood waiting before the doors, the greater the ball of fearful uncertainty grew in her belly. Her consciousness felt gripped by the dark watery undertone of dread. The sun had dipped beyond the tree line at the edge of the parish grounds. The air cooled uncomfortably on

her hands and cheeks.

"Why are you here?" she heard the nun's voice within ask her.

"To serve my Lord without restraint", she replied from her heart. The words nourished her intent. She took a deep breath and centered on that thought.

Through the door, she heard one command: "Enter." A woman's voice, but deep and masculine. The door opened heavily, as she thumbed the latch on the handle and pushed forward, into the total darkness of the vestibule.

A match struck, off to her left, and a small cone of candle flame cast a dim view of the nun standing before a cove entry. "Come to me."

Sister Christina moved toward the light, her small duffel of possessions carried at her side. She stood before the nun. Their eyes met briefly, but she quickly lowered hers. The nuns' gaze overpowered her. The eyes showed the strength of a man's, stern, like her father, whom she had also been helpless against.

What her lowered eyes glimpsed, made her start to shake with further uncertainty, but twisted back around inside her and struck another chord lower in her body. The nun wore the traditional gray veil, the starched white cowl around her face, and the triangulated white crown above her forehead.

Outside of that she was bare. The site of the nun's breasts, the absence of any pubic hair, startled her. But nothing could have disturbed her more than that dangling something that hung between the nun's legs and flashed in the flicker of the candle.

"From this point until you are informed otherwise," the nun uttered sternly, "you are to be known as number twenty-four. Walk towards that wall." The nun's bare arm, with an extended palm, gestured to her left. Sister Christina walked docilely forward towards the wall she could not see in the darkness. Another match struck.

She stood in front of another nun. This one had a round face, with cheery, full cheeks, but her eyes held an equal severity that conveyed no humor. Sister Christina's eyes lowered more slowly this time, curious to see the nun's body, her eyes transfixed on the chain that hung down between the legs with a medallion bobbing at the valley.

"Who are you?" her nun's voice feminine but potent.

" I'm sister Chris. . . "

"Who are you?" the voice snapped into Christina's rejoinder before she could finish it.

"Sister Christina" she repeated, voice wilting, knowing this wasn't the answer.

"Who are you?" this time, each word separated by a slow, distinct pause.

"I'm number twenty-four." The question was not repeated.

"Turn your head and look just past my left shoulder. Do it now."

Sister Christina peered in to the darkness, until a sudden bright flash, a camera, she realized, caught her in some startled gaze. Her view burned red for a moment, then went to total black. The low light offered by the candle slowly filtered back into her vision. A table stood to her right.

"Empty your bag." The nun pointed to the table and another candle was lit behind it. The candlelight revealed a third nun, with a lovely face. Her body stunned Sister Christina with its beauty. She turned her bag upside down onto the table. The nun picked through the few articles of underclothing, toiletries, and picked up a framed picture. "Is this your mother?" she inquired.

"Yes." Sister Christina replied brightly, hoping it might evoke a warmth from the new nun.

"She won't be of any help to you here." The nun removed the memento from the pile. "Remove your habit, and place it on the table."

By now, Sister Christina understood that she had relinquished her will, and disrobed shyly, holding her arms over her breasts and scrunching over so that her hands dropped before her sex.

"Put your hands at your sides and stand straight." Sister Christina obeyed hastily. "Do you have any diseases or impairments to your body that we should know about?"

"No."

"Any mental disorders or psychosis, or other psychological concerns?"

A long pause. "No."

The second nun came from her left. She held a candle in one hand and slowly ran its light over Sister Christina's body, a small heat tracking its path. The nun ran her soft hand over the curves of sister Christina's breasts, down her belly between her thighs, around the back, up over her bottom.

Squeezing the nape of her neck she asked, "Are you ready to begin this journey? Do you desire with all your heart to become the daughter of the Lord?"

"Yes," Sister Christina replied in a rapturous breath.

"Then put on this veil."

Sister Christina slipped her head through the opening at the bottom of the cowling that would sheath her face and to which the gray veil was attached. The veil added no warmth to the chill held in her body, nor covered any part relevant to one concerned with modesty.

"Twenty-four, Come this way!" The voice of the first nun called from across the darkness.

Sister Christina walked towards the first nun, her bare feet prickling on the coolness of the wood floor. Her flesh was still in goose bumps, little bubbles of innocent arousal from the previous nun's inspection

This time the first nun's countenance seemed a fraction less menacing to her. As she came before her the nun asked, with a direct, beatific solemnity, "Twenty-four. Are you the one?"

The nun's serene, but steely gaze, and the profound ambiguity of the question, momentarily shackled Sister Christina's thoughts.

Do you come her by your free will?"

Her mind cleared, and her resolve condensed. She remembered her mission. "Yes, sister."

"Are you willing to do anything for the Lord's pleasure and glory?"

"Yes, sister."

"Do you know that you must suffer and be purified to be made worthy?"

Sister Christina, though she was in the greatest state of fear she ever felt, desired desperately to serve this highest calling. This aspiration strengthened her resolve enough to answer again, "Yes, sister."

"Are you willing to endure and have the courage to be punished for your sins and transgressions, however the Lord sees fit?"

"I am willing."

"Step towards me then and turn around," she was commanded. The dim light went black as Sister Christina was blindfolded. The nun spun her around by her shoulders.

"We will begin the descent. There are fourteen steps. Take my hand. Remain silent."

They stepped through the cove entry, carved out of Italian marble. The stone steps on her bare feet, sent the shivers through her. She was numb with cold now. And each step in her slow descent, brought the temperature of her fear to a red-hot glow.

To be continued…

Subject: Covenant
Date: Sat, 3 Jul

Dearest Galen,

In keeping with the first covenant, I am writing to You before leaving. Please Sir, is "contact" referring to phone as well as e-mail, and does a phone message left on Your machine, count?

It was a terrific pleasure to speak with You and to hear the light and life in Your tone. I believe that our peach was given a little shave, no? I must say that I was honestly shocked at how much time had really elapsed since I had last written to You. I did not actually realize this. The first edict is good because it will make me aware of this. Thank You.

My element is the flesh also, but for the phone, the belt idea is delicious. Perhaps I should read You a poem this way.

Let me tell You again, how sorry I am that I neglected my dear Suzerain. I am trying to be as clear as I can with You, but do not venture too far in the future, as we spoke of. Nothing is festering, love. Things are so confused and crazy. This is the evil that binds me at times, as does the fascinating struggle that is my life. I am glad that I spoke to You before reading the e-reprimand. Your tone spoke volumes for itself and I hope that the sincerity of mine

explained a lot to You. I don't want to make You ever suffer, Sir. Do You forgive me?

You touched me by so eloquently expressing Your need to receive my letters. I also love the way You seduce me by certain images like: nuzzling me and licking my bloody mouth, pouncing on me, unleashing "beauty" all around me, sleek panthers racing across the plains. I also feel a strong need for Your nourishing correspondence. Unleash as much as You crave and I will be wrapped by Your will, as a cloak of Monsoon.

Like You say, I know that we will be able to wade through anything with intelligence and patience. I loved our conversation by moonlight, as I lay on the floor watching the clouds flit over the moon. I shall think of You when beauty strikes me by the cold sea as whales spray into the sky.

all my love,

Arlana

PS: What e-shots have I sent You, so that I do not send the same ones again? I have included a poem that touched me and inspired me. It I vital and honest and so apropos. The poet is a Pat Califia, a dominant lesbian. She has been described as a poet of unusual power and frankness. She writes fiction and poems which address the politics of sex, gender, and pleasure. She also is an activist for the S & M community. What a woman!

Subject: Redemption
Date: Mon, 5 July

Dear daughter,

You're tenderness wins your redemption, sweetheart. Your letter was soothing. I needed that tone again from my little daughter slut.

I always revel in your own expressions and images, loving your artists soul. I feel our connection as strong as ever. You've drawn more of my power from me in a few months than I've been able to express over my lifetime. I am grateful for the blessing of you.

You often surprise me with a title I have to cull from the dictionary(Suzerain). I delight in that honor. Your charm is large, dear, and soothes the panther's wary senses.

You show your wisdom and respect in careful attention to detail and the fine points of our covenant. You may email or call, or request I call you in a specified range of time. A phone message alone, with no further effort does not qualify for the weekly time limit.

Re: pics. I have you kneeling with leash and standing before the mirror. I welcome more of my elegant beautiful creature in the splendor of her submission

In preparation for meeting, I want you to fill out the enclosed questionnaire: a standard BDSM list. My judgment is that you don't relish such tasks, but whether you do or don't, know that this is not a request, it's an order. Trust that Papa will find this information valuable.

I want comment as well where it seems appropriate, particularly on edge-play items, or general categories that beg refinement. I also want more description of the functioning and use of your clitoris. You mentioned the don'ts, do you have do's as well. Do you desire sexual stimulation during a scene. What forms do you enjoy. Do you seek to orgasm during play, if Master allows?

I know Lothaire is on your stage again, after having "fled" in your first mention. I know you stated a deep love for him, that you spend time with him, travel with him, play with him. Are these some of the circumstances you were concerned about regarding my visit.

I never understood clearly what "circumstances" meant. Explain these. I'm not implying any subterfuge here, dear. I'm simply stating the data without knowing how it applies to our relationship.

I do not wish a visit kept in secrecy. That would create an obvious underlying tension. This is the next item to shave from the peach.

In the past, I've always had an unyielding loyalty to a personal code: never entice another man's woman. I've had it done to me by my "best" friend, and I don't know a more heinous betrayal. Offering one's sub or slave to a play partner, or having an open relationship is one thing, but I wouldn't entangle myself in a situation of deception, no matter what my feelings.

I accept your short-range perspective, and I know there are good reasons for that, but my feeling are out front. I accept the inequity and my vulnerability in this. You've stirred my feeling and emotions and desires, illuminated my dark atmosphere. You know how I feel towards you.

You resonate and enhance my noblest qualities. How can I not desire this connection with you, to the fullest extent of my passion? At the same time, developing my patience in this regard has served me and us well. It has allowed us to get so deep, without my impatience yanking it out by the roots.

It might be impossible to have a relationship with you, that served my desire to live the rest of my life with my soul-mate. I know neither of us knows if we can maintain this bliss on a short or long term basis in the realm of the flesh, and all the complexity that drags behind it.

Regardless of the future, I only feel blessed by the sacred pleasure of knowing you. That is fixed now in my heart for eternity. I cherish all of you sweet panther.

loving you,

Galen

Subject: Beauty of pain
Date: Mon, 5 Jul

Dearest,

I forgot to tell you how much I enjoyed the Califia poem. . . so
cleanly and elegantly stated, a sublime treatise on the beauty of
pain. It was like you speaking to me, dear. My desire to deliver
your relinquishment grows stronger.

... a few more thoughts for your list:

You've mentioned your desire to be bloodied. To what extent?
Through what methods? What does it signify for you?

Besides being a submissive slave, are you, a Domme to other
submissives, male or female? Sub to a domme? Are you bi-sexual?

You mentioned that your relationship with Martin had changed.
What is the current status? You stated he was your Master. How
was your relationship defined? What areas did he and did he not
control?

Tuesday, as you know dear is the 7th day. The time fly's by doesn't
it?

love,

Galen

Subject: Time does fly, my Liege
Date: Mon, 5 Jul

Dearest,

I have just returned from 7 hours on the highway. Diving in the
freezing water was exquisite. This morning I dove to 90 feet.

Thank you for Your letter, I want to savor it in my senses like chocolate melting in my mouth and to consider all the questions You pose. You honor me by remembering the details of my life and wanting to get so deep inside of me. I am grateful for that.

It is so hot here, not cool like it was near the Fjords. I must run to pick up my cat but will find my way to this terminal again very soon. I dreamt of You last night. I am glad to know that now You have moved into my subconscious. In the dream You were a teenager and very awkward looking, but quite adamant about dominating me.

Strange and marvelous. . . . I miss you like air in my tank.

Arlana

Subject: Assignment Part I
Date: Tue, 6 Jul

Hello my Blessing,

Hope that my Black Panther is well fed and purring under a shady tree, Master of all the little creatures scurrying at His presence. I might as well dive into the dauntingly huge task before me. I will fill it out in increments, as I want to be thorough.

Why not begin with Your clitoris questions. Do's: humm. . . do please stay clear as a rule, if You must, just the slightest breath of pressure of tongue or finger. I prefer all action to take place below that sensitive nub: slow, low, strong strokes of the tongue rev me up good, and when I am heated up, anything inserted while the lapping continues can surely push me over the top.

I love having pressure on my pubic bone: in general, I need this pressure 95% of the time to orgasm. Use of the hand or being pressed against the leg or pinned under the body and grinding etc,

will usually do the trick. When this pubic bone is "in the air", so to speak, it takes much longer for me to come or makes it impossible. Strange, no?

Blood: I will submit to being bloodied if this turns You on. I do find blood sexy and appreciate the sacrificial symbolism of it. It is a visceral and poignant way to give of myself. My life itself draining from me for You. Your turn-ons will become my turn-ons, dear.

If I see You thrilled at my bleeding for You, I will be thrilled and excited also. I have bled drops and bled rivers, it is up to You if I shall do so at all. It is part and parcel of the mantle I have chosen to wear, is it not? It has always been through sterile needles. I do not think I would like to be cut with a knife(threatened ok- cut no). It is rather crude and unhealthy to me, this idea. I scar too easily and do not want any permanent marks. (yet!)

I am sometimes a Dominant to other subs just because there are few people around who can Top me. I have a couple of very docile, rather soft, boys who do my housecleaning and a few close friends, male and female, that I have and may Top now and then out of affection. I sometimes do Top new people as their positive and memorable initiation to our world is important to me. At least I know that with me it will be good.

Many subs bow automatically to my strength and within the pecking order of things. It is right that they do so. I love women but am not often inspired by them. To feel deeply for another woman I need to admire her. I am passionate about intelligence, depth and personal power. Body chemistry has to be right, besides.

When these hurdles are passed, I do consider myself bi-sexual and capable of loving another female. I am quite affectionate and flirty with women in the scene. Here we all know one another and are very cozy and friendly together.

My relationship with Martin is still an open one and I hide nothing from him. He does not really want to be anyone's Master anymore.

He wants to play from time to time but generally wants to keep things on equal footing. Woe is me who so loves to mythologize!

This has put a strain on all the intimate aspects of our relationship. I find it hard to disassociate my desire for the Master from my desire for the man. They are both intertwined. I feel frustrated and misled at times but have been honest about my feelings. Things are a bit topsy-turvy as you can well imagine. Martin knows all about You and is alright with it. The boundaries of our relationship are quite broad.

Lothaire returned after his travels to Rio and Buenos Aries. We had some intense moments together and became much closer until my trip to Europe. We had a trans-Atlantic misunderstanding . I witnessed an unreasonably cold side to him that shocked and hurt me as well as undermined my trust. Something in me died over there.

Lothaire taught me much, however. Especially, he proved to me that I could fall in love again and showed me how beautiful that painful emotion can be- how worth it, it is. I am grateful to him for this and for everything he has taught me as a submissive. He brought me to another level, to a deeper refinement of thought and abandonment. I have seen him once since I returned and we had a lazy day together and did not play.

By the way, I have never really traveled with him, only a short weekend to the country once. I do not know what is happening with him either, only that I feel very different and far from him now. We never asked one another questions during the last year about our personal lives outside of what we shared, so it is unlikely that the subject of your visit would come up in our conversation.

The cold, cold sea was a marvel and I am depressed to find myself back in this hot, hot city where all is strife and complication. So many questions marks and open parentheses in my existence. I don't even feel settled and happy in my own home yet. My stomach aches with nervous knowledge of all that I must do today.

In the midst of all of this You shimmer on the horizon like a long awaited oasis and I am so very thirsty. I think of what You will do to me and am thrilled by the enticing suspense of awaiting You.

Bye for now,

Arlana

PS: hope you like the photos. . .

Subject: Blood Lust
Date: Wed, 7 Jul

My sweet little girl,

Your loving devotion and commitment to your tasks please me dear. This is a short note to acknowledge your good work, and how much I crave you. Each time I hear from my deep-sea panther, I hunger to taste you.

I do thirst for your blood, dear. I want to draw that sacrifice from you a drop at time: see it trickle delicately down your skin, mixing with the tears falling from your eyes.

I am down to the dregs of my mental energy right now, sweetheart, though my spirit and connection to yours is strong.

I will dwell on all you have thus far provided and look forward to the balance due.

your thirsty panther,

Galen

"Sister Christina" con't...

At the bottom of the stair, she was led forwards. There were no sounds, but for her breathing, and the rhythmic jangle of the nun's chains. They stopped. A hand on her shoulder, pushed her down. Her buttocks measured the temperature on the floor, a humid cold. Her blindfold was removed.

The walls were the same as the outside of the convent, but streaked with water stains from seepage. Candelabra, mounted on the walls, were spaced every four feet, illuminating the crypt. There was a ledge, a few feet above the floor that formed a small shelf, along the walls. On the ledge, along three sides of the chamber, stood the assembled Sisters of the Order of Suffering.

Their hoods were now black instead of gray, the cowling and peaked crown, black, as well. Each wore a leather mask, with slits for the eyes and nose. Every nun held a staff at her side. Each staff was adorned at the top with a silver *fleur de lys*, the flower of the Order. The Order had been founded in France during the Inquisition.

Rising before Sister Christina, on a small rampart that jutted from the ledge into the crypt, stood a nun of ominous authority. She wore the same habit, but her mask had a bridge that covered her nose, and ended there, cutting across her cheeks to the left and right. Her lips were cruelly thin. Between her legs, hung three chains. The nipples of each breast were pierced with a ring and a prominent *fleur-de-lys* bob, that pulled the nipples down slightly.

"Stand up, Twenty-four." She snarled.

So adrift was Sister Christina's mind, that had she not been the only soul to whom the command could be directly addressed, would have forgotten that she was now a number. She stood awkwardly.

"What time were you to arrive?" the nun asked.

"Around, eight." she hedged. It was foolish.

"*Around* eight?" There was a foreboding emphasis on the word

around. "Were those your exact instructions?"

"No, Sister. I was told eight o'clock."

"Keep your eyes focused on me when we speak, twenty-four. Unclasp your hands. Leave them at your sides." The nun gestured with a sweep of her bare arm around the chamber. "Look around the room. The sisters all around you have been kept waiting. They are devoted every hour of the day to serving their Lord. You have stolen their precious time, twenty-four. Look at each of them. Ask yourself, is your selfish neglect of time, more important than the devotion they offer to their Lord."

Sister Christina's gaze returned humbly to the nun before her. "No, sister," she said, and quickly lowered her gaze.

"No? Then why did you choose to be late?" The nun slammed the point of her staff onto the rampart. "Look at me twenty-four. Time past is never recovered. You owe each sister here their four minutes. They will each purge your willful tardiness through an appropriate discipline. This will be arranged this evening," she declared.

"Discipline? What type of discipline, Sister?" Sister Christina dared to ask, though her voice trembled. She felt a slight nausea gurgle up in her gullet with her words.

"Our Lord will guide us in this matter of discipline, twenty-four."

The word discipline uncovered a memory that flashed painfully bright and added to the charge the meaning of it wrought within Sister Christina's body. The complete memory, had she the leisure to recall it in total, was of her father leading her down the stairs to his basement workshop. Mama was never home during these "discipline" episodes.

On this particular occasion, at age eleven, she had returned late from her best friend's house. It had been a pajama party. One of the seven girls was from the public school. She boasted of her skill

to flirt and tease the older boys at her school. She told them, showed them actually, the functioning of the clitoris.

"I like to pinch it between my fingers. It gets bigger. Watch," she pinched and massaged her nub. "My older sister says when I feel like I've left the world, that's an orgasm. I'm still working on it. It feels really good. Try it." she encouraged the other girls.

The Catholic girls blushed, one prayed, but all watched eagerly. None would do it.

Later that night, laying quietly in her sleeping bag among the seven girls, Christina experimented. She grew flush with an ambiguous arousal, moistness seeped between her thighs. The further she withdrew from the world, the stronger her guilt became and her fear of being discovered. She heard the girl to her left roll over in her sleeping bag, facing Christina. Christina froze. She slowly looked to her left. She saw the girl's quiet face turned towards her, eyes closed in the dim light from the hall.

To be continued…

Subject: My posse
Date: Wed, 7 Jul

Dear one,

So, now you have a Cowboy, a Teenager, a Panther, a Tiger, a Pascha, a Suzerain, all stalking you. Each will have his way with you. You are doomed, sweetheart. Oh yeah! Let's not forget Papa!

I miss you dear. You agitate and excite every atom of me. You are a splendid female. I am so thankful the Mystery from the North has brought such joy and inspiration into my life, resplendent with gifts for her Lord.

If you ever wish to discuss the turmoil in your life, I am here for

counsel or comfort. This could be done by phone. I want to soothe you as well as devour you. I am neither expert at counsel nor comfort, but my heart would be there for you.

goodnight my princess,

Galen

Subject: Assignment Part II
Date: Fri, 9 Jul

Dearest Galen,

Yes my darling, You are so many men in one- all to stalk and devour me. I am reading a book on Taoist philosophy, which is doing me good right now, and is restoring some of my inner peace. I feel much better and am calmer.

Thank You for the offer of counsel. I am sure to take You up on it one day, but when I am feeling worse and You are feeling better. I am reading many of the Califia poems. They turn me on mentally and physically. Someone has gotten right down to the core of the feelings of our world and is honest about them. How refreshing, how sexy.

Your compliments inflame me and make me feel so fortunate. Thank You for seeing and thank You for believing. You are and will always remain precious to me.

Assignment con't. . .

The question about seeking to orgasm during play: This is at Your discretion. Certainly I do become quite aroused in a session depending on what is going on. If I have been a good girl, a nice orgasm(s) is/are (smiling naughtily and lustily) a lovely and loving way to close a scene. Either way, I am happy. I should mention

that I have had some training in orgasm delay, and can orgasm on command, when I am close. This develops with time and the sexual *apprentissage* of one another.

Questionnaire:

This questionnaire should be filled out by a Sub and provided to their Dom/Top before playing with them. This will provide a quick "head-start" to identifying limits, negotiating and finding common ground for play.

For each item, you need to provide two answers:

First write YES or NO next to each item to indicate if you have ever DONE that activity.

Next, indicate for each item how you FEEL about that activity by rating it on a scale of 0 to 5.

0 means you will NOT do that item under any circumstances (a hard limit).

1 indicates you have utterly no desire to do that activity and don't like doing it (in fact, may loath it) and would ordinarily object to doing it, but you would be willing to do it to please the Dominant if it they really wanted it. (sometimes called a "soft limit").

2 means you are willing to do this activity, but it has no special appeal for you.

3 means you usually like doing this activity, at least on an irregular/ occasional basis.

4 means you like doing this activity, and would like to experience it on a regular basis.

5 means the activity is a wild turn-on for you, and you would like it as often as possible.

Note any additional information which might be important for your

Dom to know.

There is intentionally some overlap between categories. Unless otherwise stated, the sub is the recipient of the activity. If you don't understand a category, ask master or search a D/s site for clarification. All info provided is strictly confidential.

Experience yes/no, Willingness, 0-5

Age Play: Yes, 3; I have some experience in this and am mentally turned on by "Daddy" figures.

Anal Sex: Yes, 3. 5; I am not a virgin there.

Asphyxiation/Breath Control: Yes, 4 on safer forms of this, 2 or less when it is damaging or very dangerous; I must be very relaxed for this- emotionally and physically. I am turned on by having a hand around my neck, my life in my Master's hand. I also enjoy having my neck held from the back. I have experienced several forms of breath control - willing delay of breath, asphyxia, a sort of throttling (painful and scary), cutting off of the blood to the brain(unconsciousness resulting), worn a latex mask (not much air getting through), body bag with little air, in stocks in a cabinet with little air. This all is very dangerous, and must be done very carefully!

Bathroom use, control: Yes, 3.5 - 4.0; if that is Your pleasure Sir.

Bestiality: No, 2.5; I have an eel fantasy/ snake fantasy. . . Dogs - 0!

Beating soft: Yes, 4.5; a perfect warm up

Beating hard: Yes, 4.5; gets those endorphins flowing and keeps bad girls in line

Blindfolds: Yes, 3.5; a normal part of play, can be suspenseful and nerve-wracking for me

Blood Play: Yes, 3.5 –4; the sacrificial lamb shall bleed on Your altar

Being Bitten: Yes, 2.5; within reason, and I do bite back (part of Panther love)

Branding: No, 1.5; this is like the wedding band but in perpetuity-for my Master and lover for life.

Bondage Light and Heavy: Yes, 4; *oui oui c'est tres bon*

Bondage Multi day: No, 3; I'd try it.

Bondage (public, under clothing) Yes, 3; sexy secret

Breast Whipping: Yes, 3.5

Caning: Yes, 4 - 4.5; I do like the cane particularly a real English cane

Cells/Closets: Yes, 3; the trunk of the car once in awhile too can be good; panic rises and falls in waves.

Clothespins: Yes, 2.75 - 3; humiliating but I guess this means that it is good

Cock Worship: Yes, 4; I love to honor the Cock God

Collars private/public: Yes, 4; I am proud of what I am

Competitions: No, 2.5 - 3; I have not done this so I am not sure if I would like it. I have a camaraderie with other subs but suppose that I am magnanimous because I feel a sense of supremacy over most. I am competitive by nature and would love to win for my Master though.

Corsets: Yes, 4; I am excited by this erotic and refined torture. Extended wear weakens me in body and spirit(a good tenderizer). I

have been told that I have a becoming corset hobble.

Cuffs: Yes, 4; of any material

Cutting: No, 1; I do not want any new scars to show.

Double Penetration: Yes, 3

Electro Torture: Yes, 2.75 - 3; in reasonable voltage and in a sensual manner

Enemas: Yes, 3; I find this very intimate.

Exercise (forced required): Yes, 3.5; Sexy for a Master who gets off on pure power

Exhibitionism: Yes, 4; I flashed a trucker just last night. I find it amusing, especially when it makes Master proud.

Hope that this is fine for now. I am going to pick up a new-hand me down computer tonight and hope to install it this weekend as well as getting hooked up early in the week. I am happy about this and begin a new contract on Monday and will soon know my schedule for the summer/fall.

I hug You tightly.

Arlana

Subject: Rrrrroarrr
Date: Mon, 12 Jul

Dear Sir,

Am I allowed to take a tiny break from the questionnaire? Are you all-right? It is my turn to miss hearing from You.

Good news, I finally have a Pentium computer at my house. I hope to have it all up and running right by the end of the week. Just think, I can drift over, naked to the terminal and begin to write to You in the middle of the night.

I have begun my contract work for a TV show here and was told that I can only find out my schedule with an advance of two weeks at a time. Still, this is not so bad, as I only work in blocks of four hours at a time(wretched literal slavery!). As it happens, I have all of next week off.

I am off to my boxing class now to work off some sadness and aggression and to fill my body with endorphins. As I hope You will fill me when You see me. I have a bit of a bug that has made me feel weak and given me a sore throat, but I hope to sweat some of the bad stuff out. I actually like the discipline and military rigidity of this type of training.

Last week when I paused to say hello to someone I knew, between the three minute bell, the coach said: "not on my time Miss!". If someone talks, the rest of the class is penalized with push-ups. Fun. I like the pain that I have to endure there. We actually scream at times. Last week, I overcame acute discomfort. Once on the other side of the pain, I became giddy and could not stop laughing. It is a different form of punishment.

Would You nurse my sore throat if I were by Your side, papa??? I am in need of TLC tonight, perhaps a spanking across the knee before an early bedtime.

bye darling,

Arlana

Subject: Hollow
Date: Tue, July 13

Dear one,

I have been in a vacuous state of mind for a few days. I feel emptied out and physically and mentally drained. Emotionally hollow. Too hollow to feel I can communicate any truth or tenderness. This is not personally directed at you. I just need to keep it honest.

That's good news about your new computer, and your new contract. I would love to soothe you, and spank you as well.

You have until Sunday, midnight to finish your task. Hopefully, by then, I will ride the pendulum back the other way. Sorry to be so meager. I didn't want to send such an uninspiring letter, but I know you were wondering where I've disappeared to.

luv,

Galen

Here's a little more…

"Sister Christina" con't.

In the basement of her house, at the back, was her father's workshop. It was filled with gadgets and contraptions, and the tools that were applied to them. The atmosphere was damp and ramshackle, a sharp contrast to the provincial orderliness of her father's business life. A dim bare bulb hung on a wire from the ceiling. The string pull chord sashayed back and forth, after her father tugged it as they entered the room.

Her father let go of her hand, and sat in the oak swivel chair by his desk. He was a narrow man, aging poorly, his soul entrapped by the meager scope of his life. He was devout and strict on matters that infringed on the rules that guided Christina's behavior.

"Why were you late?"

"Sherry's mom made us clean the house, Sir. I left as soon as I could."

" Not soon enough, apparently. You knew you would be punished, didn't you? I'm surprised. You've been such a good girl."

"I'm sorry" Christina was immediately slapped across the cheek. Her father reiterated the rule he had made early on, "When you are being disciplined, you will address me as, "Sir". Understand?"

"Yes, papa. I mean, yes sir. "

He swung the chair to his right and opened a desk drawer. His hand reached for the wooden paddle. It was a "fly-back" paddle. It once had a long gray rubber band with a small rubber ball tethered to one end, the other stapled to the paddle. Only the staple remained.

" Lay across my lap. You will take twenty strokes."

Christina positioned herself across his lap, her small hands gripping the edge of the desk. Her father raised her gray plaid skirt to her thin waist. She wore light blue, flowered panties that stretched tight across her firm young bottom. Her father's left hand pressed in the small of her back, his right brought the paddle down in a sharp smack on her bottom. Christina jerked and shrieked, a high pitched "Owwww!"

"Keep still." he ordered. His left hand pressed on her back and pushed her pubis firmly into his lap. Her squirms tightened within this restriction. By the sixth blow, eyes tearing, sobbing, the pressure from her father's left hand, she felt a new sensation between her legs. Her eyes rolled languidly.

By the tenth blow, her breath became little gasps, her squirms tightened further, focused subtly on the hard spot in her father's lap. At the fourteenth blow, she felt a flow begin between her legs. Her face was damp and flushed. A wet spot darkened in the crotch of her panties.

310

Suddenly, her father pushed her roughly off his lap, and she tumbled to the floor. She looked up at her father. He had a horrified, confused cast, rippling across the lean features of his face.

His voice quavered. "Go to your room. Now! Stay there until your mother returns. You will say nothing of your punishment. Go!" It would be the last time her father punished her.

Christina hurried up the stairs of the basement, then up the hall stairs to her room. She lay on the bed and cried into the pillow. The pillowcase soaked in her sorrow and shame. She was swept away in the confusion of a primal boundary crossed. She felt the exhilaration and then the guilt the sexually abused might encounter when they feel an aspect of sexual pleasure from their abuse, whether they want to or not.

She got up from the bed. She knelt beside it, and made the sign of the cross. "Dear Lord, if it is your will, please accept my vow to join the convent. It is all I want, Lord." She placed her head on the bed, and still kneeling, drifted asleep.

****

Sister twenty-four was led from the crypt to a small chamber. The nun leading her was about her age, a little older. She watched the firm roundness of the nun's ass, sway beneath her veil as they walked. "How strange that they dress so immodestly. How does that serve the Lord." she wondered.

Her formal Catholicism had never ventured onto this foreign branch. It was always a sin to think of your body sexually. This must serve some other purpose she thought. "Maybe the point was suffering in the cold chambers of the convent, and offering that to the Lord. Nothing sexual." she thought. She was half right.

"I am taking you for your wound, sister twenty-four. It is part of the initiation. Do not be afraid. Be honored that you have been chosen to serve our Lord, body, mind and soul. This begins your formal training."

The chamber's stone walls were painted black. A slab table of rose marble sat in the center of the room, with *fleur de lys's* carved along its granite base. Along the edges, there were wooden pegs, spaced every three feet, jutting upright along the length and width of the slab. Atop each of these was an iron eyelet, the eye about an inch in diameter. An array of candles on pedestals illuminated the slab in a flickering light.

She was led to her right to a small alcove within the chamber. Before her stood a nun, much shorter than her, and older. Her breasts would have been sagged without the rings and pendant she wore in them. Deep crows feet stamped the corners of her eyes. Her face was furrowed and ancient, but held the dignity and grace of a noble elder.

The nun lit a match to a thick braid of incense. The smell of sage, cedar and other herbs poked into sister twenty-four's senses. She felt alert, as the nun outlined her body front and back in swirls of the smoking stick.

"You are about to enter the sacred inner-circle of our order sister twenty-four." The nun placed her hand over sister twenty-four's heart, between her breasts.

"Are you the one? Are you the one, twenty-four?" The nun's voice was quiet but full of power. Her gray eyes, direct and searching, moving left and right, looking within it felt, to the secrets of her soul.

"Are you the one?" The nun's gaze injected her soul like a serum, that compels truth. She was exposed. She suddenly felt all the horror of her shame and lust, and the striking polarity to her higher devotion to serve her Lord. The nun's face shone a beatific countenance that radiated with the calmness of a sage. A slight benevolent smile appeared on her lips, in her raised cheeks, the gray eyes aglow with it.

It was a mother's look, in a tender loving moment with her newborn

infant. "Our Lord loves you for all your passions, dear. He will find no evil within you. The flesh is not a sin, dear, when offered in service to the Lord."

Twenty-four's body released a sigh, a small purr oozed from within her throat. Her eyes closed. She took a deep breath, sage tingling in her nostrils. She felt safe, her terror at everything, soothed by this beautiful sanity and love pouring from the nun.

"Are you the one, twenty-four? Are you the one of prophesy? The one who will serve our Lord as no one ever has? Do you choose this destiny? Can you offer yourself for His pleasure, now and forever?"

Sister twenty-four placed her hands over her heart, covering the nuns hand with hers. In a swoon of passion she said. " It is my sole desire."

"I welcome you to our circle, sister twenty-four." The nun embraced her. She whispered against twenty-fours teary cheeks.

"You are the one."

Another nun led her to the slab. Her short stocky frame waddled beneath the back of her veil. Her plump bottom and sturdy legs showed below its edges. Her legs were slightly bowed to allow for the chain as she walked.

"Kneel." The nun picked up a short leather collar from the slab. It was black with a small, silver *fleur de lis,* attached to a silver ring at its center. The nun wrapped it around twenty-four's neck, and fastened it at the back. It was moderately tight.

"This is a novitiates collar. It is never to be removed," she paused, "except by command from our Lord." When the nun stepped away, after fastening the collar, sister twenty-four looked up at her.

"Sister, please. It's so tight, I can barely breathe." She tried to crook a finger between her neck and the taught collar.

The nun stepped forward, tilting twenty-four's head down towards the floor. "Put your hand down from your collar. You are to keep your head bowed and eyes lowered. When you are told to look at your superiors, you will do so." The nun pushed down on her head for emphasis.

Two nuns came to her sides, their bare legs brushing against her flesh. It caused her to shiver. They lifted her under her arms, and made her stand. They led her to the base edge of the slab. "Sit down on the slab." One nun removed twenty-four's veil and cowling.

She took a small square of white cloth from a bucket of liquid, and squeezed out the excess. The nun wadded it into a ball. "Open you mouth." Sister twenty-four, looking down, had been watching as the other nun placed her in leather anklets, and a heavy metal bar that stretched her legs wide apart. She felt the pull in her thighs.

Her head was suddenly yanked back by the hair. "Open your mouth twenty-four," a sweet impatience cooing from the nuns lips. Twenty-four obeyed, and the wad of cloth filled her mouth. It's mass spread her jaws wide. Her mouth soon puckered tighter around the wad, as it absorbed the citric liquid it had been soaked in. The wad was secured with a cloth gag, twisted tight across her open mouth. It stretched back the corners of her lips.

"Until you learn control, it is best to be gagged for your punishments and rituals. Lay back."

Sister twenty-four lay back against the cool slab. She watched the chandelier in the ceiling glide across her view, as the nuns grabbed her arms and slid her towards the head of the slab. Her wrists were cuffed and secured to eyelets, stretching her arms above her head.

Sister twenty-four, her fear and devotion, a nervous tangle, struggled to breathe. The gag diminished her breath further. She was faint. She felt the muscles in her thighs about to tear, being forced so wide.

As she lay there, for what seemed a long time, the image of her Lord merged with her thoughts of discomfort: her Lord, made flesh, hanging on the cross, suffering for the sins of all time. She prayed. "Oh how you suffered for me my precious Lord. I am filled with sorrow at all the pain I have caused you. How I have denied you my full devotion. It will now be I who will lovingly suffer for you dear Lord."

To be continued…

Subject: Head better now
Date: Wed, 14 Jul

Dear little girl,

Papa's head is better now. I didn't mean to alarm my little daughter by sounding so dazed in my last letter. But I will always be honest with you, even at my own expense.

I think about us, in the context of a Master/slave relationship, with all the actual real time still to come. I consider the mental, spiritual and emotional dimensions, all the drama and theater, and try to understand how I really feel about this type of relationship. Though my real time experience as a Top continues to grow, I have not had an ongoing M/s relationship.

I don't know, yet, how an M/s relationship works day to day. There are so many variables, it seems impossible to imagine anything with certainty. The ideal is a total power exchange, total obedience, total submission. The slave is my property by contract. No limits, no safe-words. Total power with total trust. The "sensible" part of me feels that the ideal will never be manifested.

I can envision winding up in a nursing home in twenty years, hitting up drooling, invalid subs, still seeking that ideal. My more practical self accepts that a D/s relationship is a negotiation. A balancing act of all those other components of personality, style, passion, lust,

beauty and chemistry, that maintains a strong and firm tension, central to a Master/slave relationship.

It is odd to reflect on how many women are co-conspirators in this "evil" pursuit, that they've broken through those sacrosanct taboos to become so gloriously improper. People who pursue this lifestyle are incredibly courageous. It's not easy to aspire to be a slut and a slave, going against the grain of every feminist and evangelistic politically correct agenda. Not to mention the horror of family, friends and professional peers. Thank God for those who know it is exactly what they want and more and have embraced their truth.

We're placed right down there with child molesters in the view of the general public. I have personal experience in this regard. It is an intense and vehement disdain. Many people will not risk being found out. They feel they have too much at stake. Maybe their sexual truth will just go away. I did this for many years. It didn't go away.

I am forever grateful for that. I felt my Dominant urges since I was five years old, as I think back. I was a little slow to understand what that was, and once I did, it took a very long time to accept that as my true self. I couldn't face that publicly. I kept it hidden from everyone, while I fantasized constantly.

I sought out my counterpart from my early twenties. I knew I desired a truly passionate slut, who had submissive tendencies, who wouldn't feel like I was coming from way out in left field at the suggestion of bondage or spanking.

It didn't occur to me that I would ever meet a girl with experience, asking me to dominate her. I didn't know there was a scene. All I knew were the models in BDSM magazines. My god, who were these women? What is going on in their minds? They seemingly were posing voluntarily, some looking hot and turned on, begging more! My brain would sizzle from the heat of my lust.

I finally found my way, along this treacherous path. I found the courage to accept the consequences, and there have been many, to

Eye Contact Restriction: Yes, 1; been there done that. Now I want to look right into the soul and feed on the love there for my strength.

Face Slapping: Yes, 3.5

Fantasy Rape: Yes, 3; struggling is fun

Fantasy Gang Rape: No, 1; no thanks (being delivered to a football team or the like??)

Fisting Anal: No, 1; no thanks- I think this is the gay male department.

Fisting Vaginal: Yes, 3, I enjoy this a great deal.

Following Orders: Yes, 4-5; but of course!

Forced lesbianism: Yes, 2-3; I have health and personal chemistry concerns about this in a general sense.

Forced Masturbation: Yes, 3; though being touched is better.

Full Head Hoods: Yes, 3; I had a hole to breathe through. Once in a while is fine.

Gags: Cloth, Balls, Tape, Leather, Yes, 3-4; for all except cloth, a necessary part of things no?

Golden Showers: Yes, 3; can be sensual, I am not crazy about it on the face; it's fun in the shower too!

Hairbrush spankings: Yes, 3; very old world.

Hair Pulling: Yes, 3-4; gentle to strong, but not to pulling out of hair please.

Harems: No, 3; I like being the Queen bee and could be dangerous to the others in certain situations.

Head: Yes, 4-5; how can one live without it?

High Heels: Yes, 4-5; I feel sexy in them and have lots

Hot Oils on genitals: No, 1; ouch, don't know. .

Hot Waxing on genitals: No, 1; I do this on other parts of my body for grooming, not sensual to me, ok on the breasts and elsewhere.

Housework: Yes, 2; Princesses hate this.

Ice Cubes: Yes, 3

Infantilism: No, 1-2; no thanks, I like to act old enough to speak.

Japanese Bondage: Yes, 3.5; very sexy and *arrigato*. .

Interrogations: Yes, 3; shine the light on me and let her rip!

Kidnapping: No, 3.5; I would like this one day, no one has done it yet and it is a longtime fantasy.

Kneeling: Yes, 4-5; of course

Knife Play: Yes, 3.5; once in a while, nice for intimidation (I do not want scars!)

Leather Clothing: Yes, 4

Massage, giving: Yes, 3.5

Medical scenes: Yes, 3; Eurethra probes- yummm

Modeling for erotic photos, videos: Yes, 3; depending on exposure, use of photos and talent of photographer, I prefer to refrain from erotic videos (I have one, I have the only copy)

Mouth Bits: No, 3; I do not know the feeling

Mummification: No, 2-3; I have been in a vacuum body bag

Nipple Clamps: Yes, 3-4

Nipple Weights: Yes, 3

Oral, anal play, licking Master: Yes, 3-4

Over the knee spanking: Yes, 3-4

Orgasm control: Yes, 3-4

Outdoor scenes: Yes, 3.5; (note: I hate insects!) Outdoors is a nice change. .

Phone sex, serving Dom: Yes, 3; nothing beats real life

Phone sex, serving the Dom's friends: No, 3; sort of

Piercing: play: Yes, 3-4; my body retains some traumatic pain memories of this

Piercing: permanent: No, 1; I have none and will do this only for a lifetime Master/Life Partner

Prison Scenes: No, 3; sounds like fun

Pony slave: No, 3; If I did it I would want to do it for real (i. e. exertion and pulling a real cart, preferably in the English country-side)

Public exposure: Yes, 3; sure

Pussy whipping: Yes, 3.5-4

Pussy clamps: Yes, 3.5

Clamps with weights: Yes, 3.5; but not to really alter or main the

lips

Riding crops: Yes, 4; and the Master in the whole outfit…yum. .

Religious scenes: No, 3; Sister Christina??

Restrictive rules on behavior: Yes, 3.5-4; especially in training for a new Master

Latex clothes: Yes, 3.5; I have lovely stuff as I have modeled it, but am not a latex fetishist.

Saran wrapping: Yes, 3.5-4; I can panic when asphyxiated like this if the bondage is total.

Scratching: Yes, 2-3; lightly is ok but I find it rather unmanly for a man to scratch

Sensory deprivation: Yes, 3-4; I am curious about this

Serving female Domme with M. supervision: Yes, 3

Serving as Dom to other subs (supervised): Yes, 3

Shaved Pussy: Yes, 5; I find this part of good grooming and am very closely shaved.

Slutty clothing, Private: Yes, 3.75; sure

Slutty clothing, public: Yes, 4.5; to our clubs, not the street please- I am a lady

Spanking by hand: Yes, 4; I am very fond of this.

Spreader bars: Yes, 3.5-4; Basic hardware.

Stocks: Yes, 3.5

Strap on: sucking with Dom wearing: No, 1; Only in movies!!

Strap on: Yes, 3

Strap on: (**on a sub**) Yes, 3; Can be fun

Strapping, full body: Yes, 3; with the belt, or what??

Suspension, all types: Yes, 3.75-4

Supplying new partners for Dom: Yes, 2.5-3; once in a while as long as they don't supplant me.

Swallowing semen: Yes, 4; my Master's only (once health matters have been considered and cleared.)

Swallowing urine: Yes, 1.5; does nothing for me.

Swapping: No, 1; I am not into swinging.

Swinging (multiple): No, 1

Tattooing: No, 1; Nature has adorned me sufficiently, temporary ones are fun.

Tickling: Yes, 2; not erotic, but silly and funny- beware, I shall seek revenge.

Triple penetration: No, 3; all orifices at once???? human???? Hummmmm could be fun. . . . (sucking on a dildo doesn't count for me and is not a turn on), but a cock and two dildoes???

Uniforms: Yes, 4; yummmm riding boots on a man are *molto* sexy (5) as are crisp white shirts (military and poet) and black shirts with leather pants; Gloves on the Master are also a 5 (*oh mon Dieu!*)

Verbal humiliation: Yes, 3; very mild only please.

Vibrator on genitals: Yes, 4.5; or nice big dildoes

Voyeurism: Yes, 3.5; up to a point- but not an entire evening

Voyeurism: my Dom with others: Yes, 3; I like being his accomplice/assistant.

Viewing porno, (BDSM) with Master: Yes, 3.5

Wearing symbolic jewelry: Yes, 4.5-5; I find this appropriate and poetic.

Whipping: Yes, 4.5

Wooden paddles: Yes, 4; It depends on the instrument itself.

Wrestling: Yes in life, no in a scene, 2-3; I like to wrestle when horsing around and having fun- i. e. a good release of tension in the park, or with friends- it is not an erotic activity to me, but rather sportive and playful one.

Scat: No, 0; big zero there

I hope that You are not too angry with me dearest. I feel a bit ill and will lie down now. Thank You for Your message, I so enjoyed hearing Your voice. I was a bit surprised by Your e-mail but am secure in what we share and did not get carried away.

I believe that living in a S/m relationship is possible, but no one plays twenty-four hours a day. It just means that the Master can exercise his right whenever he wants and that his sub must comply. It is not that complicated, really. Both partners have to be flexible.

Things can be negotiated and that is where generosity and mercy come in. . . (right????) Don't bar me from Your affections for this small offense, please. I only read about the deadline today but had sensed that I had to finish it quickly. I believe that the questionnaire has slowed our momentum. I hope that things go back to normal.

yours,

Arlana

Subject: My new e-mail address at home
Date: Wed, 21 Jul

Dearest Galen,

Finally darling, here I am at home with my own e-mail address. I
am so glad of this. Please forward any reply that You may have sent
to my completion of assignment e-mail.

All my love,

Arlana

Subject: Strangled
Date: Thu, 22 July

Dear,

I feel strangled by my sadness and my fury right t now. This has
nothing to do with you. I will deal with your lack of adherence to
our covenant later, for you missed our one-week deadline by 24
hours. You should have called. You also exceeded my generosity
of the extended deadline for the questionnaire. Plus, the statement:
"I believe the questionnaire (an inanimate object!) has slowed our
momentum a bit", will be corrected!

I will tell you I was pleased to read your lively, intelligent, humorous, and endearing responses. It stirred my imagination, which was
the intent. I will convey my impressions at another time. I will also
tell you, that you will be disciplined for your transgressions. Probably by phone.

I've been in my divorce trial the last two days. I am totally drained,

I haven't slept in two nights, and I have even more on my mind tonight. It is a sick, dark circus. Picture me against her whole family(two sisters, her niece and her dad) sitting in court, three wives of former couple friends, one husband, three female employees from our business, her vile lawyer, and my ex.

Although the atmosphere of hatred and disgust blazing from them was not a major problem, what I heard in my ex's testimony today was. I learned she is taking herself and my sons to counseling. She is worried about the impact of them having a father who is so depraved and mentally ill that he gets his kicks from torturing women.

She was in tears now on the stand. She'd done a lot of reading, she said, and apparently this "disease" can be hereditary. So she's decided to tell my sons the horrible "truth" about their father and with counseling, she prays they will be all-right.

My poor boys! I was reprimanded by the judge for my physical outburst to her testimony. I couldn't contain my fury. But I only scratch the surface. I am too exhausted to describe all the other aspects. I won't know the outcome of the judge's decree until Monday.

I think of my two boys in their home with all her family and friends, going over the details of the trial. I hate to think of all the distorted things they will say and transmit about me to my sons. What will that do to their minds? How will they feel? What wounds will they receive that they will have to deal with later in life? And she dares to accuse me of being a sadist.

I need to talk with you by phone, it is too much to write about right now. I need a friend to talk with. I have no one with whom I can share my grief right now, who would understand more clearly what I truly feel. Call me immediately upon reading this, day or night.

Galen

(Note: Arlana and I finally spoke by phone, and these were some of her thoughts on our up and down conversation.)

Subject: So sorry about everything.
Date" Sun, 25 Jul

Dear Galen

I am so sorry about everything, about my lateness, about the trial and all the complications of our tumultuous lives. It is a shame. I am glad to have spoken to You and that we ended our winding conversation on a positive note. Do not dance away from me, do not be too unbending either. This could scare me off. Love should be pliant, caring, resilient and flexible. This has to go both ways, Master or not.

Enough of that. I believe that You have understood me. I am only concerned that I was not consoling enough for all the ordeals You are going through. I did pick a bad time to be late. When I think of it- what poor timing! Perhaps You would not have been as upset if it happened at another juncture. The judges and the ex and her family have no business in your intimate life. It sounds like a witch-hunt. If something goes on between two consenting adults, others have nothing whatsoever to say about it.

You should tell Your sons this. The truest way for them to be happy in life will be to be honest about who they are and to live that truth fully themselves. (How old are they?) Living unequivocally is all You are trying to do. I can imagine the horrible scenes of tearful recrimination. Stay cool, it is to Your advantage.

Listen to me, after that heated conversation of last night. Are there character witnesses for You or someone that the boys respect who could second what You are saying? Good luck for the decision. Call me if You need to speak again. Our issues aside, I want to be there for You.

Imagine me holding You tightly in my arms. I will fight for You.

Let us become a harbor of peace and light. The rigidity and harshness of the world should be banned in our togetherness, whatever we are to become.

Can You deal with this? Am I dreaming? I am tired. . . tired . . . tired. My disappointment weighs me down like lead around my waist when I dive: men, love, life... I crave obliteration when I contemplate abandoning my dreams. I am sending You an excerpt from another Califia poem, I hope it makes You feel better. I offer myself humbly and long to feel Your whip against my skin to wash away all the grief with a cleansing stream of hot tears.

all my love,

Arlana

by the way, what are some of the "ideas" evoked by the questionnaire???

PS: Please be well and take care of yourself for me. I regret if I sounded tense last night. It was beautiful to hear Your voice blend in with the wind, even if I ached for quiet. I will send You a poem by romantic post about Your ex and her ilk. I feel sorry for them. You, I admire. I woke with a start, screaming last night. I wish You could just hold me and that You needed me like air.

Subject: Demure
Date: Wed, 28 July

Dear,

I appreciated your tone of tenderness and regret. I crave that part of you. I don't want to hurt you (except in that other way), and I'm not happy to see you suffering in any way. We have been able to intelligently weave our way through complicated issues in the past. I hope we can continue, but I feel stuck at this impasse with you. It is time to breach it. This is the truth as best as I am able to express

328

it. How it will change our relationship, I can't predict. That will depend on you.

I don't approach this association by worrying if I might scare you off. I want you to run, if I scare you so, the way a gazelle runs when she sniffs the hunter downwind. I will let you escape, and I will also.

I feel now that it's clear to both of us that we seek different things in a long term relationship. I won't need to meet you to discover that.

Yes, I seek demure expressions when the sub is apologizing and seeking forgiveness for an acknowledged transgression of a covenant. These things are sacred for my personal mythos of a D/s relationship. It is like my religion. The rules are fair and flexible, but they are rules, and I will enforce them.

I cautioned you to be careful about making covenants with me. That you must think about them clearly and hold them sacred. When the borders are crossed I expect a supplicant to petition for mercy, and I melt in tenderness to this gift of submission. I fall deeper in love and joy, and that will be given back to my slave.

For me, this is the process of harmony. The rules are best kept simple and clear, and once the sub accepts them, enforced. You want to claim I am inflexible and unfair. I think not. I rule my kingdom, and I do so fairly and justly, as best as I am able. It's my duty to be fair.

The reluctance you show to apologize and accept responsibility for failing in your simple duty is disappointing. This is why I have withdrawn our first and only covenant. (hardly stringent).

Submission is a gift, and you are not ready to give that to me yet, or maybe never will be. I don't know. You've shown me glimpses of that side, elegantly expressed. That is what I crave in you. I fed on your intelligence, charm, beauty, submission and erotic fire.

You live on the borders in every way, like myself. This is why my

chase for you was so hot. I've sought your devotion and passion in partnership. I could have accepted you as my soul-mate. I do accept you and love you whoever you are, dear. You are such a deep dark creature, so delicious to a man like me.

I was hurt and surprised by your attitude in the beginning of our conversation last night. To hear you discuss your disillusionment with men, how lonely you are, how isolated, with no mention of our relationship, I felt like I and all the passion, love and mythic realms that I offered meant nothing to you. I felt invisible as I listened to your bitterness and cynicism.

Everything between us, in that revelation, seemed so meaningless, without value. It chilled the fire in my heart. I was included in your disdain obviously, rather than standing out as an exception.

We are in such a similar cycle. Your words regarding your current anxiety echo precisely my own when I indulge my pessimistic self. I hibernate. I can feel like I've extended my patience with life beyond reason. I can be fatigued by the merciless incoming tide of disappointment and delay. Our high points - intelligence, depth and sense of culture, eros, were a divine overlap of souls.

My judgment is that towards me, in the realm of D/s, you could be a divinely masochistic bottom, but neither a submissive and definitely not a slave. I seek a delicately woven D/s relationship full of mythos and ritual that continually renews each partner in every way, as Dominant and submissive, Master and slave.

Galen

Subject: Above the Rabble, untouched by disdain.
Date: Wed, 28 Jul

Dearest,

You are way above the rabble and the disappointment I feel. I am

sorry You took this personally. The word You used, "mythic", is very much how You figure in my life and inner landscape. It is rather like an unknown country that I want to travel to but cannot really imagine until I have landed, tasted and explored. You know that I do not allow myself to dream too far ahead into the future. This ideal has served me well so far. I do not want to burden You with my hopes and longings as You have enough to contend with. We live so far from one another . . .

I live the moment and milk that for all the complex and transient beauty that it offers. Isn't "now" what our whole lives are, a series "nows", a succession of moments? This is the way that I live my life. It is also why I do not talk too far into the future. Variables change from day to day and I have discovered that things never turn out as we expect them to. I have learnt to savor the parade of surprising marvels that life is.

I just want to live the adventure as it comes. I am absorbed in watching the unfolding of my own theater. We each have a front row seat to our own show that we cannot skip out on while we still live.

When I am hurting I withdraw even from those who would help me-bad reflex, I know, but a lot of people, even animals, do that. I should exploit the richness that You are to me. I am glad to have You. I should have told You sooner. I am telling You now. I am jarred that I hurt You. I am sorry, I was insensitive.

Yes, we are suffering alike. I am submissive, but just not every livelong moment of the day, though the fact is that in my heart I am, in every livelong atom in my body. There are just the practicalities and realities of everyday life. You must also realize that I am not a submissive woman in my regular existence. I am so in my fantasy life, as a choice.

I would not be the vital, engaging woman you know, were I truly powerless and passive. The best submissives are the strongest. Your fantasy slave sounds like a true Amazon, a giantess of a human. There is no way she could be all that and be compliant and

docile in her genuine personality. True and freely given capitulation is a gift because it is given- not because it is seized, negotiated or demanded.

I need to have my say as a human being as You do. This is personal dignity. I am of no use to myself or to anyone else without it. I have to be true to Arlana in order to respect myself and to have respect for others in turn. It sounds like You have many expectations my Suzerain, but many contradict and undermine one another.

I am enamored by the rituals and honor of our world and adhere to the precepts with loving diligence. Understanding and flexibility are great qualities in a Top, and that is why I have found You a bit uncompromising. I cannot control the movements of the Universe to suit my will, even if it is to serve Yours. It is unrealistic of You to expect me to do so.

Fantasy and actuality have to meet somewhere if your carefully nursed ideals are to be put to the life test. These cherished concepts are useless to You if they become insurmountable hurdles. They are even more damaging when they become podiums from which to criticize and exhort. It is really beneath You to do so. Do not become a species like those who criticize and persecute you. It is sad when we do this to one another personally and within the community.

My submission is a real gift even if it does not fit snugly into the illusory classification of your untested ideals, I know that I could exhilarate You.

I am very real!

Be kind now, and things will fall into place. I wish You could feel as You did before.

I am hollow without the promise of You.

Arlana

Subject: Waiting
Date: Thu, 29 Jul

Sir,

Waiting to hear from you

melting with

sadness

and

burning

with

yearning.

Arlana

Subject: Are You all right?
Date: Sat, 31 Jul

Dearest Galen,

I am thinking of You and wondering how You are. I am feeling
better about men and feel happier in general. A good friend said
that it was nice to hear me laugh again, as I had not laughed all
week. I am smiling today and hope that You are also. Please do not
leave me to languish in exile. The strangest thoughts flit through
my mind.

Did You receive my letter??

I send You a warm hug and my love,

Arlana

PS: I have attached a recent photo taken with the computer

Subject: Priorities
Date: Sun, 1 Aug

 Dear,

I am glad you are happier. Thanks for the poem and the image of "sister" Christina in Japan. It was a very similar context to the character in my story, even the costumes. I enjoy Califia's poems. She has a strong passionate fervor.

I have been at a loss as to how to proceed from here with you, or without you. Your process of holding back, though right for you, does not work for me. For me it drives all the passion and desire from the potential I felt for you. I know you are serving out your passion in other directions, so I feel too low on the list of things you prioritize in your life.

You freely state to me how strong your passion and desire is for your English friends. I don't sense I'm of the same rank. After sixteen years of my ex, I plan on being my sub's number one priority. As she will be mine. I will have royal service and respect from my slave.

You keep bickering about our issue. . . "It sounds like You have many expectations my Suzerain, but many contradict and under-mine each other..." I will correct you again. There were no contradictions. I had one expectation. Only one. Our covenant. Not so onerous, I think.

It was made with your input and agreement. "I need to have my say

as You do." This was done. You agreed the covenant would be good to keep you from going so long between contacts. You agreed you had been neglectful. I prefer to not have a tedious list of rules, but this was an example of a rule that we both agreed would be helpful.

"I found You a bit tough. . . I cannot control the movements of the Universe to suit Your will." You wouldn't have had to make nearly that effort!

Even beyond a D/s relationship, if I'm going to miss a scheduled appointment or deadline, I call on the phone, as soon as possible before hand. It is common courtesy in business and personal life. I apologize sincerely, I explain the circumstances, but do not make excuses, and reschedule at a definite time.

Our covenant had a built in flexibility, a span of 7 days within which to contact me, not a definite schedule. There was also the phone option, which increased the flexibility and ease of communication, regardless of your Internet server.

It was not a big issue that you were late and didn't attempt to contact me otherwise. It could have been long behind us, over and dealt with, with a sincere apology on your part. But you persist, and judge me as lacking generosity and kindness. "Understanding and mercy are great qualities in a Top." I do not appreciate your implication here.

What was lacking here, in my judgment, was you taking responsibility for missing an agreed upon deadline, or letting me know by phone what was going on, then, a sincere apology, offered demurely, and accepting a suitable punishment. Instead you spooked like a horse with a bad memory of a cruel rider, and still keep throwing out how tough I am, I have so many expectations, etc.

I desire no further recriminations from you on this matter. Is that clear?

I am also very busy right now. I am preparing for oral arguments in

335

the initial appeal of my divorce decree. I am at a critical juncture in my business dealings which now more than ever require my devotion. I have two other email relationships that have developed recently. I have a sub that I am training as a pain slut, every week or so (I am taking Viagra, its quite amazing, plus my impotence generally seems to be in regression.)

And the biggest irony: A woman lawyer who's an associate in the firm that represents me, and helped my on the case (She came to trial both days at no charge.) has been very supportive, considering my "deviant" behavior. She has confessed through two lengthy e-mails, that she's desired me ever since she read my D/s profile(which was part of my wife's evidence against me.(lol))

She has a Daddy/daughter fantasy, likes rough sex, wants to sit on my lap, call me Daddy, tell her what a bad girl she is, and she wants me to "hurt her pussy" and other things. The universe plays such funny jokes on us one minute, and then rips our dreams apart the next.

We have shared a wealth of our lives with each other, Arlana. I guess, like you, I can't look into the future any more.

Galen

Subject: Sad
Date: Mon, 2 Aug

Dear Galen,

Your e-mail has made me very sad. It is I who am now at a loss. I guess everyone reacts to an accumulated life response and some sums are more concentrated than others.

You mistake my living for the moment with holding back. I never hold back in life- never! I just held off on dreaming large before actually proceeding to the next phase to avoid disappointment. I am

just being myself.

I could have called, it is true, but since contracts are few this summer, I have to figure out the best time to call and the time differences, etc. I am sorry about that. Perhaps it was your displeasure that I was afraid of. I am not telling You this to excuse myself, I only thought that You should know the real story, even though this embarrasses me.

The tone of our communication has made me weary. I am not channeling my energies elsewhere. Everything is quiet on that front. It can be so lonely when you seek only the finest, and the most profound. I see that life has given You consolation from me. I am happy for You and wish you only the "royal service" and respect You deserve and have not received from me.

Arlana

Subject: Solace
Date: Tue, 3 Aug

My panther girl,

I question why I am writing this. What is my motivation at this point? Lifting these rocks, hoping to find something underneath is like lifting the dried scabs from the wounds. It is torture to not find anything beneath but blood and pus. My own and yours, but that is not what you were for me.

That is why I try to step back a bit and not give up. Why do the small things consume the big things? That hurts me more than anything, to have one small thread unravel the whole finely wrought tapestry.

I am sorry to have my efforts to elicit a clean apology and acknowledgment fail, and also hurt you, bring you sadness. And I know your hurt came from other things I said. I was careful that I spoke

337

the truth, but I know I used it like a cruel weapon. I hope you can forgive me.

I suffer from having done that, perhaps as much as you. I fought back my grief and tears, when I got your response, as I was just heading to a meeting that required a different focus. I've become expert at submerging my turbulent feelings to display a calm rationale surface. I know that you need more than anything my tenderness, dear panther girl. Again, we are so alike. Siblings of the same family of wounds.

All I wanted was to hear you say you were sorry without what felt like defiant, cruel and defensive qualifiers thrown in. I would have melted like a candle to a flame, gushing with tenderness, joy and inspiration for my royal consort, had you expressed your remorse cleanly.

I wished only that you recognized how I was flexible, generous and fair. I wanted to feel like you held our covenant sacred. You wanted and needed to honor that first ritual between us. I wanted to feel that you desired me enough to offer this.

Let me reveal one of my "shadows"(a negative thought form or message that can overtake one's divine nature): I fear I am not strong enough to succeed without the love and commitment of a soul-mate.

This "tape" is contrary to what I know of my strength, will, independence, courage, and self-sufficient nature, but still, I wrestle with this fear. Try to understand it, befriend it, tame it, give it a place of honor, so it doesn't consume me and become actualized. It amazes me to have gone this far in my life without my soul-mate, and still have accomplished what I have.

There is a part of me that feels like I've been abandoned all my life. . . by my family, my religion, culture, community. A lifelong orphan. Alone. I've made attempt after attempt to weave myself into the mainstreams, and the numerous counter-current tributaries. To belong somewhere, to fit in. I could find a bit of myself in all

these manifestations. At times even feeling or maybe only feigning passion. I kept waiting to hear a faint echo from anywhere in the universe, a signal from my home planet. A place and community where I belonged, my devoted one by my side. It is a wearying struggle to continually start over, to have spent so much time in the lonely confines of my isolate identity.

You spoke of generosity. I need yours now. I honor all that you need to be happy. I offer my generosity and tenderness, my understanding, my love, my mercy. Please offer in peace what I need, darling. There is no other woman I could ask this of. I do not desire consolations, I desire you.

Galen

Subject: Harbors of Pain
Date: Thu, 5 Aug

My darling,

I desire you so much also. Thank you for that clear, loving and lucid letter. You are so deep, our potential enormous. I should have simply offered a quiet, submissive apology. You deserve no less.

I was in a funk that week. I was also dealing with my grievances with the opposite sex and the loneliness of an unmatched soul.

I am sorry. Please forgive me. Please punish me to Your satisfaction. I have suffered so much from this already - anguish worse than whips could ever inflict. I have paid my own price.

I burned enviously when reading your last note. This shows me how deeply I care. If there is so much "blood and pus", let us learn from it, dearest. It is like going backwards to go forwards. It is the arm flexing back before the launching of the javelin, or the throwing of the shot-put. You are brave and noble, my Hetman, to even lift these rocks.

One small thread will not unravel the entire tightly woven tapestry if we do not let it. I do not want to let it. Right now I only want to look into Your eyes, feel the healing tide of love wash over me and to serve and suffer. I appreciate the truth even if it hurts.

Can we find a way for You not to be disappointed by trying to "expect"? I harbor such pain and frustration over such tests (remember I told You of a childhood friend I lost this way?) It is so distressing and unmanageable! I hope You understand this and can help us in this way.

Of course I forgive You. It was such a relief to hear Your explanation about using the truth as a weapon. You have been hurt also! I feel like crying also when I imagine You near tears. I am troubled by this. What have I done?!! I am upset with myself. I so much want to show You that I am worthy and have ended up doing the opposite. I am the one in tears now.

I did and do hold our covenant sacred. I knew that I had failed and was resigned to not being able to change that, no matter what arose. I am fearful of falling short of your ideals. Is everything ruined now? Is the dye cast? Is this all a bad sign for You?

I also wished it could have remained simple and clear cut without wide sweeping ramifications. It DOES NOT mean that I do not desire You enough. We are too attuned and intellectual for our own good at times, and woe for those wounds we share also, dear Galen. If the parameters of the soul-mate dream are wide and allow for differences and circumstance, chances become better. It is in our power to just make it so.

Will You do this for us? I will be more of what You need. I will do this for You. I am subdued by all of this. I have learnt a terrible and valuable lesson. I will fight for a place in the enclosure of love's embrace. I have tried to show You so much of this hungry hope. I shall still seize a place as friend or lover. I can be confidante and comfort also. I have never toiled quite like this.

Mysteriously, I sense that this is what I must do with you. Caution to the wind. That javelin is flying far now, my would-be subduer. If we keep this alive and come to some consensus, I might become the echo to the song You most need to hear.

Let's kiss and make up,

Arlana

Subject: Phoenix
Date: Wed, 4 Aug

My dearest sweetest panther,

You moved me so deeply with you letter. I can cry different tears and they are sweet and quenching. This is short, now, because I am so tired and my full response demands my clarity to express my joy and passionate love. You touch my heart so gently, kiss my ancient wounds so tenderly. I cherish this soul to soul embrace, and will never let go.

Do not worry my pet, every rock will be turned over and every wound healed.

All my love,

Galen.

PS: I will finish this tomorrow night. I just wanted you to awaken to my love.

Subject: From the ashes
Date: Thu, 05 Aug

......Whoops, in my excitement I sent the letter to a wrong address- well lucky ****@. com is going to get a love letter, ha –ha.

kisses,

Arlana.

Now I send it on its true path!

Dearest heart,

I nuzzle you quietly and happily. Thank you for the letter. I had not slept almost all night and am going to the countryside with two girlfriends and their two dogs. I will only be gone a couple of days, my towering spire. Soon I will be locked away within you to suffer and honor. I will run to the computer as soon as my feet enter the house. We rise from the ashes!

all my love

Arlana

Subject: My treasure, my gold
Date: Thu, 5 Aug

Dear heart,

I asked for your generosity and I have received it in abundance. Thank you my panther girl. Your tone was so soothing and concil- iatory. That posture calls for my own reasonableness and desire to create our covenants with careful consideration to both sides. I have missed your passion and your desire greatly. I needed to feel that from you most of all.

I loved your image of the javelin. It was beautiful, as are you. I am adding Hetman to my list of scoundrels, all stalking you with dark intent. They are closing in. Watch out!

We both accomplished what was needed for this to survive. We are both worthy dear, quite worthy. We've saved this still too fragile bond between us, and will make it stronger from what we have learned. But I understand, now, had confirmed, how strong and deep this bond is. We put quite a strain on it, sweetheart, and it held.

When I first got your "Sad" letter, I felt it was done with. I would just let it go. It was too complicated. Too painful. Too much hurt and damage done. The grief of feeling all the elegant beauty of what we had expressed, gone, is what brought up the tears. It was a difficult loss to bear.

You have meant so much to me. You have allowed me to share my weakest, darkest moments, without judgment. In fact you gave me strength, love, and inspiration. It kept me fighting through my despair, and I was in deep desperation, at several points over these last six months. That is where my love and admiration for you are deepest…that you ennobled me, while I was feeling nothing would save me from that obliteration you spoke of. You saved me dearest lover.

There will be no punishments or admonitions beyond what we both have already suffered, my daughter. I think it best to dispense with all covenants and all formal ritual until after we have met.

I am afraid, to be honest, of how we will settle some of these fine points to a relationship. I believe there still may be difficulties ahead. But I know now that we both have shown how our reason and desire can resolve the harshest impasse. That is a powerful ally we have now when we battle the obstacles in our path.

Please my dearest, let's solve the meeting schedule puzzle. It is time we meet, don't you think? What would be better, you coming here or me to there? I'm thinking of a Friday to a Monday, but during the week can work as well. If you wish to come here, I will buy your ticket.

You are my treasure, my gold.

keep faith luv,

Galen

Subject: My gold.
Date: Wed, 11 Aug

Dearest Galen,

You are a like a shining sword glinting in the sunlight. Sharp and forbidding, yet appealing and magnetically hypnotic. I so much want to be near perfection for You. I was so glad of Your letter. Thank You. It is a happier track that we are on indeed. I agree that we must see one another very soon. I am eager to meet You, though I am a bit afraid(as I should be right?).

If I come to you, where would I stay etc. . . How long would You like me to be there? How much notice? (not that again, right!) For a trip here, what would You like to do? Do we plan swiftly or would You like to wait for fall?

As usual, my life is up in the air, but my schedule is pretty open. I do not want to go in circles and frustrate You in the process, dear love, so please guide me to fulfill Your wishes. I am chastened and bow my head.

keeping the faith for us,

love and passion,

Arlana

Subject: Fall mystery
Date: Mon, 16 Aug

Dear heart,

Your letter was sweet. I am much more patient now, and working to suspend my poisonous expectations. Right now, it looks better to wait until fall sometime, for me. My load is quite heavy right now with things that need my devoted attention in the coming months. I also have a couple of other trips that were pending that have come to the forefront. As well, I've been thinking about attending the Living in Leather event in Florida in October, and have some friends I'd like to revisit there as well.

Your city is maybe better in the fall, as a place for mystery and romance. It is probably less complicated for you if I were to come there. I will plan to get a hotel in an area of your recommendation. So let's see how things look in September, to make a final plan.

I attended a play party in **** last week, as well as got in an accident. It was a big hassle, between towing, repair, car rental, taxi rides, up and down, but finally I have my Explorer back, and no serious injuries to deal with.

Anyway, there was a Domme giving a piercing demo at the party. I started a conversation and then began assisting and observing up-close. I finally had her pierce my pectorals in three places. It confirmed I'm not a masochist! I didn't even feel it, even when she sprayed the piercings with alcohol.

I learned a lot about procedure, safety and equipment though. One girl passed out cold, for about twenty minutes, then vomited for another twenty off to the side while the demonstration continued. She was well cared for, just sick as a dog. You mentioned your difficult time with this in a past ordeal. If you can, what exactly happened, that you might wish to avoid in the future?

I still plan to make comments on your questionnaire, as soon as I am able. I sent you something in the mail. It went out on Friday,

and should arrive soon. Hope all is well in your world, dear. I hope
to partake in making it go round very soon.

Love,

Galen

Subject: Fall fantasies
Date: Tue, 24 Aug

Dearest Tiger,

Thank you for your beautiful card and the timely amulet, which I
have kept near me and close to my heart. It is precious to me. It is
exquisite and was needed, as more adversity has been challenging
me.

I am fortified by your calm affection and steadiness. I offer You the
same with all that I am. Please forgive me for taking this long to
answer.

My mind and spirit have been fighting bravely though my body has
broken down somewhat with the stress and grief of things. My
back has become so tense that my vertebra have pinched a nerve
and I could not get up to sit at the computer. I am in pain now as I
write and I dedicate this suffering to You. I am taking care of things
and am bravely facing the pain. What would a non-masochist be
doing in my shoes at this point?

I have now cut off impeding relations and am working on knowing
and loving myself while building up my life again. This is difficult
and challenging on many fronts, as you can imagine. To survive,
one must constantly be re-invented. I am thrilled by Your upcoming
visit. Please let me know of any preparations you would like me to
make. I have missed our torrid correspondence but know that we
have gone as far as we can at the moment with that.

I feel some resigned disappointment coming from You. Am I right? If that is the price of peace and agreement, I accept it, because I know that we will become molten again together very soon. The fruits of distance and our coincidentally mutually difficult life passage at this time, did contribute to this. At least we are here for one another. This is external and cannot affect my opinion of the connection and understanding that we share. Your happiness means much to me.

I know that we will have a wonderful time together and You are right that October is a mysterious month here. The weather is still beautiful and we will be able to enjoy the outdoors(bring sweaters!). I am going to Europe to spend some time with some very special people there in September, and will be back on October 3rd. Anytime after that will be fine.

Please let me know when You will come and what You would like to plan for. You mentioned that You have questions to address from the questionnaire. Please do so at Your earliest convenience, love. Keep faith also. I lift the burdens off You that make You sound laden and heavy and caress Your soul and sensibilities so that You are bright and light again.

All my love,

Arlana

Subject: Nourish your soul
Date: Tue, 31 Aug

Dear panther,

Your last letter sounded so distressed. What is happening to my poor daughter? I hope all those external pressures, are to soon be relieved, if not already. Please take good care of yourself, nourish your body and your soul. Maybe you just need a good rest, dear.

I just had a new problem dumped on me. I had my personal signature on several loans, before a business I owned with my ex, for sixteen years, recently incorporated. My ex was awarded the business(all assets and liabilities) and our house, and about 90% of the possessions. She's purposely not paying the loans in my name, and now I have about $75,000 of her debt, that's being called due.

By the divorce decree, because I anticipated what she would do, I am still on title to our assets, and the judge gave me a lien, basically, should she default on the business loans in my name. But it's another major and expensive legal battle, should it come to that. Her parents are financing her legal "defense fund". I'm on my own.

Most of my equity is locked up, by the decree, until my sons graduate from high school in four years. She doesn't have to pay me until then. That balances out in the long term, but not in the short term. My credit is in jeopardy right now, and I don't have the capital to pay those off, at the same time I'm developing the other business ventures. I am just getting them going right now, but this new debt situation could cause me some problems in the short term. I don't know yet.

Financially right now, I'm not on solid ground, although this is generally how the life on an entrepreneur goes. I've made a lot of money in the past, but this divorce situation has me starting over again. Still, I'm a very skilled entrepreneur, savvy business promoter and manager, plus I always have faith.

My niece, who works for an airline, has offered me a standby ticket to come to Chicago. My sister wants me to come there sometime over the holidays, but I'm not big on those vacant celebrations, so I told them maybe in October. I'm going to look at extending my flight to ****, from there. I'd like to work out a time in October that we can spend three or four days together, at least a good part of the time. Right now, I'm flexible, but the sooner I can nail this down with you the more likely these plans will go smoother.

I agree that we've taken things about as far as we could via e-mail. As real and as impassioned as that has been for me, I'm finding it

too frustrating and ephemeral. I seek satisfaction of a different sort.

I'm happy you liked the talisman. I hope it can offer some solace and protection when you are in a dark or vulnerable mood. My passions are still strong and hot for you dear, but I need to put them in restraint, until we meet, so I don't get pulled into those shadows that block the light of my love for you.

All my blessings and strength,

Galen

Subject: What's the delay?
Date: Sat, 11 Sep

Dear miss panther,

Why do you delay getting back to me about finalizing plans for an October visit? These gaps in your attentiveness are so frustrating both practically and spiritually. Nonetheless, I hope you are well, if not thriving.

Thanks for the snail mail. The poem: <u>Hallucinations at 101</u>, made me lurch toward you. I wanted to grasp you, to heal my feverish cock deep in your soothing throat, ease the twitch in my hands that long to strike you, press the weight of my body and desire around you neck and smother you into relinquishment.

The picture of you, small as it was, reminded me of a Maxfield Parrish painting, my panther looks to be languidly perched on the branch in the afternoon sun. She's content after a good day of slaughter and chase. Perhaps she's bound to the branch, by rope and desire.

Are you still with me, dear? Wherever you are, I hope you are safe and joyful.

Galen

Subject: I am still with you.
Date: Mon, 13 Sep

My darling,

Things have been difficult and tiring and I am hanging by a thread.
I have never quite experienced this in my life, nor for this long.
Thank You for your queries. It means so much to me to know You
care.

I look forward to Your visit more than You know. Please plan to
come whenever it is convenient for you in October. I will be back
in town on the 3rd, from overseas and will have about a week of low
energy, disrupted sleep etc, from jet lag. So if You came anytime
after that, I would be at my best.

I am thirsty for you, for all that we are and we will share. Twitching
hands and feverish cock? Oh yes, my predatory tiger. I am excited
by the tone of Your letter. Crush me under Your body and take me
on a long and perilous journey with only You as my sustenance. I
purr and flex my claws and imagine how it will feel to be tamed by
You.

All my love,

Arlana

Subject: Your Champion
Date: Fri, 17 Sep

Dear little panther,

I wish for you to find solace and contentment, without losing the

edge that sharpens your passion and instinct for life. Your tone and description conveys your suffering in the cruel reality of circumstance, and I feel so forlorn that I cannot aid you, comfort you, slay that demon in you that wants to destroy and plunder your soul. And such a beautiful soul it is, dear.

In spirit, if not in life, I am your champion. Please know that you are to call me collect anytime, if I may soothe or distract you from the strife you feel. I am forever your friend and ally, no matter what else our fate.

My plans are not yet fully formed but I am aiming between the 2nd and 3rd week of October. My rough plan would be to spend 3 nights. Can you suggest a possible region or area of the city that would be best for proximity to you?

I will seek out a hotel in that region over the Internet, unless you have a suggestion. Something $100 US or less. I forget how the foreign exchange rate works. I think it's in my favor. If public transportation is good, or taxis, I probably won't rent a car, so that's a consideration as well.

Your pictures didn't come through completely. Just legs without a torso, and while I definitely have a fetish for nylon legs, I don't think your amputated torso was intentional. It's best to send pictures in jpg format, if possible. I would love to see the whole girl in her intriguing metal bra pose. Please resend. Also it was a huge file for one picture.

I have been getting into some deep and interesting re-exploration of my wounds and shadow with a psychic coach and counselor, who also turns out to be a Dom. It's very complex to explain where this has taken me, so I will cover more detail when we meet.

I had formerly survived crisis by a defiant act of will, to compensate for the damaged spirit that has been rendered dysfunctional most of my life. I have what is called a Sovereign wound. I am nearly drained of will. Now I must focus on healing this wound.

I carry a certain shame about this - that I am not "*apriori* omnipotent" You honor me by allowing me to be honest about all my flaws. I feel this treacherous journey is all part of my destiny. I have faith that it will all unfold well. I will find the gold in all these trials, and flourish anew as I restore the true source of my powers.

keep faith luv

Galen

Subject: Champion
Date: Wed, 22 Sep

Dearest Galen,

I thank You for your beautiful sentiments and support. I cherish Your letter and have read the first paragraph over and over. I can't tell You how soothing and strengthening Your wishes were. You helped me so much with that.

I will call You when I feel down next time. I am seeking that solace and contentment through inner exploration now (therapy). Fear not for me losing my passionate edge for living though. It is too much a part of my makeup. My "demon" is a kind of angry inertia that I am learning to identify, in order to vanquish and triumph over. It is just that too many things happened at once. I like a good fight, but cannot slay ten adversaries at a time.

Things are better now and I am distracted with preparations for my trip to Europe, which is shaping up to be an adventure of grand proportions. I am utterly drawn there. I look forward to Your visit with the anticipation of a wonderful and memorable time. It is like a dream.

I am always Your friend and ally as well darling, no matter what, no matter when or where. You are a part of me! Pick a time to visit that is most convenient for You. The leaves change in October and

should be beautiful to see.

You are right that the dollar is in your favor! And how! It is like an automatic discount. I appreciate that you are taking time and expense to come to visit me. I am very favored indeed. You will not need a car in town. It is pretty small and accessible by trains and taxi, and besides, I will have a car a lot of the time. Please note that on the 27th of October, I am working: singing at a boxing match
. . . heh . . . and will be busy all that night.

Your inner journey sounds fascinating and I look forward to hearing all about it. I must pack now. I send you lots of love and will forward the pictures you asked about; sorry they came out badly. I will be thinking of you.

Xoxo,

Arlana

Subject: Europe
Date: Fri, 1st Oct

Dearest Galen

I am here in Europe and wish I could tell You all that is going on - there is so much! It is exquisite and remarkable. I am growing and experiencing a love with Belle that is healing my soul and restoring my inspiration. To avoid going mad altogether, I have extended my stay until at least the 10th.

I have never known such rapturous euphoria. I have stumbled upon the other half of my soul. I am Belle and she is me. It is like being injected with an antidote to a fatal affliction, an instant before you were to take your last breath. This woman is in my veins now and I am throbbing with the life of her.

I hope that Your visit is near the end of the month as we spoke of. You will find me much happier, renewed and optimistic. I also will have a great many new photos to show You. I do think of You often and imagine your eyes on me as I experience certain moments of poignant intensity. I am anxious to tell you all.

all my love,

Arlana xoxoxoxo

Subject: October dates.
Dates: Sun, 10 Oct

Dear girl,

You sound joyous and inspired, as you deserve to be. I am about to meet some friends, so will keep this short. I plan to be in **** from October 18th and leave the 22nd or 23rd. I don't have an arrival time yet, and I haven't had time to check out the hotels. Thanks for taking the time to suggest the ones you did. It is most helpful.

I hope our schedules are not in conflict. I am sending this to both email addresses.

my love to you,

Galen

Subject: Dates OK
Date: Sun, 10 Oct

Dearest Tiger,

You did not tell me how YOU are. I want to know how you are feeling and what is happening with you. I am very well and ex-

tremely happy and contented. I will tell you more about it when I
see you. The dates you chose are a OK with me. I am thinking of
you and am anxious to see you. Take care! I will contact You once
I am back on North American soil.

love,

Arlana

Subject: Core wound
Date: Mon, 11 Oct

Dear sweet panther,

Thank you for wanting to know my feelings.

As always I struggle to be clear. Leaving my ex has exposed me to
so many things from my past that I didn't need to face or consider
while in the relationship. It's also added new things that I hadn't
prepared for.

My core "wound," abandonment by my birth mother and father, and
ultimately "God," is deep and difficult to heal. I struggle to reconnect with trust and faith in my worthiness and value, not to become
my worst nightmare: the verification that I am a pathetic failure,
with no purpose or value.

The greater fear is that I have transferred this to my sons, and will
fail them, lose any respect from them as a man or a father. This is
the agony of my impotence both metaphorically and actually.

That is the worst of it. I do know that there is also a part of me that
is large and divine, beautiful and beaming as a little boy and powerful, cunning, stealthy and noble as a sagely panther.

The battle rages back and forth. I have grown so much this year,
taking the fight to the strongholds of my shadows. It's opened my

thoughts to the submissive aspect of my psyche. The part I fiercely deny in my battle with life and God. I know I need to understand service and surrender to a higher authority and trust that it will not destroy, but actually enhance and redirect my power and passion to my unique purpose.

That's it in a nutshell dear, stripped of all the detail.

I am so astounded by the thought of you in my life. How it began at all, stopped and started several times, and how much I revere the power and joy of my bond with you that's withstood every blow. I am so happy and excited that our perseverance and love have put me on the path to Canada, sweet panther.

My little panther girl sounds so joyous, renewed. You deserve the reprieve and to be constantly bathed in the pleasure and excitement of life. It makes me happy that you are so vibrant. I could feel your glow right through my screen.

I still am a bit glum and border on a dark mood - more legal and financial hassles, and this relentless wait for the pieces of my life to start drawing together again. Too many things on pause, that I have no control over.

I looked up the hotels and **** looked like a decent place. I'll probably pick there, but I haven't booked it yet.

I am most excited to meet you, my little daughter, my royal consort, my sweet snake, feisty panther, all of you! I will want to devour you immediately, hungry Tiger that I am, but will nibble tenderly, sniffing for the sweetest offerings. We'll be like two cubs tangling in play. I believe I more anticipate engaging your mind and your soul, though your body is still high on my list.

By the way, are there any legal or other hassles if they inspect my toy bag (duffel, actually). I don't see why there should be unless there's a law against entry by American perverts. Do I need a passport? I hope not. Mine's expired. I don't believe so, now that I remember going to Canada many years ago. But I don't keep up

much on American-Canadian relations, except for ours! We're not at war are we?

all my love,

Galen

PS: Which airport should I arrive at?

Subject: Closer
Date: Wed, 13 Oct

Dear daughter,

Since I'm flying stand-by, there's no rush to hear back from you about the airport, etc. I am glad you got to extend your stay in Europe. I am just a short distance in time from you now, everyday I draw closer.

luv,

Galen

Subject: Prey to slaughter
Date: Fri, 15 Oct

Dear Shining girl,

Seeing the pic of you hanging like captured prey, waiting the slaughter, stirred my predatory Tiger instinct. So many torments come to mind with you in that inverted surrender. And with Belle, I presume, in love and rapture. That was sweet to view.

I realize I misstated an apology I made awhile back. I did not mean to apologize so much for feeling captured by my darkness, but for

sharing so little else. I know and appreciate greatly that you accept all these parts of me; both King and fool. You honor me, and that is so pleasing, dear.

The King is growing larger, the fool smaller. I am learning to identify and split off these relics from my wounded "little boy," and other programs, and psychically transfer the energy out of my subconscious and reflexive behavior onto other "beings" who hold that energy, separate from the King. I made them all submissives who will be honored, loved and taken care of when they surrender total control to their Master, the King.

This is a process I am developing through working with my 'coach,' who is also a Dominant. The insights I've gained through this process are personally profound. I will have a lot to share with you in this regard, including a plan I have that relates to the explosion of interest in sexual exploration and truth.

I 'prey' for you daily. Soon, I will capture you, too!

All my love,

Galen

Subject: A new wound
Date: Sat, 16 Oct

Dear,

I received an e-mail from my sons this evening. The told me they have decided not to see me anymore, until I get counseling for my "addictions," stop being "mean" to their mom, and give up all my financial interests to her so she can support them better.

I feel near tears right now, so much anger and loss, and the deepest sadness. I seek your solace and soulful support, which you are providing just by being there to listen.

My ex has obviously told them her twisted 'truth' about me. Their letter was so blatantly her, speaking through them. They've judged me harshly, solely on the point of view of their mother, never asking my side of the story, never telling me their feelings or asking me any questions.

I've attempted to stay on higher ground. This divorce is between two adults, not something to entangle your kids in. But I suspected they were being contaminated with her shit.

I've talked with my sons over this last year, and stated numerous times in e-mails how much I love them, that I know they are probably getting an ear-full from their mother and her family, to please ask me about anything that concerns them and get my side of the story, so they'd have a whole picture by which to judge. They'd always say they were fine. No questions. The story they seem to believe is twisted totally in my ex's direction, and paints me as the vilest evil.

I am so sad right now. It hurts so much. I need to let myself settle before I can respond to them. My ex has played all her cards. It won't be easy to counter her story, and regain their trust and love. I am at a great disadvantage in healing my relationship with them.

They are totally immersed, everyday in her reality. I have barely been able to see them. She's been slowly and relentlessly trashing me in front of them, ever since I left. They've been brainwashed. I always felt she was genetically engineered by the Gestapo. Below the anger, I also know how much this must hurt my sons, and I feel a greater sorrow about that.

I will deal with this. My love for them is too unrelenting to yield in defeat. The spirits are on my side in this regard, and in that I am strong. Say a prayer for me, dear to whatever spirits guide your beautiful soul. Ask them to send blessings and healing to a noble Tiger that is deeply wounded.

My precious, bless you for being there. It gave me strength and

some relief, just to write to you. You're such a tender, loving panther.

Goodnight dear,

Galen

Subject: Our alchemy
Date: Mon, 18 Oct

Dear Daughter,

I just wanted to let you know, I am doing well and have managed to not get tangled up or consumed by my sorrow over what's happening with my boys. I have received tremendous support and love from my allies. I feel strong and confident. This tragic situation they have been forced into by their mother will pass. I am past the compulsion for vengeance and hatred towards my ex. The karmic legal system will produce fair and just results.

I feel dispassion towards her. Nothing can diminish the love and compassion I feel for my sons. I know they will understand the truth of this at some point in their lives. Beneath all the drama in their environment, and their fear of going against their mother, my boys still know I love them and I know they love me, right now.

In truth, my ex knows she's going to lose this war, and she's starting to crack. She has the moral character and the ruthless, calculating terrorism of a desperate, mad dictator. She uses my children like hostages, placed as shields in front of military targets, in a cowardly attempt to keep from being bombed.

I do not need a reply to this. You are my tender ally, who I love dearly. You serve me quite well, just by being there, dear. Writing you soothes me, connects me with my strength and dignity. That is the noblest service you could provide. I just want you to continue, immersed in the magic that has captured you, until we create our

own alchemy, very soon sweet panther girl.

my love to you,

Galen

Subject: welcome home
Date: Sun, 24 Oct

Dear panther,

I called today to leave a welcome home message, but my little girl is so popular her phone message box was full. Welcome home nonetheless dear. I know you will need time to recover from your trip and will probably need to take care of business on the home front. Take care of what you need to during this week, dear. I can fend for myself while you are otherwise occupied.

I come to you a bit haggard and beat-up by this past year, physically, emotionally and spiritually. Still buried by uncertainty and the grief of all the damage wrought all around. But also more in tune with myself than I've ever been, chasing down my strength, power and vision, like a panther after his prey.

I dream of touching you on many levels, and the pleasure it will be to meet my panther sister.

love you,

Galen

PS: I arrive Tuesday at 4:25 on American Airlines.

Subject: re: Welcome Home
Date: Sun, 23 Oct

Dear Panther,

My phone message box is full and I can't face it right now. It means that there are fifty messages on it!

Thanks for trying though. My dear, you are gracious and thoughtful. You are a beautiful man, a friend, a confidant, and noble tiger brother. I will shower You with the affection, care and admiration that Your being evokes and deserves. I am happy and almost in wondrous disbelief that I will see You in the flesh tomorrow.

We have come through much. Who knows what will happen, only that it is an impressive journey. Our bond is firm; nothing frightens me. I am only sorry that I am so out of it and look like the jet-lagged zombie that I feel like. No matter, you love me from the inside out, right??

We'll both be haggard together then. It is true what they say about it being darkest before the dawn? I thought this was just a platitude, but have recently found it to be true. It only happened after I sort of gave up and settled into the dark, and then—glorious sunlight: her name is Belle. Soon You will bask too, Brave Pasha. Hope I don't fall asleep into my soup like I sort of did last night!!! You'll rouse me won't You (smile)?

Look for me, I will be there to pick You up!

Bon Voyage. See you tomorrow!

Xo Arlana

Subject: A bittersweet pleasure
Date: Sat, 30 Oct

Dear girl,

It was bittersweet, but such a pleasure nonetheless to enter your chaotic, glittering, gale force life. I know it was very difficult to manage all your other obligations, and still accommodate me with your glorious presence. I appreciate that, and feel honored.

I came to you without expectations. This was a challenge for me, before and during our visit. I am a romantic soul, and my desire is to possess and captivate a soul-mate and be swept along by her desire and returned passion. This is something that will always be a part of me. Like my best suit (leathers), I will be buried in it.

I have never had a fuller expression of my passion, lust, perversion, power, art, desire or love than you called forth from me in our elegant correspondence. In that I am blessed, and feel fortunate that it is so well documented…a testimony to the truth and beauty of it.

It is like Watson and Crick's experiment, creating the essential components of life, by firing lightning into a beaker of primordial soup. Giving hope that life and in this case intimate, soulful, committed love may someday be recreated outside the crucible of cyber reality.

Though I am sad that we will not create a love of that nature in our relationship, wherever it may be going from here, I have no regrets that I pursued you with abandon. I have grown in my understanding of how this loss affects me, the loss of my deepest desire. I am no longer bound up by it, my soul slain by it. I am more like a well-moored boat that can ride out the stiffest storm, and though buffeted about, still hold anchor.

I do admire you greatly, dear. Even more so, now that we have met. You are a magnanimous gardener of people, and cultivate a mind boggling array of relationships.

Despite your assumption, dear, you will have to take my word at this point, regarding my capacity for cruelty and the cold extraction of pleasure through sadistic torment. My tastes do tend toward the extreme, though finding a sub of such depth is not easy. My current sub is on this path, and I will patiently see how far her tolerance

both mental and physical can be stretched.

In our brief encounter, and under the circumstances, you never had the opportunity to see that side of me. I do not display that outside of a play scene. I can show that nature out of a scene to someone with whom that aspect has been accepted and desired in a broader context. We never got to that point in real time and I am sad about that!

My tenderness, which is just as authentic as my sadistic/erotic nature, should not lull your sense of the dangerous terrain ahead once the border of my realm has been crossed. The Tiger waits patiently until the prey draws close. It is a waste of energy to pursue a victim too far off, no matter how delectable. I enjoy and thrill to the paradox of the tenderness and cruelty combined. Perhaps you were daring me to show it to you, but you never lingered long within striking distance.

You know I love you dearly though, and accept you in all your deftly juggled moment to moment manifestations.

I can imagine that what I am saying will set fire to that volatile and wonderful Arabic blood coursing through your proud heart. I believe you will look at this differently than I. I honor your feelings, dearest, while holding to my own.

I was just too conflicted by the beauty and depth, emotionally and spiritually, of all that I have felt for you. When you told me that your relationship with Belle and her Master was paramount, and that your "obligation" to them required you to be "chaste," I just disconnected from you, in that moment.

For me, it would have desecrated the nobility and honor of my love for you, to just Top you, stripped of all my very real passion and joy for you. To protect my own vulnerability, I couldn't unleash my true passion, knowing that your own heart is so preoccupied.

I believe you are much more evolved in this way than I. Somehow, at the same time I say all this, there is a level in me that could step

aside from my emotional connection with you, and thrill to the pure pleasure of tormenting you.

This did rise up in me at several moments; the alignment of all these conflicts, held in delicate balance. I was so close then to the purity of my Dominant soul, that I knew I could and desired to just reach out and take you. I couldn't hold together this state of serene confidence faced with the tumult of your life and the demands on your heart, during this short visit.

My spirit has been decimated by this last year. I am still so wounded, vulnerable and insecure, but I am healing slowly. I still remain too needy and out of balance emotionally and spiritually to be able to handle my feelings for you. I would only want to possess you and horde you, and this, I realize would be a great injustice to one so free spirited and evolved as you.

But because my love and adoration of who you are is so great, and I am certain of your love and compassion for me as well, I am able to deal with this. As clumsily as that might appear at times. Please know that at heart, I am dedicated to and support your ever-spiraling growth to the highest realms of beauty and truth.

I am thrilled by the potential for our writing collaboration! Yet, this rosy vision is also laden with thorns, and we must take care how to handle it. Well, I must, I know how you crave the thorns (grin).

I only wish and pray for your highest good, dear. May you be soaked in it, on every level, in every way.

Tell Martin that I admired his courage to submit so deeply in my and others' presence. I rather enjoyed the aristocratic treatment at our meal. It suits me. I also enjoyed the brief chat he and I had while you visited with Misha. Tell Misha that I loved his crafts-manship, and I am sorry my social graces were so dim. I was jealous, I suppose, of the loss of your attention. But you were magnificent that evening. It was a special pleasure to share such an intimate event with you, despite our lack of connection on those other levels.

You were a gracious and generous host throughout my visit. I enjoyed and was fascinated and warmly welcomed by the dazzling array of characters swarming around you. I know if I return, I would be gladly received in this community. I know the secret password in your city is "Arlana".

You've got star power sweetheart. Let it shine upon the world stage.

All my blessings,

Galen

Subject: A Beautiful Meeting
Date: Sat, 30 Oct

Dearest Galen

I feel honored also, my darling. It was an excellent meeting! You are truly a romantic soul and your passions run deep. I know I only saw a very little part of who you are. You are so staid, so calm.

By God, the word is your medium! You are a seductive penman and touched me with your last e-mail. We had no expectation save to meet one another. I will not forget this time with You. Soul mates of the page or kindred sharing the pulsations of life, does it truly matter which triumphed?

We are connected and this meeting has cemented that. You have captivated me from within. The meaningful part of being is the inner. The body is a bonus, a luxury of sorts. You are very concise and controlled about love, dear. I admired how honed You are in your self-knowledge and self-possession. The Tiger is patient indeed.

Our correspondence has been an eloquent expression of deep secrets and fermenting dreams that an infrequent few dare, or are capable

of expressing. We have touched on many subjects. You were a light in the darkness for me and I am glad that I have lighted the way for you in some of your dismal moments also.

We have passed from the cyber to the flesh and that is wonderful; but I still appreciate you deeply on my screen. You speak to me so caressingly on that glowing gateway to the world.

I am not upset that you realize we will not create a love of physical nature. What matters most to me is knowing you and keeping you in my life. I have no regrets either. Bravado and heart will always be the way for people like us. Your soul has ridden out the stiffest storms and will continue to do so. You have not lost your deepest desire, only looked it in the face and smiled.

I admire you too! You should know that everyone here liked you very much. You are certainly welcome! I do love social life and humanity, but to me you are much more than "people". I am glad that you have seen many sides of me in a few short days.

I myself am becoming more extreme as time goes by. As my capacity for suffering augments and my submission deepens (something I have to profoundly thank Master **** in Europe for), my capacity for cruelty has dramatically increased. Sometimes I take a look at myself from without and even scare myself with amazed disbelief. I am a very hungry person and am not as patient as you. I need all this like air, don't you?

I also enjoy and thrill to the paradox of the tenderness and cruelty combined, but I can savor the cruelty alone. I crush the weak and melt to the strong. There is little in between. The outcome of our meeting does not upset me. It is as things should be.

I understand what you have said about desecration and that you must honor the morals of love. It is noble and poetic. I thought that I was the romantic one. Your romance is idyllic in a deep and cool way. Vulnerability makes risks more exciting, don't you think?

My heart is very big, dear. I must say that I did enjoy seeing the

ripples of hidden anger disturbing your calm countenance at times. I do think that you need healing and that perhaps you were not at your best. It is normal to be wounded and to feel vulnerable after what you have been through.

Hesitation, whatever the reason, does make me keep my distance. I can upset the emotional apple cart of the most solid. It is and was intelligently prudent of you to be cautious with someone like me. I felt your vulnerability - it would have upset me if I had made your pain worse instead of better.

The place you have occupied is now yours and can only be filled by you, for there is only one Galen. Your love, understanding and dedication have made me treasured and that is scarce in the genuine sense. The thorns are part of life. The darkness has allowed me to appreciate the light. I am eager to continue our creations. We'll be all-right, especially in cyber world.

I came by today at a bit after eleven to pick you up because the traffic was light and we could have made it quickly to the airport. You were right in saying that I was tired. I went up to your room and saw that you, and the rose I brought you on your arrival, had left. This was touchingly appropriate. You had vanished and taken with you, the necessity for a difficult goodbye. Everything is as it should be. Thank you for gracing me with your visit.

Love,

Arlana

(*Note: Arlana and I remain very close and maintain steady corre-spondence and phone connection, as well as all the channels of the spirit. Our destinies are entwined, and the mystery of our future is as intriguing to me as has been our past. Stay tuned!*)

Episode 3

Lana

Lana sent me the briefest response to an ad I had placed on a small personals site. I was tempted not to reply to Lana, but something compelled me to prod a deeper response from her.

Short replies, such as hers, had generally proven a waste of time. In my case, better than 90% of the contacts I've had proved futile, when the woman only offered a sentence or two in response. Usually, if I replied, I would never hear back from them.

Lana responded back with a little more enticing detail, and what started as a trickle, became a torrent. We became a tropical storm of raging perversity and desire that blew out as fast as it blew in. But the fury and frenzy of our briefly explored lust, love and passion were an exhilarating trial run in my quest for my soulmate/slavegirl.

Her desire for submission and to be treated like a slut were exquisite. Lana struggled with her doubts and fears about her ability to want or withstand erotic pain, and her ability to be a fulltime 24/7 submissive. Could she trust a Master not to harm her?

Our relationship brought her closer to understanding this reality than her previous cyber explorations. I was pressing for a real time encounter. I knew what I was seeking. I felt a great potential in her spirit. I was falling in love and desire. She enticed me so, with her genuinely submissive manner and a classically sexy blond appeal.

Ultimately, for all we had in common, and how close we drew to each other, we found ourselves out of phase at this point in our lives. We were both finalizing our divorces. I was clear in my intent now, to focus on developing a soulful alliance with my true counterpart. She was still exploring her newfound freedom, and the many uncharted aspects of her sexuality and desire.

This story shows the many ways shear force of passion might

overcome the issues surrounding long distance. It also painfully reveals the practical impossibility of achieving the desired outcome.

Subject: Hello
Date: Fri, 28 May

Hello,

I am responding to your ad. I'm 5'3", strawberry blonde, and 122 lbs. I'm a very attractive, submissive female. I look forward to your reply.

lana

Subject: Offer more…
Date: Fri, 28 May

lana,

I appreciate that you've responded to my ad. That in itself will rouse my curiosity, but not much else. You'll have to offer more than what you've provided to get my attention, if you desire to be taken seriously. Do you?

i. e. , What, about my ad, attracted you? What do you seek? Besides being an attractive female submissive, what else can you tell me about yourself and your submissive desires and cravings? Do you seek your Master, or just to broaden your experience? How old are you? Where are you located?

If you seek more, you need to provide more. Understand, sweetheart!

Galen

Subject: My deep desire
Date: Sat, 29 May

Hello Sir,

I'm 34. I live in the Southeast. Attached is my picture so you can
see for yourself if I am attractive. I am a paralegal and office
manager and very much used to being in control in my work.
However, I very much want to continue to explore the Master/slave
relationship. I have a deep desire to be made to totally submit
myself to a man that knows what he wants and will get it.

My experiences being a slave are online only. I am very strong-
willed and, in all honesty, I am not a very good slave. However,
with the proper training and time I can, need and want to learn to be
a good and obedient slave to a willing Master.

Thank you for considering me.

lana

Subject: Pleased
Date: Sat, 29 May

Dear lana,

I am pleased with your pic. Lovely smile, the pose with your tits
pushed forth, body bent over like an offering for Master's pleasure.
Signs of an exhibitionist. I like.

I'm not sure what ad of mine you saw. I'm on several sites, so I'll
include my full profile here, so you can better understand what I
expect. Tell me where you saw my ad. Again, what was it in my ad
that drew your interest? Tell me also what has led you, at this point
in your life, to wish to become a slave to your Master.

Galen

(my standard profile followed, with scene 1.)

Subject: Dripping
Date: Sat, 29 May

Hello Master,

You are exactly what I have so long desired but was afraid to seek. I am dripping from your story. I have so long yearned to be allowed to totally surrender; to be forced to release the slut deep inside.

I saw your ad on ****. com. It stood out because you were explicit in what you were seeking and I felt that you would recognize in me what I am and treat me accordingly.

I want to be a sex slave; to explore that deep surrender to a Dom who will take what he wants, forcing me into complete submission for his pleasure. I desire to be brought to the edge, yet always feel the safety found with my Master.

There is little doubt that I am spirited. I am very much used to being in control, yet I have this burning desire to be nothing but a whore for my Master.

I am very intelligent, professional, have a great sense of humor and feel deep passion about certain things and ideals. Because I am intelligent, or maybe just because I am strong-willed, I need someone who will teach me total obedience with patience and a firm hand.

If I was the star of your story, I would feel what she did, hesitation at fulfilling your demands, like having my tits cropped and what

else you might do to me, yet completely free. . . a wet slut, there for your pleasure alone.

I have never been spanked, whipped or tortured except in an online experience. I have never experienced real life submission in the form that I seek. Just being teased by my partner.

I had one short Master/slave relationship online but he was married and unable to give me the time that I desired. The other relationship, also online, is ending because he's getting married. So much for that. lol.

While each of these Masters allowed me to explore the feelings inside, neither of them were the strict Dom I desire. I am frankly not sure what my limits are. I think that would depend upon my comfort level with my Master.

I can only hope that I have aroused your curiosity and responded sufficiently. Please consider me. I know that you will release in me what I really am.

lana

Subject: Ooops, forgot!!
Date: Sat, 29 May

Hello again,

I was so excited by your story that my brain is clouded and I forgot to tell you what it did to me reading it. While reading it, I slipped off my bikini top (I was on the way to the pool when your mail arrived).

Almost involuntarily my legs opened and I felt such intense desire to be in your story. I rubbed my palm over my pussy and re-read your tale. Sitting on the edge of my chair. . . back arched, tits sticking out, nipples hard. . . begging for your attention.

I hope that was explicit enough for you.

lana

Subject: Desirable combination
Date: Sat, 29 May

Dear slut.

Well, you are intriguing, dear. Physically beautiful, intelligent, a
whore's heart and a slave's soul. Desirable combination. Do you
explore your spiritual nature?

You will require patience, which I possess. Your inexperience is not
a problem in itself. But it leaves a lot unknown about your ability
to tolerate erotic punishment and pain.

I've found that a slave's tolerance can be extended by "sweetening
the pain," i. e., raising the arousal level, while slowly increasing the
level of pain. When a slave goes into "subspace," if her desire is to
do so, to be so pleasing to Master, she can exceed what she considered a limit of tolerance. But everyone is different, so we'd have to
experiment a lot (grin)!

I have to go now (NBA game with some buddies). Tell me, whore,
what ways might you arouse this Master, in your darkest fantasy?
How would you desire to be used, and made to obey?

Do you have any particular fantasies or activities you crave? Verbal
humiliation, face slapping, forced oral or anal, tit and cunt torture?
Are you bi? Tell me more slut, I like it. I expect you to be the
nastiest cunt and most eager slave I've ever encountered.

Did you look up my pic?

Galen

374

Subject: Intoxicating
Date: Sat, 29 May

Dear Master,

I am so pleased you wrote back. Your story was intoxicating. It's as if you read my mind and put my desires to words. I can think of little else today except you and what you would do to me.

As for spirituality, I am a Catholic. A good little church girl with a burning desire to be a dripping wet slut. Probably all that Catholic guilt they instill in you. In all seriousness, I do go to church and for the most part, agree with the teachings of my religion.

Correct, I am untested as to my limits of pain and tolerance to fulfill you desires. I actually don't really have much of a tolerance for pain when I get hurt in r/l, lol. However, I don't think that has any bearing upon my ability and desire to please you and ache for you.

What is different about you is that you don't punish for misbehavior, but rather you appear to use your crop or whatever else purely for your own pleasure. I like that.

I do like verbal, because it demonstrates your dominance and my submission that you would talk to me that way, calling me a whore and treating me like one. This allows me to be free to be the slut that I am, there for your pleasure alone.

I can't get your story out of my head. I ache to be that slut, spread, brought to the edge and rewarded with your cum. I am very, very (I'll say it again) very good at giving oral pleasure. I love it. The thought of being suspended and being forced to devour you at the same time is so exciting to me.

Some of my fantasies involve putting on an outfit or outfits that my Master has instructed me to wear. Very revealing clothing that

makes me look and feel like a slut. My tits displayed for you, pushed up, nipples barely showing or completely exposed. . . . . pussy and ass seductively exposed.

I love stockings, with the lines, with patterns and lace, crotchless panties, thongs. Sometimes the thought of a maid's uniform or similar outfit makes me so wet. . . high slut heels. I want to wear what pleases my Master, to be on display for his viewing pleasure.

To me it is surrendering to your control to be dressed and treated this way. It all comes back to my desire to please my Master, to serve his every wish. I like the seduction of the slave in your story—made to dance, getting wet, then feeling the sting of your control and the final reward.

I also like toys being used on me and forced anal. Hard to force oral on me since I like it so much. Tit and cunt torture is kind of scary to me because of the pain. . . . but the idea of being used in that way takes my breath away with excitement and makes me squirm. I have a great desire to be spanked and whipped and teased.

I very much want to be your slut… my cunt, tits, ass and mind under your control and used for your pleasure. I am a whore and I knew that you would see that in me and treat me the way that I want and need to be treated.

I looked at your pic. I would willingly drop to my knees for you. Here is another one of me.

Thank you Master for considering me.

lana

Subject: Eager slut
Date: Sat, 29 May

Dear lana

376

It's very pleasing to know you're such an eager slut; and since I know what a depraved whore you are, you'd find I'd treat you like the sleaziest whore I've ever met. You'd definitely spend a lot of time on your knees, begging me to fuck that hot little cunt mouth.

I'd grab that pretty hair and force myself down your cock-sucking throat. I'll make you swallow my cum, too sweetheart, then lick it clean. And of course, you'll be trained to always say, "thank you, Master, for feeding me your precious cum. I love you Master," your eyes still glazed but beaming.

You catholic girls, if given the chance, turn into the biggest sluts, don't you? I guess that's why I like catholic girls, like you. I think Catholicism is great for building up all that held-back, pent-up lust (grin). I can see I'd have no trouble turning you into my fuck toy slave. I can tell you've got what it takes to be my pleasing whore.

But besides being made to do what I tell you to, I also expect you to become the part, to be and act like a slut around me, without prompt. I believe that wouldn't be a problem for a woman of your inclinations.

There are other things now that I want you to tell me. If you wrote the script, how would you see what we're exploring, developing into a r/t relationship? What would be some details of your ideal relationship? What things would need to occur before you would desire to meet in real time? How would it progress on the practical level, if you eventually sought and were invited to live with a Master?

Thanx for the new pic. You have the most radiant smile. I'd love to give you a passionate kiss and then slide my cock between those sensuous lips. Won't that be nice to taste Master's cock for the first time? Nice legs. Love to see them dressed up in "fuck me" heels and nylons attached to a whorish garter.

Mmmmm, your tits. What size are those anyway, slut? Tell me your measurements. I'll bet you'll love for me to put them in some

tight tit bondage. I also use nipple clamps and clothes pins. It will please me to place them on your tits, while I look into your eyes and see the slut within. Mmmm, time for another deep soulful kiss.

I want to keep that cunt of yours dripping wet. Maybe another little story will help.

Goodnight my sweet bitch.

Galen

Subject: Aching
Date: Sun, 30 May

Dear Master,

Your words do keep me dripping wet. My pussy tingles reading your letters, aching to be touched and entered.

If I wrote the script, I would see us meeting, me wearing what you instructed. Sitting at a booth I would feel your hand under the table, up my thigh and slide between my legs, forcing me to silently open my legs for you in the crowded restaurant.

I would feel your fingers slide into my blouse, pulling a nipple out, feel you teasing it into hardness. Watch my eyes fill with desire. You know I would want nothing more than to leave with my Master. . . to be used by you. . . to serve you.

I imagine then that you take me home and begin to teach me the sweetness of surrendering completely to you. To be the whore that you know I am. . . to learn to love your crop and beg for more. I imagine that you choose what you wish me to wear every day when we are together, that I am always to dress like a slut for you. . . always ready for you.

My measurements are 36c 27 36. I'm very tan and look like I'm

wearing my bikini when I'm naked. My pussy hair is light red, lips shaved smooth. I'm very curvy. I know I'm attractive because I see the men looking wherever I go.

My nipples are pink and long to be under your control. I've never had my tits bound or felt clamps. . . but reading what you write about it makes me squirm and drip. To watch you putting clamps on my hard nipples for your pleasure. Feel my tits squeezed by your velvet cords. . . feel the sting of your crop against them as you use my body for anything you choose, making me become the slut you know I am and training me to say thank you, Master, for every bit of it.

Will you tell me more about you. . . how many slaves you have, if any. What you do for a living. Are you married, divorced, single? Your picture made me hot because of the way you have your hand placed and the expression on your face, beckoning your slave to her knees for you.

You left me tied hand to ankle, my submissive pussy raised and open for you. . . I can feel it start to drip as I wait with anticipation and slight fear for you, wanting so much to please you, to be your sex slave, knowing you will soon delight in every part of me.

What would life be like day to day with you? I wonder, would you teach me to be a wanton slut, there to submit to my sadistic but loving Master? To let me feel safe with you, free to be that which I crave?

lana

Subject: Your devotion
Date: Sun, 30 May

dear one,

You're a sweetgirl and a delicious slut. I appreciate how you

respond to my thoughts about you, and other things.

I will tell you more about me now. Quite a lot actually. You should feel pleased, slave, that you have enticed this Master with your devotion and pleasing manner up to this point. There is a lot more I wish to learn about you as well.

As you know, I seek my submissive soul mate for a LTR. This will require the ability for absolute honesty on both sides. Coming from the heart. I need a soulful woman with a true compassionate spirit. A best friend, loyal ally, intelligent enough to give respectful feedback, be intuitive to my moods and needs emotionally, be a great listener, romantic and affectionate.

You've already proven what a whore you are (evil grin)! Do you desire to be all these things to me, as well as my sex slave?

More about me. . . *(sent her all the info about my hoax, my divorce, my experience, and the story that follows).*

This next story describes a first meeting during which you get hung upside down, with just your high heels on your long lovely legs. You get a big surprise, too, among other things.

"The Surprise"

You're driving down the freeway, on your way to your first meeting with Master. You look down at your thigh, black nylons, the straps of your garter showing under the short skirt. Your high heel, pressed against the accelerator, sends a subtle vibration up your leg. "How can I be doing this," you say to yourself. "I look like a slut!"

Then you giggle, your wicked side. "Because I really crave being this man's slut!" His letters thrill you. You can't believe you aren't disgusted as so many other women you know would be. You drive on to your destination, almost against your will.

Master has arranged for the valet at his hotel to take your car. He is a young man, handsome and athletic. He eyes you, through the

opened door, almost shocked at how sexy you look.

You step from the car, your bare upper thigh, showing above the garter. "You're here for the gentleman who spoke to me earlier. He told me to take good care of his special guest. How can I help you?"

Inside your thoughts, you are thrilled at the response to how seductive you must look. For a moment you forgot how you were dressed and were stunned by his look. You smile to yourself with a growing sense of confidence and anticipation. But you are afraid as well.

This was his last night in town. You had avoided this moment for three days. He had e-mailed you Monday that he would be in town, and had encouraged meeting. Your wicked side kept saying yes to Masters commands. It wanted to obey Master's instructions. . . to the letter!

But this other side had so many things to consider. . . there's so many crazy people. . . I don't want to be harmed. . . am I ready to do this. . . to obey. . . to offer myself for Master's pleasure. . . can I be just a slut, a shameless whore, be tied up, gagged, spanked, helpless, vulnerable. . . can I trust Master. . . give him total control. . . can I please him?

Your true sexual nature screams, Yes!! And you know, despite all your reasoned doubts, you are compelled to go forward. You accept your destiny, as your secret lust soars past your caution.

You're standing in front of room 316. You've been there several moments. You take a deep breath. The look the valet gave, crosses your mind. "Just do it!" your wicked self urges. You knock.

The door opens. Your Master greets you with warm tenderness. You cross the threshold into Master's suite, almost in a faint.

Master leads you to a cushioned armchair. He sits, holding your hand. "Please," he says in his deep sensuous voice, "sit down in my

lap." You are very nervous, but Master's warmth has seeped in.

Somehow, in your submissive heart, you know you can trust him like no other person you've ever met. You sit down, your legs crossed across his lap. You feel shy, but your arm slips naturally around his neck. you feel his arm slip around your waist with a sleight but firm pressure. You cradle your head beneath his neck, and feel safer than you've ever felt.

You feel Master's hand glide gently along the top of your thigh, until it rests on the smooth flesh above the top of your nylon. "You have obeyed well, my sweet little slut. I am very pleased that you have dressed as I expected you to. Now, stand up so that I can inspect your treasures more closely."

You stand and face Master with your head bowed. "I am happy you are pleased, Master. I want to please you so much. But I am very nervous, Sir. . . but very excited."

"I will not harm you, my slave. Quite the contrary. You will feel pleasure like you've never imagined. It's all about pleasure, my darling. You will submit yourself to me, willing to perform how-ever Master commands, step by step; but only when you are ready for each new challenge in your quest to be my total whore and sex slave."

"Now, raise your skirt so I can look at the treasure you've got between your legs. Show Master that hot little cunt, and that virgin ass I've been reading so much about."

Things progressed quickly. . . just lifting my skirt to him, so he could look at my cunt. . . it was so sexual. . . there was no turning back. Next Master made me kneel before him as he stood up. You know what happened then. Soon after, I was kneeling, bent over on my elbows, raising my ass as high as it would go, and Master used his belt. He got my ass really warm.

Before I knew it, I was hanging upside down, stripped but for my high heels, now pointing toward the ceiling. He bound my ankles to

a spreader bar. He fastened each wrist to bolts, at the bottom of the contraption I hang from. Master had brought his Tetruss portable suspension device. It works very well.

Then the doorbell rang! It sent a shiver through me. . . someone I know? Master went to the door. In walks an attractive Asian woman, dressed as I had been, and Master says, "This is willow."

"Surprise!" says willow. Master says "I hope you won't mind, lana, but I thought it might be helpful to have another woman here." As if I could've protested. . . a big ball gag in my mouth, hanging helplessly upside down. Willow went immediately to my pussy. She began by spreading my cunt lips apart, and, finding my quivering clit, began to lick me wildly.

My body began jerking around, my cunt hungry with need, for something, anything, just keep licking. . . Then she stopped. "Are you being a good little slut for Master? Master told me about those kinky fantasies you have. And about all your reluctance and hesitation. That's right, I know what a filthy little slut you desire to be. You're like I was. . . reserved, hiding it from myself and others. But, I learned. I'm not that way any more, and I doubt if you will be either!"

She held a crop in her hand. Willow focused on my dangling tits. First she had placed some very snug clips on my nipples, which had stiffened nicely with the pressure.

She whipped all over my tits. . . and it stung and made my body flinch. Master was sticking that huge dildo in and out of my throbbing cunt, and I didn't care about anything but continuing. I was hotter, more intoxicated with my lust, and this wanton expression of it, than I had ever been.

The last thing I remember is Master, lowering my legs, parallel to the floor, and ramming his bulging cock, hard up my ass, and I'm grunting with desire, while willow shoves the dildo in and out of my desperately wet cunt. I was right where I wanted to be.

Subject: Your complete toy
Date: Sun, 30 May

Hello Master,

I read every word eagerly. I will be totally honest. I desire you intensely, yet would be immobile with fear to be alone with you at this point because of the nature of what would happen between us and the implicit trust I would have to place with you to be in that position.

I was married a long time. I left my husband because he ignored me. I'm not a nag or a bitch. He simply was incapable of seeing anyone else but himself. It's quite likely that he never even truly loved me because he doesn't know how or what it means to be 1/2 of a relationship.

While my divorce is still extremely fresh and was very painful for me, I feel empty sometimes and ache for a relationship, a true friendship. I want someone to bring me flowers, take me out, pay attention to me, make me laugh, play games with me, read with me, listen to music with me and take me to bed.

My husband never would experiment with me sexually. I was uneasy voicing the fact that I would have loved to be tied up. So, I would ask him if I could tie him up and he would say no and never offer to reciprocate.

I had been with quite a few men before I married. I have no short-age of dates now, but not many more than 3 or 4 times with the same one, as my choice.

I am well aware of the liars, scams and undesirable elements of the Internet. It's sad, isn't it? You can trust no one. So many men would harm you in a minute.

I am in awe that someone like sharah would go to the lengths of

deception with you. What's the point? Was it her alone all the while or did the others actually exist?

Do you want to chat sometime back and forth rather than just email and see how it is? I'm not rushing, just wondering what you like, i. e. , is it just email?

As for the woman, willow, entering your story, I'm not thrilled by it because I am jealous and like to be the one and only one in someone's heart. However, I love women and enjoy the pleasure of a woman's body.

Topping her or being her bottom for your pleasure would excite me. Just, if you fell all over her. . . lol... I would be pissed. By knowing me, you would know I was, but I would never be so blatant as to show you any disrespect.

I was reading some of the stories on that ****. com site you sent me to see your picture. There was one by a Master and slave that really excited me. I would assume since you are on that site and in that you have an appreciation for erotic stories, you probably read it. I love reading that stuff.

Since you actually met with women that responded to your ad, please tell me what it was like. . . was it what you fantasized it would be? Why didn't it go further with any of these slaves? Were they afraid? I'm so curious. I want it so much, yet it's so dangerous, meeting a stranger and doing something like that. Please tell me more.

One thing about me is I have a lingerie fetish. I live at lingerie stores. Sexy, skimpy things. I have dozens of nighties, all colors and designs. I love to feel sexy. Some of it is very slutty, some just elegant and beautiful.

I have to confess to you, Galen, that I have been constantly excited since your first letter. Today, I have taken 2 showers and changed panties at least 3 times. I never experienced anyone like you. I would be deeply hurt at rejection from you after offering myself on

that level, so I would need a little patience from you in that way.

I could possibly be the sweetest, most attentive woman you've ever encountered. . . I am very romantic (obviously, since I left my marriage in search of it). I am attentive, appreciative, smart, and slightly stubborn. I want what I want when I want it. . . and I also have this burning desire to be a complete toy to the right person at the right time.

lana

Subject: Drawing the curtain
Date: Sun, 30 May

My dear slut,

Sorry about increasing your water and laundry bill! They're likely to keep rising.

It sounds like your ex and mine would have been a great match. Our marriages mirrored each other in many respects. Particularly, in communication and partnership, as well as sexually

I appreciate the concern for your safety and the need to build trust, before we might consider meeting.

You are so desirable, dear, the more you reveal about yourself. You look great, very sexy in lingerie. Have any pics in high heels? I'd love to ravage the sweet beauty you express in your pics. But I'd love to see you in sluttier poses and outfits. Can you accomplish that to please me?

This will not be an easy exploration for either of us. No guarantee of the desired outcome. A lot of energy to expend to find out. I greatly appreciate the energy you are putting out for me now. I am very pleased at what a well rounded person you are.

I love how slutty and nasty you are inside, and the pleasure I would have drawing out the full power and passion of the whore inside you. I would love to see your beauty placed in a training collar. You're on a leash which I hold in my hand, ankles and wrists placed in leather cuffs, and you notice this particular smile on my face as I gaze at you, preparing you for your first submission to me.

How much can we truly know of each other in just a few emails? I believe by drawing the curtain to our sexuality, it opens up the greatest intimacy and empathy. We normally do not share this level of ourselves in our everyday social relationships. Our closest allies are those we share secrets with, rather than those we hide them from.

Let's email a bit more before we switch to chat or phone.

I would want you to serve me with other slaves or Dommes, once that level of trust was established. In this regard, my feeling is that I wouldn't involve someone else in our relationship without your approval.

On another point, I am not a brutal, abusive man, though admittedly a Sadist. I am a lover and romantic at heart. It is not my purpose as a Dom to genuinely harm someone. My pleasure derives from seeing my slave submit to, accept and eventually crave torment, because it is her goal to be a total and complete slave to her Master.

How does this work day to day? I believe that evolves, as you get to know and understand each other. I don't have a big book of rules that you would follow. Though rules and expectations for both private, and when in the vanilla public, are likely to evolve. I'm into myth and ritual, as a way to strengthen bonds and give a personal, spiritual meaning to the Master/salve relationship. By way of example, a collaring ceremony.

I also enjoy a full spectrum of life, and sharing that in a romantic way with my partner—romantic dinners, drives to the coast (I'm 50 miles from the ocean). I love to share books, movies, cultural and sporting events. I also love to dance. I've got rhythm sweetheart,

and I love to see a sexy woman dance. I am going to make you dance for me, like a slut in a topless bar, giving all she's got for a nice tip.

Regarding past slaves (I'm not in a current relationship), it all boils down to chemistry. Sexually, they were all wonderful; but mentally, emotionally, spiritually, or some combination, they were not what I sought for a committed LTR.

I emphasize that this is what I seek, more than anything. I want to be in love with my slave and share every part of my life. Though we might have additional play partners, she will be my committed life partner, and probably at some stage, my wife.

These past relationships always started in email, and progressed until we both felt the desire to meet, stronger than the fear of what we might encounter. Though I'm obviously more cautious now, I still rely on my instincts to a greater extent. There are extensive protocols on many D/s sites describing how to set up a safe first meeting.

It was thrilling to turn these women into submissive sluts, to use them any way I chose, torture their tits, pussy and asses with various implements, turning them on with toys, caresses, penetration, verbally abusing them, treating them like common whores. Many just begged for more. You'll beg too!

What things would you suggest to start resolving some of the trust issues? Tell me any questions, concerns or issues, practical or otherwise that you feel are important.

"I could possibly be the sweetest, most attentive woman you've ever
encountered. . . . " I pray that be true!

Here's another story to keep you warm!

warm regards,

Galen

(I sent her 'Cocoon'.)

Subject: My addiction
Date: Mon, 31 May

Dear Master,

Your mail is so addictive. As I sit and read it, I feel my nipples harden. Tonight, I slipped off my jade green velvet nighty so I could touch them as I read your words. The "Cocoon". . . I never even imagined something like that.

The thought of clothespins on my cunt lips and being taped open, exposed for you, vulnerable, open, then feeling the sting of a crop rather than my Master's hard cock. It makes me drip to be used by you in that way, awakens the whore inside. You are driving me insane with your descriptions.

That it would please you to use me that way and that I would eventually beg you to, is so exciting. I can't stop pinching my nipples; normally pink, they're bright red now. I wonder how the pain would be to have you place clips on them or whip them for your enjoyment. My pussy drips endlessly.

I long to be your slut, to feel your control, to dance for you in ways that I never have before, to suffer for you, revealing to you my true self. Something I have never revealed to anyone. I like being a slut and I love the way you talk to me.

I hope you didn't think I was being forward, asking you to chat. I just wanted to find out what you prefer. Because I am really totally inexperienced in this, I don't really know about first meetings and things like that. I will read about it though.

Don't want you to think I am stupid (a slut, yes; I think there is a

difference. lol). I guess trust comes with time. For me, it's instinctual as well. No offense, but it strikes me as funny that you would not trust me. I am sweet as sugar and soon you'll agree. I can only hope to one day feel you.

What would you like to see in the pictures? I will see if I can arrange it for you.

lana

Subject: Basic training
Date: Mon, 31 May

My precious whore.

I'd like to see the redness of your nipples. Then I 'd tell you to lay across my lap, where I would spank your ass til it glowed in the same shade of crimson. Occasionally sliding a finger in that wet cunt and teasing your clit with my thumb. Pain and pleasure in delightful combinations.

My desire for you is strong, slut. You make me want to take you, own you, use you, objectify your body, and turn you into my obedient eager slave bitch. I know how you desire that, how you crave it, hope it comes true, somehow.

What if I only lived 15 minutes away? Your Master that close. Waiting for you to surrender, to come to me and offer yourself for my pleasure, knowing what a hot whore I'd make you be. What would you do? How long could you resist?

I want you to pose for me. As slutty as you can get away with, and still get them processed. If you have a digital camera, you can download them right into your computer. Then you could be a real slut for me, pose however I tell you.

I want you to strip for me on camera. Dress in your sluttiest outfit

(use what I've written as your model for now). Pose standing, sitting with crossed legs, showing a lot of thigh with the garter exposed, good profile of the crossed leg in heels, a "fuck me anytime you want" look right at the camera. Undo your blouse, then pull your bra down from your tits and stick them out at me. Get a dildo and show me that cum sucking cunt mouth in action.

From the chair, draw your legs up, reach around with both hands and show me your cunt, spreading the lips wide apart, always looking into the camera, with pursed lips, or slightly licking them and that smoldering look in your eyes. That'd be a good start.

Are you ready to try a little basic training sweetheart? If you are, I want you to try a couple of experiments and tell me the results. You'll need clothes pins and a leather belt about 1-2" thick. Erotic Pain 101! (lol).

You can begin to test what pain feels like, a little step at a time, while continually arousing yourself with fingers, dildo, or vibrator. Place your toys by the bed. Take a warm bath, with salts, bubbles, have a glass of wine; pamper yourself, like you were preparing for Master.

Think of me while you bathe, and how you long to be used by me. Rub your clit as you fantasize. You picture me there, telling you it's time for our little experiment. Go to your bed. Lay down. Take a clothes-pin. Drag it across your nipples. Prod your nipples with it.

Slide it down across you belly, touching your clit with it. Slide it down the slit of your cunt. Squeeze one breast. Pinch an area to one side of your nipple and let the pin clamp you there. You can adjust the tension of the pin with a rubber band wrapped around the legs, if its normal tension is too much for your first time.

Reach down and rub your clit. Use a toy if you'd like. Look at the clothespin and know that your Master is pleased. Experiment with different placements—your nipples, your thighs, your belly, under your arms, and of course they'd look so lovely clamped to your cunt lips.

I would recommend no more than 5 minutes per placement at first. There is usually a sharp sting as the blood rushes back to where the clamps bit in, but it goes away quickly.

You can also administer your own beating with the belt. Let the belt slither over your body and sensitive areas. Draw it between your legs and with both hands front and back cinch it up into your crotch.

Continually arouse yourself. Imagine me there with you, watching you, encouraging my whore to show me her obedience. "Yes Master, I'll do anything you wish, Sir. " Whip your tits, your ass, your thighs, your pussy. Gently at first, teasingly, light taps at first, and as you grow accustomed to what the sensation is like, increase the strength and frequency of the strokes.

Report to me how you felt about the experience. I am not planning on grading you here on quantity and duration. I simply want you to understand more about your body and intense sensation, mixed with erotic stimulation. Are you ready to begin training, dear slut?

I keep thinking how amazing it was that you contacted me. I went and checked that site, because I couldn't remember my ad there. I found it buried several pages in, among a 100 or more other men advertising as Dom's. The odds of you going to that site and picking me out of all that clutter is delightfully shocking, especially since the ad revealed so little about the full extent of me.

And to have you become such a delightful pleasure to connect with, I consider very good fortune. I was not so inspired when I read your brief inquiry. I wasn't certain I'd even respond to so little information. I am most glad I did.

I want you to be constantly affected by my Dominance. Carry it with you everywhere. You feel it there, lurking, attached to your mouth, your legs, your tits, your cunt, your ass, and your heart—a subtle erotic tension that surrounds you like a dark halo (angels get white, slaves dark!). I dwell with Domish delight on your offering the precious gift of yourself for my use and pleasure, understanding

that you are my whore.

I hope that in time we can meet and fulfill this destiny, can find that our souls have yearned lifetimes for each other, and that the bonds, true love and passion envelope us in the special realm of Master/slave. This is the romance I seek.

I appreciate the quality of you lana, and I'm beginning to glimpse more of you personally. I like it all so far. You do have a good sense of humor. You are a really beautiful, sexy woman, and you're a slut, too! I'm enjoying this journey.

Tell me more about how you understood your desire to be a slave. What is different now than when you first began exploring? How would you now define your goals as the slave to your Master? Don't worry about just trying to say something to please me. In this context, I want to know YOUR feelings; they are important for me to understand. I will not judge your feelings. What was the nature of your previous relationship that ended recently?

I would blend liberal doses of romance and tenderness into your first submission. My heart will be there with yours. I would not only be your Master, but also your guardian.

Warmth,

Galen

Subject: More on me
Date: Tue, 1 Jun

Hello,

Here's another picture. That's all of the lingerie pics. I hope you liked them. When you said tell you more about the relationship that ended did you mean my husband or the Master I fell in love with who had the wife? It would suck if I went off and told you about

the wrong one.

I am always excited by pictures of bondage or stories with that theme. On the Internet, I looked at a lot of that stuff but stopped after I started chatting. I found that to be a safe way to explore things and to date without having to give someone my phone number or address.

I date sporadically. Some one-nighters. If I'm out dancing and I can tell he has a hard on, sometimes I can't resist. Probably loneliness, but lust, too. Not many times have I done that. All of them were younger. All of the ones I date are younger.

Sometimes online I hook up with some 21 year old and bang him blind, lol. It's odd that I really am most turned on by being dominated, yet I have this other affect on young guys. Some phone sex, stuff like that.

I was intrigued by the thought of a D/s relationship and only in the past year have I really begun to understand the dynamics of it. The Master I am losing I spent hours on end chatting with and I ended up feeling very strongly about him. I care for him deeply. I can also feel that from him.

Although I played with another Master, it wasn't the extensive online relationship I am now losing. He was very patient with me. I am really strong-willed and although I wanted it very badly, it was hard to give up control to him. I'm not a person with a huge ego or anything, but you know a pretty blonde with a nice smile goes far. . . and I am used to getting what I want most of the time. He was not compliant and that turned me on. He was also younger, and actually not too experienced.

The other one would have cyber sex with me, which was great but he was married and the other part was lacking. So, these experiences allowed me to open up, though not totally.

I like the verbal. . . it excites me. It's so. . . damn, what's the word I want. . . I'll have to substitute a phrase; it's so "bad catholic girl".

394

Plus, in my work, if a client or whomever calls me honey or makes an advance, it pisses me off. Who would have thought I like being called a slut? I love the way you talk to me.

I'm totally unsure about the pain part of a relationship like this, but desire so much to try it; and when I read it, wow! I can't cum enough.

My goal as a slave to my Master would be to completely be able to surrender to him. . . to be taken by him (there go my nipples hardening). It's not said for your benefit but I would take pleasure in knowing that he would completely use me for his own pleasure, as his own toy, treating my pussy, my tits—all of me—as his personal property. That he would openly make me submit to his whim and make me like it, even crave it. To be a total slut and slave, mind, body and soul.

You must know the whole idea of buying the clothespins and actually putting them on me fills me with desire. I guess we shall both see how it feels.

lana

Subject: Destinations on the journey
Date: Tue, 1 Jun

Dear slut,

Like I said, catholic sluts are the best! I was actually raised as a catholic, grade school and high school. I left before I was 18 to explore a spirituality not so heavily dependent on guilt as a means of persuasion. I believe in a divine intelligence that doesn't get divided up into Christian, Muslim or Buddhist dogmas. I consider myself very spiritual.

I don't understand about having cybersex. How exactly does this work? I've never done the chat room scene.

You won't know about your appreciation for pain until you experience it. A lot will depend on the chemistry and the skills of the Master, both mental and physical. Our experiment will mostly be sensations; and, depending on how well you fantasize, the erotic nature of pain and submission may not be glimpsed in its truest sense.

As for the destinations along this journey you have begun with me, it's clear I know how to elicit your desire. I know how a whore likes to be treated, and ultimately I would use you however I desired (within your stated limits).

Even without moderate to extreme pain, there are many pleasures to enjoy. I don't doubt that your desire to be my slut, and my passion to take you into submission would make us enjoyable play partners. I don't have a sense yet what more may develop between us.

My focus will remain on the submissive who seeks what I seek—a romantic, loving D/s, r/t relationship. There are many practical reasons why this energy between you and me cannot lead to a LTR. Distance, age, your bad habits or quirks (I don't have any!), politics, domestic styles, common interests, all the things we don't know about each other.

I don't pursue a cyber slut unless I feel something more than just the sexual side. There are things I sense about you, that stir not only my sexual desire but also begins to stir my heart. As you know we are both expending a lot of energy. Energy is a precious thing. I won't expend it long on a dead end.

But nothing practical would stop me from eliminating all obstacles to take possession of my collared submissive slave. I believe in the power and magic of love.

Let me state now what I expect from you to keep this going. Agreement that we will take this to a first meeting, at some point in the not too distant future, say 2 months or less. During this time we will continue to explore and evaluate if meeting is still what we

seek. We can do email, chat or phone, although chat and phone, I've found less appealing, as far as outright D/s play goes.

But phone is very quick to explore a topic or issue in depth. BDSM is more visceral and visual for me. This is what stimulates my Dom space most readily, both lacking in chat or phone. But I'm open. Again, chemistry will be a factor. I enjoy writing email, as you know, and writing, period.

I know I want to pursue you to this level. Do you know what you want, and does it have the potential to achieve what I seek? You might feel this as pressure on you. Take it as you like, dear. I know what I want. I don't waste my, or others' time, in getting it.

Though you are a novice in BDSM, you are still one of the most exciting sexual creatures I've met online. I enjoy your attitude about being a whore. you have a strong, nasty, kinky side, and it turns me on to hear from you. Being sexily attired is one of my requirements. You pass with honors there. I enjoy your intelligence and sense of humor and adventure. You are a vibrant woman.

Goodnight sweet slut. I look forward to your response.

Galen

Another story. . .

(*Note: Sent "As Master Wishes"*)

Subject: Deep in my head
Date: Tue, 1 Jun

Hello,

I did not attend catholic school, but that does not stop the guilt from being instilled in you. I was very rebellious as a teenager and at 18 my mother sent me to live with my father.

Re: cybersex. I am used to interactive chatting where you can actually perform cybersex. If they're good and can spell well, it can be satisfying. Obviously, not the same as phone or (even better) in person.

However, it can be a window to what that person is like in bed or how they would touch you and act with you. My online Master would not do any of this with me, only talk to me. I was allowed occasionally to make the motions of climbing on his lap and kiss him or once, to suck him off through description. He also liked to watch me with another woman, either topping her or being the submissive to her.

I hated to have to share his attention with someone else, and he often used this as punishment. Even though he would only watch and she was not to address him directly, I still preferred him to myself. I wanted him to touch me, not make me touch someone else.

Perhaps if I understood more of what bringing in the second woman represented, I would resent it less. He would not elaborate. He was not as experienced as you or as old as you, so maybe those are factors which allow you to be more expressive about the entire thing. Maybe not.

I think that above all, he was—as he told me many times—totally in awe that a woman that looked like me and that possessed a brain, among other desirable personality qualities, would be willing to serve him. Who knows.

Again, I will be very honest. Ready? Here goes. I have no way of offering you any guarantee that I would feel safe enough within 2 months to meet you. It is the nature of what you would want to do with me that chills me. However, I would have no problem meeting you in public and sharing a meal, drinks and conversation.

I know that is not possible due to the distance between us, but I would like the opportunity to converse with you and look at you at

the same time. I hope you appreciate and understand my feelings, the fear. Unfortunate but true, my fear is accelerated by the story you told me that happened to you.

Even though it was a farce, I do not wish to end up in the hospital in r/l. I hate the term r/l because it implies that sharing email, chatting or talking on the phone is not reality. Just because you met me through a computer doesn't mean I am not a real person, sharing real feelings with you.

I am not as directed as you as to what I want. I have not experienced a D/s relationship in the true sense. However, what I have experienced with my online Master and the feelings that I developed as a result of giving him control, sent a powerful message to me. I know that I desire to be controlled and to be submissive.

At the same time, I want to be adored, taken care of, appreciated and loved. Remember, my husband forgot to see me standing there, so I am looking for someone to give me attention and affection, to notice if I have a new dress on and to tell me I look beautiful. Does that mean I am not your candidate? I hope not. I don't want you to stop communicating with me, although I realize if I am not your intended mate, you will.

What if I am not able to tolerate pain at the level you seek? Obviously, that worries me; that you would consider me unable to truly serve you because I may have a lower limit than another willing slut. I have read some stories online, especially since meeting you, and I can honestly say that I am unsure I could tolerate some things that others can.

Please tell me more about your encounters. What kind of limits were set? What level of pain did you achieve with someone else? That you would use a crop on my cunt lips is both terrifying and exciting. I guess I seek answers from you about the reality of it.

What is the rest of the reality of our relationship during this period? Do you mind if I continue to chat with others? Does it matter if I date or even sleep with someone? I would be very unhappy to give

up any of these activities.

I have to tell you that you are deep in my head. I look forward to your mail and read it with almost a hunger. I woke up in the night, 4 am, and came thinking of you, your words. What you would do to me? I would dress for you, be erotic for you, show you what a whore I am in your presence.

lana

Subject: Incongruity
Date: Tue, 1 Jun

Let me point out an incongruity: you'd pick up a guy you don't know in a nightclub because he has a hard on, but you fear meeting me. How many women do you think have been raped or worse by guys they picked up in bars?

After two months of exploration, intensive questioning, baring of each others' souls, you would deny the man who knows you on a deeper level than anyone you've ever met, the man to whom you desire with all your soul to submit; and yet you are more afraid of this man, than of some lust crazed puppy you met in a bar?

Do you really think I would expend all this energy and passion on you for two months just so that I could come and harm you? It would be much simpler to pick up a sleazy hooker off the street, if my thrill was to just to harm someone, and about zero chance of recrimination.

You also need to review what you really seek. I don't think its just to be a cyber slut. But maybe you just want attention. Are you just a cyber party girl, flitting from one experience to the next? I know you are afraid, if the pain aspect is what you desire in r/t, versus the titillation of anonymous play on the net.

You must realize that there is only one way to find out. If you can

find a better more compassionate Dom than I, then go for it. Or you may never do it. Will you let your fear keep you from even seeking what you truly want? Is time really the issue? Would it be three months, three years, or never, as time slips by?

By beginning your training with our 'experiment,' if you follow my instructions, you will begin to learn about your current tolerance levels. More training would follow.

Trust me, dear. As I said, there are ways to assure your safety. Plus, I can give you a nearby reference. She's a actually an attorney I met earlier this year on a business trip. It was her first experience. We met three times over the course of a week (she kept 'cumming' back for more!).

Neither of us wanted a relationship out of the deal. She just needed someone she could entrust her submissiveness to for the first time. She started out thinking she just wanted to be spanked. But she wound up begging for the full extent of my services (lol).

But my intent now is not to gain your trust, just so I can use you like the submissive slut that you are. I get quite a few responses to my ads. It is not difficult to find a play partner, one much closer than you. I told you that now I seek my life partner.

I am more interested in your heart right now dear, and your soul. If I have not struck that chord in you, as desirable as you would be to play with, we would only be wasting each other's time to continue.

Galen

Subject: Ouch!
Date: Tue, 1 Jun

Hello,

Ouch, you didn't even greet me in your email. You're frustrated,

upset or indignant that I should actually fear you. You are correct; there are many women who disappear after a one night stand. I tried in the past to choose carefully. I was driven by sheer loneliness for a warm presence and lust.

The reason I fear you is that I would want you to, and indeed you would, tie me up or bind me in some way. It is a dangerous thing to do. I'm not naive. There are all kinds. Some would actually invest time to harm someone other than the nearest hooker.

I am not, nor did I mean to imply that you would harm me. Please don't be upset with me or insulted. I want to be honest with you. If I don't tell you these concerns, how will you help me overcome them? Do you want something built on honesty or should I just say the things you want to hear?

I thought you wanted to hear how I felt, all of it. I am willing to tell you anything, things I have never told anyone, so that we can explore it together. If I didn't have any reservations regarding meeting you, wouldn't you think I was missing some vital brain cells or something?

See, you have no idea, but already you have stirred things in me. Reading your letter I feared it would be your last, and that I had upset you. I apologize.

I do want this with you, to see where is goes. Please don't stop communicating with me. I have no time limit. I just wanted you to know that it was possible that after two months I would not be ready. I don't know what two months will bring. Already I have shared so much with you.

If you are trying to hurt my feelings by telling me there is a long line answering your ads, you have succeeded. You are free to pursue whomever you choose.

I told you before I needed patience. You asked me what I wanted and I told you affection, adoration, to be taken care of, to feel safe, to be loved, to be allowed to explore that side of me that you well

know exists and that I know you could and already do bring out.

I asked you what it was like in your actual meetings so I could begin to feel more comfortable. If I was only interested in a pure cyber thing, why would I keep writing to you when you plainly would not be satisfied with that?

Please, please don't be upset with me. You're all I think about.

lana

Subject: Amends
Date: Tue, 1 Jun

My precious,

You are a sweet slut, even when you're upset.

Perhaps my tone was harsher than intended. I do not want to hurt your feelings. I respect and encourage your concern for your safety. That's exactly why I told you the story about sharah.

I was protecting you, alerting you, not knowing how cautious you might actually be. A number of women I've met on line have made it too easy. But because I know I can be trusted, I don't admonish them about the rules of safety, til after (weg!). I do want you to progress through whatever means make sense to have you feel safer than you've ever felt with anyone else.

My point was not the incongruity I expressed, but the time frame. It is not about time, I know, but about a process of eliminating doubt through tangible and instinctual evidence, and then having an adequate safety net in place. This is how I see the process. How do you see it?

I have made it quite clear the passion you have stirred in me. I desire to romance you, adore you, love you, as well as subjugate

you. To be your guide and mentor on your submissive journey. To be a partner and an ally, and to shape you into my willing slave.

From my experience, the safety issue is quite readily resolved. That can be done with references, Xerox of driver's license. You could bring an armed body guard (grin), etc…

The basis of whom I will collar as my slave is not measured by how much pain she can endure, but other qualities, more to do with her desire to serve me, to capture my heart and hold my attention, and the chemistry we share on every level. Physical tolerance is something that grows with desire.

You please me with your respectful tone and your apology, even though I know a part of you is angry and upset. You please me with your attentiveness and faithful response to my letters.

Let's continue, dear slut. I want you to do the experiment this week.

Galen

Subject: Re: Amends
Date: Wed, 2 Jun

Hello,

I patiently waited for your reply and was rewarded with a much sweeter tone from you. Yes, I apologized even though I was upset too.

To be more comfortable, I still need to know what happened with the other encounters you had. Do you make me keep asking on purpose? Want me to say, "Please?"

I will buy the clothespins. Thank you for your reply tonight. I'm sure you knew I would be waiting.

lana

PS: Did you like the new pic?

Subject: Loyalty and devotion
Date: Wed, 2 Jun

Sweet slut,

I appreciate your loyalty and devotion to our communication. You do demonstrate a very pleasing submissive quality in that regard. . . waiting, yearning for Master's words.

Speaking of lacking greetings, I noticed you switched from Dear Master to Hello. Why?

As for the pic, I see a beautiful whore who in a moment will take her fingertips and slowly spread her legs. She wants to show her Master her smooth cunt, letting him know of her availability whenever he wants to use her.

I have addressed aspects of past experiences that I thought addressed your concerns. I don't mind, and encourage you to ask any question you wish (repeatedly, if necessary (grin)). I will try again.

Limits. They have varied from sub to sub, but here's a cross section of various limits I've respected in casual play with past subs: no anal; no marks or cuts; no gags; no tying or binding of the arms and legs (in case they wanted to run out the door, dressed like a slut, tits tied tightly, nipple clamps jangling (weg)); no slapping the face; no kissing; no swallowing. Some were hard limits, which I don't push in a short term relationship.

Many had soft limits, things they might try when they were feeling more comfortable (i. e. , hornier than they could stand). Pain is subjective. Some surprised me, and themselves with what they

could tolerate when sufficiently turned on.

Some sought the subtle marks, welts and bruises, and would admire them days later and tell me how proud they were of them, like badges of honor. Many sought to have their tits surrounded in a ring of clothes pins, clamps on their nipples, and driven crazy when I put the vibrator in contact with the clothes pins on their clit and it would vibrate right to their soul.

Some asked if I would pour hot wax on their tits, belly and pussy. I'd test the temperature just like a good Daddy with a baby's bottle. I'm so considerate... Ouch! It's very hot, just right!

"I would be very unhappy to give up any of the activities." Does this refer to giving up chat, dating, and other lovers, at some point in your submission to me?

You may ask me anything further you wish, dear.

Thinking of you

Galen

Here's another story. It's a Daddy/daughter scene. I read the Don and jeri story from the site you mentioned. It was an amazing writing collaboration. And I could relate to the disciplined, sadistically playful, tormenting manner of the Master. Maybe we'll play that scene someday.

This story might seem a little harsh. I wrote it when I had a very severe, upsetting experience, not related to D/s. It was just a vent. Though I could play a scene like that with a willing partner. I wrote it to someone that I knew would not be afraid, but would enjoy it. She did. It was an experiment in creating fear, uncertainty, and putting the slave in a no-win situation.

(*Note: included 'Daddy's Home' story*)

Subject: All sides of me
Date: Wed, 2 Jun

Dear Master,

Perhaps I stopped greeting you in that way because you were less than nice to me. If you want to know all sides, I am sarcastic, independent, cannot tolerate bigotry and oddly enough, cannot stand chauvinism. Isn't that a twist? I hate that glass ceiling, being called 'honey' by someone I don't know, or perhaps someone thinking I can't balance a checkbook because I am a woman or worse, blonde, lol.

I like being taken care of but I do not want to be treated like an idiot. You understand? I don't, so maybe you can help me with this dual personality I have. I laugh. A lot. If I see someone fall, I can't help it, I bust up.

I love music. Loud, pulse pounding rap sometimes, rock of any and all types, pop, dance, disco, classical, opera, jazz, blues, some country. I like love stories and thrillers. I laugh my ass off at Ally McBeal.

I liked that Don and jeri story. I'm happy that you read it too. I probably would not want that level of pain, but I like the story; made me very hot.

Your story was chilling. I probably would not be into that extreme treatment. I don't think I want to be tortured. I don't think of myself as a masochist. More like someone who wants to be submissive but not bleeding. Is that too mild for you?

Some of the stories I have read, your last one included, seemed to project more of a disdain by the Master toward the slave. I want to be allowed to openly be a slut, a wanton whore, but not hated. I don't think the Don and jeri story contained that 'almost hatred'. If someone openly allowed you to have total power would you grow to hate them?

Please do this for me. . . pick one woman you met online and tell me about the relationship, i. e. , how you came to start writing to her, how it progressed, her age, what she wanted from you, how long before you met, how the meeting went. . . what did you do. . . how was it afterwards. . . how many times did you meet, all of that. Please.

As for dating and that other stuff, in the stage that we are in, I would not be willing to give that up. My last Master did not want me to chat online at the site that we frequented. We compromised in that I would not chat with a Master.

I was allowed to date but he didn't want to know it or for me to mention it. If he asked what I did Friday night, I left that portion out unless specifically asked. Obviously, if you and I ultimately decided we were making a lifetime commitment, I wouldn't want anyone else. For me, the second I truly find my mate, I'm turning off my computer.

How many women are you involved with like me? Which picture do you like the best? You know, when you first responded to my inquiry, you seemed almost bored and I have to smile. I hope you are no longer bored by me.

Here's a fantasy I wrote for you.

Lana's Fantasy

I imagine you coming home, after a long day. Your sweet slut greets you at the door. . . your favorite drink ready. . . you smell your favorite food. . . you're surrounded by all you derive pleasure from, including your whore.

Knowing about your bad day, I am already wearing your favorite clothes you have provided. . . tight, very short black skirt that slides up naughtily when I sit or kneel, revealing sexy stockings, a long line up the back, seductively hooked to your favorite "whore garter" . . . very high fuck me heels, making me teeter slightly. . . black lace

crotchless panties that ride sexily up either cheek of my ass. . . a
beautiful white blouse, tied at my waist, buttonless, just barely
revealing my black lace demi bra and pushing up my breasts into
two beautifully sexy mounds for your delight.

The music you prefer is playing low in the background. . . not too
loud, don't want to upset my Master on a bad day. You sit in a chair
and watch me bring your drink, knowing how much I desire you
when I am dressed like this. . . hoping but not asking that you will
let me dance for you to allow you to release your tension.

You slip your hand under my skirt, feeling the heat already. . . "You
love being dressed this way, don't you little slut?" I moan softly,
involuntarily spreading my legs. You withdraw your hand and tell
me "Not so fast. Dance for your Master, sweet slut and see if you
can relieve my headache. Be warned that I will hold you account-
able should you fail. "

I nod, turning up the music a little. I grind slowly for you, not
wanting to fail. I run my hands over my body as you like, my red
fingernails lightly touching. You tell me to lose the blouse and I
untie it slowly. "Show me your tits slut. How hard your nipples
must be from your dancing. " I know you are feeling better already
and it gives me great pleasure to help you. I pull them out, the tight
bra underneath them now, pushing them up and out.

My pink nipples stiff, the heels making them jiggle as I move for
you. At your command, I turn, still grinding, rubbing my ass, which
raises the skirt exposing the sexy garters and part of my barely
covered ass. You know how wet I am, doing this for you. How
much I want you to play with me, to use me.

You beckon me closer and pinch my nipple, pulling it, watching my
face, knowing it smarts. "You want more, don't you little slut?"
I'm melting, barely able to contain myself, but not wanting to upset
you, knowing I have to wait for you to decide.

You pull both nipples, making them bright red and I involuntarily
run my fingers to my pussy. I feel you smack my tit, and you tell

me I have to wait. I whimper at the sting. "I'm so sorry, Master, please forgive me."

You tell me to get on my hands and knees in front of you, my ass toward you. You reach over and I feel you raise my skirt. I am so wet, want you so much. You squeeze my ass, I feel your fingers spread me open, the crotchless panties allowing you to view my wetness. You hold me open and I struggle to remain still, knowing it won't please you if I move.

"I can see how wet your cunt is, slut. You would love to feel my hard cock right now wouldn't you?" I answer softy, "Yes Master."

"Not yet, sweetheart, you may get your reward, but first you need to be warmed up, don't you, slut?"

I feel your hands leave my pussy lips pulling the fabric up through my cheeks. I feel it pull on my clit, sliding deep between my cunt lips. I try hard to remain still, allowing you to play with me. "You like that don't you, my sweet little bitch. So hot you are. You're a good little whore aren't you?" I answer the question, "Yes Master. "

You pull the panties up higher, lifting my hips and I feel the sting of your hand. I moan and feel you sliding the fabric, now covered in my juice, down over my thighs, taking them off me without having my hands leave the floor.

I can't help it, and wiggle my ass ever so slightly, begging you to smack it, whip it. You know that it would make me drip with ecstasy to feel you use me. I feel you reach around to my tits and I push them out for you, wanting to feel your hands grab them, talk about them, pull my nipples, make them hard and make me moan. I know that you will attach clamps to them for your pleasure, and that it will hurt but that you will tease me endlessly until I beg for that pain.

I long to feel your power, to know that you will soon tightly bind my tits for your pure enjoyment, playing with them, using your crop on them, teasing my now dripping cunt. You don't let me cum, but

bring me achingly close, smacking my cunt, telling me what a wet slut I am.

You make me admit how much I like being your toy. How much I love and adore you and love serving you in this way. You take your cock out and tease my wet pussy mouth with it, allowing me to lick it. I whimper with the thought of sucking it.

You smack my face (not too hard) and my tits in between licks, making me ask for another smack before I get to lick it as my reward. You watch my eyes glaze with adoration and desire for you, begging you to fill my mouth, doing the same to my cunt.

Slowly you begin dipping your fingers, a toy, or whatever you choose into my wetness. You are always talking to me and smacking me or cropping me in between, making me whimper and beg for more of your whip. I know it will hurt but am driven by the desire of your touch, and my own burning cunt, to ask for more. Mixing pain and pleasure makes me hotter and hotter, slowly increasing my tolerance for you, testing what treatments I will suffer for you.

That's what I like. Is that too mild for you?

lana

(*Note: The following message was sent in an e-card*)

Subject: I am temptation
Date: Wed, 2 Jun

 My sweet whore,

You are so beautifully submissive. Your desire and courage are strong. Do not worry, or fear your ability to be a good slave for me. I will bring you along patiently. I will tease and lightly torment you, until your hunger for total surrender, your love and desire to have my pleasure your only goal, drowns you in the tumult of our

passion. I know your mind, heart and body want to obey and serve me, to be my proud slut slave. I accept you as my slut, offer you the freedom to become who you really are. I am a temptation you will not resist, your darkest desire come true.

My luv to you, dear slut.

Master Galen

Subject: re: Card
Date: Wed, 2 Jun

Master,

Thank you. Thank you. Thank you.

lana

Subject: Your lovely story
Date: Wed, 2 Jun

Precious slut,

I sent my card right before I got your mail this morning. I'm off to a meeting, and will be out all day, and then seeing my kids tonight. So I'll respond more later.

I will send a full transcript of an encounter that started online and led to a meeting, and several thereafter. I believe the contact to first meeting took less than 2 weeks. That's been about an average time.

I do not hate women. Many of the stories were inspired by the desires and needs for humiliation and pain of subs I met online or in person.

I look at it this way, during training of a sub I desire, or with just a play partner, the sub guides the experience. We start in her territory, her comfort zone, she defines her limits, her goals. I'm like a therapist, helping her find the truth about what turns her on, who she is sexually, what will give her total freedom and release.

For the woman I will call my slave, only then will I expect and take control of every part of her. She will know this in advance of course, what I expect, and will submit willingly.

I only breezed through your story because I have to leave now. It was lovely, and very sexy, as are you.

More later – luv,

Galen

Subject: Gory details
Date: Wed, 2 Jun

Hi sweet slut,

I want to play that scene you wrote. I would love to have you exhibit yourself like a whore, dressed like that, turning me on with your dance of desire, feel my cock gliding through your red lips, while you look up at me, shamelessly slutty.

I get several contacts a week. Some I ignore, some I explore a bit. There are no others like you, dear, that I pursue with both my heart and my cock. I do have a sub in Montreal, a French Arab, who's an actress and singer, and also does public BDSM scenes and model-ing. We've carried on quite a soulful journey and she was very supportive of me several months ago, when I was having a bad time with some personal issues. But I don't foresee that we are going to match as partners, though we've become very close friends and supportive allies. We've haven't met in the flesh.

I'm including a transcript of before and after correspondence from the sub I mentioned in your area. I had written her mostly from my old laptop, and I guess I never backed up those files before I sold that one. But I do have all of hers and two of mine.

You can generally get the idea from her responses what I might have said. Is this going to make you jealous my slut (grin)? Listening to another slut seeking my pleasure so blatantly.

She was not a woman who stirred my heart and I did not keep in contact, though we had talked of her coming to visit me out here to further her slut training. She was so happy to get her first experience, and I know she wished I could continue to accept her submission.

You will see that I was not involved in a passionate way, as I would be with you, my lovely whore. I also suggested to her to try the pins and belts on herself. But not as romantically as I described it to you. Be cautious how you let these letters effect you emotionally. If you have any further questions, you may ask.

This was a lot of effort for you, dear slut. I expect you to show your appreciation.

Oops! Out of time. Gotta go meet my kids.

Warmly,

Galen

Subject: Re: Gory details
Date: Thu, 3 Jun

Thank You Master,

LOL. I love the title. Yes, Master, I wanted the gory details. I'm so pleased you recognized that and sent them to me.

Yes, it smarted a little to read the things she wrote to you. I'm sure that's the gist of most of your mail. My first letter was so bland, I'm surprised you answered. I am so lucky you decided to try me.

I deeply appreciate that you took the time to put that together for me. She met you so quickly. It made me feel much more comfortable. Tell me, if you will, why you would instruct me in such a sensuous way? What is it that strikes that in you?

I can see the things you were telling her and your actual letters. I see that while much of it is like your letters to me, you are different in what you say to me. I was happy to see that difference. Otherwise, I am merely one in a revolving door of women trying to get your attention.

To show you my appreciation, I tried some things tonight you suggested. I have my daughter this week and she was sleeping, so no store. Instead, I found some binder clips. Binder clips are black clamps used in an office for documents. If you know what they are, I'm sure you feel like smacking me for acting as if you would not. I am sorry.

These were medium size, with silver openers that bend back to squeeze them open. I put rubber bands on those because they're very tight. It barely released any pressure because you can't get the band on the tip of the part you squeeze. I didn't want to disappoint you though.

I ran my bath with scented bubbles, then lit some candles. I stripped in the mirror, looking at my body, touching it lightly, thinking of you. I like the water to be so hot, I get a little flushed. I slipped in it and put the clips on the edge of the tub.

I also had wine. I thought about you and what I had written you; things you have written me, wondering what it would be like. I was slightly nervous, but the wine, the hot water and my own excitement overcame any fear of pain.

I squeezed my tits with both hands, watching the bubbles slip off, imagining you were there talking to me and that I was doing this for you as you wished. I know I whispered, "Yes Master" more than once.

I dragged the clip over my nipple and slowly opened it, looking at it. I placed it over my nipple which was so hard already. I slowly let it close until it was on completely. I loved it, feeling you there. It hurt, and I could not have kept my fingers away from my pussy for anything.

I let go of the clamp and left it on, looking at it, touching my tit. The clamp pulled my nipple down slightly and out. It hurt! I kept trying to hear you. I rubbed my clit harder. . . played with myself. I slowly put the other one on. I squeezed both tits, pushing them up, watching the clips jiggle. I had this huge desire to see myself, how you would see me. I got out of the tub and stood in the mirror, my body dripping with the suds and with something else.

I liked the way it looked. I imagined you touching the clamps, so I did, watching my nipple being pulled. When I took them both off after as long as I could stand, (which was much longer that I thought I could). I was amazed at my nipples—dark, red, huge, pulled out, marks where the clamps were. I moved the clip around my body, trying it, rubbing my pussy.

Looking in the mirror, I took a deep breath and placed the clamp on my right cunt lip. It didn't hurt nearly as much as the tip of my nipple, and I was so excited. I put the other one on the other lip, imagining you there. I took them off and stepped back into the water.

My tits ached but I was so hot. After putting the clips back on my nipples, I came so hard! It still hurt a lot but I kept hearing you, and tried so hard to please you, to suffer for you. How much you would have liked seeing me this way.

I hope this pleases you.

lana

Subject: Sweet suffering
Date: Thu, 3 Jun

Sweet slut,

I am so proud of you and pleased and excited by your efforts. I
longed to be there with you, to experience the beauty of your
virginal suffering for me. I wanted to see the first expression in
your eyes as they winced at the sharp bite of the clamp as it bit into
your erect nipple (I know those type of clamps, strong nasty little
fuckers, much stronger than clothes pins. You suffer better than
expected, slut!).

And then to see the hot burning lust as you realized what a whore
you truly are to give this decadent pleasure to your Master. I can
imagine how beautiful your dripping cunt must have looked
adorned so wickedly. I want to plunge my cock into you right now,
as a reward for your obedient submission. Then surround you in a
tender, loving, protective embrace, sealed with passionate, soothing
kisses on your cunt, nipples and mouth.

I told you that I am now seeking an affair of the heart, to find my
life partner in this exotic world of D/s. I am captured by your
beauty, your openness, desire to serve, intelligence, humor, et al.

My Domly intuition told me that your newness to pain and suffering
for pleasure would not be stronger than your desire to please me.
Apparently my intuition was correct. I always thought if a woman
can have a baby, she can easily endure the pain of being an erotic
slave girl (lol).

I am happy that you feel more comfortable now, after reading about
the sub I sent the details about. I wasn't sure how you would handle
the whole thing, emotionally. But I figured you'd be more excited
than jealous, once you focused on your desire to please me (and

yourself).

It's morning and I have a busy day. It was such a pleasure to be greeted by my slut's description of her suffering evening. I am well pleased, luv.

your Master

Galen

Subject: Re: Sweet suffering
Date: Thu, 3 Jun

Hello Master,

What a coincidence that while I am checking my mail, yours arrives. I was slightly disturbed that you also signed luv to her as well, and you used 'T.' Do I not get the pleasure of your real name?

I'm pleased that my experiment moved you. This morning, my nipples were still slightly marked, but I did that very late last night. I actually tried it again after I wrote you to see how it felt again. Tonight, I will try the belt.

I know you said that you would play my story out with me. Is it too mild for you? Did it tell you more of what I like or did you already figure all that out about me? I better be careful with you, you may know me better than I know myself in that area.

Last night I would have done just about anything to hear your voice after my bath, or to have communicated with you directly. Or, even better, to be in the room with you watching my reaction.

I could not believe the feelings and mixed emotions I had doing it. I so much wanted not to disappoint you, yet it hurt and was humiliating to do it. I marvel that I did that to myself just to write to you about it.

I think a lot of it was you being in my head. The way you instructed me to do it.   So sensual. Hearing you encouraging me in my head. Wondering how it would be for you to do that to me, knowing that you would be good to me, but at the same time, you would want me to feel it. I felt like a complete slut, ready to do anything. Honestly, I wanted to get fucked in the worst way.

Driving to work this morning, top down, short baby blue dress on that really accentuates my full breasts, sun shining, I noticed men looking (always) and had to smile openly at one cute one, thinking about what I had done the night before. I think I picked this sundress today because all I can think about is my tits and how wet I am.

I'm going to a seminar the rest of the day and will eagerly look for your reply when I get home. You must be slightly amused at how fast I am falling, aren't you? You are correct. My desire to be used and to serve you and fear of failure (obviously, I detest failure) seem to outweigh the pain I felt last night.

What did you think of her when you finally met for real? Was she what you thought? Did she please you? I know you didn't "connect" with her, but I wondered how you felt afterward.

I am a very curious and jealous slut, as I am sure you are seeing. I also wonder why she would not be willing to go out and just buy what you wanted her to wear instead of substituting something she already had. I'm not rippin' on her, I just feel that I would want to have all new things on, exactly what you want.

I know I would take the day and go to the mall and carefully choose each article, right down to the perfume, my nails, my toenails, all of it. Having it all wrapped in tissue, taking it all home, trying it on. Anticipating and waiting. People are different. Of course, I also love to shop. *smile* I would want to be perfect.

You know I already wish you were close enough to sit and have a drink with and see the way you would look at me, knowing what

you would do and that I would beg for every bit of it. Here's a deep breath: do you still travel to my area? (I know you're smiling at the way you have brought out such a willing whore in me).

Have a nice day, Master!

lana

Subject: Spanking fun
Date: Thu, 3 Jun

My good little whore,

Tonight, slut, when you use the belt, imagine it is me delivering the blows to your flesh. Dress in heels, nylons and garter only. Stand before the mirror, admire how beautiful and sexy you look. Touch yourself for pleasure and imagine I am there, giving you these instructions, knowing you will obey, watching every move.

Take the belt and drape it around the back of your neck. Take an end in each hand, with the belt between your cleavage, pulling it up and out under your tits. Just feel the pressure on your tits and view the distortion the belt creates in their shape. Release the tension when you are ready and let the belt go back to the center.

Now, cross the ends in front of you and wrap the belt around your neck like a choker. Grab both ends from behind your neck with one hand and squeeze, til you feel the pressure building in your head, not too tight, but firmly. Dip the fingers from your other hand into the folds of your cunt. Are you wet, slut! I thought so. Rub your clit. Feel the pleasure building.

When your are ready, release the belt so it's draped behind your neck again, with both ends in front. Take the buckle end of the belt in one hand, and draw the belt slowly across the back of your neck, sensuously down across your tits. Feel it slither over you like a snake. Let it slide down your torso, til the tip brushes the top of

your mound. You may touch yourself as you please, slut. I enjoy watching!

Now take the belt and draw it between your slightly spread legs. Draw it between your cunt lips and up the crack of your ass. Hold one end in front of you and with the other hand behind your back cinch the belt up firmly, so you can feel it pressing against your cunt and asshole. Holding it firmly in both hands, begin undulating your hips like you're hungrily fucking my cock, buried in you. Pull tighter on the belt, maneuver for your pleasure.

Watch yourself in the mirror. Talk to me, telling me you're so desperate to be a good whore for me. Thank me for teaching you how to be my hot slut.

Now take the belt, fold it in two, so there's a loop. Take the looped end and drag it across your nipples, make them stand erect, pinch them between your fingers if you like. Now take the loop of the belt and wrap it around your tit. Cinch it tight.

If you can, cross the ends of the belt again and take another rap on your tit, do it slut. I want you to squeeze hard, and hold it there, until your tit becomes engorged and darkens with blood. Look at yourself in the mirror. Rub your hot, wet cunt.

Now unwrap the belt, and begin striking your tits and nipples with it. Strike your belly, and then back to your tits. Keep increasing the intensity, with an occasional hard slap for the sensation (or more if you must!).

When you are ready, put the buckle in your left hand and grip the last 12-14 inches of the belt in your right. Start by slapping the inside of your thighs. Spread it around at first, start lightly. Become accustomed to the sensation. Work both thighs, starting low and working your way up to your cunt, but not on your cunt (yet!). Work your way back down each thigh.

When you start up again, strike a bit harder. Occasionally strike with force, then ease up. You thighs should be taking on a glow and

you'll feel the heat and sting lingering. When you are ready, take the edge of the belt at the tip and sensuously rub the edge across your clit and pussy, make love to it, knowing that I am watching you with a look of love and pleasure, as I see you get hotter and hotter. Do not cum!!

Now take the belt and begin to strike your pussy and clit. If you can, lay down with your knees drawn up, particularly where you can still see yourself spread in the mirror. Strike your pussy and clit mildly, playfully at first, and then increase the strength and duration on any particular spot. If you have a dildo or vibrator, or suitable vegetable (weg!), you may use it, to keep up your will for the pain. Strike until you've reached your limit.

Take the belt now, standing up with your ass to the mirror. Bend over and watch as you begin using the belt on your ass and backs of your thighs, stimulating your pussy liberally. Imagine that I have now taken the belt and am beating my hot slut's ass, enjoying the crimson glow on your marked ass, knowing you're enduring until I am ready to take you.

You may cum for me now slut, in any way you please.

I've gone by Galen for about 3 months now. I'll tell you why later. It's what I prefer. Telling her my name, T, was nothing special. Galen is more special.

Don't be upset about it, luv. Hope you enjoy your evening!!

Love (does that feel better)Your Master,

Galen

I'm off to my softball league. Enjoy your evening. I'll be waiting for your report this evening, my whore.

Subject: Re: Spanking fun!

Date: Thu, 3 Jun

Dear Master,

When you call me a whore, I get a chill. Again, I had just clicked on seconds before your mail came.

Today at that seminar, we were on a break and I went to the lounge and had coffee and cookies. I picked a sofa/chair area to sit that was unoccupied. Within less than 3 minutes, 3 men were seated with me, 2 on a couch, one in a chair and me in a chair in the middle.

I listened, smiled, thought about you, talked to them, thought about you, ate my cookies, thought about you. When I stood to go back to the class, so did the 3 of them, lol.

For a second I had to stop myself from sitting back down and then quickly standing again, just to see them. . . .hahahaha. Oh, sorry. I smiled, said goodbye. Hard for me to concentrate on anything but the memory of my nipples in those clamps.

I just came before writing this. Can you guess why? I'm sure you can. First, I got wet just reading your description of what you wanted me to do. I got a belt. Black, the longest one I own. Medium width.

I stood in the mirror in my bedroom, dressed in heels, silk stockings with a single line up the back, and a black lace garter. Very sexy! I felt and looked like a complete slut. I did as you instructed, starting with it around my neck, dragging it over my body. I felt electricity.

It was much better when I concentrated on you being here or on you holding the belt, teasing me with it. I squeezed my tit with it, watching it bulge out, my nipple so stiff, an offering to my Master. I rubbed my clit, in between squeezing my tit. I ran the cold steel of the buckle across my nipple. . . ohhh!!

I slowly drew the other end back and slapped it across my tit. It

made a sound. I had done it harder than I intended. I flinched and did it again, lighter, testing it, smacking my nipple, the underneath of my breasts, the tops, the sides. I took it a lot longer than I thought I could. Continuously sliding my hand over my pussy. I got so wet, my palm slid across my cunt like a slide. Like that, Master?

I wanted to cum, so I tested it across my thighs. Laying on my back, legs bent and open, I watched my thighs get a little red. All the while I was constantly rubbing my cunt, pressing my clit. I ran the belt across my pussy and lightly smacked it. I could barely take it on my clit and when it hit my open pussy, my legs flinched. I was getting hotter and hotter, testing it.

Finally, my tits still stinging, my thighs tingling, I stood up and turned around in the mirror and imagined you. I bent forward, reached back with the belt and smacked it against my ass, harder and harder, lighter, higher, lower. I couldn't stand it anymore. It hurt, Master, and I needed to cum.

Afterward, I looked at my body. Definite criss-cross marks on my ass. I traced them with my finger. My tits were red, nipples hard and very dark red. While I was cumming, I could feel the sting of you everywhere. You are making me a much bigger whore than I thought I was.

After it was over, I felt strange. Definitely stinging and humiliated that I did that. I don't know what to think of it. I'm confused in my head I guess. I liked it and I was incredibly wet doing it.

I look forward to hearing from you.

lana

Subject: Precious tramp
Date: Thu, 4 Jun

424

My precious tramp,

I am very proud of how my slave bitch is learning to suffer for me. It is difficult to be so far away, when I know how strong you are in your efforts to pleasure Me. I am more than pleased, dear; I am impressed and moved by your obedience, your devotion, your passion to be my slave.

You are getting a glimpse now of what a whore you really are. You didn't know before we met that you would move so far, so fast into my realm, where your sole purpose and desire is to be my willing slut, a sex slave for her Master.

I know how this is driving your need to be fucked, isn't it slut? I know you desire Master's cock inside of you. Where do you want it, bitch? Never mind, I'll tell you. I want you to bend over and offer me your ass. Would you like that slut? Bend over! Spread your cheeks! Tell me that you're my whore, and to "fuck me up my ass Master, please!"

I reach for my elk hide flogger. "Your lovely ass isn't ready yet my bitch. Stand perfectly still, slut. I want to turn that ass crimson. I want to feel the heat rising from it when I touch it. When it's the right temperature and hue, then I will let you beg me to fuck your slave's ass. Is that okay with you slut? You don't have a problem with that, do you?"

I realize I must give my blessing if you need to go out and get fucked this weekend. I will not make you suffer neglect, if you feel the need to release. I do not give this blessing lightly. I do not want you to fuck anyone else. It is not a command! I want to possess you entirely.

But that is premature at this point. It would not displease me if you desired only me. But I am open to a surrogate, with these conditions: one night stand, only; you can't suck his cock; and I've got to throw in a little torture for condoning your desire, since you like having a cock fucking your cunt mouth. Just say no!

425

Plus you have the perfect brush-off, if he wants to see you again. "My Master only gave me permission to see you once. I'm so sorry but there is nothing I can do but obey and be my Master's slave. I'm sure you understand," lol!

Maybe it would be simpler if you just found another slut like yourself, and made it with her.

I don't have any short term plans to come to Your area on business. Why, should I be thinking about some other purpose to cum to Your area, slut? Do you think it strange that I suggest you get fucked? It is not done without a certain pain.

I want you to feel wonderful about this journey. Ask yourself, is it true? Is that desire to be a whore, a tramp for the right Master, truly you? We already know the answer. Though many people would scorn your decision to accept this truth about you, there is a growing community of people, thanks to the Internet, who are exploring these strange desires. You are not alone.

What you feel is normal. Look how many people, millions in this country, certainly, who are clandestinely exploring this life. It is true for them. They want to express it, to embrace it without scorn or ridicule. The mantra is safe, sane and consensual. There is a dignity and a spirituality to it. Two or more people agreeing that they want this pleasure. Why not, dear slut? It is our truth.

It is a greater love and intimacy than will ever be achieved by those conforming to the social norm because they are too afraid to be truly themselves. Feel wonderful sweetheart. I love you for being who you are for me.

I want you to fuck your ass for me. Do you have a dildo or other appropriate toy? You might want to have two dildos, one for your ass and one to use on your mouth or cunt. It is late and I'm too tired to think about this now. Maybe you can offer some ideas.

Sweet dreams, my whore.

Galen

Master,

I have only had anal sex a few times. Once with the married guy
that broke my heart, a couple times with my husband. The most I
enjoyed it was with the married guy. I wanted to do that for him
and it was slow and easy. The others with my ex were long ago, too
long to count, lol. I'm not sure about it at all. When I have sex, I
like it hard, fast and deep; but I'm not sure about having anal sex
like that.

I see now that if I want to know something from you, it's likely I
have to ask you more than once. Not a problem, I know what I
require answers to and will hound you as long as you let me.

Is the scene I sent you too mild for you? This is really what I prefer,
I think. Who knows? I also asked you some questions re: how it
was to meet that other sub and experience that with her for real.

If the opportunity presents itself, it's likely I will have sex this
weekend. I appreciate that you understand. I'm sure there is a 22
year old who would be eternally grateful, lol.

My final divorce hearing is next week. I can't sleep and food is
totally unappealing. Now, I'm a little sick, sore throat. I guess if I
do have sex, it will probably be after the hearing.

I am really upset about my marriage and the whole thing. You
know, if you start to focus on whether that person actually ever
loved you, it's very difficult to try and believe that he did. There
were a few things he had to do to keep us together instead of crying
about them, after I left.

He did nothing while I was right there next to him and made 10,000 promises after I was gone. If he didn't care while I was there, why would he care later. It's not like I required massive doses of attention. I just wanted to get flowers sometimes, have him do something I wanted to do instead of us always doing what he wanted.

He never took any interest in what interested me, so, to me, I must not have been important enough to him for him to bother to share with me. Anyway, I miss my home, my stuff and my old life sometimes. Okay, sorry to tell you all that. It's very much on my mind because it's almost done.

Look forward to hearing from you.

lana

Subject: Deep passionate kisses
Date: Fri. , 4 Jun

Sweetheart,

I appreciate that you share your sorrow. I wish I was there to hold you and comfort you, provide tender deep passionate kisses, arrive at your door with flowers (and my bag of tricks). Our respective marriages and divorces have many parallels. I left everything behind, and have grieved the loss of all that was built in 16 years.

My ex has been trying to destroy me in many ways, with my kids, our friends and financially. I will tell you more if you wish. I just can feel the difficulties you face now. Know that I am here for you dear, to offer any comfort I can, to provide an ear to listen. Besides being a kinky pervert, I am also a soulful, compassionate, and tender man.

You are wise to prod gently when I don't answer your questions right away. I put a lot of energy in responding to you, and often run out before I cover everything. I will hold nothing back from you.

There will be no deception. I left that behind in my past relationship as well.

You move me, dear. Your courage to try to please me has succeeded beyond measure. I am proud and happy at how you have succeeded, and enjoy the discovery of your beautiful whoredom.

I have to leave now, so will answer further at my next opportunity tonight or tomorrow. But briefly, you story was beautiful and exciting, not too mild for this stage. I feel confident if it is your desire, you will grow into the ways of a pleasure slave. You show great potential.

As for anal, I believe you will find, as with our other "experiments", that we will proceed slowly, sensuously, with liberal doses of pussy stimulation and lubrication. But know that I will not force you to do anything that does not ultimately bring you pleasure, no matter how humiliating or painful it may be on other levels. This is the paradox of being a submissive slave.

Feel me there, holding you, loving you, supporting you as you move through the painful finality of your divorce.

Love,

Galen

Subject: Re: Flowers from my heart
Date: Fri, 4 Jun

Master,

Thank you for the flowers (*note: I had sent her an e-card bouquet*). My husband never sent me flowers; just once when I had our daughter. The day after I moved out, two dozen roses arrived in a crystal vase. I was so mad, I called him and told them he was lucky I didn't smash them over his fucking head. So, one thing I am

looking for is flowers.

I know I can offer a lot in a relationship. I am a very attentive, very giving person. However, I must have a return this time. I will not settle for less.

I called my ex today. No reason. Maybe looking for a reason not to have to make it final on Monday. I'm so disappointed in him. I am going to get past it, but I blame him for the 3 of us not being able to have what we set out to obtain.

I was married ten years, so I know what it's like to dismantle it all. My husband wouldn't give me our daughter, so we share her, rotating custody weekly. For now, she's 4 and it works. Later, it won't and we will have to deal with it. With any luck he'll get married and give her to me permanently.

A counselor for my daughter said this was okay and in fact, good for her at this stage. I could have fought him, but I'm not like that and he has every right to her as do I. Lately, all I do is cry. I was doing much better, but not today.

Tell me more about your marriage, if you like. It allows me to know you better. Do you find that you think about me when you are not reading your mail?

Since I am keeping track, the remaining unanswered question box contains the unanswered questions about your meeting the other sub. I'd like to know how you felt about her when you met—what you did; how you liked it; was it after meeting her that you decided you were not interested in a relationship or before? Did she find you attractive? Of course, I ask all this with a please and a smile.

lana

PS: you can tell I'm not feeling happy, an entire letter w/ no sex - what is the
world coming to?

Subject: Courage dear
Date: Thu, 4 Jun

Dear lana,

Within you is a power. You can feel it, access it. It is your courage, your fierceness to get what you want and deserve, your determination, your passion, your daughter! Draw on the power of these allies. Feel their strength. Feel your anger. Strip the vengeance from its fire and turn it's power on what you want.

You have to overpower your fear and doubt and remorse about your marriage. You can't go back. Men like that rarely change (I won't say never).

I believe it is important to prepare yourself for Monday. Grieve now if it will help, but by Sunday you want to develop and focus on the new beginning. This step opens the door for you to discover the relationship that you truly want.

You are being set free. How joyous is that. You are not to blame. It doesn't matter now who is. I want you to enter that courtroom radiating your dignity and grace. Don't buy into the melodrama of him and you, don't be bated into a scene.

Hopefully you will have some loving support there with you. I say this, not because I am so wise that I can follow my own advice, not get sucked in by my own pathos. But I know I can and do draw on different parts of myself when I need support. I wish I was there to cheer you up.

Do I think of you. Of course I do. How could I not? We've exchanged twenty some letters in a week. I believe you are maybe concerned that I have the revolving door you mentioned with slaves piling up at the entrance, while I dangle you and dozens of others online.

My current situation is as I stated in a previous reply. I think about you all the time. I thought about you last night when I played softball. I smile when I think about you. I saw a couple tonight in a bar, sitting close, she reaching over with her hand to tenderly turn his face to hers, then whisper something in his ear, her cheek pressed against his. I imagined you sitting so close to me, touching me so lovingly.

I spend too much time I shouldn't, writing these letters to you, when I should be focused on my business things. I am devoting my attention to you dear, because of the many fine qualities you possess as a human, a woman and a slut. I like all you've shared so far. It's been exhilarating, hasn't it?

Because you have been so devoted, are respectful, intelligent, superbly erotic, have the desire to be the best slut that's ever been, you stir my passion. So far, nothing has shown up to diminish my pursuit of you.

<"Since I am keeping track, the remaining unanswered question box contains the questions about meeting the other sub. I'd like to know how you felt
about her when you met; what you did; how you liked it; was it after meeting
her that you decided you were not interested in a relationship or before?
Did she find you attractive? Of course, I ask all this with a please and a
smile.">

See, I copied the questions, so I don't miss any. Your respect and graceful way of asking does win my attention.

I felt she was a little heavier than stated, not bad looking. She was late without calling my cell. I sat in the lobby waiting. When she arrived I gave her a warm hug. Then I told her. "You're late. If you decide to be with me tonight, you will receive a punishment." She tried to argue and make excuses. A silly thing to do.

432

I firmly told her that I don't accept excuses about agreements we make. She apologized and we went to the bar. We sat in an isolated booth. I complimented her on how sexy she looked. I told her to cross her legs, so I could see her legs and high heels. I already knew she was going to go to my room. We talked, mostly me.

She had 38" tits cupped in a low cut black lace bra, and her top showed them to advantage after she removed her jacket. There was a small tattoo of a butterfly, I believe, above her left breast. I outlined it with my fingernail. "Nice tits. I'm going to reach in and feel them. Is that OK with you?"

Then, I had her spread her legs slightly. "I'm going to feel your pussy, now." It was absolutely dripping. She flushed as she knew I knew. "You're wet slut," I smiled. I took her to my room.

"Go stand by the bed." I went and sat down on a chair by the bed. "Sit down. Spread your legs, and slide your panties to the side and show me that wet cunt."

Then I proceeded more or less like this: I had her kneel before me, introduced her mouth to my cock. She was hungry. I had her kneel on all fours on the bed. Had her raise her skirt above her ass, and spanked her good with my hand. I gave her twenty hard strokes on each cheek. This was her punishment for being 20 minutes late. I had her change position sideways to me, so I could fuck her mouth again, while I finished her punishment.

I had her stand as I sat, and I took a vibe dildo and played with it on her clit. I had her strip to her bra, garter, heels and nylons. I stood up, pulled her tits from her bra, pulled on the nipples, and then placed the small clamps on them. I put a ball gag in her mouth, and mildly whipped her tits and pussy.

I keep having to prompt her to say, "Yes, Master," instead of just "Yes," when I asked her something. And "Thank you, Master." I can go on and on, but you get the idea. She went further than she expected and as you can tell from her letters, was anxious for more.

433

There was bondage in different positions, dildos, no anal, clothes-pins on pussy and tits. She liked rough treatment on her tits. I left bruises. She told me she liked having them. Personally, I felt little spark for her.

She didn't interest me intellectually, and she had little romantic style. She was not provocative in any way, did nothing to drive my passion other than give herself over to me to do what I wished. At the time I wasn't as strongly committed to finding my soulmate. She wouldn't have been a candidate.

I knew this for sure after I met her. I want a woman with soul, who constantly desires to turn me on, stroke my vanity, spur me on, tell me how hot she is for me, who openly espouses what a slut she will be for me. She was very shy and repressed in that way. She was too nervous perhaps to let herself go mentally.

I seek, no require, the mental aspects. I felt fine about it afterwards. I enjoy my work <weg>. She expressed no thoughts about whether I was handsome, intelligent, funny, powerful or anything other than that she wanted more, and I met with her two more times that week. So I guess she liked me. I know she liked what I did to her.

That's it for now, sweet. Since there are so many details piling up that I would like to comment on and you have questions as well, I want you to think about phone contact for its expediency. I will tell you that I am not big on phone sex. It is not as much fun as the real thing, so I find I have to really work at it to get into it. But it's much quicker than email for practical discussion, though I love getting your emails.

I know you are down right now. I hope it cheers you up to know I am thinking of you, desiring you. Consider that you have a bright happy future ahead of you. Be brave my sweet slut.

Galen

Subject: Re: Courage dear
Date: Sat, 5 Jun

Hello Master,

I feel much better today. It's finally sinking in that I am not going back home. My ex is not going to change. Every so often I feel a panic attack and start questioning the whole #%$#@ process. Then I speak to him on the phone, and all the answers are right there.

Why would I keep hoping this guy would bring me flowers some day or even see me? Part of it is that he never was taught to consider anyone else. It only mattered what he wanted.

He's not going to the divorce hearing. Just me and an associate from our office. I prepared the agreement, had my lawyer do all the papers for me. All the spouse did was sign. I don't have to go to work that day unless I feel like it. My boss is very supportive of me.

Your letter made me feel so good. I too spend quite a bit of time writing to you. Thank you for all of the information re: your relationship with her. That helps me feel more comfortable. You can tell she's a lawyer, late for her own date, always with an excuse.

I have had phone sex on many occasions. Apparently, I cum loud, hahaha!! Since I am not in the habit of cumming with other women, I don't have much to compare to, except the movies, lol. Anyway, sometimes it's just really the desire to talk to someone that you have shared time with online.

I asked you more about your marriage but it's not in the question box because I more wanted you to know I was interested. Those are things only talked about at particular times when you feel like it, I know.

I have no idea how I would be in person with someone like you. Maybe I would freeze up as she did, maybe not. I am an expressive

435

person. I know the verbal part of a D/s relationship greatly excites me so it's hard to imagine I would not openly state my desire to be a slut, beg for more, always use "Master."

I love that you would talk to me that way. It's more controlling than the actual physical part. I like the dress aspect of it, the seductiveness. Mmmmm now I'm getting wet, thinking about it all.

Just to refill the question box, Master, please tell me, what if the sub begins to cry, do you feel bad and ease up, or only if she uses the safe word? Did she use it or did you mutually end?

I too, love your letters.

For the record, I do find you to be compassionate, humorous and intelligent. Have a nice day, Master. I will be thinking of you.

lana

PS: Here's a picture of me with all my clothes on. That's a switch.

Subject: Ring, ring, ring
Date: Sat, 5 Jun

Master,

I thought about the phone contact. I can only hope you are what you say you are and won't trace my number and come here and kill me, lol. Who would answer your email if you did that anyway?

I'll have to bet on the fact that you would miss me too much to harm me. I don't know why I should fear you, you're quite upfront about what you like. I probably should more fear the one that doesn't express himself. If I should fear you, what would that fear be?

"deep breath"—my number is xxx-xxx-xxxx.

lana

Subject: D/s theater
Date: Thu, 5 Jun

dear slut,

A thought on D/s.

It's all about theater. I think D/s is a lot like the theater. In the
theater, the serious actor is a unique person, who plays any number
of roles. But no matter the role, they are an actor through and
through. They live and breathe the theater, but they've got bills to
pay, shit to deal with, personal crisis, and maybe other pleasures
outside the theater. I want to live and breathe the D/s lifestyle.

I believe this is how a relationship would start out. You rehearse
before you take the stage for a live performance. Then you find out
if the connection between partners is strong enough to bring this to
the level of a 24/7 Master/slave orientation. But that would take
some time to develop.

Might we do that together, someday? How do you picture the
relationship you seek. You know the term slave implies giving up
everything, every decision made by the Master. Where would you
say you were between that extreme and an equal partner?

In the 20 years I knew my wife, I rarely made her laugh. My jokes
went over her head, usually. She had no subtlety. I hated her for
that. It took away the natural joy I possessed. I try to take things
lightly, find the humor in the day to day calamities. I'm basically
high on adventure, low on drama.

I sought an intuitive connection where just a glance or a gesture
confirmed the deep bond of our souls. Her intuition was that of a
Gestapo interrogator, always sniffing for trouble, checking my

pockets when I returned from a trip, going through my desk drawers.

I never had an affair. Two prostitutes, one in Hong Kong after a night of drunken debauchery with some Chinese buddies. And once in Atlanta, about 6 months before I left her. That was actually the key to my leaving - long story, I'll tell you later.

My turn – questions:

What was the difference in your caution in meeting me versus the married guy? Same thing with the chat room guys you phone sexed with. Did you give them your number?

By the way, I don't encourage giving out your number initially. There are probably ways to track down your address. Get the guy's number and call where you can block caller id, or from a location that doesn't matter.

Tell me about you and phone sex. Did it involve BDSM? How do you turn a man on over the phone? What do you say, act like? What do they do that turns you on?

You mentioned you would top or bottom with another sub. Are you clear on that? Have you had sex with a woman, with a woman and a man? Do you desire to? In relation to D/s, do you desire to switch, with a man or a woman?

Sweetheart, I wouldn't let you freeze-up. I'm going to melt you down til there's nothing left but that hot fucking whore, I know you long to be.

Tell me things you did with the previous Masters. How did you get connected the first time? How did they Dominate you? How did you show your submissiveness? How do they differ from my encounter so far with you?

To what extent do you desire verbal abuse, humiliation? Write a sentence or several of dialogue that would be to the edge of what

would still make you wet.

Have you ever worn a ball gag? How would you feel about that?
Are you a screamer(lol)? Would you like having your hands tied
above your head, around a pole, or from a rafter, standing in your
slutwear, while I prepare you for a cropping or flogging, or various
penetrations and clamps?

Tears: some subs seek tears. Turns them on. It's emotional as well
as physical. Actually it can turn me on. Crying is so vulnerable. It
reveals physical and mental resistance has ceased. The sub's
surrendered and is relying on my mercy.

Tears are a release. I believe they wash away the pain of negative
emotions. Usually a preponderance like that would come up in pre-
scene discussion and negotiation. If I didn't know beforehand, and
a sub started wailing on me, it would spook me and I'd stop whatever and talk to her "out of scene."

"CUT!!!" If she's having trouble, I'll stop the scene and provide
whatever care and comfort I am capable of. If she's really OK,
"ACTION!!!" (picture me as CB Demille, in nothing but my riding
boots, monocle, and riding crop, slapping my boot impatiently-lol).

Safewords are mandatory. If I have any concern that she's not
paying attention to her own body, too "subspaced" out (subs call it
'flying'), I'll ask if she remembers her safeword, and make her
repeat it to me.

Glad you're feeling better my slut, and that I can still make you wet.

Tell me when the best times to call are.

Galen

Subject: Box is empty
Date: Sun, 6 Jun

Master,

Wow, is this my penalty for opening up a question box?

I need time to think about where I am between being a slave and equal partner.

My caution with you is more because of the nature of what we would be doing, surrendering to you. I was very cautious with the married Dom. We chatted hours on end then on the phone and shared letters. I knew that guy was not going to hurt me physically; I could feel it.

If I have known someone awhile, I may be more open to giving them my number. Again, I go to the same chat sites and see many of the same people there. If I get to know someone and feel comfortable, I may be open to phone sex.

Usually I call using a phone card, which cannot be traced. If I have spoken to them on the phone more than once I might give them my number in return. There are very few. I have developed relationships with some that are not based in sex.

Over the phone, it depends. I might take the lead and question them about what they like; tell them what I look like, stuff like that. Or, he might start asking me things or telling me things he would like to do with me and we will both go from there.

I have "phoned" (lol) being tied up, or tie them up. I have spoken to each of the other Masters on the phone; 2 or 3 times with the first one (the married one). He wanted to hear me beg. It was very hot. A few times with the last one. We talked openly and also got off. It's always different.

I can tell you that I have been told I should be a phone sex operator for a living, lol. Do you think it's bad that I have done that? I'm in my sexual prime. I can tell you that sometimes I am totally driven by my need to get laid. I think the phone and the Internet are safer

than one night stands and I need contact. It's very lonely sometimes when you're in this stage of a break up. You know that.

I have been with a woman once, when I was 18 or 19. She and I and 2 guys were drinking. She was flirting with me. The guys egged us on and she and I undressed each other, kissed, and touched while they watched. The guys jumped in before we could really do anything, guess they couldn't wait, lol. Anyway, we coupled off and did it in the same bed but not interacting.

I was with 2 guys once too. That same year. (Before I got married). I knew them both. Honestly, I can't remember how it started, but it ended up with one in my mouth, one behind me. I liked it.

I might be open to being with another woman. I am a jealous person, so I'm not sure about that aspect if the guy involved was my lover. If he's not, no problem, I'd do it in a minute. I love women's bodies though and would love to share that experience.

Being a sub to a woman? Not sure. I probably would do it to please someone else but I would have to trust her. Online I have dommed women for the last Master and vice versa. I have been the mistress to a couple guys. I know a 21 year old I met online, great guy. I mean, really nice and we phone/email and switch. He prefers being the sub and I like that with him. I like to hear him beg.

He's pretty damn good at being the Dom too, probably because he himself is a sub. We also play mutually, which I like too. I've been talking to him for about 10-11 months and we consider each other close friends. Again, I am trying to be totally honest with you. Most of the guys I interact with online are young and have the same sex drive I do, lol.

I met both Masters in the same chat room. The first one was also the second person I ever cybered online. The night we first met, he called me slave, which totally turned me on. He has this way about him that would bring me to my knees. Before we had even talked a few minutes, he asked me to show my loyalty and do it with a room

of guys out in the open so he could watch. I did, which surprised him and me.

From there we started meeting frequently, more than 2-3 times a week and had cyber sex. He liked me to beg, tied me up, spanked me. No whipping, no clamps. He more preferred bringing other guys into it. Not for him, but for me. Mostly because he knew I wanted him, so he would make me do it with someone I didn't know, then with him.

The second Master is the most recent one. I believe I told you. We would chat. He would give me assignments, i.e.., be naked at home, flash, take pictures for him. He made me buy a dog collar and wear it for him. I developed very strong feelings for each of these guys and still feel that way.

They differ from you in that we have never chatted, strictly email. I like chatting because it's an instant response. You can get to know someone pretty well. I would like to do that with you.

Damn, you're really making me work here today. You know, I went out last night dancing and didn't get home until 5. I danced for a long time, hours. I had a snafu, actually. I was dancing with this gorgeous guy, getting along well, let him touch me a little. He was built, dark, great face. Lol, you gave your permission and I was thinking I could fuck that guy all night.

In walks this other guy that I date occasionally. No relationship, we go out though maybe once a week, maybe less. Never slept with him. So awkward. The 2nd guy was openly not pleased. I told him we have no ties to each other and reminded him that I go out and that I have been honest about it. I ended up going home alone, lol. My choice though.

Anyway, back to my work. Where is that $^$## question box, anything left in it? Oh yeah, verbal. I never want to be called stupid. I find that line of verbalization to be mean and it only irritates me.

442

I like being called a whore (by you), a slut. You call me a sweet bitch and I like it. It's more the way it's used than the words. If you called me a stupid bitch or a fucking cunt, I would be more likely to leave or perhaps consider smacking you darlin'. (There's that sarcastic side, sorry).

However, if you said to me, "Come here, you sexy cunt," I would run to you. If you were teasing me and touching me and said things like "You like that, don't you slut? You're such a little whore for me; tell me slut, tell me how wet your cunt is" stuff like that. As long as it's not mean.

The verbal part is a big part of it for me, but it has to be done correctly. I have to know you respect me as a person so "stupid" or "idiot" is out. I like being called a "bad girl" or "slut" or "slave", as long as it's sexual, not mean. For you, I know you would talk to me and I would willingly admit to you that I am a slut, your whore, telling you how hot I am, begging you for more. What do you like?

Never wore a ball gag. What do you like about that? If I can, I like to be loud in bed. I am not a silent cummer by any means, lol. You'll know if I like it. As for being a screamer, if you started whipping me, I might. Who knows. I would like having my hands tied above me, waiting for you. The anticipation.

I know that when I look at pictures of bondage, I prefer the ones where the guy is in them as opposed to just a woman tied up. It makes me wet to think of being tied and you talking to me, with the gag or without, touching me, spreading me, feeling how wet I am, being your toy, playing with me, whipping me, dressed for you, used by you. Will you write me another story? *smile* Please, Master?

What is the balance for you in a true relationship between having a slave and an equal partner?

You may call whenever you wish. You yourself have some questions in your box now.

443

I hope that I answered everything to your satisfaction. The more you know, the more I wonder what you think of me.

lana

Subject: re: My box of Q's
Date: Mon, 7 Jun

Master,

Well, I give you my phone number and then don't hear from you. I had to fight the irrational fear that you were instead on your way to greet me in person. I know that isn't true. Hope all is well.

lana

Subject: My mission
Date: Mon, 7 Jun

dear lana,

I've made it clear what I seek.

Because your first long letters were so effusively submissive and slutty, and you identified me as what you had always longed for, I continued.

I am not seeking an email, cyber, phone, or chat sex relationship. I don't have the time for that, only real time is fulfilling to me. I know what I seek. I probed for an emotional and spiritual connection with you, beyond our sexuality, but we haven't connected on that level. Either you didn't feel that level with me, or you don't seek that level with me. You effused numerous times at how strong you felt for your other "friends" and still feel in fact. This isn't just about kinky sex for me. Isn't that funny to hear that from a man?

444

I don't think you're ready for me, sweetheart. I believe you're a sexy, kinky girl, but at this point, not a submissive seeking a LTR, real time with a true Master. I don't say that because of your inexperience. I think you're a woman ready to explore her fantasies, sow her oats. You may wind up not wanting to be a slave at all, before you settle on what you really want.

I do like you and meant every word of desire, affection and compassion for you, but my mission is to find my soulmate, not just generate reams of futile titillation.

I suggest if you really want to try a D/s experience, find someone local. There are probably 500 Doms (a least that's what they'll claim in their ads, be careful) within 20 minutes of you. Look in alt.com, or bondage.com. If I make it to your neighborhood sometime soon, I'll let you know. If you're free, we could probably have a lot of fun for an evening or two.

Best regards,

Galen

Subject: Please don't disappear!
Date: Mon, 7 Jun

Galen,

Now, please tell me why you have said this? I wait for you to call. . . . no call. What is different now? I wish you would explain. Is that wrong that I feel strongly still about past relationships? That's not a bad thing.

Please do not disappear without talking to me. What have I done? I don't understand. I love your letters. I think of you constantly. Please don't do that to me, Galen. I don't understand.

lana

Subject: Please!!
Date: Mon, 7 Jun

ouch Galen. . . . please explain. I wanted to get to know you more,
share with you.

Subject: I am begging you!!
Date: Mon, 7 Jun

Galen,

lol, sorry, I'll just one line you to death. I keep re-reading your
letter, trying to find what upset you. I don't understand it at all. I
just want to go slow. It's easier for you, you are more directed at
what you desire and you have tried it before.

I wish you would not run off. I spend a great deal of time thinking
about you. I mean, not just fantasizing, but really thinking what it
would be like to be with you; to wake up with you; to live like that,
taken care of by you, respected by you, free to be that which I
desire. I don't get it, I'm walking around wondering all this and
waiting for your mail and you tell me it's not there for you?

Please forgive me whatever I have done to displease you. I desire
to know more about you, to feel you. I've never encountered
anyone like you. Please, Galen, please, give me a chance. I just
had that hearing this morning and the whole process took a great
toll on me as you can tell in my letters. It's over now, and I feel
more like myself.

With great humiliation, I am begging you to reconsider. I am a
loving, giving, attentive woman and have much to offer you. Please
explore it with me.

lana

Subject: Sorry, please call back!
Date: Mon, 7 Jun

Here I am again. Sorry I missed your call. Please try again. If I am online, call my cell @ xxx. xxx. xxxx Thank you. I am waiting. Please!

Subject: Please call
Date: Mon, 7 Jun

I am waiting. Your voice went right through me. My sister had called to see if I was okay. But the line is free now. Please call!.

Subject: Ring, ring. . .
Date: Tue, 8 Jun

Master,

I'm so pleased you called and we had an opportunity to talk. I enjoyed it very much. I guess we both know a lot more about each other, now. How did you feel about it? Was I what you thought or different? I much prefer the personal interaction.

While you and I can trade jokes in the mail and connect, there is so much more to be shared, i.e.., the french-fry thing. . . . that would have been lost in the mail somewhere. I laughed about that today. I knew you had a sense of humor. I also wasn't able to "hear" you tell me something in email and I found that quite attractive about you, the way you told something.

I was so pleased that you called, Galen. To me, it was what I was looking for to make you real to me. I can't be afraid of someone that laughs with me late at night. You understand? I hope you smiled about it today, too.

I went to sleep smiling. I had been laying on the floor in my living room talking to you. When we hung up, I was so spent, I just laid there on my side, face on the rug, thinking about you and our conversation.

The sexual side of the call was heaven but as you said, you knew that was not the problem anyway. It was so intense hearing you, imagining you there. Gives me a shiver even now.

Your voice was so great. In short, it was excellent to talk to you and I hope you knew that while we were talking.

lana

Subject: Re: You've received an e-card from Galen!
Date: Wed, 9 Jun

Master,

Thank you so much for the flowers. How flattering to know you listen. How different to know I matter.

Your voice really sends shivers through me. I really enjoyed all the things we talked about last night. You must know I wanted to cum but you didn't say anything and I didn't want to push my luck. Hard to talk to you without that tingling.

lana

Subject: lana's story

Date: Fri, 11 Jun

"The Second Time"

You heard the cab pull up out front. You felt Him. Your toes curled
in your high heels. You squeezed one knee towards the other,
slightly bent, and it provided a pleasant pressure between your legs.
You took a deep breath, and ran your hands over your breasts. You
felt the ridges where your nipples stood out, waiting.

"My Master," you whispered with a sigh.

This was his second visit. He said rather than meet him at the
airport, you would wait for him at home. This morning he had
emailed your instructions. He closed the letter with: Follow them
carefully, understand whore? It wasn't a question.

Master had shown you on his first visit that he was a strict and
exacting man. You had made a mistake that displeased Master. You
shivered as you remembered the punishment. But you understood.

"It is Master's right to punish me when I'm a bad girl. I will learn
to be a good slut girl to please my Master." The rewards, you knew,
were all you sought. "What a whore I am for him." You smiled.

Master had instructed you to wear a slutty low cut, micro dress, that
left no doubt what's it's occupant was willing to be used for. It was
jet black. You had purchased a new lace push up bra with matching
garter, attached to black seamed nylons. Your nails were done in
deep red. You were heavily perfumed, the fragrance barely masking
the sweet musk from your shaved slit, smooth as calf's skin.

You wore the thick, leather, training collar Master had left for you.
You had purchased a dog leash with a black leather grip and 6 foot
silver chain, as instructed. You held the leash now, and pulled it
from the side, resisting with your neck. That provided the slight
choking pressure that swelled your desire.

You stopped your hand as it began to reach for that sweet spot

between your legs. "Do NOT touch your self, til I give you permission. Don't disobey me." Though it was written, you heard the tone of it. The harsh emphasis on don't.

Master had left behind a variety of toys and such on his first visit. A large black dildo, a red phallic vibrator, two dozen clothes pins, their bite softened somewhat by rubber bands around the ends.

"For Master's pleasure, and my pride, I'm going to do without the rubber bands," you thought, "at least some of them." You remembered the bite of them as they formed a circle around your breasts, and then you shivered, remembering the things Master did to your pussy, and you'd forgotten all about the pins.

The wrist and ankle cuffs were aligned on the coffee table by the couch, with the other toys, the black crop, two sets of clips, both of which had adorned your pussy lips. "Your cunt looks lovely, dear slut." He had jangled the chain that attached to each clip, and you nearly fell over when he bent down and kissed his whore's cunt tenderly.

You now wore the butt plug He had left for you. Master's instructions made this requirement quite clear. You remembered the first time He had taken you there.

It had involved a bit of patience and preparation to remove your resistance, the first time, but soon you gave your ass willingly for Master's pleasure. Like everything else, he had brought you to that point, where you wanted, needed, begged for Master to fuck your slut's ass.

"Go ahead, fuck your slut's ass all you want Master," you had said.

He had smacked you hard across the ass. "I don't need you permission, now do I, sweetheart?" he said, smacking you sharply again.

Master had explained that using the butt plug, would keep your ass open and ready for him whenever he chose. You liked it best when Master had put you on your back, knees tucked back. Master had

given you the big black dildo.

"Fuck your cunt my little bitch. Do it, slut. I want to watch you fuck yourself."

You happily obeyed. You barely noticed Master put on the latex glove. He had coated it with KY Jelly. He placed his index finger on your asshole and rubbed it in a tight circular motion. The sensation made you slow your frantic fucking and you moaned. Master slapped your ass hard.

"Did I tell you to stop slut. Come on you hot little bitch. Fuck that cunt. Do you like the feeling here?" He pressed just through the opening.

You gasped, "Yes Master."

You began to pant, as he let his finger glide into your ass, very slowly. You pounded your cunt harder and arched your back causing his finger to slide to its full depth. He slowly withdrew and you chased after it, gliding your ass forward, and then he pushed back hard, his fist mashing into your ass cheeks.

You, pleading, "Yes Master, please Master. Don't stop."

Then Master had grabbed your hips roughly in both hands, positioning you for the insertion. He made you look in his blue penetrating eyes, taking possession of your soul. He entered you and you nearly came. You left the dildo buried in your cunt and rubbed your clit in fury.

Master began to take long, slow, deep strokes, telling you that you were his total whore now. That your ass was another fuck hole for his pleasure.

"Isn't that right, my slut?"

"Yes Master. Oh yes Master." Your mind was lost in the frenzy of your lust. "I am so glad I am your whore. My ass is to be fucked

whenever it pleases, you Sir."

You feel Master's body start to tense, his strokes hard and deep, his grip fierce. You push back wanting his cum, anointing your ass as his property. He comes just as you reach the edge and tumble into the deep cavern of your bliss.

The doorbell rings and startles you back to the present moment. "Master's here," you whisper in near rapture, thinking of the rapture to come.

That one was just for you, lana. Miss me sweetheart? I miss you. Can you tell?

Oh, about the other nite when I left you hanging. OKAY, you can come now (lol)!

Galen

Subject: Uh oh
Date: Fri, 11 Jun

Master,

Uh oh! I did cum in between receipt of this last letter and your last call. Long and hard thinking about the first time you called me. I hope that you are not displeased. I love hearing you and couldn't help it.

Thank you so much for writing a story just for me. As soon as I saw the re: line of the letter, I sat down and read every word 3x. Wow. . . so intense you are. I felt my pussy start to drip as soon as I was reading it. I couldn't resist and reached down, rubbing my clit, and felt my nipples get hard.

All those toys! You know that made me nervous and excited at the

same time. What a feeling that is, fear and stimulation. Your story was woven like 2 stories, one a little tease to me about what had already happened and one a preview of more.

I would want you to have my ass as a gift to you. It's just in the offering that I would be reluctant. I know you would help me with that as you have already shown me. I would want to look into your eyes as you take me, to feel us become one.

I have missed you, Master. You pop into my head at different times throughout the day. Tonight I am going dancing with a group of women. That will be lots of fun, I'm sure, lots of laughing.

Tomorrow night I have a date. You and I have not talked about this, however, I would not keep something from you. I have not been out with him before. I met him recently. He's 23 and very attractive. I suggested a movie because I felt during my conversations with him that we probably have little to talk about. I'm going because I had already agreed and because I need to get out.

What is your feeling? I date frequently but hardly the same one too many times. Is this a problem?

How did your all guy retreat go? What are your plans for the weekend? Tell me, Master, do you still like to go out at night? Would we be able to do that?

Did you consider if we could cook together? Of course, if I was in close proximity to you, I would be hoping you would touch me and unless you made me stop, I would brush against you, but I would try to keep my mind on the cooking if that is what you wished. I wonder what that would be like, to want you so badly, but to have to wait for you to decide.

Yesterday, I wore a beautiful Claiborne, cream, summer suit. Short sleeved jacket, short skirt with little slits on each side. Underneath, no blouse, just a gold push up bra and matching panties, thigh-hi stockings and brown heels. Mmmmmm, I felt hot all day. I would love to have slowly undressed for you, felt you looking at me,

knowing what you would want from me and what I would willingly give you.

I will be thinking about you.

lana

Subject: Whack! whack! whack!
Date: Mon, 11 Jun

my sweet whore,

Hmmm. . . cumming without permission! I'm going to extract a bright red punishment on my slut's ass when I get my hands on it. "Bend over my little bitch!"(grin) Whack, Whack, Whack! (about 20 strokes on each cheek should be sufficient.) "Thank you Master", you will reply.

At this point I will impose no rules on you. I'm not in a position to enforce them. I don't want you to die of frustration, or just become outright bitchy before we meet (lol).

 At some point if we continue, I will expect you to turn over decisions about your extracurricular sexual activities to your Master. Then you will ask permission, and will be expected to honor and obey your Master's decision.

It doesn't make me feel great about your chasing all these young bucks around. I appreciate your honesty, and concern with my feelings. I don't think I care to know. I try to contain my jealous feelings, to be reasonable, understanding, though I am not perfect at it.

But if you don't tell me I may become suspicious, and that's no good either. But I realize your need. Both us are free to pursue our needs, since we are both so far apart.

I don't date vanilla women. I go out occasionally, but it is futile to expect to run into a submissive in a nightclub, as that hasn't happened in my 30 years of cruising the bars.

It would be fun to take my slut out dancing. Watching others see how sexy you are and devoted in your dancing and affections to Master. I would be so proud to exhibit you thusly. I'd also like to take you to a bondage nightclub, or a topless bar, and make you watch while one of those sluts danced for me. Maybe I would allow one to dance for you, while I watch and encourage.

I will offer you a phone date this week sometime. Let me know the best time. I know you have your daughter with you. You will be required to have your belt, clothespins, and a dildo, or appropriate substitute and be suitably attired. I want to hear how well you obey my commands.

Enjoy yourself til then my beautiful whore.

Galen

Subject: I don't chase
Date: Sat, 12 Jun

Galen,

For the record. . . . I do not chase young bucks. I don't chase anyone. You should know I don't need to do the chasing. I know you may be mildly put off, but it is true, we are very far away from each other and no, I don't want to sit home alone. I could have remained married. I hope you're having a great Saturday. *smile*

lana

Subject: I am offended!

Date: Mon, 12 Jun

lana,

Not a very friendly tone. Highly displeasing in fact. I consider that a sarcastic smile at the end. I am offended.

I was just being honest in my feelings. I feel my attitude was rather liberal. You were offended by the "chasing" concept? Sorry if I put the wrong spin on it. I simply meant emotionally, I could feel a certain pang from thinking of you with other men. Those were my honest feelings, and did indicate the growing feelings I had for you. I stated that it was my issue to deal with, not yours. I am a Master, but also a human.

The "die of frustration, bitchy and young bucks" were said with humor. Do you really think that would be my statement, if I was seriously displeased. . . out chasing young bucks??? You've made it quite clear as to how much attention you receive and attract. I know you don't have to chase.

The point about sexual decisions was stated "at some point", which we are not close to. That would come with a commitment on both parts. I had placed no restrictions on you. I was in fact quite considerate of your needs.

I looked forward to your reply today, and discussion of our phone date. You have disappointed me with your cool, terse arrogance. Is this the attitude with which you expect to serve and excite a Master?

Despite your rude intrusion, I will enjoy my Saturday and my life.

Galen

Subject: I am so sorry. . . . .
Date: Sat, 12 Jun

Galen,

I apologize. I should not have been like that to you. It was not meant to be sarcastic. I was actually only playing with you. It was a tease to you.

I too would not like to hear if you were having a great time in someone else's company, but I know that is quite possible and indeed likely because of the distance between us. This relationship should not end on a sour note, Galen. I certainly would not like it to end because of me. I greatly enjoy talking to you. You must sense that when we have spoken. I am enjoying exploring this with you. I did not mean to displease you.

Please, I would get on my knees and tell you how sorry I am that I offended you or hurt you.

Please, Galen. I am so sorry. Please, I would never intentionally offend you or want to displease you. Please. I feel so badly that you opened my mail, knowing how much I look forward to your mail, and that I made you unhappy.

Please allow me to make it up to you.

lana

Subject: I am sorry. . . very
Date: Sat, 12 Jun

Dear Galen,

Your words hurt very much and I am sure they are meant to hurt, as you must feel hurt yourself to say them. You have become very special to me. I would gladly talk to you, listen to you for hours on end. I did mean it as a tease.

I admit, I re-read it and I'm sorry for my words. I did not mean it to

offend you. I greatly appreciate the time you expend on me. I was deeply honored that you wrote a story just for me. I am very, very, very sorry.

Please, Galen, I didn't mean to upset you. My mistake, totally and completely. I offer you no further disclaimers or excuses. I am wholeheartedly sorry. I see that you are not the same as anyone I know or have encountered and I will keep that foremost in my mind when communicating with you.

Please don't go away. I would crawl to you on my hands and knees and beg your forgiveness. I will be better for you. I promise you that you will not see a side of me again that displeases you.

Please accept my apology. I made a terrible mistake without thinking of the consequences. Please, Galen, I would not even assume to call you Master since I am sure you are done with me and I don't deserve that pleasure from you.

If you so choose to never communicate with me again, please at least know that I am very sorry. I did not mean it in the way in which it was taken, but I do take full responsibility for offending you. You are correct, it was wrong.

I am not a waste of time and I do have much to offer.

lana

Subject: Rollercoaster
Date: Sat, 12 Jun

Dear Galen,

Okay. Apparently you are not going to communicate with me any further. I understand. I cut the date short, hoping you would have emailed me back. If it was not going to work out between us, I wish it would not be because I said something stupid to you.

Again, I offer you my apologies. It makes me very sad. I've been on such an emotional rollercoaster and evidently still am. I so much enjoyed you. I'm sorry, Galen.

lana

Subject: Please
Date: Sun, 13 Jun

Dear Galen,

I didn't mean to offend you. Please!!

I crawl to you on my hands and knees, dressed in my skimpiest black dress, cut so low, I'm almost out of it. I'm hoping you will be pleased to at least look at me. The dress is riding up as I crawl, showing the bottom of each garter, so much hoping my Master will forgive me my transgression.

I bring with me your crop held between my teeth. Pleading with you briefly with my eyes, hoping to find a glimmer of understanding in your eyes. Hoping this outfit will stir you to decide to punish me rather than turn your back so coldly.

I drop the crop at your feet and brush my body like a cat against your leg. "I am so sorry, Master. I promise you I will do better to please you. I need you to teach me how to be a good slave to her Master."

I turn my ass to you, slowly pulling up the hem of the dress over my thighs, which are encased in black nylon, your favorite pair with the lines up the back, pulling the dress up over my ass, showing you the black garters. I'm shaking but need to show you I am repentant, ready for my punishment.

I drop my shoulders down low, spreading my legs for you. "Please,

Master Galen, I am so sorry. Please punish me! As hard as you deem fit, so I will learn. I beg you to use the crop on me."

I am so nervous at the thought of being hurt but the pain of you turning away is far, far worse. "I'm a bad slave, Master, but I will learn to be better." I am submissively bent before you.

You bring tears to my eyes. Please don't go!

lana

Subject: My terms
Date: Mon, 14 Jun

lana,

If you were my collared slave and I was there, you would have been slapped across the face, dragged roughly by your hair, and led to the closest chair, for an old fashioned paddling on your bare behind. Punished like a bratty little girl. I would have used my leather paddle, shaped like a rounded but small racket. Why hurt my hand? This could take awhile.

I would admonish you verbally, in the strongest, most punishing terms. During your punishment, I would check the bad slut's cunt. If it was wet. . . "I see slut's still insolent enough to think this if for her pleasure." I redouble my efforts on your ass.

Your ass jumps with every blow, now. It's making you cry. "Please Master. I'm so sorry. I was a bad little bitch." I continue to paddle you. "Oh Master, please forgive me. You have a right to punish me. I am your slave and I caused you displeasure." Every sentence is punctuated by your sobs of grief and pain.

Finally I stop and rest my hand gently on your burning cheeks. "Be still now." I say quietly. "And ponder your act and your punish-

ment."

"Thank you for punishing me, Master," you moan with complete sincerity.

You are making persistent efforts to appease me. Perhaps you are capable of becoming a good slave slut, whose greatest desire is to be pleasing to her Master. This is where the line is drawn.

This is not like a vanilla relationship or dating, where you hold the power. In the Master/slave aspect of this relationship, you have no power other than your safewords and stated limits. You will have given up control. It is not taken from you, but offered freely. It is your desire to be a pleasing, submissive whore.

There are rules of behavior and decorum. When they are broken, you are punished. You willingly accept that you deserve punishment, to encourage your commitment to being Master's pleasing slave. You must accept this fact if you truly desire to continue. Do you desire and can you surrender to this level?

I am still displeased that you adhere to the statement that your offending letter was meant playfully. You may believe you were being so. What you commented on in your next letters did not convince me, though.

I reread them several times. Your explanation of playfulness could not be found in what I read there. But since you have shown your sincerity in being forgiven and have asked to be punished for it, as I expect when you have misbehaved, I can forgive you, without further discussion.

If you feel strongly that you are correct in what your intention was, you have permission to try to convince me otherwise. Either way I will forgive you. But in the future always take care to be clear in your intention. I will expect this always, whether I am displeased by your intention or not.

I would allow you to beg for your punishment, as you so submis-

sively expressed in your letter. But since I am not there, I will devise something appropriate.

If you desire to continue, know that this is the first level of control that you offer me. Anytime you do not show proper respect in your attitude and manner, are inconsiderate, bratty, manipulative or the like, you will agree to be properly punished.

And if I decide that you have to beg for punishment, you will do so without hesitation. If I command you after your punishment to make me cum in your whore's mouth, you will do so eagerly, begging for Master's cum in your mouth. "Swallow it, slut, every drop. "

Then I would take you in my arms, and soothe you tenderly. "Master forgives you, dear."

In other areas, outside of the submission and proper behavior towards me, it would be as before. We can have fun, and address all the other issues for your further training and surrender that will decide where this goes.

I appreciated your sincere efforts to continue.

Oh, one other thing. From now on, always address me sweetly in your greetings, at least with dear, and I will be pleased (from the start anyway).

Do you accept continuing under my terms?

Galen

Subject: Thank you
Date: Wed, 16 Jun

Dear Galen,

Thank you for calling me last night. I appreciate it very much. When I read your letter, I understood about the punishment. But I thought that you were asking me the "big picture" question relative to was I ready for a true, total D/s relationship.

I do not mean that I thought you were saying you were ready for that with me, I just thought you were asking if I could say I was ready to commit to that style of relationship. That is why I stood still so to speak rather than reply to you.

Now that you have explained it to me, I can respond appropriately. I understand completely with regard to you punishing me for my transgression. I would willingly, and indeed, I did ask you for it. It took me a while to get to that point, but I did.

I am afraid of the pain. I imagine it's much like a child knowing they are going to get in trouble, dreading it, but still knowing it is going to happen. I am not a child but still I dread it.

Even when I wrote it to you and asked you to punish me, actually tried to entice you to punish me rather than walk away, I felt a dread that you would respond. That is why I crawled to you, hoping that would show you I was sincere and understood that part of the relationship. I do understand. I want to learn and I want you to teach me.

I am so pleased that you would consider training me and putting the long-term portion of the relationship aside for now. I know that you are clear what you are looking for and I want you to know that I appreciate your time in allowing me to explore what I want.

To reiterate, I totally understand the D/s side of the relationship in that if I am not pleasing to you, you will certainly let me know. I will take more time responding to you and will work harder for you.

I have my daughter this week, so the date is difficult. Would you consider waiting until next week? I'm afraid she would wake up again in the night. I am also afraid that you will punish me, but I will not run away. I want to experience what you have to offer.

I hope you understand the dating thing with me. If the guy is my age or older that is when you would have to worry. Someone in their early 20's is not going to hold my attention and in fact, that is exactly why I am out with them, because I don't want my attention held. I should have explained that to you earlier. I apologize.

lana

PS: I started this letter yesterday. I apologize that it took so long. Work is very busy and then I had to see my ex last night, so I went to bed
early.

Subject: re: Thank you
Date: Thu, 17 Jun

dear lana,

I appreciated the sentiments in your letter. . . that you understand, now, this initial level of submission to me. It is a pleasure to have you surrender that to me, and though you are afraid, accept that you deserve and ask for a proper punishment.

It is pleasing that you understand that you beg best for forgiveness, as a slut does, hoping to humbly entice Master, to release her from the worst torment - Master's displeasure. It maintains the erotic element that is the essence of a Master/slave relationship, especially when it comes to the slave's punishment.

I'm not in a good mood now. I have to go to a deposition tomorrow at my lawyer's in the morning. My wife and her lawyer will be there. I haven't seen her in over 6 months. It is painful to be exposed to her energy, so hateful, scornful, so hurt herself, and it's created this vicious attack by her on every area of my life from my kids, my friends, my family, business issues. It's really fucked up.

This is probably affecting why I feel that my energy for our exchange has flattened out. Backing off from the hot pursuit was the right thing to do. I understand what you told me in our phone conversation about your needs, right after being divorced. You are not ready for a total commitment. That is reality.

But it removes the element of passion, feeling a slave's desire for me in that soulful way, that makes it more difficult. That passion is what drives me in the creative, absolutely erotic mindspace of my Dominance.

I know I do care about you lana. I felt the pain and sorrow of this last week as well.

If I was nearby to train you in person, it would be much different. I said I would train you, and I will. But I think how that occurs will need to be thought out, a path and a process that is clearly defined and agreed upon.

It will be up to you to define the pace and the areas of exploration you desire. As long as it remains interesting, we will likely continue your training. We each are free to end the training at any time.

If we do contact by phone, I will give your punishment for your recent transgression, but after that what occurs will be generally and always defined by you. I will expect you to describe in significant detail, what you want to try physically and how you want to be made to feel emotionally. I will put you in a scene using this information. This is how each contact would occur.

What are your thoughts?

Galen

Subject: How sad
Date: Fri, 18 Jun

Dear Master Galen,

I feel I know you so well. We have shared so much in such a short time, Galen. As short as the time period is that we have known each other, I knew some things about your last letter.

I knew that your lack of response was not a good sign. I was laying in bed last night contemplating writing you to see if you were displeased with my letter. I decided that it was not my place to push you for a reply and remembered that you told me previously you could not write me everyday.

I also knew that when I saw the "re" line was simply a reply to my "re:" line, you were not overly-joyed. If we were in the same area, I imagine I would detect these moods in you in person by your face or your voice. I also knew from your greeting that it might be a letter that was going to be painful to read.

Leaving all that aside, I definitely know and understand your pain and frustration with your spouse and an impending deposition with her sitting there. I am so sorry that you are experiencing that today. It's unfortunate that she cannot just recognize that it's over and leave the desire to hurt you behind. Sad that she doesn't realize that the very most pain you can cause your child is to tear down their parent in their eyes.

So, you know I'm not ready, yet we both know I want to know about a relationship with you. This is the part of your letter that prompted me to use "how sad" in my re: line. I can feel your level of interest drop.

It's very painful to me to know that I am disappointing you. I don't want to displease you, Master. I want to be exactly what you are looking for, yet, I am not sure I can be. Reality! Such an ugly word.

When you talk to me on the phone, do you feel pleasure and interest and excitement and a closeness? I feel it. I don't want to detain you from your quest. I appreciate that you would be willing to train me, but I know that is not what you wanted from me.

I wish I could call you and talk to you about it. This letter writing of deeper feelings is difficult at best. Sexually, I can write to you all day long and ohhhh, no question, I could read from you all day. However, we have this stumbling block to resolve.

I also felt a pain last weekend, so perhaps you would call me if you wanted to and we could talk. I am unclear as to what you are leading to. You know I hate being stupid, but I read your letter twice and I hope that you would be agreeable to explaining it to me. As is my position in this relationship, I wait for you. I say all of this with a smile, Master, a sincere, submissive smile.

Here's another picture in case you wanted to see my face smile at you.

lana xo

(*Note: I called lana and with sadness, we decided to cease further contact.*)

Episode 4

Kate

Toward the end of my divorce proceedings, my fate took an unexpected turn, like a twist in a well-crafted novel. It entwined me in a poignant irony that restored my faith in the warped, trickster humor of the universe. Only this time the trick was played on my ex.

Kate was a 30 year-old associate at my divorce lawyer's firm. My ex had proffered 'evidence' that was intended to prove beyond a doubt that I was a dangerous, violent, and abusive sex addict beyond help. This 'evidence' supposedly cast me as a disgusting, vile pervert, and an unfit parent.

She had discovered a three-page D/s ad and profile with my photo, that I had placed on a personals site. She downloaded and printed it, along with several kinky stories and other correspondence, and entered it as evidence in our divorce trial. My lawyer received a copy. My ex also sent a copy to my sister in the Midwest. Kate was assisting on my case, and consequently read the "evidence." It turned out her interest in my case was more than legal.

At that point in my life, I was widely ostracized from my previous social and professional circles and in some quarters, outright scorned. I had little support anywhere. Throughout my divorce proceedings—including depositions and a two-day trial—I noted how supportive and nonjudgmental Kate was. I greatly appreciated her friendliness and compassion during the brief moments I talked with her during my seven-month legal ordeal. I liked her greatly as a person and a sharp lawyer.

I had no thoughts about her, beyond that. Her dress and manner were conservative and professional. I could tell she was a little shy, despite her confidence, humor and intelligence. I got no hint of her sexuality from her words or manner. In the context of the circumstances I was in, finding a D/s partner was not on my scanner. Kate flew in below my radar.

Shortly after my trial, Kate called and told me the judge had issued his orders for division of property and child custody. It was late afternoon, and she said she would be working into the evening. She suggested I stop by to review the judge's decision. I sensed right away, what was about to happen.

I went to her office, and as I expected, she was the only one there. After we reviewed the judge's opinion and discussed the implications, she asked if I would have a drink with her at a local bar. I accepted, waiting to understand exactly what this woman—who was about to become more than my lawyer—had in mind.

What she confessed to me over drinks was like answering the door some evening and there's that guy from the old TV series holding a check for a million dollars with my name on it. Inside my head, I was smiling ear to ear, as she revealed the secret fantasies she'd had since her preteens. She revealed her desires to be spanked, bitten, bound, raped, to sit on her "Daddy's" lap and be scolded for being a bad little girl, and more.

My smile wasn't a lecherous one. I initially turned down her request that I train her as a submissive, be her guide on her journey through the steamy jungles of her sexuality. While I honored her courage and trust to confide her secret to me, I felt our circumstances were too complicated and risky to allow that possibility.

My inner smile came from the sweet taste of irony. The evidence my ex had thought would destroy and humiliate me in the eyes of my family, friends and the court, caught the eyes and desires of a kindred soul.

Her longing to be with me persisted through email and eventually, we negotiated the complexities of our circumstance and her training began. She's turned out to be one of the nastiest, bad little girls I know, as well as a very close friend and intimate ally.

Some of our 'play' might disturb those who don't understand the dynamics of role-play founded on the guidelines of a safe, sane and consensual relationship. Despite our mutual perversity and the way

it's acted out, we have the most tender of feelings for each other. We have provided each other unconditional support and humor through the harshest moments in the other aspects of our lives.

Subject: correct address?
Date: Tue, 27 Jul

Dear Galen:

I want to make sure I have your correct email address this time before I
write you a letter. Would you write back and confirm that you got this note?

I really enjoyed seeing you today and feeling your body heat on my leg, too. I hope my forwardness didn't offend you.

I am a little devastated about having sent my last email to you to the wrong address. I wrote some deeply personal things in it, and didn't want anyone to see it but you.

I await your response.

kate

Subject: correct address.
Date: Tue, 27 Jul

Dear kate:

Address on target, you may proceed. I wasn't offended.

Galen

Subject: confidential
Date: Wed, 28 Jul

Hi Galen.

Sorry it took me so long to get this email to you. I tried to send one on Saturday as you know but (as you also know) I sent it to the wrong recipient. I could have sworn you told me to use your first and middle initials.

I am now waiting for my boss to come running into my office with a copy of the letter, screaming, "what the hell is this!?!?!?" Because of the professional-ethical issues involved, I could really be in deep shit for sending such expository emails to you—a client.

I am very interested in you as you probably can tell. I am intrigued by and drawn to your sexuality. I have always fantasized about the kind of sexual play that I think you like. The only problem is that I'm not really sure exactly what it is that you do, or like to do.

Like I said, I never read the controversial letters, other than the one that begins "Dear Daddy," and your personal ad. But those don't really make it clear to me what is involved. I hope that it doesn't involve beating a woman up, because I am not into that, I'm sure.

I know that I love to be spanked, bitten, pinched, scolded, held down, and to have a man's fist wrapped firmly around my hair, pulling and yanking me into submission. I also like to call my lover 'Daddy' and think of him as an authority figure. I want him to call me baby, little girl, bad girl, and similar names, and nasty names, too, which I'll leave to your imagination.

I long to be tied up by a dominant man (one that I trust); but I have only been tied up once, and just my wrists, and I had to practically beg my husband to do it. He seemed to get no thrill out of it at all, and so there was really no thrill in it for me.

When I was only about 12 years old, I started fantasizing about

471

having a man tie me up, spank me, and bite me. Like you, I was very sexual very early. I remember that thinking about being tied up, spanked, and fondled made me really wet, even then; and right now I am excited thinking about it.

It has always really turned me on to call my partner 'Daddy' and to think of him as my Daddy. It's not that I desire to be with or fantasize about my actual father. What I really want is a lover who considers me his special, precious little girl; a lover who will protect me, defend me, guide me and cherish me in ways similar to the prototypical father figure of popular culture. He is overprotective and controlling. He is vicious, jealous and even paranoid when he suspects that anyone has designs to violate or corrupt his little girl.

But my fantasy Daddy goes far beyond the overprotective father in popular culture. He also exercises full privileges with his little girl, and his jealousy really stems from his hot, perverted lust for her and his need to control and to own her, mind, body and soul. He controls her in ways that only a strong, fatherly, authority figure can; these ways range from tender to cruel, from compassionate and fair to tyrannical, depending on his whim.

Daddies sit on top and daughters on the bottom, in the natural hierarchy. From this vantage point, there is no question that the Daddy can rule, compel and control his daughter, who is weaker and smaller, also by nature. So, the imagery of Daddy/daughter fits well into my desire to be forced, taken, and controlled by my partner, in defined contexts and settings. This imagery excites and arouses me, sexually, as well as provides a strong sense of comfort and security in my otherwise unsafe world.

But I really need a partner who wants all that, too. Otherwise, I have to coach him too much; that feels ingenuine and the thrill wanes, because he is supposed to be dominant and telling me what to do.

I have always wanted a partner who makes decisions for me, especially about sex and related matters. In a Dominant/submissive relationship, does the girl *ever* get to tell the man what to do?

Please tell me how that works. What if she needs tenderness and gentle sex, sometimes? Is there a place for that in a 'D/s' relationship?

I understand that you said, 'it's whatever the partners decide,' but I want to know what you think about this. Also, you told me that the partners say things to each other, in public for example, to create tension between them, but that only they know the real meaning of the words uttered. Tell me more about this, like what kind of words these might be. . .

In my marriage, I have had bits and pieces of a Dominant/submissive relationship; but only in the sexual realm, and only insofar as I have coached my husband to don the role of dominant sex partner. Otherwise, I make all the decisions about everything, and it is not by choice. I am a strong personality, and he is a weak personality and so it's just the way the chips fall most of the time.

I do like to be bossy sometimes, and to get my way. But most of the time I would rather follow a man's lead, especially in personal and intimate matters. I just haven't been fortunate enough to meet the man who can lead me and dominate me the way I need it. I nearly always desire rough sex. But when I have to ask for it, it kind of loses its appeal.

I have always wanted a man to tie me up and take me, viciously. I never once felt that it was wrong for me to want that. Instead, I believe that it is very natural for me to want a man to dominate me and get physically, intimately aggressive with me. I have always needed a lot of guidance and control, and I have just never really gotten any. So, I had to learn to do it myself. But I really want the security that comes with someone keeping me in-check.

Well, this letter only covers some of what I want to say to you. I really can't believe that I am sharing these matters with you, or with anyone for that matter. But it feels great to reveal what I have held inside for my whole life to someone who understands. I know that you will keep all of this in confidence, and I appreciate that about you.

Please write back soon. I am eager to have an exchange with you on these subjects. I am also really eager to spend more time with you in person, if you don't mind.

Sincerely,

kate

Subject: Confidential reply
Date: Tue, 27 Jul

Dear kate,

How ironic that I have a lawyer who's also a Daddy/daughter slut. Maybe you could start a submissive lawyer club (grin). Think there're any others like you in this town? I've actually met two other lawyers through the Internet.

You've shared a very intimate portrait of your sexuality (gp25 must have been shocked, or turned on—I wonder which). I admire your courage and honesty.

I am intrigued by your fantasies. Playing Daddy/daughter can be a lot of fun. Rough sex is fun. In the D/s lifestyle, there are all levels and styles, from mild to extreme. I participate in the mild and the extreme, at times tender, others cruel. I am an erotic Sadist. I enjoy verbally humiliating and inflicting pain on my sub, treating her like a whore and a slut, taking total control of her for my pleasure (within her stated limits), appreciating her reaction and endurance.

I am not an abusive man, out of 'scene'. I have no wish to truly harm someone. Women who enjoy erotic pain as a path to ecstasy fascinate me. The key to endurance, I've found, is to sweeten the pain with relentless sexual stimulation. The pain and pleasure mix together into an intoxicating blend; that state of mind (there is a strong mental aspect to D/s) is called subspace, by many. Or 'flying'

is a term common to many subs.

Not every sub is a major masochist, nor is every masochist a submissive. And there are many blends of the two. People's fetishes and styles, I've found, are endless.

I personally like the combination of slut and slave, for me a very pleasing and erotic combination. This translates easily into a Daddy/daughter style. I believe I like my daughters in their mid-teens range, when their sexuality has become demonstrable. She's a slut but she's also my submissive little girl. Daddy likes to make her feed on his cock and his cum. She's a real hungry little slut girl, always begging Daddy to use her any way he wants. She's a good little fuck bitch for her Daddy.

I think I appreciate a Daddy/daughter scene because it allows a full range of tenderness and depravity. I have no desire to abuse an actual teenager, but the power of playing out those fantasies is compelling.

D/s can go much farther than sexual fantasy and physical and mental sensation. In a Master/slave relationship the slave gives up control to her Master. They may draw-up an actual contract (Better review any contracts with Paul, or the other lady lawyer in your firm, just to protect your interests!). The contract can range from becoming the Master's property, to being micro-managed with rules, responsibilities and punishments. It can be monogamous or a Master might have a number of live-in or outside slaves. It has been startling to find how far some slaves will go to please and obey their Master; but it is all consensual.

Submission is often termed a gift. The Master does not force anything from the slave. She offers it freely to a worthy Master. I don't feel it very practical or fun to be a micro-manager. I haven't yet been in a Master/slave relationship. What I would create will not occur until I do. It would be a combination of the two personalities involved.

It would of course include my control of the slave's sexuality. I

would expect that she be respectful and courteous, and devoted at all times. She would present her point of view with a humble demeanor. And the core of her life would revolve around pleasing me. After being married 16 years to my ex, I deserve royal treatment (grin).

Another aspect is play and training vs. a long-term relationship (LTR). This isn't like vanilla relationships, where the woman is supposed to be a virgin. This lifestyle requires practice for both the Dom and the submissive. This is why many people choose play partners, though they might not be right for a LTR.

Many women, from the ads I've seen on net, are looking for their one true love before they'll accept any training at all. In my opinion, expecting to start a LTR with someone whose never experienced any BDSM, makes no sense at all. There's no way of knowing if your kinks will match up, no matter what a new submissive thinks she wants, until you actually try it.

That's why I think some experience helps the sub understand what she does and doesn't enjoy and more readily narrow the field of her many choices for a Dom. It just saves a lot of "courting" time. There are probably 20 or more Doms for every sub on Internet personals sites.

But Kate, I don't think it's a good idea for you and I to become involved. I have both ethical and practical reasons for not becoming involved with a married woman. Plus you are my lawyer, or at least within the same law firm, and that raises the legal aspect.

Carrying on affairs becomes so complicated (I don't speak from experience, but observation. I was never unfaithful to My ex, unfortunately (grin)). The deception and secrecy, while perhaps providing a certain thrill initially, I feel soon deteriorates into guilt and other complications. I don't enjoy stealing another man's woman. Peer loyalty, I guess. When I was younger, my 'best friend' did it to me. It was a painful betrayal by both the woman and my friend.

So where does that leave us? I will aid you, as I can, by answering questions and offering feedback on your thoughts. I have several email relationships right now that take up a fair amount of my dwindling available time. The rest must be devoted to getting my ass out of hock.

I feel you should continue your personal quest to find your truth and create the freedom to explore and express it. But you must come to terms in some way with your current relationship.

You have been a loyal and non-judgmental ally during this ordeal I've gone through with My ex. I want you to know how much I appreciate that. You've been such a good little girl!

Galen

Subject: Confidential
Date: Fri, 30 Jul

Dear Galen:

Thank you very much for writing back. I don't think there's a submissive lawyers club in this town. Submission is not a revered quality in an advocate, I'm afraid!

If gp25 hates lawyers, he has probably already forwarded my letter to the state bar and the ABA. It's only a matter of time before the sex police come knocking down my door.

I eagerly awaited your response and when it came I savored every word and every image it stirred in my mind. I read it over and over. But the part about not wanting to get 'involved' with me made me sad because it reminded me how stuck I feel in terms of my marriage. There's more to it than I let on, and I want to tell you about that (I hope you won't mind).

I knew I wanted to leave my marriage about two years ago. The

reasons I haven't left are complex. First, I have tried to salvage the marriage; I invested ten years of my life trying to make the relationship work.

For example, I have repeatedly suggested and requested counseling and have had about a million heart-to-hearts, where I explain that I am not happy, and so on. But he never once has resolved to heal or change the relationship. He just is the most unmotivated personality, and he appears to have no desire to grow as a person or a partner. We share no spiritual connection.

I am a very vibrant personality, I think. I want to have deep and meaningful exchanges with my partner; but my husband cannot rise to the occasion, though I have tried to work on that with him as well. Then there is the pity-related reasoning

The long and short of it is that he is not employed right now, and is (I believe) depressed about that. I am just waiting for him to get a job so that I don't have that guilt of kicking him when he's down. Also, he is a really introverted person—an isolationist with very few friends and really no family; so I feel badly for him in that regard.

Last month I told him that he needs to look for work in the city and that he should move down there if he gets a good offer. I believe—job or no job—I won't give him past October. I have talked to my parents about everything, too, and they stand behind me and support me completely in my decision to end the relationship.

I am not thinking that I want to get "involved" with anybody right now so far as commitments go. But I really, really want to be intimate with you, Galen. I have since I first read your personal ad. Of course intimacy is a large component of involvement, but I don't know if that's the definition you had in mind.

Of course, I fully accept it if you either don't want intimacy with me at all, or don't want it until I give my hubby the boot. I really want you; I know I would really please you and that you would please me. And I would love to please you in various ways. As for the professional/ethics component of it, I am willing to take my

chances and violate the code of professional ethics because I am such a naughty girl.

Your letter left me sitting here with wet panties. Your words made me so wet and made me throb for you. My hot pussy juices came running onto my thighs while I walked over to the courthouse; and when I stood in front of the judge all I could think about was how wet my pussy was and how much I wanted to give it you. I thought about my naughty secret and it turned me on even more that nobody knew but me and you. I hope that someday you can feel how wet you make me, Galen.

I have a tight little hole and I love to shave my pussy bare for my Daddy. I would so love it if you asked me to sit on your lap, and made me submit to your plans for me. I would let you do almost anything to me and would love it, I am sure. I love to be on top and I love to take it doggy style. I have a really nice throat and mouth for you, too. But I have never swallowed, and don't know if I could do it, although I would be willing to try.

I want to know what it is like to be with a man who enjoys the same sexual dynamics as I do. I really want that man to be you because I trust you, I like you an awful lot, you make me feel very safe, and I become aroused in your presence.

I also know that I would feel so liberated not having to ask for what I desire from you in terms of the particulars, because I think that what you want from me is what I want for myself. Does that make sense? I would love to beg you to hurt my pussy and to teach me how to please you.

You know, when I was only about 17 years old, I got a copy of the Marquis De Sade because I was so intrigued by the subject of Dominant/submissive dynamics between men and women, and wanted to learn more about them. I had long since forgotten about that book, but remembered it recently. Have you read it? I should read it again, because most of it probably didn't even make sense to me back then.

I want you to know that I am way too scared and uncomfortable with the idea of meeting a man over the Internet, or through some S&M club thing, and am not inclined to do so. So I feel very lucky to have met you like I did.

Please forgive my forwardness, and please be firm with me if you don't want me to pursue intimacy with you now or ever. I would appreciate your response and will respect your wishes. Even though you already told me that you aren't interested in getting involved with a married person, I wanted to respond since I really didn't give you the whole sorry picture of my marriage and how close I really am to divorce.

If you write me back, I promise to write you again if you ask me to. Please do.

Thank you again, very, very much for writing to me. I loved reading your letter and believe me that I will read it again and again. I am going to print it and hide it where nobody can find it. I will delete it so that I won't get into trouble. You are a wonderful writer and I hope that you will write me more letters, but only if that is what you want.

Sincerely and very fondly,

Kate

Subject: Flattered
Date: Fri, 30 Jul

Dear kate,

As much as you tempt and flatter me by what you promise for me, I still adhere to my previous position. Believe me, for a man of my nature that is not easy, especially when you offer yourself so openly and generously.

I understand the position you are in. I know the difficulty and complexity of it. I can offer no advice but to do what you feel in your heart and trust that you will survive no matter what pain and complication comes with it.

Warmly,

Galen

(*Note: After not talking for several weeks, Kate called one afternoon to update me on my divorce proceedings. Towards the end of our conversation she asked if I would meet her some place discreet for a drink. She told me that she had come to terms with her decision to leave her husband. They had a discussion in which she revealed her desire to end the marriage. She said that he wasn't surprised, and that he had agreed to move out within a month.*

She claimed that she just wanted to talk. I agreed to meet her and told her to pick a place and a time. You can probably guess where the currents of her repressed passion led her.

We met, and after talking for an hour, I reached under her skirt. She was dripping all over the seat of the secluded booth where we sat. I did the Domly thing and took her back to my lair, to verify this little slut's intention.)

Subject: Private
Date: Mon, 16 Aug

Dear Galen:

I had such a nice, nice time last night. I really didn't expect any of it, and so I was very pleasantly surprised that you wanted to touch me and to feel how wet my pussy gets when I am with you.

When I finally got to touch you the way I have fantasized about

touching you, it made me very happy and content. I only regret that I didn't seize the opportunity to play with some of your toys. I hope you still would like to tie me up and punish me for wanting to suck your big hot cock so badly. I'm sure that I need you to use that leather thing with the strap on it; and I am sure that I need that collar around my neck, and I might need you to put a clip on my clit.

I loved every minute of last night, except going home. My favorite parts of last night were kissing you, and when you grabbed at my hair and pulled, and when you put your hands around my neck, and when you slapped my face. I also loved sucking and sitting on your big hard cock, which really felt so nice inside of me... and your skin felt so nice against mine . . .

I would like to see you this weekend coming up if that's all right with you. Please write me back and give me something nasty to think about all day, okay?

Sincerely,

kate

Subject: Last night
Date: Tue, 17 Aug

Dear Galen:

I hope you don't mind that I am emailing you again. I just wanted to say that even though I said I wasn't expecting what happened on Sunday, I wished for it and wanted you very badly. I just didn't expect that you would want to be intimate with me because of what you said previously about not getting mixed up with me.

I am very glad you changed your mind, at least on Sunday. You could teach me a lot about myself, and I am eager to learn. I fantasized about you in my hot tub last night. I pretended that you

made me hold on to my orgasm until I begged you to let me cum. Then, when I came, I came so hard and really lost my head.

Please write back, okay?

kate

Subject: Rougher?
Date: Tue, 17 Aug

Dear kate,

Quite a nasty little slut, aren't you? I enjoyed using you like my slut daughter. I enjoyed making you take my cock deep into your throat, forcing you to hold it there. Turning you into my whore.

It turned me on yanking you by the hair and slapping your face, watching your reaction, how it changed your face into a glow of docile obedience, acceptance, desire. You obviously like it rough. I wonder how rough. Did we just scratch the surface in that regard? Did I slap you hard enough, often enough? Or did you really desire more?

I'm not sure about my plans for the weekend. I may go up to the city on Friday to visit some friends. I may stay over Saturday. If that's the case, we'll make another arrangement. I should have this figured out before the end of the week. Tell me your situation again.

Kate, I want to caution you, that I do not want you to become reliant on me, or get attached to me. We will do this under my terms, or we can't do it at all. That doesn't mean that I don't like you, or don't find you exciting to play with. I know that I've explained this. I don't want to be into anything complicated right now.

Think toys!

Galen

Dear Galen:

I do like it rough; and yes, I think we just scratched the surface. In candor, I can't say how rough I like it because I just don't have any experience with bondage and S/m. All I have are my fantasies. I think I would like to be slapped harder, because I felt, in that moment, that I desired more and harder.

Your tenderness and your dominance made me melt, and feel that I could finally let go of so much sexual tension and desire that I have held inside for what seems like a lifetime. I believe that, yes, I would like to play rougher with you. Please tell me more about what I could do and what you want to do. Then I can tell you whether it sounds like something I would like (though I anticipate it will).

I feel inclined to obey and please you, so I believe that I am willing to try most of what you recommend. I think that you will suggest really nasty, slutty things for me to do. My problem is that I have only a vague idea about what your suggestions might be.

As for my situation this weekend, I have plans to go out of town for a bike trip with some friends. I leave sometime Friday afternoon. I told my husband that I am going for the whole weekend and won't be back until Sunday or Monday. I told my friends that I am probably leaving Saturday afternoon, though, because I decided that I could have more fun with you.

I hope that you, too, will return Saturday because I am so anxious to play with you and your toys again, soon. I have a very horny and hot little pussy that needs to be managed. Please let me know when you firm up your plans.

Galen, I don't intend to or even want to become reliant on you. My goal is, for now, to be self-reliant. That will take a great deal of time, I believe, given my current situation. It would be foolish and unrealistic for me to become reliant on and attached to any man at this juncture.

Plus, I don't believe it would be in my best interests to jump immediately from one relationship into another; in fact, I have vowed not to do so. I imagine that you feel the same way about your life right now.

My primary focus is on wrapping-up my existing relationship as expediently and sensitively as I can manage; and the inherent demands of motherhood, and of trying to adapt to a pretty stressful new career also require a great deal of my attention and energy.

I don't have a ton of time for additional activities, but what extra time I have, I would like to spend some of it connecting with you and exploring myself and my fantasies with you. I think you are a really sweet, handsome, and interesting man. I find you very exciting.

Plus, I think that you can please me in the way I want to be pleased by a Man; and I won't deny my craving to satisfy you completely. But, while I can definitely avoid becoming reliant on you, I would lie if I said that I could just shut down my emotions and refrain from getting even a little attached to you, over time.

Galen, if and when I feel that I am becoming attached to you I promise to tell you so that you can choose what is right for you. Is this all right with you? Can my position meet your requirements and expectations?

Sincerely,

kate

Subject: Weekend
Date: Fri, 20 Aug

Dear Galen:

I got your message. I would love to meet you in the city on Saturday night. I will be tied up until about 5 p.m. tomorrow. When I get back to my friends' house, I will call you on your cell phone. I don't want to make a hotel reservation on my credit card (for obvious reasons). So, why don't you do it.

I don't have a cell phone but you can call me at my friends', no problem. Why don't you call me sometime tomorrow and leave a message about where and what time to meet you. If I have any problems or questions, I can call you back.

What is a crop? I think I know what a 'flogger' is—a whip, right?

I am really excited (and also kind of nervous, too) about seeing you. I want you to hurt me, but there must be a limit, where it becomes too much. If I tell you that it is too much and that I really mean it, I trust you will let up. I feel that I can trust you, Galen, but can we discuss this when we meet.

kate

Subject: Oops
Date: Sat, 21 Aug

Dear Galen:

I don't know how I did it, but I left your email somewhere (at work I think) and I deleted it from my mailbox. It had your cell phone number and I don't otherwise know it. Please email it to me again. I will call you when I get back tomorrow, or else you can call me here and tell me where and when to go. Please don't email my

address because I forgot my password and can't access my account; instead, email this address.

Sincerely,

kate

Subject: Re: Oops
Date: Sat, 21 Aug

Dear spacegirl,

Sounds like you'll require a little mental discipline as well! Lucky for you we live in the age of electronic communication.

I am at the Hilton, room 754. Why don't you plan to be here by 7pm.

Don't be late.

Galen

Subject: Private
Date: Mon, 23 Aug

Dear Galen:

I just found the lost email. I noticed this morning that I hadn't deleted it from my box, so I figured that I hadn't even printed it. Then, this afternoon, I opened a client's file and there it was situated prominently right in front. I am *so* happy and relieved that I found it and not someone else at the office.

That was very bad and irresponsible of me to leave it like that. I

could get fired or even disbarred if the wrong people found out about my activities with you, and I know you do not need further distress in your life either. I am really sorry that I put us both in such a situation. I need a severe punishment from my Daddy. I'm sure you agree. Why don't you tell me how you can correct my carelessness.

I have to go right now, but I really want to tell you what I think of your toys, because I do have an opinion about them, and I have ideas about what I would like you to do with them.

Sincerely,

kate xx

Subject: From chronically wet
Date: Tue, 24 Aug

Dear Galen:

You and your toys make me feel so submissive and eager to please you. It feels kind of like a drug or some kind of a giving up, where I feel so completely compelled to let you take me over. This feeling comes so profoundly; and I feel it in my pussy, in my mind and all over my skin, all at the same time. I experience it like a powerful psycho-sexual high.

The high is like a ladder, where, in the past I saw the top, and wanted to get there—really badly; but I could only get up a few steps, and only in my private fantasies. I still can't believe the things that I have done with you.

I really want you to tie me up, Galen. You know I need it, don't you? I liked your soft ties; I liked the rough ones.

I am such a bad girl with a vibrator on my clit . . . when I feel my pussy throb and my clit burn at the same time, I am more submis-

sive than at any other time I know of. I would love to have the vibrator, the ties, and be held down, all at once. I do have more fantasies involving you and your gear, and will share them with you later.

Write me back, please.

kate

Subject: Get wetter
Date: Tue, 24 Aug

My sweet little bitch,

This is a special place you are exploring, isn't it? I applaud your courage and appreciate the sincerity of your submissiveness. Beyond the toys, I find the mental landscape of submission to be greatly enticing. I recognize that part of you, and it thrills me to find a partner so well suited for this style of exploration, both physical and mental.

I have only glimpsed, really, all that you can be and desire in your submission to me. You've pleased me very much, thus far. It can take a while for my intuition (and yours) to lock in, to where I see it clearly and know exactly where and how to take you. Knowing more details (as you have been providing) about your fantasies and how you feel about what is happening, feeds more data to my intuitive, creative Dominant nature.

I will take what I want, but I also enjoy hitting your hot buttons (among other things). There's nothing more exciting than knowing I'm becoming like a supreme God to my sub, as I drive her further and further into the frenzy of her lust. Giving it all up, as you say.

I do know, slut, how badly you need it. I know how desperately my submissive little bitch needs it rough, needs to be used, forced, hurt, and degraded by her Daddy. I want you to be chronically wet for

me. I had already planned out several rope bondage scenarios to put you in, and the dildos and vibrators held an important position. You know the position I mean, don't you?

I am also moved by your loyalty, defense and devotion to me at your office. I am honored by the risks you take for me. But I don't want you to jeopardize your career or job, by pushing beyond the limit. I have not been treated very well throughout the ordeals of this last year. You've been very soothing and sweet. Your understanding and support have nourished me. I really want to thank you for that.

Why don't you see if you can arrange some time out of the office late afternoon, sometime soon?

I'm including a story called 'Cocoon'. I had met a woman online who said she had a confinement fetish, to be put in closets, trunks etc. That inspired this story. It might not be practical to do this exactly, I just enjoyed writing it. I truly feel a passion for writing, no matter what the topic.

Warmly,

Galen

Subject: Marks on my titties
Date: Tue, 24 Aug

Dear Galen:

Thank you very, very much for your letter. I savored every word and every image. I crave to sit down and write you a long letter about my fantasies, and I promise that I will, but I have to go to work now.

I am going swimming at lunch today; and when I do, I will probably think of your story about gasping for air and the cocoon. That story

was amazing. Your writing talent impresses me very much. I would like to talk to you more about it. I can't imagine myself being in the situation of the woman in that story, though.

Why don't you tell me how the Master feels in that situation, and maybe I could better understand the dynamics, and appreciate the woman's role more. I appreciated the nastiness and the sensuality of the story.

The purple marks on my titties finally started to fade today. I love going into the bathroom, closing the door, and looking at them. I love to touch myself when I look, and to feel my moist pussy start to throb when I think of how you put those marks on me. I need for you to bite and pinch me so hard that you leave your mark any-where on my body (that my clothes can cover up).

I still need to repent for my carelessness around your letter. Have you planned my punishment? I dread it and I and crave it at the same time, Galen.

I would like to accommodate you by getting away from work early one afternoon soon. I will really try, okay? Once my husband moves out I can better accommodate your wishes regarding me and my time. I know that will happen by October; and, at the rate we are already working through things, I believe it will be sooner.

Can we leave the afternoon up in the air for now, and then plan on meeting Sunday when you get back from out of town?

Very sincerely yours,

kate

Subject: Here I come.
Date: Fri, 27 Aug

Dear Galen,

I am leaving to meet you now. I get nervous and excited when I see you. I think I get nervous because I understand that I pretty much have to let you punish me whenever and however you want to; but I never know when or how it is going to play out.

See you in a few minutes . . .

kate

Subject: Re: Confidential reply
Date: Fri, 27 Aug

Dear slut,

You were sweet to write me a note before we met last night.

You are correct that I will punish you and use you whenever and however I choose. I know you crave harsher punishment. It will delight me to turn up the heat, give my bitch the torment she seeks, make you suffer for me. That is my nature. I get pleasure from hurting you, making that pain turn into a sexual high, watching how it transforms your face into submissive beauty. I will explore your tolerance and desire for pain further at our next meeting.

Also, I will provide your punishment for your error with your letter to me. I am strict about punishing bad behavior. Do not expect it to be pleasant, although 'punishing' a pain slut like you always poses a challenge!

I enjoy force fucking my little daughter's cuntmouth. I will make you serve me that way on a regular basis. I know my whore is keeping herself wet thinking about Sunday.

See you then,

Galen

p.s. Here's another story. It's a bit more extreme, and has a Daddy/ daughter context. I wrote it the evening after my ex discovered my HIV test results. It was my way of purging frustration.

(Note: Sent " Daddy's Home story.)

Subject: Private
Date: Fri, 27 Aug

Dear Galen:

I loved the story you sent me. It left me dripping wet and thinking about you and your Dominance and how much I love my experience and experiments with you. I think maybe I need to buy panty liners and just wear them all the time, because every time I talk to you, get an email from you, read your stories, or even just think about you, my pussy starts to salivate.

I thought about my fantasies last night after I left your house. I am sorry that I didn't share them with you when you requested. You just kind of caught me off guard. One is that you bind my knees and wrists together really tightly; then you torment my clit, slap me over and over and over, on my face, titties, and legs.

You scold me for being such a bad girl and you tell me how I might become your good, sweet little girl by taking your big raging cock as deeply as you can drive it up into me. I want you to make me really bad, and then fix me by making me good. I am not really sure how you might do this, but I trust that you can. I am very anxious for Sunday to come . . .

I suppose I want a Daddy because Daddies are supposed to comfort their daughters in special ways. And even though they aren't supposed to put their hands down their little daughters' panties, they are so aroused by having their little girl, there on their lap, feeling her hot little young, innocent crotch pressed up against Daddy's

less, and she needs a Daddy to supervise and control her. She needs Daddy to affirm that she has value, because all she really cares about is whether her Daddy is happy with her, and whether he adores her.

Do you think that all these thoughts and images are beautiful? I do. . .

Please send me another story. You really do write beautifully. How uncanny that you know so much about how I think and operate, and what I want. How do you know me so well and you don't even know me at all?? It deeply intrigues me that you could fantasize about sexual scenarios that so parallel my very own fantasies.

I actually thought I just made these things up in my head, and that they must be so unique and strange that others couldn't actually be thinking of or wanting the same things. I don't think I had these ideas put into my head from any outside source. So my fantasies always seemed like a private secret that nobody knew. But I see that you know, Galen.

Write me back, please, if you have a chance. Hearing from you gives me a rush.

kate xxooo

Subject: Wet secret
Date: Mon, 30 Aug

I have a secret between my legs
It held you in its wet, warm embrace
and can't come back from that place

My hole is still wet for you today, Daddy.

Subject: Reflecting
Date: Tue, 31 Aug

Dear daughter,

You were such a bad girl on Sunday; the more ways I used you, the
wetter you got. You're such a slut, even punishment and pain make
you wet. But you will require further abuse and torment for having
me fuck you instead of torture you further. There are still quite a
few things I have in mind for you, that I have yet to do to you.

I appreciated how much torment you can take. I enjoy using you
that way. It seems we're still a ways from your limits in that regard,
though I do plan to push you further this weekend. You looked
wonderful in the ball gag, by the way, the way it held your mouth in
permanent cock sucking position.

I want you to buy or bring high heels (3.5" minimum, preferably
with an ankle strap), black nylons, garter belt and matching push-up
bra. You will present yourself to me in a short skirt and blouse that
can be opened in the front, or a short dress.

I have sent information to the party host about our request to attend
this Friday. I await her reply. We have reservations at the Hilton,
downtown.

I'm curious about your relationship with your girlfriend. Do you
have some type of fantasy about her? Are you thinking that I might
train her, or her and you together? Do you have any urge to domme
or be dommed by another woman? Or, are you just wanting to help
introduce her to D/s in a general sense with no personal involvement?

When we get to the city, I'm going to take you to a BDSM shop. I
have to replace the missing ankle cuff, so I can place you in the
spreader bar.

Here's another story for you.

Hot regards,

Galen

(Note: I sent 'Daddy's Daydream'.)

Subject: Friday
Date: Tue, 31 Aug

Dear Galen:

My friend unequivocally stated that she has no desire to go to the party. I was somewhat surprised. I have no sexual feelings toward her. I only intended to have her come along for curiosity and interest related reasons. I wish she did want to go, though.

But I still want you to take me along with you, if you can. Why do I need to dress like a slut to go to the party? Tell me about that. Tell me what I am going to do at the party. Can I just quietly watch and observe? Please tell me your thoughts on this.

Was I right to make reservations for only one night? Write me back please,

kate

Subject: Dress like a slut
Date: Tue, 31 Aug

Dear slut,

Did I say you needed to dress like a slut to go to the party? You need to dress like a slut whether we go or not. It can be a sophisticated look, without looking trashy, or like a street whore.

My thought on this wasn't in relation to the party. I didn't plan to participate actively in the party. I would have discussed this with you beforehand. Although the idea of surprising you—making you submit to me in front of others—might have been a fun idea, I haven't taken that level of control over you where I would expect you to do what I tell you anytime and place.

You will have to have some interaction with the people I know, just as a courtesy. But generally, I will make it known that I must be asked permission from others who may wish to talk with you.

I assumed from the start that we were spending two nights. You never mentioned otherwise. I didn't notice the reservation was for one night. I feel you need to be clearer on what your intention is. Let me know.

Galen

Subject: More questions
Date: Tue, 31 Aug

Dear Galen:

I read your story, which held me captivated to the end. I haven't fantasized about dominating another woman, and frankly, thinking about it does not arouse me at all. I have thought a little about being dominated by a woman under the direction and supervision of a man though, and for his pleasure.

Galen, your stories excite and arouse me. They also make me feel silly, embarrassed, weak, vulnerable and corrupt, too. And I like to feel all of those ways, although not at all times. It is something like a persona, because I don the emotions and feelings that go along with my little pussy girl persona when I am with the right person, wanting or needing to feel safe.

At other times, I need to feel strong on my own, and to dominate

something or someone—out of practical necessity. These two personas don't coexist well together. They are kind of schitzoid. Maybe your ideas about a 'persona' are different than what I'm thinking about here.

Please tell me if it is not okay that I email you so many times.

Sincerely,

kate

Subject: Reply
Date: Wed, 1 Sept

Dear little pussy girl,

I view your emails to me as a sign of devotion, desire, respect, submission, need, perversity, and decadence. I welcome them.

I liked your thoughts about separating the parts within you into distinct personas. I think when done consciously and symbolically it represents a healthy schizophrenia. I'll tell you more about this on the ride to the city.

Making you submit to another woman, telling her how I want her to use you, slap you, fuck your mouth with a strap-on, flog your ass and tits, make you eat her cunt; these are all pleasant thoughts.

Warm regards,

Galen

Subject: Weekend
Date: Wed, 1 Sep

Dear Daddy:

I am very distracted thinking about you and about what you might do to me this weekend. I trust that you will take care of me the way that you know I need it.

I called the hotel and got reservations for Friday and Saturday nights. I hope this pleases you.

Remember that dream I told you about, the one I had right before we became romantic, where you were fucking my throat and I couldn't breathe? I have never had anybody do that to me before, or even force their cock into my mouth like you have. And what seems really uncanny is that when you do it, it feels just like it did in my dream; and when you describe it in your stories, you describe it just the way it felt to me in my dream. It's as if I knew what was coming, even though I really didn't know yet.

Would you want to come over to my house and hot tub with me? I would really like that. I can't wait to see you, touch you, smell you and taste you again, Galen.

I think that I would like to have a female to do those things to me that you mentioned in your letter, but only if you would be there. Did you have someone in mind? I think I would need to get really psychologically prepared for it, so I am not saying that I believe I could do it tomorrow, or this week. But I am interested. I don't think I could eat her pussy though. I have tried that before and did not like it very much.

Do you believe that I can or will do all of the things that you have in mind for me? That I can be the filthy little slut girl that you desire? What do you most want to take from me? Can you tell me some of the things you want to do with me that you haven't done yet (other than hog tying me, which you have already explained to me)? Or will you surprise me?

I am scared, but I have so much desire to experience all that you have planned for me that I keep wanting to come back for more and

more and more. You told me that you would give me a 12-week course in bondage and obedience; what does it take to get an 'A' in your class? When 12 weeks are up, what are the most important lessons and tasks that I should have learned? Tell me, please.

I did like it last night when you told me what to do. It felt very good, like I could let go of some responsibility that I really didn't want to have. I don't know why this is, but everyone always expects me to plan and orchestrate things. I am not blameless, of course, in creating this reputation for myself. But I don't want that burden in every facet of my life, like I have had far too long now.

You know, I only recently learned to say 'no' when I need to, and to recognize when I need to say no. This lesson has liberated me a great deal and enabled me to become more independent and strong by being more realistic about what I want, what I need, and what I can do. Saying no has also enabled me to avoid countless situations where others have sought to place me in that decision-making role when I don't wish to take on that role.

Sincerely,

kate

p. s. I woke up with a very wet pussy this morning, thinking about your body and how much I wanted to see and touch it, and how much I craved to straddle your lap, Daddy. I wish that you were here right now to help take care of my pussy, which desperately needs you right now.

Subject: Musings
Date: Thu, 2 Sep

Dear slut daughter,

The ideal goal for your training is to turn you into a total whore and slave. One that cultivates her slut/slave persona, eagerly offers her

body for punishment and pain, her mind for degradation and humiliation.

I will mold you into a girl who offers every pleasure her Master desires, seeks to obey Him without question, respects Him, adores Him, supports Him, serves as His ally and a source of strength and inspiration, provides tender solace and compassion when needed, offers her complete surrender and eagerly desires to serve Him faithfully in every way.

This requires a state of mind where you have accepted this as your greatest desire. A state of mind that is shrouded in a sense of pride, and rid of shame or guilt. You live your decadence, take pleasure in it, create the freedom you seek by giving up control, and find your greatest pleasure in serving and pleasing your Master.

That is a glimpse of an ideal. Whether you or anyone can attain that level of surrender is not known to me; but it is my target. Life is more complex than that. Perhaps at some point, it might become the slave's goal to give up total control in every aspect of her life. She becomes her Master's property, with total trust in his power over her.

But that's not where things start. It is an explorative journey, to discover the truth about your desire—the reality versus the fantasy. I am not clear exactly what shape an ongoing relationship would take. What I would choose to control or not, what would be negotiated, before a commitment by the sub to give up areas of control.

Where the dividing line falls, between the sexual drama and play, and living as a Master/slave on a day to day basis in all aspects, can only be discovered by doing. Some people are only into 'bedroom bondage' and are 'vanilla' in every other aspect. Others choose, and the slave accepts, to live as an abused house pet, a slave of the lowest order. Difficult to understand the pleasure in that, perhaps, but this is some people's reality.

You've been a very good student. You've pleased me in a variety of ways. I wouldn't have guessed what a nasty slut you are, with such

a delightfully perverted desire for rough sex. When we first met, I
thought you were a shy and repressed girl, though intelligent,
respectful and supportive. See what a poor judge of character I am?
We'll talk more about your questions on the ride up to the city.

Here's another story. See you tomorrow.

Galen

(Note: I sent 'As Master Wishes'.)

Subject: Humiliated
Date: Thu, 2 Sep

Dear Galen,

I want you to know that I bought a garter, push-up bra and panty
hose per your instructions. I am very fond of them already and
hope that you will also be pleased. It was hard for me to even ask
the clerk where I could find these things. I felt embarrassed and
kind of humiliated telling her I needed them.

After that difficult part though, I had fun trying them on and picking
them out. It felt very, very strange seeing myself dressed like that.
My pussy was already wet from thinking about you on the way
there; and when I contemplated how I was doing these things
because you directed me to, I got very, very excited and just wanted
to submit to you and let you take me however you wished.

I couldn't find the kind of shoes you described. Maybe women
don't wear those kind of shoes anymore. But I only looked in two
stores. I will continue my search today, though. I am trying really
hard and I do understand that I must come up with something that
will please you.

Thank you very much for sending me the story. I loved it. How
many stories are there? I hope that you have one-hundred more, at

least. When did you write it? I have more questions for you. I hope I don't forget them when I see you.

I felt really isolated and restrained last night, dealing with my husband's and my separation. I did go into the hot tub, though. I fantasized about you, Galen. I talked to you and told you that I was gong to sit on your lap and fuck you. I begged you to bite me, to hurt me and to kiss me. I had a nasty orgasm and moaned like a bad little girl. I moaned for you, my Daddy; I wanted you so much.

Bye for now.

kate

Subject: Another chance to humiliate the slut
Date: Thu, 2 Sep

Dear slut girl,

I like the thought that you were humiliated to give a stranger a glimpse of your slut girl nature. I wonder what the sales clerk thought of you. She has to understand that there is only one reason for a girl to purchase those items. Now she knows you're that kind of girl. What if she could read your mind, and see the full extent of what a submissive whore you really are? Would she have been shocked?

If you got pantyhose, dear, that doesn't work. You need nylons. One for each leg! They attach to the garter—unless you misnamed what you got. Most stores won't have the heels you'll be getting. It's like a specialty item for special girls.

There's a place in town that offers the style of high heels I expect you to wear. They supply most of the topless dancers in town, among others, and should have a range from slutty to classy. You might call them and ask about their selection and quality.

Oh boy! Another chance to humiliate the slut, by requiring her to ask embarrassing questions. We'll discuss and review the other thoughts in your letter tomorrow. I've got to go get stuff done now.

I know you will please me (you may expect punishment when you don't). I understand how badly you want me to use you, punish you, hurt you, make you obey, make you do unspeakable acts just for my enjoyment, fuck your dripping pussy, ram my cock down my daughter's cuntmouth. Be patient little daughter.

Galen

Subject: Correct me
Date: Mon, 6 Sep

Dear Galen;

I believe that I left my glasses in your car. I realize that you must think I am irresponsible with my stuff, but the truth is that it is out of character for me to misplace things so often. I believe you could correct this new trend by some form of discipline.

By the way, Sir, I want you to fuck my little cunt until it's so raw that it hurts. I desire all the sweet and severe punishment that you have to dish out to my pussy, my mouth, my titties, my ass, and any part of my body or soul.

Our sexual encounters have brought me to a whole new level of experience, of living. I never imagined I could feel so sexually stimulated, or be with someone who could excite my body and my fantasies so wildly, and to whom I could safely disclose my true desires.

I am so lucky that you want my hot pussy and my cunt mouth, Daddy. My pussy longs madly for your big hot rod. I want to be your bad, bad, bad girl, Daddy, so that you have to rough me up and punish me.

If I accept my punishment from you then I am your good girl. Is this right Daddy? You redeem me with punishment, and my pussy drips and drips with desire for you to ram your strength and power between my thighs and into my dripping cunthole.

Very, very sweetly and steamy,

Your little pussy girl

Subject: Without restraint
Date: Mon, 6 Sep

Dear slut daughter,

Yes, when you willingly and eagerly seek pain and punishment, you are Daddy's good little girl. I want to explore my daughter's desires for rough treatment, pain, pleasure and submission to a further extent.

It excites me to have a little whore like you, who craves to be abused by me, and loves it. My little girl's face takes on such a lusty, rapturous beauty, when Daddy strikes her. Oddly, hurting you and knowing how it makes you wet to be so used, elicits profound tenderness.

As promised, we will pay more attention to your pussy and ass in our next rendezvous, plus some bondage of course. I want you to focus on the erotic potential of these acts. I want your desire to please me, to be greater than your fears and concerns. Give this to your Daddy, for his pleasure. Feel the power and pleasure of surrender to your Dominant Daddy.

I want your submission without restraint. I want you to want it like a whore wants it. By the way, my little girl looks like a real slut in her high heels. Did you feel how sexy they made you look?

506

Nasty regards,

Daddy

(*Note: I included the story "Daddy's Home"*)

Subject: Kiss me
Date: Tue, 7 Sep

Dearest Galen:

Thank you so much for emailing me back. I am always very
excited to receive your letters and stories. They send me spiraling
down into my most base thoughts and desires. I agree with everything you wrote. Your sweetness and your dominance make me
melt and make me long to rush right to you, rip off your clothes,
and lick, kiss, and suck you all over.

You also sent me a very nasty story about a girl who quite obviously
longs to please her Daddy and be his good little bitch in ways that
only a truly dirty slut can. This story was very dirty and sexy and,
of course, it made my pussy throb and drip. Please send me more
stories. Why do the toys in your stories look just like the ones in
your toy bag? What is a butt plug? What does it look like? What is
it made out of?

I have a meeting until 9 p.m. tonight, but can swing by your house
afterwards to pick up my stuff. Please let me know if this won't
work.

Your nasty wet pussy girl xo

Subject: This evening
Date: Tue, 7 Sep

So slut,

I believe you left your glasses on purpose, just so you could come over, because you want to be used. Isn't that right bitch!? How long can you stay?

Galen

Subject: Next time
Date: Wed, 08 Sep

Dear decadent slut,

I really enjoy how eager you are for degradation, humiliation and erotic torture and submission. You're well suited to the role of a whore who'll do anything to please her Dom. I have been cautious, not wanting to push you too fast, or too hard. But you always say, "Can't you do it harder?" Next time will be very hard.

I plan to put you into bondage again, which made you look beautifully submissive and compliant. I will crop, slap, pinch, clamp and clip your tits until you have to use your safeword. I need to know just how hard this little bitch can take it. It will be my pleasure to discover this through trial and error. Tell me your schedule for Sunday.

Galen

Subject: Your doll
Date: Thu, 9 Sep

Dear Daddy:

So you plan on giving it to me very hard soon? Should I be afraid? Should I wear my high heels and garter belt for you, Daddy? Do

you want your daughter to play dress up for you? Will you play with me like a doll? I can't wait until you use me again, until you break me down some more for your pleasure. I love it, want it, and need it desperately!

kate

Subject: Fucktoy
Date: Thu, 9 Sep

Dear bitch girl,

I do plan to give you a hard time on Sunday. You asked for it, remember slut? Your fear or not, is not my concern. You're a whore. I expect you to dress like one, because I find it appealing. You can be as slutty and enticing as you like.

Like a doll, hmmmm . . . give me some ideas that that provoked in your dirty daughter's mind. What kind of fucktoy could you be as a doll? I look forward to my sweet daughter begging Daddy to use her, hurt her, play with his little fuck dolly. Be assured, little girl, that I will break you down further into your devout, depraved submission.

I want you to be here at six on Sunday. You can make me dinner, though I am challenged in the kitchen utensil and cookware department. Since you're not a slave (yet), you give me a shopping list and I'll pick up the food. A slave would get to do it all.

See you then,

Galen

Subject: Slut or slave
Date: Thu, 9 Sep

Dear Daddy:

Please have these items on hand: gorgonzola cheese, walnut oil, and balsamic vinegar.

I will get the rest of the stuff I need to cook for you. I am going to make gnocchi. Tell me, Sir, which pasta sauce would you prefer— roasted red pepper, carrot and garlic cream sauce, or pesto?

Daddy, when I read your email about what you would do to me this weekend, my pussy began to flow like a raging river. I am so hot for you now . . .

Galen, I realize that you might be joking, to some extent, about being a slave who does everything for her Master; but, honestly, I don't have the time, inclination, or energy to be somebody's slave 24/7—even yours, and you would be the best Master any slave could ever wish for, I'm sure.

I would, however, enjoy being a sex slave to a worthy Master, and would also eagerly submit to getting bossed around and roughed up even outside the bedroom. We can talk more about this later, all right?

I will bring the Nietzsche book on Sunday. The essay I think you would find interesting is called "The Genealogy of Morals." I am confident that it will touch you deeply, and will ring very familiar. I believe it will match up with your intuitive feelings, and your observations about your world, human nature, and your struggle with the cultural forces and value systems that work against your individual nature, and even our collective nature as humans.

Your slut truly

Subject: Your questions
Date: Thu, 9 Sept

510

Dear daughter,

Daddy's tired now, but I wanted to get back to you on some of your questions.

I look forward to being served your culinary pleasure. I consume pesto twice a week. The red pepper sounds interesting, but I've never had a carrot sauce. I'll go with that.

I am teasing you about being a slave. Your response about being a willing sex slave, and serving out of the bedroom (bossed around and roughed up) would be a good thing to explore and clarify. I also want to discuss adding some ritual and protocol to your behavior when you're with me in private.

I want to begin to extend your role beyond just our sex play. Just like in rough play, there are boundaries and limits that need to be understood to allow the play to become exciting and psychically powerful. The same can be applied to our total time together in a Dom/sub dynamic. I want to understand what your needs and thoughts are.

I guess it's time I read Nietzsche. I'm sure I'll find it interesting. Daddy likes that his little girl is so smart and competent, among other things.

Looking forward to seeing you Sunday.

Galen

Subject: Eager to serve you
Date: Fri, 10 Sep

Daddy Darling:

Thank you for your response to my mail. I do hope that you enjoy

511

what I prepare you for dinner.

You said that you wanted to discuss ritual and protocol for my behavior with you in private. I am curious and somewhat intimidated by this suggestion and by the thoughts it provokes. I am dying to know how you would plan to conform my behavior, and exactly what kind of behavior you have in mind.

Can you give me a clue? Or will you make me wait?? From what information you gave me, I understand that you believe your rules will strike me as exciting and psychically powerful. I trust you very much and believe that you are right about these things. I, too, want to understand your needs and your thoughts on these topics, and I look forward to taking your direction.

Thank you very much for acknowledging my intellect and competence. It flatters me deeply that you perceive me that way; but Daddy I am also a dumb little cunt, too, and wouldn't want you to overlook that. I want to have it both ways, if that is all right with you.

I began reading your book manuscript. You write very well and have a great talent for stimulating your reader's imagination, passion, thought, creativity, drive, and will. I wanted to feel your hand up my skirt and your fingers pressing hard onto my pussy through my panties while I read your story.

Do I even have to tell you how wet your little girl's pussy became thinking about you carrying out all those scenarios you wrote about? You are very brave to write what you wrote, in terms of revealing your deepest, most private thoughts, experiences, and beliefs. And you are willing to reveal it to a public audience. I don't believe that I could ever bring myself to do that.

I am still having a really hard time with the idea of anal sex and it is giving me a lot of grief. Can we talk about that on Sunday, please? I want to kiss you . . .

Sincerely,

512

Your dumb little cunt

Subject: What you need
Date: Fri, 10 Sep

Dear dumb little cunt,

I know what a stupid little whore you are, and that my little cunt daughter needs to be treated that way by Daddy. I think it's fun to degrade, humiliate and abuse my dumb cunt of a daughter. Daddy's been thinking about his little bitch's titties and how I long to torture them and observe how my little girl reacts to Daddy's perverse pleasure in doing so. Don't worry, Daddy won't overlook my responsibility to make you suffer for me.

I don't want you to feel afraid of how Daddy want's to penetrate his little girl's ass. You won't be forced to do anything you are uncomfortable with. But I do want to introduce some stimulation and perhaps mild penetration, maybe my finger while you are bound and clamped and fucking yourself with a dildo. I'll put the head of the vibrator right on your ass hole and test your reaction. My little daughter might be surprised at what she'll accept and desire, once her cunt is dripping with lust.

Thanks for your warm reception to my manuscript. I do feel vulnerable in several ways by letting you read it, not always showing myself as strong and competent. But my journey now is the truth, both good and bad.

I will let your imagination play with my comments on ritual until Sunday. But your input will be important to this process as well.

Thinking nasty thoughts about you.

Daddy

Subject: Reflecting on events
Date: Mon, 13 Sep

Dear Sir:

Thank you for allowing me to serve you last night. As always, you were brilliant company. Did you love the way I sucked your big, thick, hard cock, putting every inch of it down into my throat like Daddy's good little cuntmouth girl?

I also enjoyed my punishment for being late. I probably deserve even harsher scolding, slapping and pushing for not leaving when I was told to last night; I am sure that I do, and it wouldn't serve me well for you to just ignore my transgressions.

But did you really want me to go home last night, Daddy? Or did you want me to stay, so that I could repeatedly wake you up with your cock in my mouth during the night? I just couldn't tell what you wanted from me, especially when you rammed your rod deep into my dripping pussy after you told me to leave.

Have a nice time delivering your speech today. I know your audience will enjoy it, and hope they will be open to your message.

Did I please you yesterday? I probably didn't behave the way you wanted me to. I think I need more direction and guidance from You in that department. What do you think? I really liked making you dinner. I also really enjoyed wearing the clamps you placed on my tits; and the rope bondage turned me on completely.

I want more, Daddy. When do I get more bondage and punishment? I think I need it more than ever. Can we meet later this week? Please write back, Daddy. I want to hear from you because my pussy is sopping wet and it craves that stimulation I get when I read your nasty thoughts.

kate xx

Subject: Putting you in your place.
Date: Wed, 15 Sep

Dear slut,

You've accumulated a number of small transgressions that I will
deal with on Friday. Just to keep you in line. Discipline is good. A
slut like you needs to be kept in your place—on your knees usually,
with your cuntmouth eagerly begging Daddy to fuck it hard and
deep.

Friday, I also plan to get back on track with your training via more
elaborate bondage, whipping, more clamps, etc. This time your
cunt will be exposed and tortured for my pleasure. I want to see
how it reacts to being clamped, spanked and whipped with my
pussy flogger.

During this, I will make you use the dildo and vibrator, and while
you're doing so I will paddle your ass red. I will penetrate your ass
with my index finger or similarly sized object. All this will be done
to you while you're blindfolded. Perhaps this will reduce some
anxiety, though I am not really concerned about your anxiety. My
pleasure and enjoyment in using you is what's important. Is that
clear?

You can make me dinner, and are to make yourself available for my
pleasure throughout the evening.

I feel there is more to be revealed about your desire to be slapped
around and choked. Tell me how this plays out in your deepest
fantasies. I'm still trying to guage your limits and your desire
around this. How far can we take it? I expect you to answer me
explicitly.

What was your physical and mental response when I mildly probed
your ass while I fucked you the other night?

Yours in pain and pleasure,

Galen

Subject: Nasty thoughts about you
Date: Wed, 15 Sep

Dear Sweet, Strong, Daddy:

I cannot contain my urge to write you a letter after you got me going on the phone today. I couldn't concentrate very well today at work, because I was consumed by filthy, sexy day dreams about you. I will try to get them off my chest here.

I also don't want to make demands of you, and that's not my intention here; but I want to tell you something that I need you to do to me: I want you to punish me so severely that you leave marks all over my body (parts that can be covered by clothes, please).

I want, if it pleases you, for you to tell me how I earned my punishment and how I can please you better in the future. This would reinforce my submission to you and would arouse me so much so that I would probably go crazy. I also long for you to bite the back of my neck so brutally that you leave bite marks and bruises.

Would you deny your naughty girl this opportunity for discipline and punishment that she longs for, needs, and deserves? Would dominating me in this way fulfill your desire? Would you enjoy inflicting that kind of pain onto your whore of a girl? Would you get really hard and excited doing these things to me??? Please tell me, Daddy!!

After you punish me, could you please make me take the dildo you showed me the other night up my wet pussy while you bite me some more? Then, do you think that you could please make me beg and plead for you to lick my clit and suck it while you pinch me and

pull at my hair?

And then, I would beg and plead with you to fuck my throbbing, dripping, nasty little pussy hole with your big, hot, raging cock, which I absolutely adore. What else would you need to do to me, Daddy? What more could I do for you? I know there must be more, and you always have the best, most exciting ideas about how to use and humiliate me.

Why didn't you push me to the point of using my safeword on Sunday? Did you feel I wasn't ready to be taken that far? Your threats keep me in a constant state of reflection and tension, which thrills me.

Very sincerely and warmly,

kate

Subject: Tonight
Date: Fri, 17 Sep

Dearest Daddy:

I want you to know that I am very excited about seeing you tonight. I also have a lot of angst wondering about your plans for me. I know that you will treat me like a whore and punish me like a bad, bad girl; but there's a part of me that's reluctant and afraid of how that experience will unfold (though you say that my fear is not your concern).

I know that you want to treat me like your slave daughter; and I know that you will do whatever derives you pleasure and will use me in whatever way that suits and excites you. And I want that, badly. I want you to take whatever you want, Daddy. I will try my very hardest to endure whatever you inflict, and will desperately try to please and satisfy you. Please don't be too hard on me, Daddy.

Last night I sat in my hot tub and fantasized about you. You collared me and held onto the collar. You brought me to my knees and fucked my cunt mouth while you held me by the collar and my hair. You also made me press my pussy up against the water jet and have a nasty little girl orgasm right in front of You, which I loved. It made me moan and pant like a bitch. There was more, but I don't really have time to write about it right now.

I also talked to myself a bit about my fantasies, at your suggestion. I got a few answers, though some were terribly vague and un-formed. I will tell you later if you want to hear.

I will prepare your dinner tonight, Sir. I have to go now. But you might be interested to know that ever since you fingered my pussy hole yesterday, it has been dripping, throbbing, and steaming hot, and all I can do is think about the nasty things that I want to do to you and that I long for you to do to me.

Until tonight . . .

kate xxx

Subject: My ass
Date: Sun, 19 Sep 1999

Dear Daddy:

I just wanted to answer your question about my reaction to having your finger up my ass recently. It felt very nice to have your finger up my tight virgin ass hole. It felt really soothing, nasty, and made me pant and moan, Daddy. Almost anything feels nice and turns me on, as long as something is shoved up my pussy hole or rubbing against my clit at the same time. That plug you have, though, looks way too big for my butt. What do you think, Daddy?

I had a nice time visiting with you and sleeping in Daddy's bed. It felt too good. I will invite you to my house for dinner next, and to

spend the night. I hope that you will honor me with your presence and I will be exceptionally submissive if you come over. I plan to masturbate right in front of you in the hot tub, at your direction.

I am going to write a story about my little horny girl with the secretly dripping wet pussy. I have gotten a clearer vision of her lately. You are very sweet to offer to play out my fantasies with me. I do want to take advantage of your offer, as long as it still stands.

This morning when you fucked me so aggressively, I imagined that you were raping my virgin pussy hole. My clit and hips quivered and I was speechless. You were entirely focused on shooting your hot cum in my filthy little cunthole because you know what a horny slut I am, and because you want to fuck Your little bitch, Daddy, and use my hole for Your pleasure. That's true, isn't it?

I need more spankings, Daddy. I have been so, so, so bad to gush hot pussy juice all over your naked lap, your cock, and your fingers. I love rubbing my bare pussy all over you, Daddy. I want to cry out for you every time my pussy starts throbbing and leaking. I want you to punish me in the shower, Daddy. I want you to whip me while I fuck myself with the shower head. I have a lot of fantasies that I want to share with you. That's just one.

I had better run. Dear Daddy, would you please write me back and tell me what you would most like to do to me that you haven't done yet? I would love to hear from you on that, and on any other subject for that matter.

Your baby pussy daughter

Subject: Peep show
Date: Tue, 21 Sep

Dear Galen:

If you don't have lunch plans, could we meet somewhere, at some

time designated by you, Daddy? I wore a special bra in your honor today and will show it to you if you meet me. I also want you to look under my skirt and I plan to give you more than one opportunity to do so.

Let me know if you get this message in time.

Sincerely,

Your daughter

Subject: Bad girl!
Date: Tue, 21 Sep

Dear slut girl,

Daddy's been out of town since yesterday, and won't return until late afternoon. Sorry to miss the peep show. You're a very bad girl, to suggest such things to your Daddy and I feel you need some severe punishment right on your slutty, dripping cunt.

I know you're a whore and can't help it. So, even though you leave me no choice but to rape you—when you exhibit yourself so shamelessly (Daddy's only human after all)—such bad behavior will require a stern spanking and other painful tortures that I will inflict.

Regards,

Daddy

Subject: Spanking, etc . . .
Date: Tue, 21 Sep

Dear slut,

520

I think your first anal training went very well. I am sure my little daughter's ass will be able to, and then yearn to have my cock deep up it. But I will keep your training slow and gentle. The ass is one of the most dense never centers in the body.

Think of the possibilities, once you are relaxed and we have worked to stretch the little bitch's ass a little more each time. And as you say, Daddy will give you permission to fuck yourself with the dildo and vibrator at the same time I'm inserting something up your ass. Soon my little slut will have three holes to offer for Daddy's pleasure.

So you liked how I raped your tight cunt the other morning? At times I'll enjoy using you, suddenly, ruthlessly, just taking out my animal need on your willing body. I will use you any time I choose, in the way I choose.

If you hold to your promise to be exceptionally submissive, I will come for dinner. Actually, I will enforce the promise myself. Whip you while you fuck yourself with the showerhead? No problem. I'll whip you hard until you cum.

Don't worry bitch, when I get you in total privacy, I'm going to paddle and spank my whore's ass good. You've got a lot coming, that I have been saving up for you. Spanking you and other punishments will help you behave like a proper submissive daughter. When is Daddy's submissive little girl going to be available for him to use again?

Warm regards,

Galen

Subject: Please scold me.
Date: Wed, 22 Sep

Dear Galen:

About your letters—I best loved the part where you admonished me for behaving like a nasty bad girl, and told me that you would punish me for it and would teach me how to behave like a 'proper submissive daughter."

And your suggestion that, with 'slow and gentle training,' I will be able to take your cock up my ass, intrigued me. Even though I am not so confident as you are about it, your confidence did inspire me a lot and motivate me to want to try to work up to it.

I can't wait until you get me in total privacy so that you can spank my ass really, really good, as you promised. My pussy drips and longs for you, Daddy.

Your hot little slut xx

Subject: About my duties
Date: Mon, 27 Sep

Dear Sir,

May I please say a few words about yesterday when you pulled down my pants, bent me over the sink and raped my cunt? I really deserved all of it. You need to give me pain like that and I have to accommodate you. You pounded my hole harder and deeper than it ever got it before, and the pain almost made me cry.

I feel that I must submit like a trapped animal when you want to fuck me and use my body for your pleasure, because you're the Daddy and I'm just the little girl and I don't have many choices. But I know that you aren't going to hurt me more than I can take it, Dear Daddy, so I try to please you so that you'll not be too hard on me.

But what if I really, really, really was a very bad, bad, bad girl, and deserved it completely; would you then hurt me so bad that I would

never be so bad again? I don't know what I might do to disappoint
you so, but I bet if I did you would really show me, Daddy,
wouldn't you?

Please write me back and tell me if you're happy with my pussy; I
want to hear it. And after I read your response, as to my cunt and
my throat, and whatever else about my body, I will go into the hot
tub and think very, very bad little cuntgirl thoughts about you and
your big fucking cock fucking me all over and your hands all over
me—grabbing me, slapping me, pulling my hair, pinching.

You really turn me on when you hold my head down while I take
you down my throat, or when you hold my head down on the bed or
the table. Tell me about what it does for you. It makes me feel
totally vulnerable and weak while you feel so so strong over me,
taking me. I want to be taken and be made to surrender. That's one
of the most satisfying aspects of sex for me.

kate

Subject: Daddy
Date: Tue, 28 Sep

Dear Daddy:

I had a very nice time with you last night. You were sweet to hold
me and be so tender with me when I was feeling kind of sad and
exasperated with everything that's going on in my life right now.

I am concerned that you are encouraging me to get attached to you
now, Daddy; and, in light of what we said our boundaries were at
the outset of our sexual involvement, I think that we should talk
about this soon.

I feel like I am looking to you for support and comfort and want to
at least understand what I am doing here, and stay aware of myself
in this process so that I don't lose touch with my needs, motives and

actions concerning you. I need to set some boundaries for myself around this, but am unsure what they should be.

I am also afraid of getting attached at this time, but cannot deny that it is starting tohappen for me, and I promised that I would tell you if this happened. What are your thoughts and feelings about it? Please be honest with me and don't hold back your opinion.

I really would like to hear from you. You probably think that I am kind of an email pest, but apparently that isn't stopping me from being one.

One last thing. . .you love shoving your fully hard cock all the way down my cunt throat, don't you? I can tell how it pleases you to do that, how it satisfies you. Maybe you can put your finger up my ass next time you fuck me from behind, which I hope will be very soon. Have a nice visit with your kids tonight.

Sincerely,

Your horny girl

Subject: Nonattachment.
Date: Tue, 28 Sep

Dear daughter,

Those are certainly complex and important questions for such a little girl to be concerned about. You are a smart girl.

The same thoughts are on my mind. The longer we continue to see each other the more these types of questions will arise, and become increasingly complex and creep into immediacy. It is good to re-examine our original intent.

I will say that I am enjoying your company immensely. I enjoy

talking with you, hanging out with you. I feel we are just beginning to explore the D/s, the Daddy/daughter, BDSM, and rough sex; but every encounter has been exciting and satisfying. You have also been so supportive of me, tender, kind, generous, flattering and I have a great appreciation of you for that as well.

I feel both our individual situations and the unique way our situations overlap make it complicated to understand what the future would allow us in a relationship. Ultimately, we may find ourselves on different paths, but I'm not looking that far ahead right now.

I enjoy the romance that we are sharing. I feel I need to stay open to non-attachment as well. I don't claim to understand how to do that dance very well, but I feel that is really the only way this experience between us should proceed, until either of us can't continue in that emotional ambiguity any longer. I am open to a boundary discussion.

Daddy's tired now. I had a very good day as well. I feel much clearer, stronger. You should know that your coming to me last night and the pleasure of your company were valuable to me.

In closing, I will say that my daughter's throat is so good to Daddy. There are times when I have just fucked it so hard, so deep, forcing your head down, using you fiercely, with my pleasure my only concern. Your eagerness to serve me in this way pleases me. I have never fucked a slut's throat so hard, as my little daughter's. I see you have a growing interest in being trained anally. It will be my pleasure to continue your education.

Warmly,

Daddy

Subject: Wise Daddy
Date: Wed, 29 Sep

Dear Daddy:

You are sweet. I appreciate your letter to me very, very much. You are so smart and wise about things. Your response made me more comfortable with the situation between us. I like the idea of talking about boundaries, and about expectations.

I want each of us to avoid making assumptions about the other, or making assumptions about the nature of this relationship between us. That way, we can be on the same page, or at least know that we aren't. More about that later.

What's more important right now is the fact that my cunt is throbbing and is very, very steamy wet right now. Oh!! I just can't stand it!! I want to moan and whimper for you to tear off my panties and rape me, Daddy.

Right this second I would kiss you all over your chest and belly; then I would kiss and lick all over your hips and around your groin. When I finish there, my mouth would drool for your hard, throbbing cock to penetrate it; and my lips would latch onto the tip of your dick and suck, suck, suck and tongue it, around and around, until it grew even harder and more huge, and throbbed even more.

You wouldn't stand for it and would have to thrust my head down into your pelvis so that my throat and neck engulfed your whole rod, my sweet, cruel Daddy. I would have to keep my tongue and throat going and focused on Your pleasure. I would only come up for air when I absolutely had to because I don't dare interrupt Your pleasure.

You also would use one of those leather straps on me while I suck you and if I begin to lose momentum you would remind me of my place and of my responsibility to please You without reserve. You would also put me on my back and pound fuck my mouth like a whore's pussy and I would love it like a whore.

I enjoy reading your work. I had a very wet pussy by the time I finished reading the last piece you sent me, and longed for your

hands and cock to make use of my wetness in ways only You can. I am trying to please you, and hope that I am succeeding. A little girl longs to please her Daddy and keep him on her good side so that he will indulge her and treat her kindly.

But we both know that a little girl also wants desperately to be put in her place and reminded of her place constantly by her strong, strict and sometimes cruel Daddy. Naughty, spoiled little girls want to be second only to their Daddies, and they want their Daddies to need and to want their pussies, their mouths, and their titties and nipples; little girls also need to be fucked brutally by their Daddies on nearly a daily basis.

Little girls so desire for their Daddies to penetrate their little pussies with big, foreign objects and to examine their little girls' reactions to their Daddies using them in this way. Little girls want their Daddies to be perverted and to corrupt their little girls' virtue.

They also want their Daddies to sneak up on them and attack them, trap them, and rape them no matter what the little girl says she wants. Did you know that little girls wanted so much???? But that's not all, because they want even more.

Sincerely,

Your horny little bad girl

Subject: Reflecting on last night . . .
Date: Sun, 3 Oct

Dear Galen:

Thank you again for a nice time last night and this morning. I am still wet and have been thinking about rubbing the vibrator wildly on my throbbing clit while you finger my asshole and scold me for being such a whore. I did find some solace in my hot tub this morning, though. But, as usual, no amount of pussy and clit

stimulation ever seems to be enough for this slut.

Sincerely,

Your nasty little whore.

Subject: Tonight?
Date: Sun, 3 Oct

Dear slut:
If you wish to come over, what time? I enjoyed our evening as well.

Galen

Subject: Wet daughter
Date: Sun, 3 Oct

Sir:

What if I come by at about 8 or 8:30 p.m.? I would really like to take you out for a drink tonight; what do you think? Maybe you just want to stay at your house and don't want any hassle? Please tell me what you want, Sir.

I know that you have to punish me because my dog busted the screen door last night and you had to fix it. I will graciously accept any punishment you inflict.

I am also a bad girl for thinking that I can make you fuck me when I want it. I need to be taught a lesson about being more submissive and respectful. I should probably have to beg you to finger my pussy and my ass hole; and maybe you should even force me to beg and plead with you before you indulge me in that way.

But I also want to beg and plead with you not to shove your finger

528

in my ass, or not to take my panties down; would you then react by hitting and slapping me and by scolding me severely me for not being totally submissive??

I also want you to trick me into letting you touch my cunt through my pants, and my titties through my top, if it would please you to indulge this whore in that way. Then, once you see that I like it, you slap me so hard because you realize that I am a total, dirty whore, and not an innocent little girl like I wanted you to believe that I was.

Your slippery, dripping cuntgirl

Subject: Your transgressions.
Date: Sun, 3 Oct

Dear slut,

You do deserve and need some painful punishments for all those transgressions, inappropriate desires and such nasty, slutty thoughts.

Be here by 8:30 tonight. I think the above will take precedent over meeting for a drink in public, don't you?

Daddy

Subject: Rain
Date: Wed, 6 Oct

Dear Galen:

I definitely felt better after talking to you today. I am grateful for you, for your patience, understanding, and good advice. I did obey you and took a minute or two to get some perspective after we hung up, and I felt much, much better after that and after our conversation, really.

I absolutely needed to talk about the stuff concerning my husband and get feedback (maybe the problem is that he won't talk about it with me, and when I try to talk to him, it just hurts and annoys me so much because he can't talk about anything).

I didn't spend the time I really needed to spend on these issues in my women's group last night, and I just hadn't finished dealing with it (not that I think I am now 'finished' with it, but at least I got a lot of it out of my system for the present). Thank you, Daddy, for being interested in my stuff. You help make me feel safer and less alone, which naturally feels really very, very nice to me.

I really love the way you touch me, too. I still don't understand how you know all the right ways to do it, and how you know all the best things to say to get me excited and make me feel so, so good.

Your obvious pleasure and excitement that you derive from punishing me turns me on completely. I wish that I understood why I like all that punishment and rough treatment so much. I want to show you my appreciation by doing my best to give you much pleasure.

The rain outside is cozy to me. Do you like it? I wish that you were here right now, Galen.

Sincerely,

Your slutty baby with a very wet, longing pussy that needs you desperately. . .

Subject: Thinking of You.
Date: Thu, 7 Oct

Dearest Galen:

Do you think about me a lot? I only ask because it seems that I think about you quite a lot.

530

I have a big deadline coming up next week at work. In a sick way, I am excited by the pressure. It is reminiscent of my craving for punishment.

Anyway, I was thinking about you and writing some poems about you. The poems honor You, your Manhood, and your power over me. They try to describe those images in beautiful ways, because the feelings they stir in me are among life's ultimate treasures.

Gotta go. I can almost hear your voice and feel your breath against my neck right now.

Very truly,

Your cunt

Subject: Dressing like your whore
Date: Wed, 13 Oct

Dear Strong, Sweet, Strict, and Merciful Daddy:

I wore my garter and nylons to work today without any panties. This has made me horny and wet throughout much of today. I've found, however, that I do better at work when I don't create these kinds of distractions for myself. So, next time I might think twice before wearing this again to work.

I wait with great anticipation to see you later today, though I hope it is sooner rather than later. I want to sniff your scent and feel your skin. I want to feel the hard, pounding warmth of your stiff cock against my panties and then against my skin. I want you to punish me and rape me tonight, and be really rough with me, Daddy, if it pleases you. I have been very, very bad today.

Will you make me tell you what I was thinking, Sir, while I was in court today with my skirt and no panties, and that garter belt

hugging my hips? I know that you will and that you will conclude that I am just a hopelessly filthy little whore who needs her Daddy to discipline her.

Daddies need to show their little girls how to be good and submissive by roughing them up and showing them how weak they are compared to their Daddies; don't you think???

Galen, you are definitely my favorite Daddy of all time and I really appreciate you and all the happiness, excitement and satisfaction that you have given me during the past several months. You're Mastering my pussy!

Yours truly,

kate

(*Note: Kate drove me 100 miles to the closest major airport, where I was to depart for my trip to see my sister and Arlana(see chapter 3)).*

Subject: Red toy
Date: Thu, 14 Oct

Dear Daddy:

Thank you so very much for the wonderful gift of your red toy, which I used on the drive home today. I had the hardest, nastiest orgasm and it made me very, very happy. I smiled and even laughed afterwards at the thought that I could cum just anywhere.

I imagine that you are well rested now and looking forward to your vacation in Canada. That is how I see you, and I hope that it is so.

Little girl

Subject: Blessing
Date: Fri, 15 Oct

Dear little slut,

Daddy takes delight in what a whore you are. What a decadent little
bitch you are. I so enjoy degrading and abusing you, slapping and
beating you, hurting your tits, and your slippery cunt, forcing my
cock down your cunt throat. You are such a bad girl, for invoking
Daddy's perversion to turn his daughter into a pain slut. Not that
it's been difficult.

You have been a blessing in my life in many ways. I've never had a
woman be so supportive and tender to me. I would have felt so
lonely and isolated over the past months, without the pleasure of my
little daughter.

It might have been unbearable, as it has still been a terrible time in
many ways, these last six months. I thought I had endured all that I
could before I left my marriage. But I have endured, thanks to you
and others who have been so lovingly supportive to me.

It's deep soap here, already. I am gathering my strength to stay
above it, and try to bring about some good, here. My sister is in
deep pain and is so angry at the world, so consumed by bitterness
and loneliness. I will try my best to help her.

You are a submissive angel of mercy!

Bless you,

Daddy

Subject: Dearest Daddy
Date: Sun, 17 Oct 1999 16:52:31 EDT

Dear Daddy:

Hi. I really need my Daddy tonight. I need more than just one spanking. I think I need about 100 slaps, smacks and swats all over my bad girl skin. My pussy is slippery and wet right now for you. Too bad you can't run your hands and fingers all over it. I want you to run your finger around and around my clit and my cunt hole. This would cause me to squirm uncontrollably, Daddy.

You would see me lose control and would want to hit me and punish me in many ways to show me how you control my pleasure and my suffering. I would love every minute of it, too, Daddy, because I would be so aroused. I want to kiss, suck and lick your big cock. Mmmmm . . . I think that might make you smile and feel very pleased with your little daughter, yes?

Do you want to put my pussy and ass in bondage and paddle me all over, Daddy? You know I need, deserve and want it, don't you? I also need to be slapped in the face when I don't say what pleases you or when I talk back to you. I need you to teach me how to behave like a good daughter for her Daddy. I want to be a good girl. I want to be a bad girl.

I am really enjoying the red toy, Daddy. It gives me so much pleasure. And when I rub it on myself I pretend you are right at my side saying nasty and perverted things to me while I play with my little girl pussy.

Then, I just lose it and have my dirty orgasm and I moan and groan for you Daddy, as I lose control to You. I just let my clit take over and all I can think of is fucking, being smothered by a Your total control, all the stimulation to my clit, my hot throbbing cunthole, and how I want to rub my clit all over my Daddy's lap. I wish you were here right now so I could show you.

Well, how is your vacation? I hope that you ended up having some closeness with your sister and other relatives; how has that gone? What have you been up to? Will you still see Arlana? When? Are you feeling peaceful mostly? Or have you had a lot of angst?

My husband is all moved out. His attitude has been mostly grumpy and difficult these last couple of weeks, and those characteristics were at an all time high this weekend.

Today's arrival seemed like a great relief. I have a lot of relief and happiness about this day. But, I also had a moment of feeling an overwhelming loss and sadness and then kind of a numbness. Tomorrow night when my son goes to his dad's, I think that things will seem very, very strange. This is one of those times of transition where there are good and bad parts and I just have to experience both.

If you aren't too busy, could you call me tonight after 10:00 p.m.? I would love to hear your voice. Would you talk dirty to me while I play with the toy??

One last thought. I am sure that you haven't forgotten this, but I am still having some worries about it. Please, if fate has it that you must put your cock in some other girl's pussy (or other hole below the belt) please, Daddy, please, use a condom, or even two condoms. My hole and bill of health are clean and there's no way I want to jeopardize that. Since you are my Daddy, isn't it natural that you want to protect me?

Daddy's hot little pussy girl

Subject: Toygirl
Date: Sun, 17 October

Dear little slut,

It's about 11pm here. I won't make it to 12 p.m. I'm so sleepy, so I won't call tonight. Plus, my sister only has a phone in her living room, and with her there it would not be easy to talk about anything, but especially about what a naughty little girl you are.

535

I will certainly take the measures to insure my little bitch understands clearly, that she is at Daddy's mercy, fair or not. When we are together again, you can be assured that your cunt, ass and tits will be whipped hard. And if your cunt is wet as a result, Daddy will beat his little cunt daughter harder. Then I will use you for my pleasure, just as I beat you for my pleasure. I wish I could do that to you right now. You're being such a slut, abusing Daddy's toy so frequently.

How can Daddy's girl be such a whore, wishing to be slapped around, beaten, and to have her mouth used like a cunt? I'm going to punish my little girl severely when I get back. You are such a fucking whore.

I miss my sweet little tender girl. I am both sad and happy about being here, and my life in general. I feel I'm on the brink, but haven't a clue about what fate lies over the edge.

Tomorrow night, when you are alone, think of me thinking of you, in all of the above ways, both tender and cruel. Grieve truly. Let it out. Know that your Daddy is with you in spirit, supports and understands you, and his body will be back soon.

Good night little girl. You are in my thoughts and prayers.

Love,

Daddy

Subject: Missing you
Date: Mon, 18 Oct

Dear Galen:

I didn't hear from you today at work. I left early, though. I am at home working on another appeal. I miss you an awful lot and that is why I am writing to you. I want to ask you, no to beg you, to

please call me tonight Daddy. I want to hear your voice.

Your bad, bad little girl

Subject: Impulsive slip of my tongue/fingers
Date: Mon, 18 Oct

Daddy—

I apologize for begging you to call me tonight. You realize, of course, that you need not call. I realize you are busy. Although it would please me to hear from you when you get a chance to call me, I didn't mean to put you in any position to feel like I need you to call, because I don't need you to. I feel that I may have sent the wrong message in that respect. If I did, I am sorry.

My cunt is steaming hot and has been constantly since last night, when I played with my new toy, again. I really love it and can't believe that I have never had one and used it A LOT. This might have kept me out of bad relationships, but I don't know.

Anyway, my pussy was so slippery, so dripping wet. I just had to lick my fingers after I rubbed myself so intensely. How I wished you had your fingers up my ass and pussy, Galen, while I pressed and wiggled the vibrator on my clit. I found out something new about my orgasm. I will tell you later. I have to go.

kate

Subject: Checking up on you.
Date: Mon, 18 Oct

Dear little bitch,

Sorry I haven't been able to phone. The situation isn't good here

for that, as I said. I had hoped to catch you today, when I called in, but Paul was there, so I talked with him. I decided that it would not be discrete to ask for you afterwards. I felt you there, though and wished I could have spoken to my little girl.

I appreciate how considerate you are, to have sent me your second email. You are a wise soul, to have so evolved how you think about things. I will communicate with you everything you wish to know when I return, regardless of whether I am able to call or email before then.

I am leaving tomorrow for Canada. I imagine on some level, that you might feel jealous and hurt in some way. I understand that you might feel more vulnerable right now, because of your own circumstances. I admire your courage and honesty to deal with this openly. You are still Daddy's special little slut, and he both cares about you and looks forward to using his little bitch, very soon.

Warmly,

Daddy.

p.s. Daddy promises to practice safe sex, if that were necessary. I give you my word.

Subject: Weekend
Date: Thu, 21 Oct

Dear Daddy:

I filed for a thirty-day extension of time on the appeal. So, this weekend I can rest and not worry about it. I hate to put it off, but really need some time off, so I am sure I did the right thing under the circumstances. Paul was sweet and understanding, as usual.

I wrote you a long letter. I had to explore my feelings for you because of all the conflicting emotions and thoughts I have on the

topic, especially very recently. I sorted out some of it just by writing about it, but I need to share it with you, eventually, so that you can draw your own conclusions and make your own informed decisions about me and you.

I can give it to you on Saturday, or if you want to read it sooner, just let me know and I can send it. In any event, I can pick you up at the airport and then even enjoy the weekend without any work (unbelievable!).

Your bad little girl xxoo

Subject: Dear little one
Date: Thu, 21 Oct

I was just about to send the letter below, when I saw your email. Good girl for doing what you had to do to take the pressure off. I am glad you can meet me on Saturday! Your long letter sounds a little ominous, but I know your intent, as is mine, is to be honest and clear. You can send the letter along. I will deal with it no matter what it concludes.

Dear little one,

I was sad that you are feeling so down right now, and I am not there to soothe you. I know how bleak life can feel, and lonely and hopeless. I want you to know you have my love and support, I care about you, find you desirable and stimulating, sexy, and deliciously perverted.

I know you are a loving, dedicated mother to your children, both human and canine. Plus you are a damn good lawyer, and a compassionate, noble human being. Dwell on all the good in your life, dear, for it is large.

You might be happy to know that I will not have sex with Arlana, and will probably not even play with her. This is too complicated to

explain here. This may not give you comfort, but it is said with that intent. Our relationship is evolving into one of soulful allies, and I am having a great time on that level. She is well connected with the scene in London, Canada and San Francisco, knows a lot of media, and authors, and is going to help promote the book when it is finished.

I hope you will soon feel strong and happy again. I hope to be able to contribute to that cause, very soon. I'll call or email my final travel plans. I miss you and hope that we can arrange to see each other Saturday night.

Warmly,

Galen

Subject: 2 letters
Date: Fri, 22 Oct

Dear, Sweet, Strong Daddy:

I will send this letter, as I promised. I wrote it yesterday before I got your letter. A lot of it sounds rambling and unfocussed, but I struggled with the daunting task of trying to put my very conflicting feelings into words. I resolved a good deal of the conflict just by acknowledging it.

I know I thanked you already, but I have to say again how much warmth and joy your letter brought me yesterday. I was just starting to feel more like myself anyway, and your sentiments and words carried me further down my healing path. You helped me to re-member the good in my life.

I am very grateful to you, and for you. I really did hug your letter, really, really tightly, and for a long while, too. Your kind words made me smile, made me feel stronger, and made me feel much more content.

I hadn't wanted to disrupt your vacation and understood that you needed time away. I hope that sharing my troubles with you didn't undermine your needs and goals for your trip. All I can offer you, if I did that, is my body for your pleasure and revenge . . .

I am very excited about seeing and serving you tomorrow night, Galen. I know you understand just what I need, so I won't resist. Please understand that I am not altogether my usual self; and I ask for your forgiveness, in advance, for being somewhat weak right now.

I can't wait to put my arms around you and sit on your lap, Daddy, and to feel your arms wrapped around me. I want to feel you bite me. I want you to mark me like your property, to whip me, suck me and to make me suffer for you. I want to feel you all the way up inside of me, Daddy, no matter how much it hurts. I crave it.

I will run that vibrator all over my pussy lips and my clit right in front of you. You will have to punish me because I am such a dirty whore for wanting to stimulate myself to the point of losing all control and cumming all over my panties and my sheets like a dripping, nasty little slut girl. And I really want you to see me be so bad, Daddy. Do you like putting your finger up my ass? I dream about that, want that.

I await tomorrow with great anticipation. I hope you have a peaceful and safe journey home.

kate

Here's the letter I wrote yesterday:

_____

Dear Daddy:

Thanks for calling me today and spending time trying to console me. You are very sweet and I sincerely appreciate your advice and insight. I just need to stick this out and I'm sure that in time I will

feel more of the positive effects of the situation I have chosen for myself. I have absolutely no doubt that I have made the right decision regarding my marriage, but I did not expect that the consequences would include all this sadness and adjustment.

I find that my sadness really stems from my inexperience at being alone, on my own. I resist it but I crave it, too. I know that I need to learn about myself, develop my individuality and all those important character-building things; but, due to my inexperience and circumstances up until now, I am not experienced at flying solo.

The time I made my husband go to my first day of my first college class ever, serves as a pretty good example of what a frightened baby I am about facing new experiences alone; I just have never chosen to operate that way.

I do believe in the positive and necessary aspects of being a strong, independent person; but during these past few days, all that I have found in this experience presents me with grief, despair and a stinging feeling of alone-ness. I know that I will come through this phase a much stronger and wiser soul, and that belief provides some hope during this trying time.

In truth, your absence during this time is really for the best; if you were here, I would certainly try to run away from all the pain and struggle by distracting myself with you. While it sounds appealing and comforting, and even though I long for that, it would just undermine my opportunity to make this transition by toughing it out on my own. Each day has been a little easier and I am sure that means that I am getting stronger.

I realize now that I have repressed a lot of the pain and sadness surrounding the loss of my relationship with my husband. It has been difficult coming to terms with the knowledge that I will not continue on with him in my life, that I do not want to continue that way. Inherent in this truth is my realization that I have suffered inside of myself so deeply and for so long about this relationship. Much of my grief stems from that understanding.

I often let things eat me up, make me sick, sometimes, before I deal with them. This makes me feel so sad, so weak and so helpless. I want to be stronger. But recognizing the sources of my pain helps me feel better because at least I stay present with myself, listen to myself and stay engaged in processing the sadness; and I become stronger.

I really am more confused now than ever about my feelings toward you as well. On the one hand, I really care for you deeply and I long to be with you. I think of you very, very frequently, and am always amazed at how I so frequently slip into sweet daydreams about you, regardless of where I am or who is around.

You are on my mind so much—too much I am sure. I have tried really hard to set boundaries around my contact with you for this reason, but, as I told you, I have not been successful. I have been too emotionally driven and impulsive to set the boundary in the first instance, let alone to respect it.

I want you desperately; but I don't want to want you so much that I have to suffer grief over it when you leave, or when I want to be with you and can't. I suspect that the reason that I am having such a problem at this moment with my feelings toward you, Galen, is because I have judged my weak reaction to my alone-ness as a sign of unhealthy dependence.

My longing for you reminds me that I am weak somehow. I even attribute my decision to stay so long in my dysfunctional marriage as a symptom of this weakness My weakness has made it very hard for me this week to cope with just being alone. So on some level, these strong feelings that I have for you feel very threatening to me.

I promised myself that I would not get involved with you or anyone for at least a year after I ended my relationship with my husband. I rationalized, though, that I could get sexually involved with you and could avoid any significant attachment.

That might have worked for a short while, but at this point, I have failed to live up to my expectations. I have considered, planned,

over and over, to just tell you that I need to stop seeing you, or need to see you only once in a while, or would not see you until I split up with my husband; but I never follow through and I never even decide that it is what I want, because it is not really what I want.

I just sometimes feel that I need to step back so that I can figure out what it is I am doing. My desires to be close to you, to experience the sexual encounters with you, to be pleased by you and to please you, cause me to continue pursuing you.

Since you went away, I have resented myself and you (sorry) because now, I feel like not only am I struggling to keep my strong feelings toward you at bay (my own failing struggle to keep from becoming attached to you), but recently I have felt the added pain of knowing that I am directing my tender sentiments at a person who wants to go and be with somebody else.

I realize that it is more complex than that, but that's one way I see it. Even as I write this I wonder if I will have the courage to send it to you. I don't want to feel this way, I don't want to feel jealousy about you while I am trying to not feel too strongly toward you, which I feel I need to do in order to protect myself. Does this make sense to you?

I want to not care about all these things; I want to have the ability to just shut the feelings on and off when it serves me. I want to be able to not care about you going to meet Arlana; and I don't want to miss you. But, none of those 'wants' are true for me. That's not how I feel. I feel hurt, confused and angry. So, the long and short of it is that this is a bigger dilemma than I anticipated.

I want to deal with this situation honestly, even if it means that you may decide that we shouldn't be lovers anymore. I know that you warned me not to become attached to you, and I really have tried to keep things in check with that. But my attachment level has deepened with time and the truth is that now I feel a strong attachment to you.

It could be that it feels more intense just because of the other

circumstances in my life right now, the other struggles and changes; maybe my bond with you has taken on greater proportion and significance, as some kind of a diversion mechanism, I don't know. But if that is the case, I need to be really cautious, because I want to get my intentions straight where you are concerned.

I can't pretend to completely understand what is going on in my head about you. I just know that I have deeper feelings for you than I planned on having at the outset, when we agreed to non-attachment, and I really need to take everything very, very slowly, and to spend a lot of time getting strong in myself and in my independence. My feelings toward you seem beautiful and at the same time threatening to me.

So, in closing, I will say that I look forward to seeing you on Saturday. I want to hug and kiss you and to feel you right up against me. I want you to spank me and to hold me and to hurt me and to fuck me, Daddy.

Well, this letter was going to be one or two sentences, but I really needed to get all this off of my chest in order to move ahead. I won't blame you if you decide that the time has come to cut me off if you don't want to deal with my attachment issues.

Your very bad, good girl

Subject: Tonight
Date: Sat, 23 Oct

Dear daughter,

Thank you for your heartfelt letters, your courage and honesty at expressing and coping with all your conflicted feelings right now. I understand, daughter, and support you in whatever direction you need to take this relationship between us.

I, too, have struggled with my feelings for you. We are both in a

vulnerable state right now. I just want you to know how much I care about you and appreciate you.

I am leaving for the airport shortly. I hope the standby status goes smoothly, and that I return home in a timely fashion. I can't wait to see you.

Warm regards,

Daddy

Subject: Hot clit
Date: Mon, 25 Oct

Dear Daddy:

You are so kind, Master, for supporting my desperate and frenzied need for stimulation this morning by your red toy. Having you hold me and use my titties, pinch them, bite them, and scold me for being a wet slut who just wants to spread her slippery pussy lips open for her strong Daddy . . .

I want to come to you right now and suck on your cock like a fucking whore. Then, after I sucked you long and hard, you would grab me, push me, and throw me down and slap me; then you'd spread my legs apart VERY forcefully and spank my pussy before your would bang my hole with your fingers—as many of them as you could ram in there—and your hand, too, if you could. Then, your cock would be raging because I would be cumming by now and you would probably turn me over and want to take me like a dog!!

Sweetly,

Your little girl

Subject: Your animal
Date: Tue, 26 Oct

Dear Daddy:

I went into the hot tub last night after I finished working. I fantasized about you and I came so hard, moaning and groaning like a
animal. I have never masturbated so much in my whole life as I
have during the past months since I met you and discovered the toy.
You do make me so nasty, Daddy. Please, tell me why I am such a
whore.

I can't wait until you put my pussy and ass in bondage for work
tomorrow. It will make me so hot and wet for you, Daddy. Maybe
at lunch time tomorrow I can go to your house and get raped by
you, Daddy; what do you think?

I look forward to seeing you tonight. You are the kindest, sweetest
Daddy in the world; you take care of my pussy so well and have
been so patient in teaching me how to behave like a submissive
daughter should behave for her Daddy. I want to please you and
your big cock, Daddy . . . I have to go but I have a big kiss that I
will save for you until later.

Your little fuck bitch

Subject: Longing for Daddy
Date: Tue, 26 Oct

Dear Daddy:

I am having trouble concentrating. All I can think of is your cock,
your hands, your voice and your mouth. What a weak slut I am.

I would love to read a nasty email from you. Will you send me one,
please? Just a short one???

Your bad, bad, bad girl.

p.s. I loved it so much when you scolded me so harshly and spanked my pussy the other day while I got off on your vibrator. Thank you so much for giving me so much satisfaction, Daddy. I'm sure that I don't deserve to be treated so well by you Daddy, since I am just such a bad little whore, made to be used and fucked and punished by her Daddy. Maybe I should pretend not to like it so much??

Subject: Please tell me
Date: Wed, 27 Oct

Dearest Daddy:

I have had such a very, very busy day today. I can't wait to get home and rest. You wore me out completely last night. My pussy, tits and neck and shoulders hurt today. My whole body feels used and abused, Daddy. It serves as a constant reminder today that you are in charge of my pain and my pleasure. When you come in my bed and fondle my pussy and my tits you leave me no choice but to behave like a filthy little slut.

I am ashamed of how wet my hole was last night, and of how the punishment you inflicted on me made me want to get punished more and get fucked so hard, so badly. I also feel very whorish and impure for wanting to slam my cunt and ass so hard against your cock while you fucked me like a dog bitch, like a fucking whore. I could not even begin to control myself, Daddy.

I plan to get right in the hot tub when I arrive home this evening, to soothe my sore body. I won't stop there though, Daddy. . . I will also press my ass and cunt so hard right up against the jets so that I can cum while I fantasize about you and all the very cruel and nasty things you do to me, you will do to me, and all the filthy, slutty things you make me do for you.

I really have enjoyed every moment that we have spent together, Daddy. You are so, so sweet and so stimulating to be around. I love what you say and do to me. I love your ideas and your visions. You are such a wonderful Daddy to me.

Sincerely,

Your very own fuckdoll

Subject: Telling you
Date: Wed, 27 Oct

Dear little fuck bitch,

You were a pleasure last night. I enjoyed torturing my little girl's tits, using the floggers and crop. You didn't like the crop very much, did you? You will find no sympathy, here, and can expect to have your tits cropped regularly. In suffering this, you serve me.

Your tits looked lovely tightly-bound, the array of clothespins, the butterfly clamps and then the weights. I took my sadistic pleasure in removing them and watching how much pain you wanted to submit to for me.

Next time, you are to look at me directly, as I remove each one. You will not deny me that pleasure. Consider this a command from your Master. Another dick-tate from your Lord, like the one that requires you to lick and suck your cum from my cock, after I've used my whore's cunt.

You looked terribly slutty, high heels, black briefs, poised against the wall, facing it with your ass sticking out for your paddling. Daddy believes his daughter's ass needs a good whipping on a regular basis for all the nasty, bad girl thoughts she dwells on everyday.

I'm thinking though, that I may need to start lighter, with my hand

or the small flogger and slowly build to the heavier equipment. I believe you could go far in your tolerance to take a beating that Daddy could give you, if we patiently find the right pathway. What do you think, daughter?

You can expect your torment to continue and increase at our next meeting.

Warmly (think bottom),

Daddy

Subject: Thank you
Date: Thu, 28 Oct

Dear Daddy:

Thank you so very much for the letter. It made my pussy drip for you. . .

Are you saying that you think the paddle is too much for my ass, Daddy? Why would you think this? Maybe I misunderstood. You suggested that your hand and the small flogger would provide a more appropriate means of punishing and beating this little girl at the outset. Is that right? With all due respect, Sir, I think that I can take whatever you dish out.

Well, I do want you to punish and beat me, since I am a girl who needs constantreminding of my place. You must know how much and how often I need your lessons and reminders. I want you to teach me my place; I need it. I am a spoiled and manipulative little girl and you will break me down into a submissive cunt for her Daddy.

All I can seem to think about is getting punished and fucked by you, my Daddy. You are such a benevolent, capable Daddy, so sweet, so handsome and so strong. I crave punishment from You. I want you

550

again and again, Dear Master. I want you to tie me up and take total and complete control over my body and mind. That would be bliss.

Truly Your slut

Subject: Hi Daddy.
Date: Fri, 29 Oct

Dear Daddy:

I was just reading your last letter to me. I still have questions about the part that reads:

> " I may need to start lighter, with my hand or the small flogger and slowly build to the heavier equipment. I believe you could go far in your tolerance. . ."

Well, my Daddy, I have a different sense of what you mean now. Is it that, during a session of my obedience training/punishment, you will begin by using your hand and then the frayed whip and then work up to the paddle and other "heavy equipment"?—i.e.., work up to all that during a single session? And drag it out longer that way, thinking that I can endure more if you approach it that way??

I think you do mean that, as opposed to what I thought you meant before, which was to suspend further paddling indefinitely until you got me more used to the other, 'lighter' means of torture and discipline.

The latter is not really what I desire, Daddy. I really do want to suffer, severely, for you. I want to show you how far I will go for you, and in return what I really want, is to know that you will take care of my pussy, and allow me to be my slutty little whore self for you, Daddy.

I need to be who I am, and I am just starting to really feel fulfilled,

sexually, for the very first time in my whole entire life; and I love it and I don't want to lose that. I cherish you, Daddy, for coming into my life and giving me this opportunity to serve you and to be ravaged by you! I desperately need you to bite me so, so hard the next time you see me.

I also love when you degrade me by talking to me like I am your little girl and your submissive whore. That, Daddy, pleases me so very much and invariably renders my pussy dripping, sopping wet. You must know that you can fuck my cunt and my mouth anytime Daddy, and that I am always ready and eager to give myself up to you.

I also want you to take it from me and force me to give it to you. . . but that is hard for me to play out because, since I am such a fucking horny slut by nature, I just tend to immediately want to offer it right up to you.

Maybe I should work a little bit on pretending that I don't want it. What do you think about that approach? Would you like that, or not? I also think that sometime I would like for you to sneak up on me, blindfold me, and then beat and rape me.

I know that I am a perverted, sick little girl, but thank goodness that I have such an understanding and indulgent Daddy to keep me in check.

Your devoted little girl

p.s. I loved the feel of your body next to mine all night long last night. Did you like sleeping in my new bed?? I liked having you there.

Subject: My dirty hole.
Date: Tue, 2 Nov

Dear Daddy:

552

I really loved all the dirty fucking this morning my Dear, Strong Daddy. And I love the Tetruss.

(*Note, the Tetruss is a portable, lightweight, freestanding suspension platform I invented and designed. Go to* <u>www.tetruss.com</u>*)*

Subject: You are Master
Date: Tue, 2 Nov

Dear Daddy:

I want you to know that I am thinking about you right now . . . about your big hard cock and your power over me. . . about your desire to punish and degrade me . . . and about your perverted wish to turn me into a submissive pain slut. I desire all that, and more. I love to suck and lick your cock after you use my pussy, and I appreciate that it is your rule, a requirement that I must follow.

I know that I am just a cunt, Daddy, and that you need to hurt and use my body for your satisfaction and amusement. It suits this slut that way. I want to be my Daddy's little slutty whore, with an insatiable appetite for pain, degradation, humiliation . . . I have an insatiable appetite for your cock, Master, any way I can get it.

Why does my pussy get so wet even when you don't even touch it? It must be for all the slutty, whorish, bad little girl thoughts that are constantly reeling around in my corrupt little head.

I would be honored and humbled for you to hurt and degrade me, my Daddy. I can't wait until you finish the Tetruss, so that you can carry out your plans for me. I know they are decadent and hope they are endless . . .

I imagine feeling your naked body rubbing all over mine. I melt when you scold me, and my cunt hole tightens up and throbs for you, Daddy, when you touch me and speak to me sternly, or sweetly.

I think that eventually I could cum at Your command; or, at least just from hearing you speak really, really, really nasty and threatening to me.

Thank you for inviting me to accompany you out of town. Can I be your little daughter next time we are alone together again? That is, if you will indulge me in that way. I think that you should lecture me about my attitude and purpose, and that you should make me say things to you about what a lowly little cunt I am, and what my purpose in life is (because I think I know, but need you to clarify things for me).

I think sweet thoughts about you. I melt as I imagine all the aggressive things you will do to me. . .

Your warm, wet, tight, throbbing sucking fuck hole girl

Subject: Housewarming
Date: Sun, 7 Nov

Dear Daddy:

I am all moved out except for a couple of items. I will try to go by and pick them up on the way home from work this evening. I hope to hear from you soon, and that you won't forget to call, like I did. I am so sorry for doing that. I hope that I can earn your complete forgiveness.

Would you bring me a housewarming gift tonight? Show up at my door; I will tuck the key beneath my mat. The housewarming gift cums when you climb into my bed and find your little girl waiting for you under the sheets . . . wearing just my warm, wet panties. Then you can give it to me!!

Thank you for punishing my body, Daddy. You left marks so that I couldn't forget what a submissive pain whore I am for you.

554

I am thinking about you, your energy, your body, your soul. I hope that your project is coming along very, very well right now.

I want to squeeze you cock as hard as I can with my cunt walls; I want you to command me to do it, and then to scold me for doing it. This fucking whore wants to take your whole cock in her pussy, and her mouth.

Will you stick your finger in my butt, Daddy? That makes me feel like a totally submissive bitch who can't do anything about what her Daddy does to her body and just has to take it and then cum all over her Daddy's hands and lap.

Yours truly,

whore daughter

Subject: Deserving
Date: Mon, 8 Nov

Dear Daddy:

Since you told me about your boys' letter, saying they don't want to see you, I have been very concerned about you. I want to help you and I want your boys to know that the information they've received is false. Of course, there is not much, if anything, that I can do to that end, but it is what I believe would be best for them. Their circumstance is so, so sad, Galen.

I know how much you love your children and how much you want them to know
that, and to know that you are not a sick man, or a threat to them. I also believe that if they knew the facts they could have respect for you again and could see you again for the kind and loving father that you are.

Those letters you wrote them in response were beautiful and I am

555

very surprised that they didn't come around at least a little bit after receiving them.

Of course, I cannot replace your children, and wouldn't want to. I also know that the situation with your boys must cause you to feel a painful and even hopeless emptiness inside at times. But Daddy, I hope that my longing and demonstrations of wanting to be your devoted little daughter can help you feel cherished, needed, and loved while you face this temporary fiasco with your boys.

I want you to know that I care a great deal for you and I want to comfort you and to give you so much pleasure. I want to hold onto you very tightly and demonstrate how I feel for you.

I hope to see you when you come into the office today. Like I said, I have a client at 4pm. Would you still like to come to my house tomorrow night?? If so, I will go into work a little late on Wednesday so that we can have a little extra time together before your trip. I anticipate that you will return from your weekend feeling stronger and more at peace.

Maybe, too, you will bring the Tetruss back with you. I hope so, Daddy. I am excited about it. When you return, I will be your slave when we're together. What should I do to prepare for that?

Your little girl xo

Subject: Bye
Date: Wed, 10 Nov

Dear Daddy:

Bye, again. It was sweet to hear your voice for a brief moment when I accidentally picked up the wrong line. I don't usually demand to know who is on the other end, but I knew it was you, Daddy, when you answered 'Yes' to my question. You have a beautiful voice that melts me. It makes my pussy melt into pure,

wet sweetness for Daddy.

I believe that you will have a great weekend and will feel better when you return. I will miss you . . . I will wish for you on Sunday, Galen. I might have to write you a letter while you are away and send it to you.

I am very, very sorry that your toy bag got ripped off and also about all the other shit you have to deal with right now. I love trying to make you feel better, though. Your happiness and pleasure bring me happiness.

All day today my pussy has dripped for your cock. I have walked around like a wet little whore ready for her Master to fuck and use her body, because that is what I am, what I am for, and what I need.

Your cock worshipping slave girl

Subject: Naughty girl
Date: Wed, 17 Nov

Dear Daddy:

I am sorry that I drank too much last night. I expected that you would tie me up and stick those needles into me. I was scared about it and I did try to get loaded so that I wouldn't feel it as much. I know that is not very courageous of me. It also means that I should check in with myself about what it means for me and what are my specific issues with piercing play.

I believe that I can do it, even though I am afraid. I also thought that if I got kind of loaded you would put that anal plug in me and I would be able to take it. I am sorry if I disappoint you. I disappointed myself, and wish that I hadn't drank so much.

I will be your bad girl to punish this weekend. I will bend right over for my ass beating and will stick my face out for slapping on

command. Daddy, do you need to mark me all up so that you can admire how submissive a slut your daughter is? I hope so, and will eagerly accept whatever punishment suits you.

I found all three vibrators. They're all right here. But it's about a million percent more satisfying when you are here with me, watching me cum all over that fucking dildo. I can't stop thinking about your fingers and hands, your lips, your voice, your chest and shoulders, and your big stiff cock rubbing up against me, Daddy. I want you to rub it on me, and corrupt me. I want you to strip me of my virtue, to make me hot and crazy like a bitch in heat.

I love to feel your hands on me, right this moment. I can't wait to lay in my bed tonight and think about you making me feel so nasty and making me want to rub my pussy all over your lap.

Thank you for licking my pussy last night, Daddy. I liked it very much. I only like it for about thirty seconds, though. After that, I get distracted and bored. I hope you don't find me rude for telling you this, but I know you like me to tell you everything, not keep secrets. I would like to feel you bite my clit and my pussy. Please let me know what you think about that.

What I want this minute is to feel your skin against mine.

Fondly,

Your daughter.

Subject: sub missy
Date: Thu, 18 Nov

Dear Daddy:

I have considered your question—how do I envision my submissive role in a D/s relationship; or, at least I think that was your question. Here are some of my thoughts on ways to demonstrate my submis-

sion:

· Not question your authority; Daddy is always right and if I challenge you, I should do so with respect and fear because I can expect
punishment for insolent behavior;

· Kneel before you to address you when you are sitting down, and
when you tell me to kneel;

· Call you Daddy, Master, or Sir, some of the time, and always when
you tell me to;

· Be ever ready and willing to accept what you do to my body;

· No lying and if I lie I have no more than 24 hours to confess;

· Allow you to speak down to me, to demean me, humiliate me, and
thank you for it;

Wear what you direct me to wear; and,

· Give you the physical pleasures you ask for, and initiate physically
  pleasing acts and services to you even when not requested (ask
  permission, first)

The list is non-exhaustive. Would you please write me and tell me
your own ideas on this topic. I am not challenging or questioning
you in any way here, but haven't I been a good submissive girl for
you? I am sure that I have done some things to displease or disappoint you. I can tell that you expect more than I have given. Please
tell me what it is so that I can understand what you want, and so that
I can know whether I can fulfill your expectations, or whether they
are not realistic for me.

I am afraid that I may not be submissive enough for you, that I
cannot meet your needs. I am forward and assertive by nature,
perhaps too much so for a Dominant Master/Daddy like you. If this
is the case, it is good, I suppose, that we figure it out sooner rather
than later. It is a good idea that we discuss these things.

Like you, I want everything out in the open. So tell me, please, what is on your mind, alright? I could probably be a little more submissive, but, again, I need your input, guidance and teaching.

I need your patience, as I can't even pretend to be well versed in the ways of submission. Maybe I need to revisit that website again, CastleRealm, the one about submissive behavior, relationships, etc. . . I am kind of at a loss though, not sure what it is that you want, or if I could give what you require.

One last thing, wouldn't a too-submissive girl be boring for you? I probably just don't understand these dynamics very well, and maybe my ideas of submission aren't on the same page with yours. Teach me, Daddy.

Sincerely,

Your little girl, who is trying very hard to please you, Daddy. xo

Subject: My feelings
Date: Thu, 18 Nov

Dear little girl,

I want to clear some static I feel between us. First, know that I do care about you, greatly. I enjoy your company, your friendship, your overtly sexual nature.

I feel the need for some clarity about our emotional relationship. I don't think this is an easy issue to deal with. I want to feel the closeness that I do with you. I do miss you when I don't see you. Neither of us, as we've expressed, desires to become dependent on the other.

This is what I want to check in with you about. I feel this topic needs to be kept near the surface, and examined on a regular basis,

to give us the opportunity to keep it from falling into our shadow emotions, which, I believe can destroy a relationship. I want to know what you feel right now about this. I know this issue came up for you when I was visiting Arlana.

This is the realm where the dance is delicate. I don't want to trample on it. It will require our highest effort to remain close and independent and keep our relationship in the moment. I feel there are a number of circumstances in our lives that prevent me from looking too far ahead in my relationship with you. The legal issues, your son, family, friends and peers, and some differences in our goals and desires for a D/s relationship. These are topics that I feel I need to revisit with you.

As far as the D/s aspects of our relationship, my needs are to delve further into developing you as my submissive, on more than just the sexual level. That does not mean I need that aspect on a 24/7 basis, whenever we are together. But it does include some further ritualizing of how you relate to me at designated times, as a service oriented pleasure slave, respectful and demure in manner. This is an important part of a D/s relationship for me. I want to hear your thoughts in this regard. What do you want?

I also want to tell you that I have been contacted by a submissive in the city, who seeks training. Someone I met at one of the play parties told her about me. She has had a few play partners, with two other couples, actually, though she's not bisexual. She is 39 years old, divorced, and has four kids that she has on weekends. I have talked with her several times. She says she is a bedroom submissive, desires to keep her independence, isn't seeking more than a casual relationship, and wants the opportunity to explore her needs, likes and dislikes with someone she can trust.

I am planning to meet her and see what happens. If sexual contact is involved I will take the necessary precautions. I don't see her as a potential partner, beyond training her. The long distance aspect, four kids, etc., aren't what I am looking for in that regard. I want to be open with you about this. I want your honesty and courage in dealing with this.

With regards to the other night and your drinking . . . I understand why you did that. I think, perhaps, you should turn control of your alcohol intake over to me, when we are together.

I had planned on initiating you in play piercing of your breasts, to start, that night. I would start with one needle, and we'd see how you took it. I will help you relax, and we'll deal with any fear you have by talking it through. I will be tender with my little girl. I am not out to scare you. I want you to suffer and submit to me joyfully. I will proceed with training you to accept me anally, with the same care.

I hope that checking in on our feelings will lead us farther on our path, wherever it may be leading, little girl. I am your good Daddy. I know how to use my little girl, how to make her pussy get so wet. I know the beauty of her desire and decadence to shine forth from the deepest reaches of her naughty soul.

Let's talk soon about our plans for tomorrow. I do want you to stop by here and test out the new version of the Tetruss. Maybe we can have dinner here and then go to your place later. I bought a steak that's sitting in the fridge. What else might you like to put together? I know you are not a meat eater, except for Daddy's meat, which I know you enjoy raw.

I would also take the opportunity this weekend to get a lot of work done, as I know that is the mode you need to be in as well. I enjoy when we both do our work together.

You are still my nasty, bad little slut girl.

Sweetly,

Daddy

p.s. I also wanted to tell you that I am not big on phone sex, sweetgirl. I find no pleasure in it. I enjoy the physical reality too much.

Subject: My reply
Date: Fri 19 Nov

I hadn't felt any static between us, Daddy, but maybe you picked up on my resistance to your wish to expand my slave role beyond the bedroom. I am ambivalent about your suggestion that we have a 'slave day' every now and then, and that on those days I would be your total slut and slave, ready and willing to please you, focused on and anticipating your desires. It sounds fun in some ways, but also intimidating and demeaning.

Part of me resists because I don't feel very submissive on other levels beyond the sexual. Part of me resists because I have felt very awkward on past occasions when you have asked me to behave like a passive, humble slave, and have requested that I serve you like a maid would serve her employer. In fact, on many levels these images are repugnant to me and I feel that I am above waiting on a man hand and foot.

I am adverse to the idea of disappointing you or pushing you away; and I fear
that sharing my true feelings and opinions about your desires and expectations regarding my submission will have that effect. But I want honesty between us. At this moment, I feel that for me to play that role to you would be a substantial sacrifice that I am not sure I am ready to make.

I am naturally reluctant to be a slave—even an occasional slave—and especially so in light of your suggestion that you now plan to meet another woman, potentially for intimacy with her. My resistance and my willingness to play slave are tied into my level of comfort and commitment to you. I like the way our relationship is evolving so far, but I feel that there is much to be seen and experienced before I can know where it might be leading.

I see that it could be fun and adventurous for you to meet with this

woman, Galen. On the other hand, it hurts me to think of you being intimate with another woman. But I can hardly justify discouraging you from exploring your interests or pursuing other women, even if I believe that your decision to do so would hurt me.

I can't ask you to conduct yourself as if we are committed, monogamous partners, when I, myself am not prepared to make that sort of pledge right now, to you or anyone.

As for clarifying our emotional relationship, the only light I can shed on it will probably just illuminate its inherent ambiguities. I have great ambivalence concerning my emotional attachment to you. I do feel very close to you, and I want to feel close to you. I think of you all the time and I miss you so much when I don't see you. Yet, I regularly warn myself to keep my distance from you, to refrain from getting too attached.

On some level, I think that your age and your expectations concerning a D/s relationship pose far too many risks and pitfalls for me to take on. I find myself telling myself that, in the long run, we could never make each other happy; that I couldn't make you happy, couldn't meet your expectations, and that I would end up resenting you for placing too many demands and expectations on me. I fear that I would also feel too pressured and would end up having no time for self-care, which I need a lot of. It could be too much for me to bear, I think.

At this point, I want to remain close with you, but independent from you. I, too, want and need to keep our relationship in the moment; anything else is largely unrealistic at this point in light of the timing and our overall circumstances.

I am thankful that you prompt me to check in with myself and with you, about our feelings, circumstances, expectations, and desires. I am not happy that you plan to meet another woman; but I won't discourage you. I am not sure how I will deal with it, if it happens.

I will have to take a wait and see approach.

Sincerely,

Kate

Subject: Reminders
Date: Sat, 27 Nov

Dear Sir:

My bruised ass hurts as I sit here writing you this note. My tits are tender and also bear bruises from your infliction of pain and punishment on me. My neck also has a very tender, sore spot from your gnawing. Do you want to eat my flesh??

The residual pains and discomforts serve as a constant reminder of Your dominance over me. I feel very secure knowing that you are taking care of my discipline.

I just wanted to share these thoughts with You, Daddy.

submissively Yours,

kate

Subject: Hi & goodnight.
Date: Sat, 27 Nov

Dearest Daddy:

It's pretty late, but I wanted to send you a little message, to say goodnight and to tell you again what a nice Thanksgiving I had with you. I really wanted to spend it with you, Sir, and I am thankful that I could. You are a very sweet, strong Daddy.

I really meant every word I said about you being so smart and so full of insight. When I told you that I have never had romance and intimacy with a man as smart, spiritual and insightful as you are, I meant it, completely. You are also the most soulful and creative person I have met in a long time, maybe ever.

In case I didn't mention it last night, I am very, very thankful to have the opportunity to share my thoughts and ideas with someone like you, who really seems to understand me, and to care.

I want to tell you one more thing. I know you've told me that I haven't seen your full sexual performance, that at times you still have difficulty maintaining an erection, but I do believe that you are a fabulous lover with me and want you to know that you have satisfied me enormously over the past months.

Did I tell you that on our next meeting, I would very much like for you to pierce my titties? Do you plan to tie me up when you do it?? I was thinking my knees or ankles. . .

I hope that your night was fun. Did you go to the play party? I would really like to come with you again sometime; please invite me. Maybe you could play with me at the party. Why don't you come up with an idea about that, and tell me what you think. What could I do at the party that would make you proud of me??

Do you think that I am learning how to be a good submissive for you Daddy?? I found the large butt plug on my floor after you left. I wanted to put it in, I knew that would make you proud. But, I just couldn't because it looks so big and I was afraid. When you are here, and insert it into me yourself, it's easier for me to take it. In fact, I really was surprised at how much easier it was to take the small butt plug up my little girl ass than I thought it would be. Were you proud of me, Daddy??

Okay, I am going to go to bed. I bet you are asleep right now, all warm and soft in bed. I can smell you and feel you in my mind. Mmmmmm. . . . Oh, and I will look at CastleRealm tonight before I

go to bed. Maybe I will learn something that will help me satisfy your most passionate and perverse desires.

Your little pussy slut. xo

Subject: Good morning
Date: Mon, 29 Nov

Hi Daddy!

I want to apologize for waking you up this morning. I just whispered your name to see if you were awake already, so that I wouldn't miss the opportunity to touch and kiss you before I left for work. I hope that you got right back to sleep and had sweet dreams about my pussy and my mouth.

May I spend the night at your house tomorrow night? You gave me great pleasure last night, Sir, by pumping my mouth and my cunt with your big, thick cock. I literally almost completely lose my self control when I feel and see your hard on, Daddy.

I know that just proves what a fucking whore I am, and I am ashamed of myself for it. I am so thankful, though, that my Daddy appreciates it, and can keep me in line and give me a safe place to release my slutty, whorish nature.

When you slap, grab or pinch me while you are fucking me, Daddy, my pussy becomes even wetter, throbs even harder, as I lose more and more control over myself. I feel like an animal, and like a hot little fuck girl, made just for Daddy's pleasure. You have total control over me during these moments, Daddy; I have no choice in the matter, nor do I desire a choice. I joyfully and dutifully accept what you dish out.

I want you to use my holes, but most especially my pussy hole because its when you enter that hole that I feel most erotic, and most cherished.

567

If it would please you, Master, would you please write your little slave girl an email? That would make me smile and feel very warm . . . I would love it!!!!

Very fondly,

Your little girl xo

Subject: Bad, bad little girl
Date: Wed, 1 Dec

Dear Daddy:

Last night, I couldn't help myself and I played with your toy that you left for me. I realize that I should have asked your permission, since I had a guest in my home; but it was late and I didn't think of it at the time. I am sure that nobody knew, as I was very, very quiet and even locked my door. I hope that you are not angry with or disappointed in me, Sir.

I discovered a new way to make my pussy throb and tickle and cum so incredibly hard that I just can hardly stand it. I fantasized all about you, Daddy, while I played with my pussy. . .

You brutally ripped apart my pussy lips and spread them as far as they could go to expose my raw little clit. . . You made me rub my clit and tug at it with the toy and it felt incredibly good. Then, when I could not hold back any longer, I asked your permission to cum, but you scolded me so cruelly, and reminded me that I was a fucking dirty little girl whore.

And as I began to cum, I removed the toy and pressed my fingers down onto my clit. I felt hard pulsating and throbbing sensations on my clit and pussy. I wanted you to feel it so badly, Sir, and wished you were there to enjoy your filthy little girl whore.

I miss you and hope that you are feeling hopeful and strong today my Dear, Strong Daddy Galen.

Lovingly, admiringly, affectionately Yours,

kate

p.s. While I rubbed my clit, I heard you tell me that I had no choice but to submit to you, and that I must lay very, very still when you play with my pussy, that I have to touch my own cunt in front of you, at your command, and make myself cum in front of you. You scolded me for being such a bad, bad little girl. I heard you saying all those nasty, sweet, perverted things that you say, and that I dream about hearing you say.

Subject: Not out of town.
Date: Thu, 2 Dec

Dear Daddy:

I don't have to go to out of town for my client tomorrow!! The other lawyer and I were able to work out a settlement in her case by phone. I am ecstatic about that. I want to spend time with you tomorrow and this weekend, too.

I have very, very little work this weekend, and could even get away with doing none!! This pleases me completely, since the appeals I have been doing have swallowed up the past two weekends.

What are your thoughts on spending time with me this weekend? Is that what you would like? Do you want to drive up to the pass and go cross country skiing??? I would love that. We would need to go to the rental place early tomorrow, though, to get skis and boots.

I realize this must sound somewhat narcissistic and self-absorbed, but was there some punishment/revenge element or motive in your not wanting to engage with me last night while I had fucked myself

with the toy?? Or were you simply too tired to play?? Will you tell me, because in my twisted mind I am thinking that something is wrong because of it. Please be patient with me, Daddy, and indulge me by telling me.

I realize that these thoughts are somewhat babyish and insecure. I can't deny that, and even agree that I can act and think those ways at times. It would feel good to hear from you today, Daddy, now or later. Please?

I hope that you are getting things done—or not—but at least taking care of yourself and believing in yourself. I believe that you can do whatever you set out to do, by the way, and I have a great deal of respect and admiration for you. I also feel love for you, Galen.

Your sweet little slut daughter

Subject: This weekend
Date: Thu, 2 Dec

Dear daughter,

I am glad you don't have to go out of town. You have worked very hard and you deserve a break. Let's talk about the possibility of cc skiing this weekend. It might be fun.

I was severely depressed all day yesterday before I came over. I just couldn't shake that physical and spiritually devastated feeling. It wasn't logical. It really felt like I had ingested some kind of depression drug that, once taken, I couldn't sober up from, whether I wanted to or not.

I felt much better last night and was thankful for your warm welcome and delicious dinner. It was just what I needed. But you must know that much imbalance during the day left me drained emotionally and my "perversion quotient" was about zero.

Of course, I did have a few dregs of energy left, just enough to use you, and drain off the last of any physical energy I had. So, it wasn't due to anything on your part, that I didn't actively participate in your pleasure with the toy (it didn't seem to inhibit your efforts, any!(grin)).

I am getting some things done, although when you are removing a mountain with a spoon, it doesn't look like much is being accomplished. I am, however, feeling much better today.

I just feel so devastated at times about the loss of my sons. I worry so about the damage they may be suffering inside, the wounds they will have to carry with them now. I feel helpless and don't know what to do.

I know I need to stay patient and trust that the truth will win out over the lies. I just want them to know how much I love them, and that their Dad isn't this evil creature I have been portrayed as.

Your belief in me makes me stronger.

Warmly,

Galen

Subject: Re: this weekend
Date: Thu, 2 Dec

Daddy:

Thank you for writing me back. I so enjoy getting email from you. It always brings me great joy. I also thank you for clearing things up about last night. I assumed that, logically, it was what you said. I believe that it is just as you explained and can put my paranoid, center-of-the-universe delusions aside now. Thank you.

You are such a sweet Daddy and so dedicated to your kids. It

makes me want to sit on your lap and tell you that I am scared and that I need you to comfort me. That sounds silly when I read it, but it is true. I am scared and I do want your protection, your strong, comforting influence and energy.

I am still shocked that your boys have not taken advantage of the opportunity to spend more time with you—a parent who loves them and has so much to offer. I realize though that your ex's influence is strong and oppressive on them right now, and that they have to live under her roof, day to day.

Well, thank you again, Master, for writing me back. I am truly sorry for your sadness and devastation yesterday. I am very glad to help you at all to perk up, and I appreciate your acknowledgment of that.

Sincerely,

Your little girl

Subject: Master
Date: Mon, 6 Dec

Dear Pussy Master:

Your cock worshipping whore (me) thanks you from the bottom of her depraved heart and soul for allowing me to play with myself in your presence and with the vibrator last night. I am a terribly nasty little fuck, loving to rub my cunt and clit so fiercely with that toy; thinking about my pussy, and your cock, so often, being preoccupied with sexually stimulating myself like a nymph slut.

I am ashamed to admit how much I love to make myself cum in front of you using that vibrator, and how much it turns me on for you to scold me and degrade me, to slap me and to hurt my body while I keep on stimulating myself with the toy. Do you think I am a sick little girl, Daddy? Can you rehabilitate me? Do you want

to?? I need more punishment, and soon.

I had a very nice time this weekend, being with you the whole time. Will we have a Master/slave day soon? When?

I need to go, now. You are so cute, Daddy. I love your lips and your hairy arms, and your big, nasty cock, especially when you rub it between my thighs and hit my face with it when I am worshipping it with my mouth.

Your sorry little slut xo

Subject:
Date: Wed, 8 Dec

Dear little daughter,

I am having a very hard time right now. I just got another letter of rejection from my sons, in answer to my appeal that they discuss with me their concerns about me.

My ex is so fucked for pulling them down into her shit. Right now, I'm not sure of the best way to deal with this.

I also feel bad to some extent about hurting your feelings, which I know will be the case, because I did visit the sub I told you about, last night. I "played" with her, and also had sex. I didn't use protection as she had been married until last year, and I am the first man she has had sex with since her husband. I saw no reason not to trust her about this and this was the decision I made.

So, today I am feeling some guilt about this. It is not my intention to hurt you, or to drive you away, or to make you angry. I hope you understand how much I care about you, and yes even love you, however that can be defined under our circumstances.

But I have chosen this lifestyle, and have paid some heavy dues to

get here. Having different play partners and learning and perfecting my style as a Dom are important to me. It's not something I have done to cause you distress. This is just the way I intend to be. We both also know and have discussed the challenges our individual paths create for us, in terms of looking into the future toward a long-term relationship.

I enjoy our time together so much, the sexual as well as just being with you moment to moment. I hope that you and I both can deal with this somehow, without all those terrible feelings of guilt and jealousy and hurt, even though that may be impossible.

I will be home later this afternoon, if you want to call or email me about tonight. Also my group doesn't meet tomorrow night, so I am free all evening.

If this challenge isn't too great to overcome, I also got the invite last night from Bruce to the New Years Eve fetish party we had discussed. It is a dinner party for 55 people. I would like to invite you to accompany me.

Let me know your feelings, daughter, no matter what they are.

Your Daddy

Subject: Grief, loss
Date: Wed, 8 Dec

Dear Galen:

I am very sorry about your boys' positions and harsh words. I know you grieve deeply for them. Your ex's conduct in feeding them whatever 'information' she has, is inexcusable and vicious. You and your boys deserve far better.

I, too, am grieving, terribly so, after reading your letter.

I resent your decision to disclose this by email rather than face to face. But I do honor your decision to do whatever you need to remain true to yourself. I know that you are trying to follow your heart and to create a meaningful path for yourself, and I respect you for that. Not least, I appreciate 100% your honesty in telling me the truth right away.

I understood our agreement to be protected sex outside of each other. Your decision to proceed differently has a great impact on me, too, and I need to sort things out around this.

In fact, I need to sort out a lot of things right now about my needs, wants, goals, decisions, reactions, truths, etc., around you, your decision, and what they mean for me. I just need to deal with this in my own way. I don't know, really, what that will be, because I am deeply torn and numb still over what your disclosure brought up for me.

I do know that I need time to sort things out, to process things. I didn't believe that we could get through this unscathed, though, when you told me that you planned to do this; and I was hoping that you would decide against it. But this is your life, your path and I am in no position to direct it.

My feelings toward you had deepened and I have felt complex and highly charged emotions and feelings with you, for you. With you I have experienced such deep, tender, sweet, fond, cherishing, trusting, admiring, soothing, submissive, honoring, joyful, intimate, sexual, comforting, secure, desirous, passionate, adoring, raw, and animal-instinct-charged sentiments and emotions; and all at once.

I have wanted to tell you many times that I love you, but the words scare me, make me feel totally vulnerable, and at the same time are inadequate to describe the deep feelings that I have had toward you.

In retrospect, though, I don't think those words would have made any difference in what has transpired; and, if anything I would probably feel even worse right now for having shared those feelings with you expressly, and then finding out about last night.

I do understand and believe that you care for me, and of course I know that you did not have sex with this woman whom you just met last night to hurt me. Nonetheless, I am hurt. I don't expect that I can feel the same closeness that I felt with you in the past, though I wish sincerely that weren't so.

Although I have barely begun to sort out my feelings around what has transpired and its aftermath, I am fairly confident that my needs and goals for a LTR don't include outside relationships, at least not outside the presence of the partners. But I also understand that I am not, at this time, ready to be in, or to profess to be in, a long-term relationship with you or anyone.

I also understand that you have your own needs and desires, and that you need to do what you believe to be right for you or else you can't be true to yourself; and you must be true to yourself or else you can't be true to another person. If a long-term relationship, for you, must include having sex with other partners in this way, then I am pretty certain that a LTR between us is not in our future.

I am so, so sad, Galen. I don't feel that I have anyone to turn to but myself about this matter. I do have a lot of compassion for myself, but it is hard to comfort myself when I am largely consumed by grief and loss. And I can't even articulate what exactly is lost, but I understand that it is something that has become profoundly special and important to me.

I need time. I hurt so badly right now.

kate

(*Note: Kate and I met face to face and worked through our issues about this situation. We are still close friends, lovers, allies, and still struggle to define exactly how to love each other without sacrificing who we are as individuals, and with the knowledge that our paths may diverge due to circumstance. And of course, I am still her sadistic Daddy Dom, and she is my naughty, slutty little daughter.*)

D/s and BDSM Resources

There are thousands of web sites relating to every aspect of BDSM. The resources listed below are either particularly focussed or they are a very good general resources. Each of them has extensive links that will point you in about any conceivable direction you might wish to explore on your journey into D/s.

Galen's Realm http://www.GalensRealm.com

Submit your Secrets – a safe place to reveal your darkest secret fantasies http://www.GalensRealm.com

About.com Guide to BDSM
http://bdsm.about.com/culture/adult/bdsm/msub11.htm

Alt.com(D/s personals) http://alt.com

BDSM Events Page http://www.thebdsmeventspage.com

BDSM online - huge resource and info site
http://www.bdsm-online.com

Bondage.com (D/s personals) http://bondage.com

Caryl's BDSM http://home.earthlink.net/~drkdesyre/indexB.html

Castle Realm D/s Resource Center http://www.castlerealm.com/

Deviant's Dictionary http://www.queernet.org/deviant/

Different Loving Home Page
http://gloria-brame.com/diflove.htm

Ds Kiosk Community Resource Site http://cuffs.com/

D/s World http://www.bdsmlife.net/dsworld//main.html

Erotica Readers Assoc. http://wwwerotica-readers.com

Femmerotic Portal http://www.femmerotic.com

Jane's Guide http://Janesguide.com

Nerve   http://nerve.com

Offline/Online BDSM Safety
http://www.flick-the-switch.com/safety.htm

Quality SM   http://www.qualitysm.com

Socirety of Human Sexuality   http://www.sexuality.org

Stephen's BDSM Page   http://sandm.com

SubNation   http://www.mouse-works.com/subnation/